THE MEDIA AND THE MILITARY

Dr Peter Young served as a regular soldier in Special Forces and Intelligence. He saw combat with 22 SAS as a troop commander in Malaya during the Emergency. He served two tours of Vietnam in Intelligence and Special Forces, the first with the CIA, the second as Assistant Military Attaché in Saigon.

He is a former Defence Editor of *The Australian* and Defence and Foreign Affairs Editor for *Network Ten Television* (Australia), working out of the Parliamentary Press Gallery. He was founding Editor and Publisher of the *Pacific Defence Reporter* and served for a year as the television representative on the Media Response Group of the Australian Defence Media Advisory Group.

He is Associate Professor in Defence Media Studies at Griffith University, and President of the International Defence Media Association. He holds a bachelorship in war and policy studies, a masters in defence studies and a doctorate on the topic of defence and the media.

Peter Jesser served as a regular soldier in the Australian Army. He was attached to the Papua New Guinea Defence Force as an adviser for two years and was selected for twelve months' higher education in the United States.

He is currently an academic working in the areas of management and defence studies. He is Secretary of the International Defence Media Association.

He holds a bachelorship in business (distinction), a masters of science in management and policy, and a masters in defence studies. He is completing a doctorate on the topic of the media and United Nations peacekeeping.

The Media and the Military

From the Crimea to Desert Strike

Peter Young
Associate Professor in Defence Media Studies
Centre for the Study of Australia–Asia Relations
Griffith University
Australia

and

Peter Jesser
Secretary
International Defence Media Association
Australia

St. Martin's Press
New York

THE MEDIA AND THE MILITARY
Copyright © 1997 by Peter Young and Peter Jesser

St. Martin's Press, Scholarly and Reference Division, 175 Fifth Avenue, New York, N.Y. 10010

First published in the United States of America in 1997

This book is printed on paper suitable for recycling and made from fully managed and sustained forest sources.

Printed in Hong Kong

ISBN 0–312–21011–6
ISBN 0–312–21012–4

Library of Congress Cataloging-in-Publication Data
Young, Peter R.
The media and the military : from the Crimea to Desert Strike /
Peter Young and Peter Jesser.
p. cm.
Includes bibliographical references (p.   ) and index.
ISBN 0–312–21011–6 (cloth). — ISBN 0–312–21012–4 (paper)
1. Armed Forces and mass media—History. I. Jesser, Peter.
II. Title.
P96.A75Y68 1997
355.3'42—dc21   97–24399
                                                        CIP

Dedicated to Phillip Knightley
the man who first posed the question of
the public's right to know in time of conflict, in
The First Casualty

Contents

Acknowledgments

This book could not have been completed without the support and encouragement of Rochelle Jesser and Ruth Young. Each contributed in a major part to the research, proofreading and final compilation. Great thanks are due for their patience and understanding over a long period.

Thanks are also due to Naomi Jesser for her proofreading and ever helpful suggestions, and to Sheree Bailey who went beyond the call of duty in her constant support and assistance with the word processing.

1

The Changed Nature of War and Duties of the Citizen in Time of War

Early in 1991, television audiences around the world were transfixed by images of the Gulf war in progress – cruise missiles thundering skywards from battleship launch tubes, gun-camera video of laser-guided weapons finding their mark, the crackling voices of pilots engaged in air combat, and triumphant columns of allied armour rolling across a landscape of burning oilfields. There was hardly a body in sight. It might almost have been a bloodless war.

The film footage is now filed away, sealing the history of the Gulf conflict. But it is not a complete record. The military's system of media management effectively prevented the real story from being told. In May 1991, as the full extent of media manipulation became clear, the American Society of Newspaper Editors was moved to describe the military's handling of the media in the Gulf as '... the international humiliation of the profession of journalism.'[1]

This book addresses that uneasy relationship between, on the one hand, the media's perceived duty of serving the public's right to know in time of war and, on the other, its obligation to observe the proper constraints of 'operational security' demanded by the military in Western liberal democracies. It follows the progress of defence journalism from the Crimea in the 1850s to Operation Desert Strike in September 1996.

The charge levelled against the military is that the cooperative arrangements arrived at for managing the media, designed to accommodate the public's right to know, have been overridden by the military's perceived need to limit and manipulate the media in order to enlist and maintain national and international public support. This has come about because of the changed nature of war following the advent of nuclear, biological and chemical warfare. The new approach to war is likely to see 'limited conflicts' such as that in the Gulf become the norm. Such limited conflicts pose no threat to the wellbeing of the average citizen, let alone any threat to his or her physical survival or the survival of the state. As a consequence, the citizens of Western democracies are no longer bound by the patriotic imperative of unquestioning duty to the state which applied in wars of survival, and are able to exercise freedom of choice.

It is this emerging freedom of choice which has made public opinion a priority target for governments in their quest for the legitimacy and public support needed to wage war against an enemy who poses none of the traditional threats that rallied support in earlier wars of survival.   In this chapter we examine the changed nature of war and the way those changes have shaped national and international dimensions of confrontation. We then look at the reaction within Western liberal democracies which appear to be imposing draconian military restrictions on access, transport and communications in their attempts to contain the 'media threat' in time of limited conflict. We also consider the relevance of existing theory on citizens' rights and obligations imposed by the social contract, theory which is currently rooted in the twentieth century notion of 'patriotic' wars of survival.

The argument we will develop rests on two major premises. The first is that the penalties inherent in nuclear, biological and chemical warfare have made it more likely that future international confrontations involving major powers will be decided through limited conflict. The second is that, stemming from this changed nature of war, existing social contract theory is no longer relevant, in that the basic presumption of a direct threat to either the individual or the nation no longer holds.

When combined, these premises raise questions about the military's need to enlist and maintain national and international support, regardless of the military's ability to restrict or even contain the new high technology global media. Can governments afford the political penalty of imposing censorship or denial of information to an electronic age audience which has come to expect that every side of every issue will be examined and addressed through the immediacy of television? Conversely, would this better educated and informed public be prepared to forego that 'right', especially if a significant section of the community chose to oppose government policy? This leads us to ask whether the media have a duty to cater to that public opposition and, last but not least, whether journalists should enter into the sort of cooperative arrangements presently being offered by the military. The ramifications are significant, considering both the military's past record of being less than forthcoming in time of peace and the emerging politico-military policies of management and manipulation of the media.

The Changed Nature of War

Clausewitz defined war as 'an act of violence intended to compel our opponent to fulfil our will.'[2] The definition presents war as an extension of politics, with the military aspect taking precedence once diplomacy or politics have failed. In the view of Clausewitz and the realist school, war is a rational instrument of national policy: as Rapaport interprets it, the decision to wage war ought to be 'rational', in that it should be cost effective, it ought to be 'instrumental' in that it is waged to achieve a defined goal, and it should be 'national' in the sense that the objective advances the cause of the national state, with the entire resources of the state mobilised towards that aim.[3] It is generally accepted that this definition of war anticipates an end with complete military victory for one side or the other.

While some, such as Hammond, drawing on Clausewitz's unfinished revision of Book 1, believe that Clausewitz had foreseen limited conflict in which the political aim could dominate,[4] conventional Clausewitzian thinking has fostered the idea that armed forces should be deployed with the predominant aim of achieving a military victory.[5] Over the past century, however, war has progressively become so costly and destructive that, even before the advent of the nuclear age, it was, according to Rapaport's interpretation of Clausewitz, in danger of becoming 'irrational'; the stalemate on the Western Front in 1917 is often quoted as an example.[6]

This cost benefit approach of strictly state to state military conflicts fought by professional armies was displaced to some extent by the emergence of patriotic nationalism during World War I, and by the revolutionary ideologies that followed it and continued into World War II. In these conflicts, the massive short-term cost was seen to be worth the long-term political gain.[7]

This set the scene for the great change, immediately following the end of World War II, when the international community was confronted with a round of wars of insurgency which were waged under the shadow of nuclear confrontation. In the main, these wars defied Clausewitz's theory of the supremacy of the military; they afforded a prime example of political issues becoming paramount. As Algeria and more recently Afghanistan have demonstrated, a mobilised people need not triumph on the battlefield – they need only maintain their resistance. The wars in Algeria and Afghanistan were fought at low levels of operations with strictly limited weaponry and limitations of geography. Because of this, despite the presence – in most cases – of an external directing or supporting ideological patron state, only in the case of Korea and to a lesser extent Vietnam, was there any risk of escalation to nuclear confrontation. But, as such struggles became more ideological, the risks of escalation or, as happened in Vietnam, the cost in wealth and psychological commitment sounded strong warnings against open ended engagements.[8]

Beyond these examples, the development of the post-World War II nuclear threat and the awesome penalties of mutually assured destruction virtually outlawed the nationalistic confrontations of the past. For the first time there was the prospect – either through incident or accident – of war which could destroy civilisation. As a result, total nuclear war became a military absurdity and the enormous economic cost of maintaining the necessary offensive capability for deterrence was in danger of becoming politically counter-productive. This led to moves by the superpowers to agree to strategic arms limitations beginning with the Interim Offensive Agreement (SALT 1) in 1972, expanding to the 1987 Intermediate Range Nuclear Force Treaty and continuing in current negotiations for reductions in nuclear weaponry.

From this it is clear that the nature of war has changed. In fact as early as 1957, the then future United States Secretary of State, Henry Kissinger, realised that, in the face of the nuclear penalties, all future international ambitions would have to be achieved through limited war. And limited conflict, he argued, would have to be managed as part of a politico-military continuum.[9]

This concept has since become formalised under the heading of 'Low Intensity Conflict' – a descriptor which was developed in the United States in the 1970s to describe a new style of politico-military activity short of modern conventional warfare. Low Intensity Conflict describes a range of situations from peacekeeping and displays of force, up to conventional military operations with limited objectives and of short duration.[10]

In the United States, limited conflict has been defined as 'political military confrontation between contending states or groups below conventional war and above the routine peaceful competition among states.' Such conflicts could be localised yet have regional or global security implications. They would usually be of limited duration, using political, economic and information instruments as well as the military.[11] The British definition of limited conflict is described in similar terms as a limited politico-military struggle to achieve political, social, economic or psychological objectives. It is often protracted and ranges from diplomatic, economic and psycho-social pressures through terrorism and insurgency. It is often characterised by constraints on weaponry, tactics and levels of violence.[12] The only unclassified Australian definition is even more succinct, defining limited war as embracing 'a host of threats and hostile acts which may confront a nation from terrorism to full scale national invasion.'[13]

In 1981, the Australian Parliament's Joint Committee on Foreign Affairs and Defence defined low level contingencies as those which can be addressed within the peacetime organisation and structure of the Defence Force. The Committee specified a list of eleven low level and five intermediate contingencies that might threaten Australia and these, though primarily of a defensive nature, when taken together generally follow the American and British definitions.[14]

The United States Navy has refined the definition further, coming up with a concept called CALOW – Contingency and Limited Objective Warfare. This distinguishes between the low end of the scale of military operations, such as anti-narcotics or counter terrorism, and the upper end, where violence could become war.[15]

In O'Brien's *Conduct of Just and Limited Wars*, analysts such as Kissinger, Halpin and Deitchman have produced a consensus that affords an acceptable set of broad guidelines for involvement in such conflicts. O'Brien summarises these as political primacy over the military instrument, limited objectives, and voluntary imposition of rules of engagement. These voluntary limitations would include the avoidance of direct superpower confrontation, no nuclear weapons other than limited tactical or theatre weapons, the geographical containment of the conflict, 'fight and negotiate' strategies with the introduction of third party negotiators and inspectors, a will to avoid escalation, and restraint in the use of the psychological instrument (that is, the full mobilisation of government resources for reporting, explaining or justifying its belligerence).[16]

Such limited conflicts can hardly be expected to generate the sort of universal support given to wars conducted by nation states in the past.

The problem of national support for limited conflict becomes even greater if the conflict is conducted by regular volunteer forces isolated from the wider community and operating in geographically remote areas. Campaigns waged without the involvement of conscripts generally have little or no impact on the day to day living of the majority of the home population. The legitimacy of an action may also be open to question, making the individual's decision whether or not to support the government an intellectual choice only, without any of the imperatives of self interest inherent in wars of survival. As a result, we might reasonably expect such conflicts to be opposed by a significant section of the home community. As with the war in Vietnam, the weight of dissent and the media coverage it attracts might be large enough to constitute a rejection of the mandate to govern inherent in the social contract, threatening the legitimacy of the government.

In summary, while the threat of escalation in any conflict can never be absolutely discounted, the destructive potential of nuclear warfare means that national confrontations of the past, of the sort which might be termed patriotic or wars of survival, are now simply too costly to contemplate. Consequently, the nature of war and the shape of international conflict has changed to one of limited conflict. These limited conflicts demand high levels of public support and that support is eagerly sought by the belligerents.

At the same time, the obligation of the citizen to support the conflict objectives of his or her government is no longer what was expected in wars of survival. It is to this question of the changed nature of the obligations of the citizen that we now turn.

The Concept of the Social Contract

Throughout history, war has been central to the emergence, conduct and survival of the state in all its forms, from the tribe to the modern nation state. In turn, the origins of the state rest on the social contract, whereby men and women gathered together and subordinated their individual rights in order to gain a common defence of life and property and the other benefits that flowed from cooperation and association. However, no matter what political organisation emerged, everything revolved around the tacit bargain of consent and the voluntary abrogation of rights on the part of the individual and the community in support of the common good, with defence as the most pressing issue. This abrogation of rights was limited only by the ruler's mandate, which could be withdrawn if the government or state exceeded what was generally considered reasonable demands.[17]

From these early times, the first demand on a monarch or leader under the social contract was to protect the peace, to repel invasion, and to wage war in the interests of the group. Without exception, it was accepted that the ruler had the right to command the citizen's duty of obedience in time of war.

This view was accepted right up until the Renaissance and well into the seventeenth century. The prospect of subjugation, slavery and death – the penalty for defeat which prevailed in those times – provided strong reinforcement for the concept that all should cooperate in defence of the national interest, whatever the nature of government. So well entrenched was this concept in thought on government-citizen relations that it has prevailed to the present day, easily surviving the scrutiny of the early libertarians and the emergence of the democratic state.

John Locke, for example, believed that the most urgent concern of the body politic was for external security and that the ultimate objective of external policy was to '... establish a relative superiority of economic and military power vis a vis other states.' The state's right to make war, he argued, should merely be limited to its employment '... only in defence of the commonwealth from foreign injury.' War, Locke stressed, 'admits of no plurality of Governors.' Along with the conduct of foreign affairs, war was an undoubted prerogative of the ruler, and as such overrode any other rights under the social contract which had drawn men together in the first place.[18]

Hobbes argued that war was to be avoided where possible but, if necessary, had to be faced for the common good. It then became '... the obligation of the citizen to authorise all the sovereign's actions, including their defence against a common enemy.'[19] Similarly, Rousseau believed in the concept of duty to the state in time of war, stating that when a man laid down his life in defence of the state, all he was doing was handing back the very boon he had received at its hands.[20]

Other social contract theoreticians have favoured Locke's approach. Bentham was suspicious of defence and foreign conquest, but he accepted that territorial integrity had to be defended and that this might involve sacrifices in support of the common and greater good. The state, he said 'towered over the citizen', who had a duty to sacrifice life and property for the survival of the state.[21]

Care must be taken to relate the opinions of each of these political theorists to the times in which they lived, for it is accepted that there is strong religious, political or personal bias in all of their writings. However, while most argued for increasing personal rights and freedoms, without exception they identified an over-riding obligation and abrogation of rights to the state in time of war. Based on the tenets of social contract theory which prevailed up until the nineteenth century, therefore, any war designed to protect the nation was a 'just' war on both philosophical and religious grounds. As such it was not open to challenge.

This concept of an over-riding obligation to the state in time of war survived the industrial revolution. Nationalism, however, replaced the earlier imperative of survival and, largely through the emergence of a popular press, the new urban industrial class was encouraged to share in national and imperial glory.[22] Although there were some who opposed predominantly colonial wars, such as the Boer War and the Belgian excesses in the Congo that took place during this period, for the main part this opposition was unpopular, limited and, as a result, easily isolated.[23]

There was a strong anti-conscription debate in an egalitarian Australia, led to some extent by an Irish-oriented clergy. There were isolated protests in France. But the concept of patriotic and nationalistic obligation to the state in time of war survived World War I. It survived despite casualties on a scale never encountered before. Beyond that, the belligerents enjoyed widespread popular support. This was despite restrictions on almost every aspect of life and the fact that, for most people in their home countries, there was little real threat to survival.[24] Marwick argues that this continued support was only achieved through a policy of outright and almost unbelievable propaganda.[25]

Even with the 1917 Russian revolution, there was no major challenge to the concept of a prior duty and obligation to the state in time of war. The newborn communist regime in Russia quickly reverted to the concept of an overriding duty to the state in time of danger, with Lenin advising every citizen that life and property should be placed in the service of the State in defence of the fatherland.[26]

It was much the same in World War II, when the citizen's obligations in time of war were taken for granted. This time however, the acceptance of an obligation to the state was reinforced by the fact that each of the major participants saw the war as being 'just'. In Great Britain in the early days, and certainly in Soviet Russia and later Germany, the war also rapidly became a war of survival, with the threat of death and destruction shared equally by the civilians and frontline soldiers. In the case of the democracies, the population readily accepted the abrogation of their rights, including that of a free press.[27]

Since then, other than the challenge posed by the Vietnam war, the concepts of the citizen's rights and duties in time of war have remained largely unchanged. Among contemporary political thinkers, only Rawls comes close to addressing the wider implication of limited conflicts which might engender divided loyalties; these he terms 'unjust' wars. Even then, however, Rawls' main focus has been on the issues confronting conscientious objectors.[28] Rawls' argument rests on a form of social contract in which the citizen owes no political obligations, only natural duties based on an individual concept of justice as fairness, in the circumstances in which an agreement or contract is reached. This idea of justice as fairness, he argues, need not be confined to relations within a political community, but could be extended to international relations. Rawls considers that these principles would include the equality of nations, the right of self-determination, the right of self-defence against external attack, the duty to observe treaties, the excessive use of violence in war, a strict and limited definition of national interest, and the exclusion of economic gains, territorial expansion and national glory as justifiable reasons for war.

In Rawls' opinion, the citizen might properly appeal to this principle of fairness to justify conscientious refusal to take part in what he or she perceives to be an unjust war. By extension, a soldier might refuse to engage in certain acts if he or she reasonably and conscientiously believed that those acts violate the principles of international justice. However, the crux of Rawls' argument as it applies here is that the citizen's natural duty *not* to be made the agent of grave injustice and evil to another outweighs his or her duty to obey the government. This means that if a war is perceived by the citizen to be unjust in its aims or conduct, then the citizen has the right to refuse military service on the grounds that he or she must disregard the legal duty when it conflicts with the natural duty not to damage the basic liberties of his or her own or another society. As Parekh interprets it, 'Rawls believes that the aims of modern states in waging war are now *so likely to be unjust that one might rightly abjure military service altogether in the foreseeable future*' (emphasis added).[29]

While this remains pioneering theory, it is the only new thinking of its kind in the field. For a government involved in a limited conflict that might outlive the initial patriotic euphoria that normally accompanies such involvements, the implications are enormous. Given the new focus on individual rights in most Western liberal democracies, Rawls' views should not be discounted. Despite the warnings sounded by the round of post-World War II conflicts of self-determination, Vietnam and, later, the Gulf, the reality is, as Parekh put it:

... that political philosophical discussion on property, citizenship and the relations between Government and the economy, social

classes and even war, continues to be dominated by the categories
and assumptions inherited from our nineteenth century forebears.[30]

Elitist and Libertarian Theories

Libertarian theory generally rests on arguments put forward by classical
democratic theorists such as Rousseau, Hume and J.S. Mill, who believed
that freedom of speech in all its forms is essential if there is to be
informed debate. The public, they argued, cannot form adequate
judgements or participate effectively in the workings of democracy
without being fully informed. This argument has taken on added weight
with the growth of the modern media. The media plays an increasingly
important role in providing near instant comprehensive coverage of
events and also determines, to some extent, the climate of opinion within
which those in power make their decisions.[31]

The need for an informed public is accepted to such an extent that
accountability and open scrutiny of government is seen as a measure of
legitimacy in a democratic society. As a result, these rights are often
guaranteed in democracies, either as part of a written constitution or by
convention.[32] In reality, freedom of speech and of the press are accepted
as an absolute right only in parliamentary forums. Nevertheless, for all
practical purpose – and despite the ever present tensions between the
press, bureaucrats and politicians – there have to be powerful reasons
before these conventions are breached to any major degree. This has been
reinforced in recent years by the introduction of Freedom of Information
legislation in many Western liberal democracies, even though these rights
have been immediately whittled away by financial, bureaucratic and
political restrictions.[33]

A more restricted view of the libertarian belief in the right of citizens
to be informed on every issue is advanced the theory of democratic
elitism. This theory argues that a democratically elected leadership and
its bureaucratic advisers are entitled to the protection of confidentiality
and freedom of privileged discussion once they have been given a
mandate to govern. The opposing views are summed up in Schumpeter's
statement that 'the elector's work is done once he has voted.'[34] This
position accepts the value of democratic elections as a safeguard against
the abuse of power by political elites, but argues that effective and
efficient government cannot be achieved without some degree of secrecy
in areas such as defence and foreign affairs. This locus of secrecy is
deemed necessary in forums as disparate as local government authorities
and the United Nations, on the basis that few administrators or law

makers would be prepared to examine or propose extreme options or advance unpopular solutions if they knew that their deliberations would be open to public scrutiny.[35]

Elitist Authoritarianism in Time of War

When the libertarian and democratic elitist theories are put to the test in time of war, however, the struggle becomes unequal.

The libertarians see the media as an important part of the information process. They can rightly point to support in principle from the majority of the population, in their claim that the media should be free and unfettered *except in time of 'just' conflict.* But the reality is that, in time of war – any war – this principle has been ignored by the public in both the United States and the United Kingdom; opinion polls have shown overwhelming popular support for constraints on the media during recent limited conflicts.[36]

This position plays into the hands of authoritarian elitists who see the media as a potentially dangerous interloper in the process of government and erect barriers of prior restraint through the threat of legal action. They manipulate access by imposing controls and deny information by the use of security classifications in areas such as defence and foreign affairs.[37] The danger to democracy arises because almost every commentator or authority comes to accept the government's right to secrecy and freedom from scrutiny of their actions in matters of defence and foreign affairs.[38] Generally, however, mainstream commentators have accepted the government argument of the need for a locus of secrecy when it comes to defence.

This elitist approach to the dissemination of information is echoed in major international forums. While these may pay lip service to wider freedoms, they retreat when it comes to guaranteeing freedoms in time of conflict. In almost every instance, before such organisations as the United Nations and the Council of Europe, the general ambit claim has been for a free and open media. In each case, however, freedoms have been limited by some form of wording that allows them to be overridden by individual national governments. Thus, the 1954 United Nations Convention on Human Rights states, in what is little more than an open invitation to censorship, that the exercise of the freedom of speech carries '... duties and obligations which may be subject to formalities, conditions, restrictions or penalties as are prescribed by law and necessary in a democratic society.'[39]

The same caveat appeared in the 1966 United Nations International Covenant on Economic and Social and Cultural Rights, allowing individual nations to ignore rights and freedoms 'in the interests of national security.' These limitations were given express sanction in the International Covenant on Civil and Political Rights, adopted by the United Nations the same year, on the basis of the 'exigencies of the situation'. Under Article 19 of this document, the limitation of national security is imposed on the freedom to '... seek and impart information and ideas of all kinds ... either orally, in writing, or print, in the form of art or through any other media.' Article IV of the 1969 Draft United Nations Convention on the Gathering and Transmission of News, which claimed as its ambit 'the right of the people to be informed', afforded open acceptance of the right of nations to impose censorship. In Article II it also allowed the right of any nation to derogate from its obligations under the convention in time of war.[40]

In summary, despite the different forums and changing times, the message remains the same: social contract theory and the expectations under that theory which prevailed in wars of survival have not changed. Despite the internationalisation of the problem, and with the partial exception of Rawls, current political theory has not progressed beyond the outdated argument that the state is pre-eminent in time of war or conflict. It is still held to be the natural duty of the citizen and the media to rally in defence of what is claimed as the common interests of security and survival in any conflict. It is an attitude we shall see demonstrated in each of our case studies as Western liberal democracies fell back on outdated theory once they had committed their military forces to war. While this has happened, the military itself has cynically treated a cooperative media as yet another obstacle that must be dealt with by whatever means available, irrespective of public acceptance of the 'rightness' of the conflict.

The Media-Military Dilemma

A prime example of outdated thinking on the dilemma presented to the media in catering to the information needs of the modern, thinking citizen, is offered in the comment made by the then Australian Prime Minister, Malcolm Fraser in the Australian 1978 *Protective Security Handbook*. In the foreword to that publication, Fraser stated:

> It is hardly necessary to explain why nations must keep secret their
> defence arrangements and there are equally important areas where

confidentiality in the national interest must prevail over private or public rights to information.[41]

This approach has been taken up by the military forces in all Western liberal democracies and is fundamental to their imposition of cooperative restrictions on the media in return for access and support in the field. At the tactical level it is difficult not to agree with them, nor with Mr Bill Hayden, a former Australian shadow minister for defence, who stated the case for the field commander when he observed that 'It does not seem to me unreasonable to require clearance before reports are published or broadcast on strategic or tactical deployments, military intelligence, force levels, casualties, logistics, reinforcements, weapon systems, potential weaknesses and the like.'[42]

This attitude is understandable, but it rests on the outdated theory of the media, along with the citizen, placing itself at the service of the nation in time of threat. What should be the case when we are faced with limited conflict, when, as we have argued, a large part of the population might not support involvement in the conflict? In this case, as Woodward put it when examining the role of the media in these new forms of conflict:

> The media potentially becomes a free and independent player with the capacity to influence both the conduct of hostilities and, particularly through its impact on popular sentiment, the direction of government policy... it has the capacity, and the media would say, the responsibility to analyse critically not only the government's objectives but also the military strategy being pursued and the details of operations at the tactical level while hostilities are continuing.[43]

An equally important point is the speed and global reach of the new internationalised media – a reach which could well allow coverage by other nations not bound by considerations of operational security. Such coverage, including input from the Internet, would be beyond sanction, but fully able to feed footage into a global system, allowing rapid relay to both combatants and their home nations. While the belligerents could place restrictions on media in the field, censorship would be almost impossible to maintain in the face of expectations in the home nation.

In addition, with freedom of travel and communication unaffected by a limited war, alternative sources of information would include international travel with its accompanying passage of ideas and journals, the posted arrival of independent newspapers, international broadcasts and satellite transmissions. There is also the digital telephone and the Internet, the jamming of which would present both political and technical problems. Beyond these lies the impact of the amateur video.

Consequently, the global spread of information would be almost impossible to contain, short of policies of outright deception and misinformation, or the restrictive measures open to a government *only* in time of a war of survival. As an example, there is anecdotal evidence that the Soviet people became aware of the failure of the war in Afghanistan from word of mouth news that accompanied the return of army conscripts drawn from all over the republics.

To counter these arguments, the reality is that in most, if not all international conflicts, the target audience is ranged on one side of the issue. As a result, the source of most of the news presented to them is also drawn from one side. Beyond that, the media tend to mirror audience expectations; and given the competition between media outlets, there is strong pressure for conformity. This conformity is reinforced by a steady stream of official and unofficial news from the government or governments on either home side of the conflict, and creates an initial advantage for military and government in control of the media. Further, as Pilger points out:

> Unlike totalitarian states, the narrow conformity of information and opinion in the 'free' media is mostly idsidious: its sameness implicit, ingrained, even celebrated as 'objective' and 'balanced'. This makes reading between the lines difficult and propaganda far more effective than its former cold war counterpart.[44]

The dilemma for the military is that, despite this tendency to conformity, the potential remains for the media to break free of these strictures.

The Global Media and the New Electronic Audience

The biggest problem confronting the military is the unprecedented advance in communications technology that have largely made the reporter independent of the military. Here it is necessary to highlight the difference between covering conflicts with strong local media infrastructures, which might reasonably provide support for the journalist, and those such as the Gulf war, where capabilities were limited. Satellite transmission of television and telephone, and radio transmission of video, have been the major innovations. In addition to the normal satellite borne voice and data systems, underdeveloped areas are being increasingly linked into Remote Area Network Data systems (RAND), which allows data and voice to be transmitted over standard high frequency radio capable of being linked into national and international circuits. Other advances in compressed video signal and computer driven and enhanced satellite (Inmarsat) CODEC technology using a 50 kilogram terminal now enable real-time seaborne transmission from anywhere on the globe. In addition, this technology allows the transmission of colour still images taken off video footage. Work has been done on a multibeam single antenna capable of simultaneously picking up signals from up to 20 satellites.[45]

Each of these advances, in particular satellite borne and micro-wave and optical fibre transmitted systems, is moving towards miniaturisation which will allow further mobility. Most networks presently use truck-borne satellite transmitters because of the peacetime lack of restriction on access. These systems, along with lesser distance microwave line of sight link systems, are a familiar sight at major news events. The networks routinely fly such systems into remote areas by transport aircraft, as was done to provide coverage of the anniversary of the ending of the Vietnam war.

However, media interest lies with miniaturisation because, despite their technical independence, large systems remain dependent on the military for access to airports and operational support. Nevertheless, it is now technically possible to equip reporters with a three man crew-borne portable solar powered system that can be packed into three large suitcase sized packs. This will soon be reduced even further. Further refinements in video camera technology could see the video-journalist become completely independent in the near future. Work is already underway on remote control pan and tilt head systems called 'Journocam'. The entire system could be assembled using existing technology at an estimated cost of $5,000. According to recent research, it could be carried in a single package the size of a normal briefcase.[46]

This mobility limits even further the ability of the military to block transmissions through electronic jamming, as was demonstrated by an Australian journalist, George Negus, who in recent years reported live from a trip across the then Soviet Union. In a similar manner, Greenpeace was able to send acceptable live television footage worldwide from Muraroa Atoll, using compressed digital high speed data links. Similar systems have been used for global boat races using ISDN multiplexus high-band video conferencing links.[47] The independence and mobility conferred by such systems restricts field censorship to physical sanction. This was demonstrated during the Gulf war, when Peter Arnett used direct satellite telephone voice communications to report from Baghdad.[48]

The capacity to support this type of reporting is not in doubt. The United States has requested the United Nations affiliated International Telecommunications Union, to allocate international frequencies for a low earth orbit network of satellites which could provide global digital voice, facsimile and cellular telephone links.[49] The major American networks now have access to private media satellites, despite American legislation which prohibits private ownership.[50] The great advances in satellites, digital phones and other modern communications linked to the Internet are likely to further foster public awareness of world events. And knowing that the public knows can be a powerful restraint on governments and the military. The use of satellite-borne home video coverage and digital mobile phones by foreign correspondents during the May 1992 riots in Bangkok is credited with reining in the Thai military.[51]

Current predictions are for the cost effectiveness of the new technologies of fibre optics, satellite transmission and decoding, computer enhanced imagery, and digital switching and editing to increase at least a millionfold over the next decade. A single chip could exceed the computing power of twenty existing supercomputers. Existing fibre optic links can transmit more than a thousand million characters per second.[52]

This computing power and fibre optic technology is only years away from widespread public affordability and application. The new technologies will provide individual access to information presently only available to the major media networks. Future audiences will be able to shape the nature of what they see on television by the selection of camera angles and instant replays. They will also be able to participate; instant polling participation is already available in game shows. The audience will be able to select its viewing from a wide range of specialist cable networks, both national and international. When combined with miniaturised, personal computer based telecommunications, these technologies will empower the individual to an unprecedented extent.[53]

This technical reach of the media is matched by the almost total penetration of radio and television within Western liberal democracies. Radio was accepted as having a saturation audience in most Western nations as early as 1948. A near-total home penetration of television was achieved in the United States in 1980, with 99 per cent, or 77.8 million American homes having television sets, 85 per cent of them colour. The latest statistics show multiple ownership within households, but this is incidental to the fact that *complete* penetration of television was achieved in the United States and Western Europe a decade ago. Similar penetration has now been achieved in most other developed countries, with the Third World rapidly achieving the same status.

This level of electronic media penetration means that a whole generation in most Western countries has grown up with radio and television. In the case of television, the audience accepts it as the most credible source of news.[54] This generation is also far better educated and informed than their parents. Literacy is near universal and the majority of students finish high school equivalent, with an increasing number going on to tertiary studies. Many see themselves as far more worldly and cynical than their parents.[55] Reliance on the media, and its role in the lives of this new audience, has taken on such momentum that it would now be extremely difficult for governments to attempt to limit it – especially the burgeoning Internet which not only provides instant, uncensored information, but also images.

A further problem undermining the social contract concept of supportive media coverage in war, is that levels of popular support for conflict and the military have declined in recent years. Though warning that the potential significance of these changes is not yet well documented, in a study of changing Australian opinions on defence, McAllister and Makkai argue that Australian public opinion and opinion in most other Western democracies is now less favourably disposed towards defence than at any time since the end of World War II. They suggest that this has been brought about by fundamental changes in social and political values in Western democracies, and from the different experiences and life chances of their populations. McAllister and Makkai point to evidence that these two trends – the improving international climate and changing values – are converging to radically transform popular attitudes towards the military in many societies.[56]

The changed nature of war has thus largely freed the citizen of the obligations governments could call upon in earlier wars of national survival, and the populace now expects, as a right, informational access on any aspect of any issue. A better educated and more critical citizen audience has become used to, if not dependent on, having the necessary information presented through the immediacy of a mainly electronic internationalised media. That media, in turn, has the potential to become independent of both national and military control.

The military response to the increasing technical independence of the media and its role as 'middleman' to public opinion has been to offer a system of media-military cooperation. In general, the military provides access, transport and communications, working out of a central media unit, in return for agreement by correspondents to submit their copy for scrutiny solely on the grounds of 'operational security'. In Australia this is organised by the Defence Media Advisory Group (DMAG) made up of media organisations and the military, which provides accredited correspondents (ACCOR). This is backed up by a dedicated Media Support Unit equipped with a wide range of communications. Similar systems are in effect in most other Western military forces.

The success of this form of cooperative arrangement relies, however, first on the remoteness of the campaign and, second, on its duration. Remoteness favours the military, while a lengthy conflict favours the media. Operations in areas far from civilian support infrastructures – such as the Falklands – give total advantage to the military. The difficult access and lack of local media infrastructure in Grenada and Panama favoured the military, while the Gulf provided the relative isolation of the desert. These factors increase the dependence of the media on the military and have generally resulted in greater exploitation by the military. But time is a major constraint. The advantage of remoteness quickly dissipates if the military cannot maintain momentum and seize victory quickly; for, as the advantage slips away, so the media emerges as an independent and highly competitive factor in the battle for public opinion.

Conclusion

In the past, the mandate and legitimacy of the central authority has been enhanced in time of war by the near universal perception of the need for common defence by a population facing a direct threat, either to their liberty or their physical survival. But it becomes a very different picture in time of limited conflict, especially when the conflict may have little bearing on the welfare or lifestyle of the majority of the people. Involvement may even be actively rejected by a significant proportion of the population. This raises the question of what duties and obligations are incumbent upon a citizen if, in his or her informed judgement, the conflict, or the reasons behind it, pose no threat to the common good.

The question becomes increasingly salient when it is considered that governments are constrained in their conduct of such conflicts, in that they need to limit the ambit of conflict and are effectively denied the propaganda weapons of the past. It is especially so when the conflict takes place in what would otherwise be considered peacetime, with all the concomitant constitutional guarantees of freedom of the press. An additional problem involves attempts to reign in the information expectations of the most informed, educated and critical audience the world has ever seen - an audience which now has access to individual video and voice links through the Internet and which will be served by an increasingly internationalised media backed up by exponential improvements in communications technology. The argument is negated to some extent by the success of the military in containing the media during the Falklands, Grenada, Panama and, more recently, in the Gulf conflict.

But this form of containment can only be maintained for a limited time and does not affect the main argument.

To date, other than within a very limited circle, media actors have given little thought to the theoretical and empirical issues raised by this situation. The military, on the other hand have long appreciated the problem and have come up with uniform systems across the Western world, to harness the media in cooperative arrangements which operate to the military's best advantage. The problem, as our case studies demonstrate, is that while the military have paid due deference to the rights of the media and the public in this changed environment, the cooperative arrangements they have established afford them the advantage. In almost every situation, this advantage has been exploited to the full, aided by the tendency of the media to mirror audience expectations.

But the military did not arrive at this happy circumstance of control by chance. An examination of the background and growth of the problem of the media on the battlefield reveals the attitudes that have resulted in this present situation of cooperative yet exploitative military control.

2

The Evolution of the Conflict between the Media and the Military

Until the emergence of the printing press, public opinion was governed by the teachings of the Church or the demands of the State. Public opinion was moulded by these authorities, who dominated what representative machinery existed, and who could be relied upon to represent their own interests.[1]

With the advent of the printing press and, importantly, the printing of newspapers, this situation changed. Once the printed word was freed of the shackles of licence and censorship which the state had used as its first line of defence, an avenue existed for the expression of public opinion. This public opinion, in turn, developed into a political force *external* to parliament or any other authority.[2] As Sir James MacIntosh remarked in 1803, when newspapers were beginning to emerge as a power:

> The multiplication of newspapers has produced a gradual revolution in our government by increasing the number of those who exercise some sort of judgement on public affairs.[3]

But MacIntosh was still speaking of a newspaper industry limited by the means of production and distribution, and which in the main catered to a political elite. The breakthrough that put newspapers within reach of the wider population came with the invention of the steam press in the early 1800s followed by the rotary press in 1846. When combined with linotype composition, devised by Mergenthaler in 1844, these innovations allowed up to 30,000 copies of an average-sized newspaper to be printed in one hour. The introduction in 1880 of the half tone system of reproducing photographs freed newspapers of the limitations of engraving and opened the way to the near immediate advantages of pictorial material.[4]

These improvements in production were matched by rapid strides in the means of gathering and disseminating information. The introduction of the electric telegraph and Samuel Morse's code saw transmission across the English Channel in 1851, and spanning the Atlantic Ocean in 1866. In 1877 Edison patented his phonograph and by the turn of the century, the telephone was in widespread use. In 1882 the first wireless communication was made between the Isle of Wight and the English mainland. In 1899 this was followed by the first practical demonstration of Marconi's wireless. In Australia, the electric telegraph linked Sydney to Melbourne and Adelaide in 1858, with the first cables from Great Britain in 1872 and the first wireless transmission in 1903.[5]

These developments in the gathering of information and production techniques were accompanied by the growth of the railways and later the petrol engine, which facilitated rapid distribution of printed news. More importantly, the process of information dissemination was assisted by the concentration of workers into the cities, as part of the great social change brought about by the industrial revolution. In Britain, the introduction of compulsory education from around 1880 onwards provided an increasingly literate population anxious for news and entertainment. There were similar developments in most other Western industrialised nations.[6] In addition, political reform led to a massive increase in newly-franchised voters who presented both a market and a target. Economies of scale led to a steady reduction in unit cost and increased circulation of publications. Over the next half century, newspapers such as Lord Northcliffe's *Daily Mail* could lay claim to daily circulation figures of over half a million.[7]

This marriage of an educated constituency with the means to inform it soon showed an effect on politics. A new mass audience had been created and the battle to influence the populace began, with the reader identified as a target to be swayed through the power of the press. At first these first forays into the manipulation of public opinion excluded defence matters, where nationalism and patriotism still ruled and the media never strayed far from representing views of government. But it seemed unlikely that the situation could remain that way for ever.

Long before the arrival of the mass media, truth had been accepted as the first casualty of war. It was understood that governments or military leaders would attempt to manipulate public opinion in support of their war aims and, while such control had been relatively easy to impose prior to the advent of a modern press media, the presence of reporters on the battlefield signalled a change in relationships. The media's capacity to acquire and disseminate independent information meant that the government's ability to control public opinion in time of war, and the military's ability to limit information, was considerably weakened. The fact that this new media could present views other than the war aims of the government of the day – in what were mainly nationalistic wars – was immediately seen to be inimical to the interests of the state. Certainly, it was anathema to the military. As a result, censorship, or at least the limitation of information, rapidly became an accepted adjunct to the conduct of war. From the very start this was rationalised as nothing more than a proper limitation on information that might be prejudicial to the operational security of the troops involved. This catch-all cry of 'operational security', which is still embraced in Western democracies, was first used by Sir Arthur Wellesley who, at the time of the Napoleonic Wars, complained in a letter to the War Office:

> I beg draw your Lordship's attention to the frequent paragraphs in the English Newspapers describing the position and numbers, the objects, the means of attaining them possessed by the Armies in Spain and Portugal... This intelligence must have reached the enemy at the same time as it did me, at a moment at which it was most important that he should not receive it.[8]

Formalised military censorship was not introduced until later in the nineteenth century, but the dilemma of whether to withhold strategically important facts or to report them in the national interest existed from the very beginning.[9] Newspapers had long retained serving officers to report on their campaigns, but the emergence of the professional journalist who bore no responsibility to the profession of arms or the cause at hand, provided the catalyst for change.

The first professional war correspondent was Henry Crabb Robinson, who covered Napoleon's campaigns along the River Elbe in 1807 and the action at Corrunna in the Peninsular campaign the following year for the London *Times*. He was followed by Charles Lewis Guneiso of the *Morning Post* who provided a comprehensive and balanced coverage of the Spanish Civil War of 1835–7.[10] But it was William Howard Russell of the London *Times* who gave the first real demonstration of the power and problems inherent in modern war reporting.

From the Crimea to the Colonies: 1850–1860

Russell was not alone when he was sent to cover the Crimea. Other correspondents included Thomas Chenery also of the *Times*, Nicholas Woods of the *Morning Herald* and J.A. Crowe of the *Illustrated London News*. But it was Russell, in partnership with his equally talented editor, John Thadeus Delane, who caught the public's attention.[11] In a series of objective reports that gained a wide following back in England, Russell recorded the incredible hardships suffered by the ill-prepared and poorly equipped troops in the long siege before Sebastopol. More telling were his reports of the horrors that awaited the almost 30 per cent of the 56,000 allied forces who went to hospital through cholera, dysentery or malaria:

> The dead laid out as they died, were laying side by side with the living and the latter presented a spectacle beyond all imagination. The commonest accessories of a hospital were wanting, there was not the least attention paid to decency or cleanliness – the stench was appalling... the sick appeared to be tended by the sick and the dying by the dying.[12]

Descriptions of the shocking conditions under which the men fought and died demonstrated the power of the war correspondent. The public catalogue of failure led to Delane setting up the fund that sent Florence Nightingale out to reform the hospital system, while the revelations about the conduct of the war, backed up by the editorials written by Delane himself, aroused public opinion to such an extent that it led to the fall of the Aberdeen government in 1855. Still, the hostility encountered both at the front and in London was at times intense, with Russell being denounced as a charlatan and Delane coming under heavy political pressure. But truth prevailed, and Russell, along with Chenery, set the standard by which succeeding war correspondents would be judged.

Russell also pioneered entry into the grey area of operational security. Despite offering to have his dispatches cleared by the military, he was accused of aiding Russian intelligence through his reporting. Raglan, who had not been spared by Russell over the conditions of the medical services, caustically reported to his superiors that '... the enemy had no need of a secret service, all they had to do was to read the *Times*.'[13] As a result, Russell had to live at the front with suspicions fostered among the soldiers that he might have been responsible for their casualties. He also faced great political pressure and press harassment at home as the High Command reached for the only weapon it had – accusations of espionage

But Russell was vindicated and went on to cover the Indian Mutiny. George Warrington Steevens of the *Daily Mail* followed in his footsteps in the Sudan, while others covered the forty-nine British colonial campaigns or expeditions that were mounted between 1856 and 1897.[14] This pattern was repeated in the French, Dutch and German press as they covered their own colonial or expansionist clashes. However, without exception, the correspondents who accompanied these colonial or punitive expeditions supported the armies they were sent to cover. They had to, because they were hired by imperialist-minded proprietors to cater to a populist and jingoistic readership, avid for the thrills and excitement of war.[15]

The Golden Age of War Reporting: 1860–1910

The colonial campaigns may have made good reading, but it was the American Civil War (1861–65), the Franco-Prussian War (1870), the Sudan (1898), the Boer War (1899–1902), and the Russo-Japanese War (1904-05) which were to prove the real testing ground of the war correspondent and military alike. In America, this period took in the Spanish American War (1898) along with some smaller conflicts. The military on each occasion had to contend with the very real issues of security and the mobilisation of national and international public opinion. The correspondent, with his new technologies of cable communications, photography and even cinematography, presented a new and major worry. The problem was countered by formalised and stricter censorship, and increasing control over the levels of access, transport and support afforded to correspondents. In particular, access to military communications was limited.

This period, which Knightley terms the 'golden age' of defence reporting,[16] saw papers following the flag in the sure knowledge that wars generated circulation. And despite the developing restrictions, they continued to sway public opinion. The reports of J.A. MacGahan in the London *Daily Mail*, revealing the Turkish atrocities during the Bulgarian uprising of 1876, played a major part in invoking international condemnation of Turkey. Later, during the Japanese invasion of Manchuria in 1894, James Creelman, an American who had first come to prominence in the Spanish American War, wrote so graphically of the Japanese atrocities at Port Arthur that he is credited with turning American opinion against Japan.[17]

But all that was in the future. The American Civil War was where technology began to show its effect.

The American Civil War

Russell was only one of many hundreds of reporters who covered the American Civil War, but he was one of the few to take an unbiased view. Again, he was the pioneer in bearing the brunt of official displeasure when breaking unwelcome news.

A prime example was reaction to Russell's factual coverage of the battle of Bull Run, once it was reported back to the United States from Britain. As Delane wrote when praising Russell's coverage, 'My fear is only that the U.S. will not be able to bear the truth so plainly told.'[18] According to Russell's diary, Delane's warning was an understatement. The resulting furore over what was regarded as unpatriotic reporting came from every quarter in the North. Russell received assassination threats, libellous articles were written about him, and he was given the nickname 'Bull Run Russell'.[19]

The attitude of the military differed between commanders, but both Russell and the equally eminent photographer, Matthew Brady, reported universal distrust for the American press. And it would seem that the military had good cause.[20] Russell was continually shocked by the lies told by the press of both North and South.[21] The majority of the American correspondents were under the age of 30, poorly paid, and employed by demanding and unscrupulous editors who wanted news at any price. Russell, however, continued to report what he saw. The result was that he continued to be a trailblazer, this time as the reporter 'wearing out his welcome.' His factual reports became so embarrassing that his accreditation was eventually withdrawn by both sides. It was at this point that, unable any longer to ply his trade, he returned home.

In 1862, soon after Russell had left, the North set up a formal system of censorship. The United States Secretary for War, Edwin M. Stanton helped set the pattern for the future when he deliberately held up news of the surrender at Harpers Ferry (1862) and altered the North's casualty figures at Petersburg (1864–1865), reducing Grant's losses by a third. He also suspended the publication of Northern newspapers and began arresting editors and threatening proprietors with court-martial if they did not support the government. He even issued orders for one correspondent to be shot for refusing to hand over a dispatch.[22]

In 1864, Stanton began the practice of issuing daily 'war bulletins', addressed ostensibly to the Chief Military Authority in New York, but circulated through Associated Press.[23] At the same time, a now familiar pattern was set by some commanders who formed close alliances with journalists for the career benefits of having their exploits publicised. Others took exception to the way actions were reported. General Meade, paraded one journalist through the ranks to the tune of the Rogue's March, sitting backwards on an old horse, with the placard 'Libeller of the Press' tied to his chest. Meade was subsequently blackballed by the media corps for the rest of the war.[24]

The American Civil War also saw the first real battle for international support through the media, with both sides engaging in overt and covert propaganda for their cause.

Without the industrial resources of the North, the Confederacy realised that its logistic salvation lay with Britain. In an effort to sway public opinion in favour of their cause, the South sent an agent whose task was to suborn the British press, apparently to good effect. Lincoln countered by widening the issue from state's rights versus federalism to the far more appealing issue of the abolition of slavery.[25]

These were new and interesting developments in audience manipulation. But, in media-military relations, the biggest impact of the American Civil War lay in the formalisation of patterns of censorship and indirect political and military control. The growth in communications and photography, plus vast improvements in newspaper production and distribution, had created an enormous capacity for information dissemination matched by an avid public appetite for war reporting.

The Franco-Prussian War

While the United States had been occupied with its Civil War, powers on the continent had mobilised on a much larger scale for wars of national confrontation.

In 1870, an indignant France declared war on Germany, following a supposed snub of their ambassador by King William of Prussia during negotiations over the vacant throne of Spain. The French saw it as a matter of honour, but Count Otto Von Bismarck, the Prussian Chancellor, saw it as an opportunity. The Prussian Chief of General Staff, General Von Moltke, had modernised his armies and built up a railway system to support troops in the field. Within eighteen days, Prussia had mobilised and deployed a force of over a million men. The press also began to mobilise for a war which would see the full arsenal of media management strategies applied by the belligerents, from complete censorship on the French side, to deliberate media exploitation and manipulation by the Germans.

Napoleon III, the French Emperor, unwisely refused to have any foreign correspondents with his army. According to Russell, one of the reasons could have been the War Ministry's awareness that neutral observers might identify deficiencies which correspondents of the French press either could not detect or were afraid to report.[26]

Bismarck, on the other hand, recognised the value of a friendly press, not least in England. As a result, both Russell and Archibald Forbes, two of the most notable journalists of the day, followed the Germans. Forbes set new standards in organising telegraphic communications, reporting events in London within twenty-four hours of their happening. Labouchere, another English reporter, with a reputation as something of a dilettante, sent out copy by air, using hot air balloons. These advances pointed the way to the future but, beyond that, there was little to be learned. The French press was limited by a jingoistic and patriotic mood that would brook nothing less than optimistic reporting. The German press, however, had little need of censorship in its reporting of continuing and rapid victories.

The most important lesson to come out of the war was the way in which Bismarck totally repudiated an interview Russell had with the Prussian Crown Prince, regarding the meeting between the King and Napoleon. Despite the fact that Bismarck himself admitted to a misunderstanding at the time, Russell's reputation for accurate reporting was sacrificed in the national interest. Russell himself could do little more than bite his tongue, since to do otherwise would have been to betray his source. It was too late when Russell was later shown to be correct. It was also a pattern of official deception that was to be repeated time after time in the following years as the media became more internationalised.[27]

The Sudan

By the time Kitchener was dispatched to the Sudan in 1898, a clear understanding of the power of the press was reflected in a hardening of the military's attitude towards the correspondent. Kitchener imposed strict censorship and limited access to reports of only 200 words a day on the telegraph for the twenty-six correspondents who accompanied him. He held the reporters in absolute contempt, referring to them on one occasion as 'drunken swabs.' His policy was to give them no assistance or information whatsoever. It was only after representations had been made by the editor of the London *Times* to the government that correspondents were allowed to accompany the troops within the area of operations.[28] But, despite these difficulties, the conflict was little more than the victory of machine guns over spears, and was to be the last of the old style imperial wars where jingoism was the guiding light in reporting.

From the Sudan on, it was to be a far more serious game. The press could be controlled, but its power to influence public opinion could also be exploited. The correspondent was now seen, and used, as an extension of policy in an attempt to win international support.

The Boer War

When General Redvers Buller sailed in the *Dunottar Castle*, in October 1899, to quash the Boer Republics in South Africa, he took with him a veritable army of correspondents. At the height of the campaign there were over 300 journalists in the field, representing British, American and European newspapers. The London *Times* at one point had twenty representatives.[29] The campaign also attracted a contingent of press photographers and Buller took with him the first ever British war cinematographers. The release of early newsreels of the action caused enormous public excitement, especially a segment recording an incident in which a British Red Cross team came under enemy fire while attending to the wounded. It was later revealed to be a fake, staged by paid actors on Hampstead Heath and sponsored by the government to whip up public support. This was the first example of what was to be a continuing pattern of the government use of this form of news media for propaganda purposes.[30]

Roberts, who replaced Buller in January 1900, instituted a series of regular briefings and communiques. He also imposed strict censorship at the point of access to the military telegraph. As Roberts rightly pointed out, information on dispositions and intentions, or other factors such as morale, could be back in the European capitals within the hour, providing vital information to a sophisticated enemy like the Boers. France and Germany, in particular, were hostile to the British and were sure to pass information on.

This first exercise of censorship on a major scale set the pattern for the military bias that has been a concern ever since. The problem was summed up by Edgar Wallace of the *Daily Mail*, when he complained:

> If I wanted to cable from here that the situation was unusually optimistic, do you think that the censor here would offer any objection to it going? But if I wished to send the truth that the country around is full of boers and rebels are joining the commandoes daily, would the censor pass that without being called to book by Kitchener in three weeks time ... So much for censorship.[31]

In addition to censorship, correspondents were manipulated by the military into sending dispatches acceptable to the commander. Baden Powell, the commander at Mafeking allowed journalists entry into the besieged city but refused to let them out on the basis that they might evade his censorship and report on rumour which was at odds with his depiction of a gallant stand by a small group of beleaguered sons of the empire. One aspect of the situation he was particularly anxious to hide was the almost starvation rations afforded by him to the black population, whose only other alternative was to run the gauntlet of the Boers. When this was reported by Hamilton of the London *Times* in a smuggled dispatch, the paper simply refused to print it because it was at odds with the almost hysterical popular support for Baden Powell. It was a perfect example of the limitations faced by the media in that they seldom dared to go beyond reflecting public expectations.[32]

The Boer war can be seen to have preceded the Vietnam war in its cyclical pattern of jingoism, patriotism, questioning, and then doubt within the home nation, as the Boers turned the conflict into an unpopular protracted war of insurgency.[33] Kitchener's response was to tighten censorship and make it an offence for soldiers to discuss the conduct of the war with correspondents. By the beginning of 1901 however, military frustration and public concern over the treatment of the Boers led to calls for a negotiated settlement. This was achieved in April 1902. It led to a near breakdown in military-press relations as Kitchener threw a security blanket over the talks. The news of a successful peace was broken only when Wallace used an informant and a visual code to signal the outcome of the peace talks. Wallace and the *Daily Mail* scooped the world. Wallace's reward from Kitchener was to have his accreditation removed. It was to be a lifetime ban that would last and exclude him from reporting World War I.[34]

The Boer war furthered a developing pattern. That pattern was one of strict censorship through control over the means of communications, the imposition of military bias in censorship, and punitive measures against journalists who did not meet military expectations. These limitations became almost insurmountable in combination with home editors who dared not move beyond prevailing public opinion. All that was missing to complete the picture was disinformation and misinformation, but that was to come.

The Russo-Japanese War

The 'golden age' of war reporting came to an abrupt end when, in 1904, Japan challenged the might of Russia over its claims to Manchuria. More than a hundred correspondents presented themselves in Tokyo for accreditation. Lacking a free press themselves, the Japanese simply did not know how to handle the problem. The answer was a stratagem that has since taken root around the world – that of the elusive visa.

The problem was made a diplomatic one, with the several national ambassadors having to apply for visas on behalf of individual correspondents. The applications were then conveniently lost in the Japanese bureaucracy. As a result of this move, fewer that twenty foreign correspondents are believed to have covered the war. The Japanese press, in contrast, was deployed in large numbers, albeit constrained by the same patriotic limitations that had hampered national coverage in other conflicts.

Apart from the obvious cultural differences displayed by foreign correspondents, the Japanese suspected most journalists of being spies. As Knightley points out, the ease with which some changed their calling from journalist to government agent gave some credence to this suspicion, as it does to the present day.[35] The conflict also demonstrated, for the first time, the value of radio. Lionel James of the London *Times* secretly installed a radio transmitter aboard a chartered yacht. With official approval, which some believe included using it on behalf of Japanese intelligence, he successfully reported on the naval war. The Japanese, however, retained control of his shore link and banned his broadcasts when he had served their purpose.[36]

Beyond this first known use of radio, the biggest lesson learned from the military point of view was the efficacy of absolute, or near absolute, denial of access. Another lesson learned was that the day of the geographically-limited battlefield was over. The Japanese waged war on fronts of more than 150 kilometres (90 miles). These distances presented new challenges for the war correspondent. In the future, journalists would be as dependent on the army for transport as they already were for communications. This led to the emergence of a new breed of correspondent – the analyst – such as Charles a'Court Repington, who covered World War I in detail for the London *Times* while remaining in London. Commenting on this new role, Repington wrote:

> I had seen from the outset that more useful work could be done by a man who remained at the London nerve centre, than war correspondents of the old type who sought to repeat the feats of Russell, Archibald Forbes and Steevens at the seat of war. I knew

they would be shepherded, almost imprisoned and prevented from telling the truth owing to the regulations which had been established in all Armies to muzzle the press, whereas in London, I had no censorship to control me and could speak my mind.[37]

Repington was right in everything, other than being able to foresee the absolute control of public information on which to base those judgements; this was demonstrated more than seventy-five years later during the Gulf conflict. Repington's clear analysis of the conduct of the war, however, far outstripped the limited reporting of those remaining in the field.

The success of the Japanese policy of exclusion was borne out by the fact that only the Italian war correspondent, Luigi Barzini and two news agency men remained to see the war out. Of these, Barzini was the only one permitted to move outside the Japanese military headquarters. Even then, he was allowed out only under the escort of a military attache.[38]

Along with other nations, the British had sent a team of military observers to this conflict. The policy of censorship by absolute denial, and the freedom of action it afforded the commander, was not lost on them. It is believed to have played a major part in formulating British policy during the next great test, the Great War of 1914–1918, involving the European powers of France, Great Britain, Germany and Russia.[39]

The Great War: Patriotism and Still More Patriotism

Given the hindsight of history, there is little to recommend World War I, except the individual gallantry and sacrifice of those concerned. It was mismanaged butchery on a massive scale, yet the truth of the war aims, the conduct of war, and the losses were mostly concealed from the home nations by the media, both print and film, under the guise of patriotism. The largest share of the blame for this must rest with the war correspondents on each side who, as Knightley put it:

... were in a position to know more than most men of the nature of the war of attrition on the Western Front, yet they identified themselves absolutely with the armies in the field; they protected the high command from criticism, wrote jauntily about life in the trenches, kept an inspired silence about the slaughter and allowed themselves to be absorbed by the propaganda machine.[40]

There is some excuse for this grave charge, in that for some time there had been calls for restrictions on the press in time of war. In November 1904, the British Minister for War, Arnold-Foster, in an internal war office memo, had foreshadowed some form of limitations based on the experiences gained during the Russo-Japanese war.[41] This was followed up at a subsequent meeting of the Committee of Imperial Defence, where a war office minute entitled 'Control of the Press in Time of War or Threat' drew up plans for restricting the reporting of military matters in time of war or national emergency. As a result, a Joint Military Press Committee was introduced in 1912 and, following the outbreak of war in 1914, a War Press Bureau was formed headed by F.E. Smith, later Lord Birkenhead.[42]

The war office plans for media management were abandoned, however, when Kitchener, with his entrenched attitudes towards correspondents, assumed command of the British Army. One of Kitchener's first orders was to follow the French policy of absolute exclusion of the media and he ordered the withdrawal of all correspondents. As a result, the British Expeditionary Force (BEF) was deployed to France without a single journalist attached.[43]

Under Kitchener's orders, any correspondent found in the field was to be arrested and have his passport withdrawn. Because of this, the only independent British coverage of the first few weeks of the war was provided by a London *Times* correspondent, Arthur Moore, in France en route to Serbia, and Hamilton Fyfe of the *Daily Mail*. Both these correspondents were able to observe the initial clash and retreat from Mons. Moore's accurate reporting of the heavy losses suffered by the British was printed in the *Times* under the headline, 'Broken British Regiments Battling Against Odds', along with a reprint of a piece by Fyfe, headlined 'German Tidal Wave, Our Soldiers Overwhelmed.'[44] The Amiens Dispatch, as it became known, was immediately (and quite wrongly) denied by Kitchener, and the *Times* was berated by the other leading British newspapers for printing inaccurate and unpatriotic alarmist war news. Both pieces, however, had been cleared by the London-based censor. In fact, the censor had re-instated much of what the *Times* had deleted, in the belief that a warning exposé would help recruiting. This offered some defence, but the damage had been done and for a while freedom of the press hung in the balance.

The government's answer to this problem was the appointment of a military officer, Colonel Ernest Swinton, to write 'eyewitness' accounts from France, for use by the press. Items were vetted by the Chief of Intelligence, the various General Officers Commanding involved in the particular piece and, according to some accounts, by Kitchener himself.[45] Weekly publications such as *The Illustrated War News* and *The Great War* were employed also to present an idealised view of allied war efforts and to propagandise against the enemy, making good use of photographs, drawings and maps.[46] The bowdlerised and sanitised 'eyewitness' reports, which lasted to mid-1915, satisfied neither the press nor the public – primarily because Repington, acting in his role as 'armchair' correspondent, was consistently outguessing them. Repington's success in revealing such issues as the shocking ammunition shortages, led to the *Times* being openly burned and picketed, with placards condemning it as an 'Ally of the Hun.'[47] But, as Repington was proved right, public unease over the lack of news, and dissatisfaction with the official 'eyewitness' reports, brought increasing pressure from journalists and the politically influential Newspaper Proprietors Association for a more active and independent press coverage. As Phillip Gibbs of the *Daily Chronicle* wrote in April 1915:

> Even the enormous impregnable stupidity of our High Command in all matters of psychology was penetrated by a vague notion that a few 'writing fellows' might be sent out with permission to follow the armies in the field, under the strictest censorship, in order to silence the clamour for more news.[48]

As a result of this pressure for greater press freedom, from May 1915 to the end of the war, correspondents were placed on attachment with the British armies in Flanders, the Middle East and Gallipoli. This group was to include in their ranks photographers, war artists and, especially, film makers, who in the age of Chaplin were to play an increasingly important role.

At the same time, this access was matched by a growth in government controls. In 1917 a Ministry of Information was formed under Lord Beaverbrook. The following year a rival organisation, the Department of Enemy Propaganda, was created under Lord Northcliffe.[49] In the climate of World War I, however, the controls were largely unnecessary, since the overwhelming patriotism and sense of duty among the media in the field resulted in total commitment to the government's war aims. Gibbs explained the situation in his post-war memoirs:

> We identified ourselves absolutely with the Armies in the field.... We wiped out of our minds all thoughts of personal scoops and all temptation to write one word which would make the task of officers and men more difficult or dangerous. There was no need of censorship of our dispatches. We were our own censors.[50]

This attitude was to conceal from the British and French publics the realities of poor planning and the resultant mechanised slaughter which was to be the hallmark of the Great War. Not only did correspondents not report the truth, but in the main they willingly participated in propaganda and what could be described only as a massive conspiracy to keep news of the real course of the war from the public. It was much the same in Germany, where the war effort came first. The aim of both governments was to foster hatred of the enemy. This early form of 'demonisation' was based mainly on atrocity stories, most of which subsequently proved to be unfounded.

Both sides, while keeping their own populations in the dark, also went on the offensive to fight their case in the overseas media, with the United States their main target. The prize was either continued American neutrality for the Germans, or intervention on behalf of the Allies. Despite exploiting the heavy Germanic population in the United States, the Germans were beaten hands down by a media campaign organised by the British secret service. There were specific factors such as the sinking of the Lusitania but, according to Frederick Palmer who represented three American newspapers in London, overall it was the British effort within the American media had brought the United States into the war.[51]

There were also some critics who would not be silenced. In particular, there was the Australian, (Sir) Keith Murdoch, aided by Ellis Ashmead Bartlett, and in a more restrained manner, the official Australian war historian, C.E.W. Bean. Despite the same pressures of patriotism, the accurate reporting of these individuals played a major role in drawing the attention of the Australian public and government to the realities of the situation in Gallipoli. But their actions, which in the case of Murdoch went as far as the British war cabinet, were devoted to the welfare of their own nationals and the conduct and levels of support of Australian operations.[52] The Americans, too, once they were committed, presented a much more critical approach. But again criticism was generally limited in favour of the overall war aims and the gallantry of their national contingent.

In Britain, Repington, in his regular *Times* column, 'The Military Situation', was one of the few who looked at the broader issues of freedom of the press and the need for an informed public. He commented that 'The ignorance of the people because of censorship, is unbelievable.'[53] But that ignorance was carefully fostered and protected by the media, despite losses of up to 5 million French servicemen, 60,000 British soldiers in one hour at Paschaendale, and an estimated 3 million German combatants. The pattern of uncritical patriotic support by the media was by then too entrenched, and both journalists and politicians were too committed to back off. As the British Prime Minister, Lloyd George, put it in December 1917, 'If people really knew, the war would be stopped tomorrow. But of course they don't know and can't know. The correspondents don't write and the censor would not pass the truth.'[54]   Letters from the front which got past the censors, however, painted a more realistic picture. Jack Watts (killed in action in France during World War I) wrote to his sister on 30 May 1916:

> You might not believe it ... but a man is considered jolly lucky if he gets a wound that is considered bad enough for him to be sent to England. This place is hell and it is going to be worse before long. So you can understand when you read in the papers about the happy wounded heros [sic]. They are happy because they know they do not have to go back to the trenches again for a while.[55]

The tragedy of it all was that the troops in their millions knew the realities, but even they found it difficult to persuade their families.[56]

The major lesson to be learned from this conflict is that the media is largely powerless in the face of the combination of political strictures and public expectations in what can be termed 'patriotic' wars. Certainly the closing of the ranks and abrogation of individual rights, including that of a free press in favour of an over-riding national interest of survival, might validly be accepted in the case of France, and later Germany, under the terms of the ancient social contract. It is difficult, however, to accept the level of restriction and complicity in hiding the truth, and infringement of freedom of the press, that took place in Britain, especially in the early days of the war. World War I provided a graphic demonstration of the fact that one of the limitations on a free press remains the acceptability of news to the audience and, in this case, the mood of the audience was one of patriotic optimism. Whether, as in the case of the objective reporting by the *Times*, early on in the war, the media could have gone against the trend and survived, is debatable.

A further and final factor is the lack of parliamentary debate or fact finding committees at the end of the war. Everyone was content to leave things as they were, take their knighthoods, of which more than forty were awarded to the war correspondents, and concentrate instead on remembrance of the gallantry and sacrifice of those involved.

Spain and Abyssinia: Partisan Propaganda

The inter-war period saw little development either in reporting or technology. In the case of Abyssinia, the Italian media was as committed as that of the Allies during World War I and constrained by national expectations of Empire. More than 120 foreign correspondents gathered in Addis Ababa, but they were limited by language, transport, distance, heat, disease, and chaotic and uncertain communications. Those who chose to accompany the Italians were encouraged by the Ministry of Press and Propaganda, but rebuffed by the army. In the event, the dozen or so foreign correspondents who remained to the end, along with the Italian contingent, provided a faithful interpretation of the eventual Italian victory.

There was little in the way of lessons to be learned, other than an expanded use of military radio communications, which was in the main denied to the correspondents. There was also the warning to be on the winning side, since the Italians promptly expelled all those correspondents who had been accredited to Abyssinia.[57]

Abyssinia, however, was little more than the prelude to the Spanish Civil War (1936–1939), which in turn was a practice run for World War II. In Spain, both the Fascists and Communists enjoyed absolute partisan reporting from those who covered the conflict. It was one long propaganda battle, with little of it based on reality. As George Orwell put it when looking back in 1943:

> I saw newspaper reports which did not bear any relation to the facts, not even the relationship which is implied in an ordinary lie. I saw great battles reported where there had been no fighting and complete silence where hundreds of men had been killed.... I saw newspapers in London retailing those lies and eager intellectuals building emotional superstructures over events that had never happened.[58]

Little had changed in the reporting other than the exchange of ideology for patriotism as the cover for partisan reporting. The left covered the left and the right the right; and, despite their commitment, both were still subjected to rigorous censorship.

The conflict showed no major advances in the methods of news collection or communication, even though correspondents had access to a greatly improved international telephone and cable service. Radio was beginning to gain widespread acceptance in the Western world, but there is little evidence of its sustained or coherent use for direct broadcasting. The cinema, in particular the newsreels, emerged as an important source of information with a high level of credibility; but beyond a steady output of propaganda films from both sides, the war remained remote from the public.

The major advance seems to have been in the range of media used for dissemination of propaganda. This now included film, the novel, posters, photography in its own right, and art. The statement made by Picasso in his painting of the suffering of Guernica, for example, effectively drew attention to high level bombing carried out by the German Condor

Legion, while Robert Capa's famous, albeit faked, photograph of a soldier supposedly caught at the moment of being shot dead, drew attention to the heroism of the Republican forces.[59]

World War II: More of the Same

The ideological battle between democracy and National Socialism (Nazi) philosophy began in 1933, soon after Hitler came to power. It was a battle primarily fought in the newspapers and newsreels. Many foresaw an ultimate struggle, however, and it was against this background that, in 1935, the Committee of Imperial Defence set up a sub-committee to plan for the control of information in time of war.[60] The Committee's recommendation was that the task should be handled by a single ministry with responsibility for coordinating all aspects of propaganda and information.[61] As a result of this planning, two days before the declaration of war in 1939, a Ministry of Information was created with an establishment of nearly a thousand personnel. Under the Emergency Powers (Defence) Act, the new Ministry was given unlimited powers to censor every press, commercial or private message leaving Britain by mail, cable, wireless or telephone. All persons, including newspaper editors, were '... prohibited from obtaining, recording, communicating to any other person or publishing information which might be useful to the enemy.'[62]

Despite these far ranging powers, the ministry suffered from a lack of cooperation from the services and, more importantly, was sidelined by Churchill himself. Despite his journalistic background, Churchill saw the media as a security risk and consistently bypassed the press on important issues by broadcasting direct to the nation or making statements in Parliament.[63] To make matters worse, the first clumsy efforts at emulating the 'eyewitness' system of World War I was a failure for much the same reasons it had failed in 1914–15, and the early attempts to field war correspondents descended into a shambles, complete with contemptuous cavalry officer escorts and complaints from correspondents that the navy afforded nothing while the army and air force misled them. It took the Ministry almost two years to get a uniform censorship code in place.[64]

The Germans were better prepared. They provided a wide range of services to correspondents from neutral countries, as long as they adhered to the pro-German line. They also went to extreme lengths to influence American public opinion, with a surprising openness. This may have been because, in the early days of the war, the message they had to sell was one of unqualified success.

Inside Germany itself, the media was seen as simply another weapon of war. Journalists, artists, broadcasters, cinematographers and photographers were enlisted into military units known as Propagandakompien. Their task was to use their civilian skills to inform both the military and the home population. The fact that they were in uniform as part of the normal military organisation meant that there was no question of the need for censorship or neutral or objective reporting. A glance at any copy of the German internal military publication, *SIGNAL*, which covered every front, and the high praise still afforded the radio stations they set up in every theatre of war, bears testament to the effectiveness of these units. They were also active in enemy propaganda. Any questions of objectivity were, and still are, answered with the assertion that they were engaged initially in a patriotic war and later a fight for survival – imperatives that brooked no opposition.[65]

In contrast, the Russian campaign – perhaps the definitive patriotic war – remained largely unreported despite some of the biggest battles of World War II. When Russia entered the war against Germany, her part in the struggle began to gain coverage, but mainly through the blatant propaganda efforts of committed left-wing journalists aimed at enlisting support for Stalin and the opening of a second front. More evidence may now be forthcoming, but at present it is safe to say that the exigencies of the struggle, plus the ruthless censorship and news management of the Soviet leadership, revealed little of the events of the war to the Russian people. Most media outputs were little more than carefully orchestrated propaganda for home consumption, similar to that used to enlist international support. As Brzezenski and Huntingdon state, 'The Soviet citizen had access only to official sources of information designed to elicit from him the desirable political reaction.'[66]

Other societies could be managed in much the same way. Dunkirk was the watershed for the British. No one had prepared the public for such a disaster; certainly not the muzzled and committed media, none of whom – apart from one freelance journalist, David Divine – was present at the evacuation. The evacuation itself was presented through the medium of government-controlled film and radio coverage as a major propaganda victory over adversity.[67] Much the same can be said for the Battle of Britain and the Blitz. A largely subservient and ill-informed media retailed the optimism peddled wholesale by the Ministry of Information and the services.[68] The Blitz and the Battle of Britain were also well served by a large American media contingent who, from an analysis of their reporting, were predominantly pro-British. And not even they were allowed to exercise any opinion on the frightful losses being taken by Britain in the battle of the Atlantic convoys. This information was simply classified and not made available until the issue became a media non-event.[69]

American correspondents came under the same strict censorship following the bombing of Pearl Harbor and the entry of America into the war. After the attack, the US Navy at first refused to divulge the names of the sunken vessels, which included the two battleships, *Arizona* and *Okalahoma*. This, as Collier puts it, was '... despite the fact that correspondents could see both ships, along with the *California* fifty feet down in the clear water.'[70] But this attitude changed as the United States military came to appreciate the value of war correspondents in informing the home nation of the conduct of the war. Japan, meanwhile, operating under the code of Bushido, tolerated no alternative views, and initially was prepared to treat all foreign correspondents as spies. In the event, they were tolerated, but the limited access they were granted was no better than during the Russo-Japanese or Manchurian wars.[71]

For the British, the turning of the tide in the Middle East, after the series of disasters in the early part of the war, led to improvements in the handling of correspondents. This was primarily because of the need to broadcast those successes to boost morale on the home front. Many of the improvements , such as mobile censors and priority air carriage of copy, was due to the attitude of commanders who were determined that the mistakes they had seen in World War I should not be repeated. In 1942, General Alexander, the then Commander in North Africa, summed up the military position:

> The press correspondent is just as good a fellow as any military officer or man who knows a great many secrets, and he will never let you down, on purpose, but he may let you down if he is not in the picture, merely because his duty to his paper forces him to write something, and that something may be dangerous. Therefore he must be kept in the picture.[72]

Montgomery was also an enthusiastic supporter of the war correspondent, in line with his strong commitment to morale. As Desmond Hawkins, who served as a BBC correspondent with Montgomery throughout most of the European campaign, put it:

> It was largely because of Monty's endorsement that our war reporting unit went into Normandy in such strength, and, for the first time in war with adequate equipment. Monty sensed the importance of keeping the public at home and the worldwide audience in day by day, even hour by hour touch with the progress of his armies.[73]

On the larger scene, Eisenhower took much the same view:

> I regard war correspondents as quasi staff officers, and I want to emphasise that, in my opinion, each newsman has a greater responsibility than that of a competitive newsman. I am not prepared to treat you as my enemies. If I thought you were, I tell you here and now, I would do nothing for you, I trust you... As staff officers however your first duty is a military duty, and the one fact which you must bear in mind is to disclose nothing which would help the enemy.[74]

Meanwhile in the Pacific, General MacArthur was to prove himself adept at using the media. The realities of a complete lack of preparedness was hidden through the strictest censorship and public concern glossed over by public relations optimism. As Royle puts it:

> Most of the journalists were critical of the lack of preparation for the defence of Port Moresby but they were permitted to say little. To them it was clear that official stories which spoke of the build-up of great allied armies were little more than a public relations' bluff. The reality, they knew, was rather different.[75]

There was also an attitude that the military should not be questioned. Chester Wilmot, who had made a name for himself as a correspondent in the Middle East, clashed with the Australian Commander, General Thomas Blamey. Blamey informed Wilmot that it was not part of the war correspondent's job to be critical of the Australian high command; criticism promoted the wrong image of the Australian war effort. Blamey later withdrew Wilmot's accreditation in retaliation for his coverage of the campaigns in Papua and New Guinea, with the comment that, 'We should give thousands of pounds to have someone in your position in Japan trying to undermine the C-in-C there. Your accreditation to Allied land forces is forthwith cancelled. You will return to Australia at once.'[76]

In the main however, the Australian military had a captive and generally supportive press. Kenneth Slessor wrote while covering the Australians in the Middle East in 1942, that 'Every correspondent wants to help the effort to win the war, and *wouldn't mind colouring his dispatches to suit the Plan*' (emphasis added).[77]

This repeat of the World War I ethos, with journalists willing to see themselves as part of the overall war effort, was widespread. And who could blame them, faced as they were in reporting – at least in Britain and Australia – to audiences facing the prospect of invasion. The depth of collusion in cooperation with government is suggested by new evidence that the respected news agency, Reuters, worked closely with Foreign

Affairs in Britain, in 'black' operations involving propaganda, counter-propaganda, misinformation and deception.[78]

The growth in the number of war correspondents on both sides, and their uncritical acceptance of their respective causes, was not matched by any major advances in media communications technology. The newsreel and radio emerged as the major means of communications. Film afforded a perceived credibility, while radio broadcasts such as Chester Wilmot's coverage out of Arnhem and Dimbleby's in-flight commentary from a bombing raid over Berlin, provided immediacy. Both sources suffered the self-censorship of committed journalists as well as military and government censorship. But beyond the introduction of a lightweight portable recording machine weighing around 18 kilograms (40 pounds), which provided one hour's commentary on twelve double-sided disks, improvement in long distance military radio communications, and the development of wireless transmission of photographs, little real change took place in the reporter's armoury. The correspondent was still reliant on the military for transmission of material.[79] Governments, however, emerged from the war with a much more sophisticated feel for the utility of censorship and information management.

At the end of the war, the Americans ceased censorship almost immediately. Although a valuable lesson had been learned, a strong, confident and victorious democracy was not prepared to accept anything less. In Britain, however, the Ministry of Information was to linger much longer.[80] In Australia also, the politicians and bureaucracy had taken to censorship like bears to honey, and restrictions were retained well after there was any military or operational need. A group of courageous editors and publishers had to risk heavy jail sentences and the closure of their publications by taking their case to the Australian High Court before censorship was eventually phased out.[81]

As for the performance of the correspondents themselves, the institutions they represented, and the wider issues of freedom of the press, there is little to be learned. Bound up in the patriotic demands and expectations of nations fighting for their survival, correspondents on each side had little choice other than to support the war aims of their government as they had during World War I. They were also limited by the requirement of their news outlets to reflect the patriotic spirit of their audiences. For the most part, allied correspondents appear to have accepted operational censorship and the very real limitations of communications without complaint. There were, it seems, few problems in the working relationship, other than the normal ones of frustration and exasperation, as well as those of a personal nature. What was important was the emergence – on both sides of the Atlantic – of a new commitment in time of war to home propaganda and the strictest of censorship which brooked no opposition and carried heavy sanctions if it was challenged.

It would be wrong to lay too much blame at the door of the profession, since in Russia the people were fighting for their lives, and in America and Britain they were on a crusade against the commonly perceived evil of national socialism. Add to that the imperatives of patriotism and the very real limitations of secrecy and classification, and there is a case to treat the performance of the press in World War II with more respect. The final judgement however might best be left to Charles Lynch, a Canadian war correspondent quoted by Knightley. Lynch observed that it was:

> ... humiliating to look back at what we wrote during the war. It was crap – and I don't exclude the Ernie Pyles or the Alan Mooreheads. We were a propaganda arm of our governments. At the start the censors enforced that, but by the end, we were our own censors. We were cheerleaders. I suppose there wasn't an alternative at the time. It was total war. But, for God's sake, let's not glorify our role. It wasn't good journalism. It wasn't journalism at all.[82]

Conclusion

In summary, the end of World War II marked the culmination of one hundred and fifty years in which the relationship between the media and the military had been shaped by the twin forces of changing technology, which permitted more immediate and critical reporting of events, and the efforts of the military and governments to limit both access to conflicts and the freedom of the press in time of war.

The nineteenth century opened with strong-willed, independent journalists roaming the trouble spots of the world, feeding back the excitement of imperial successes to an avid and growing daily press readership. From the Crimean War onwards, this was recognised by both military commanders in the field and political leaders in their nation's capitals as a new and alarming factor. For the first time, the military was open to independent scrutiny while politicians were exposed to possibly adverse public opinion. The immediate remedy was the imposition of censorship and the use of such sanctions as restrictions on access, transport, and above all, military communications.

In the main, this scrutiny and the public opinion that stemmed from it was supportive of the armed forces in what were primarily colonial or punitive expeditions. The war correspondent had little choice but to present jingoistic material, for the emerging popular press catered directly to the nationalistic and patriotic expectations of the new literate urban classes brought into being through industrialisation. It was only when conflicts became internationalised and confronted the reader with political choice that the alarm bells began to ring. The American Civil War was viewed with interest in Britain, but the Boer War brought the problem home.

For the first time, the war correspondent began to play a policy role in his ability to sway not only national, but international opinion. This was met by further, and increased, restrictions on access, transport and communications. And because of the correspondent's growing impact on public opinion, the application of sanctions was widened to include the sort of professional banishment afforded Russell of the *Times* in America when his reporting became too objective. The military was also quick to exploit the increased difficulties of access brought about by the widening of the area of operations, as demonstrated in Manchuria. In addition, the benefits of a policy of exclusion, as practised by the Japanese in the Russo-Japanese War, was not lost on Western military observers.

The danger to the authorities posed by objective and impartial war reporting was stopped in its tracks in World War I by the even greater limitations of patriotism. The feelings of nationalism and patriotism infecting the populations of each of the belligerents admitted no point of view other than that of gallantry, optimism and an absolute commitment to the war aims of the government. This resulted in a massive conspiracy of deception on the part of the media, the military and the governments of the major nations involved.

The inter-war years saw a hesitant move back to the swashbuckling days of the golden years of war reporting in the Abyssinian campaign, but the revival did not survive the exclusionist policies of the Italians and their lack of cooperation with those who attempted to cover the conflict. What remained of the free press spark was extinguished in the Spanish Civil War. The restrictions of patriotism and national commitment that had typified World War I were now overtaken by an equally stifling ideological commitment that reduced reporting of the war in Spain to little more than a propaganda battle.

The outbreak of World War II saw nation states with competing ideologies ranged against each other. Patriotism quickly became the guiding force again, with the media harnessed and exploited as part of the national war effort in a pattern common to all of the belligerents.

The tools of the trade changed little over this period. Advances were made in radio communications, recording systems and cinematography, but use of these technologies remained at a relatively primitive level because of restrictions of size and range. What advantages they gave the war correspondent were quickly subsumed by improved censorship systems, and accreditation and selective military control over access, transport and long range means of communication.

This was a situation that was to remain unchanged until the emergence of two factors that were to revolutionise the world of media communications. The first was the advent of popular television as a global medium and as a technical revolution in the means of information transmission. The second was the round of wars of post-colonial self determination which afforded home nation populations the luxury of opinion without patriotic penalty, and which permitted a demand for coverage free of the constraints of patriotism or ideology. It is to this catalyst for change that we now turn as we examine the alarm bell conflicts of Korea, Indochina and Algeria.

3

Post-War Self Determination: The Unheeded Warning

The end of World War II unleashed a tidal wave of de-colonisation, legitimised by the terms of the Atlantic Charter. The Charter, signed in August 1941 by President Franklin D. Roosevelt of the United States and Prime Minister Winston Churchill of Great Britain, afforded – among other things – the right of self-determination to all nations.[1] It was a right which was eagerly sought.

The claims of many peoples to independence from the major colonial powers of France, the Netherlands and Britain were based primarily on promises of post-war reform which had been held out during the conflict in return for support for the allied cause.[2] Some nations subsequently gained independence through peaceful transition; for others it was achieved only after protracted limited conflict.[3]

In this chapter, discussion will be limited to the examples of Indochina and Algeria, where independence was gained through conflict, and Korea, which may be regarded as the 'bridge' between World War II and the new style of warfare.

There were many other conflicts over this period which could have been considered. These include the Mau Mau uprising in Kenya, the rebellion of the communist-dominated Malayan People's Liberation Army, the Indonesian fight against the Dutch for independence, and the Greek-led EOKA movement in Cyprus. All have been rejected because, in each case, they were generally successful with relatively few casualties incurred by the Western nations involved. They were also fought far from the home nations in the West and faced no major opposition there, even though the deployments involved national servicemen. Indeed, each of these conflicts appears to have been accepted by their respective publics and media as an extension of the aims of World War II. In the case of Malaya, the operation could be seen as a reversion to the pre-war role of Empire policing. As a result, there was not the level of dissent that might have triggered a revision of the citizens' duties or obligations to their respective governments, nor any questioning of the media which generally carried out its World War II role of patriotic support for the military.[4]

Indochina and Algeria were the exceptions. These were true limited conflicts fought against politically sophisticated opponents – wars fought over issues that generated such widespread dissent in the home nation that they either threatened revolution or caused it. There is the contrast, too, between the one war fought in a remote area half way around the world, and the other waged on the doorstep of France. More importantly both these conflicts demonstrated the emergence of a media which, up until that time, had been supportive of the military in patriotic wars, but now found itself free of the earlier limitations and able to report what it saw. Equally, for the first time, an audience in a Western democracy could choose whether or not to support its government's war aims, free of the pressures of patriotism or the imperatives of survival. It was here that a new problem in media-military relations emerged, but was largely ignored.

These two campaigns, along with Korea, provide a convenient chronological sequence that demonstrates the matching development of the reach and immediacy of communications technology, and the independence that advances in technology afforded the correspondent. It was in these campaigns that the alarm bells were rung for the changed and changing expectations of the duties and obligations of the citizen in time of limited conflict, and for the military forces of Western liberal democracies.

Before we can examine our two minor case studies, however, and follow the development of a free media reporting to a free and sophisticated audience, we must first deal with Korea.

Korea was the first example of post-nuclear limited conflict. It was limited by geography and weaponry, and the fighting and outcome presented no direct threat to the home nations of the allied forces involved. Korea can best be described as the link between patriotic wars and true limited conflict since it encompassed a wider freedom of personal choice in the home nations than had been seen before. It also exhibited technical developments in the means of media communications and a depth of international coverage never before encountered in conflict.

Korea: The Beginning of the Questioning

Korea, the large peninsula that juts out of Manchuria towards Japan, has had a long history of subjugation, first by the Chinese and then the Japanese.[5]

At the Cairo meeting of Churchill, Chiang Kai Shek and Roosevelt in 1943, it was agreed that post-war Korea should be given its independence. The decision was re-affirmed at Yalta by Stalin. As part of the combined allied effort against Japan, it was also agreed that Soviet troops should occupy northern Korea down to the 38th parallel and the United States military should occupy the southern half. The Soviets moved in over the last two weeks of August 1945 and the Americans two weeks later. During that interval the Soviets installed a communist government under Kim Il Sung. The Americans responded by setting up a rival democratically elected but nevertheless authoritarian government in the South, headed by Syngman Rhee.[6]

On 25 June 1950, following agreement between Mao Tse Tung and Stalin, the vastly superior forces of the North invaded South Korea. Within a month the North held all of Korea except for a small pocket around the southern port of Pusan. Despite the fact that South Korea was not a member of the United Nations and ineligible for help under its Charter, the United States exploited a boycott of the Security Council by the Soviet Union and moved a motion of condemnation through the United Nations. They then arranged for a United Nations force to be sent to defend South Korea.[7] President Truman threw the full weight of the United States military into the conflict under General MacArthur, who was appointed Commander-in-Chief of the United Nations Force.

The force, which was to reach over half a million in 1951, was made up mainly of American, British Commonwealth, Turkish, Thai and Belgian troops, with token forces from twelve other nations.[8]

Despite the implied risk of nuclear confrontation and the deployments of the nineteen participating nations, Korea was, according to Royle, '... the worst reported war of modern times.'[9] But such was the interest in the early stages of the conflict that there were some 270 foreign correspondents in country. Most were there to cover their own national contingents, but it was the American media which dominated the war coverage, especially after the brilliantly conceived amphibious landings at Inchon. Only Alan Winnington and Wilfred Burchett covered the war from the communist point of view as part of the allied press corps.

In the first few months, the military saw the role of the correspondents in the same light as it had in World War II – 'patriotically' reporting in support of their own side. As a result journalists were initially restricted only by a voluntary code aimed at preserving operational security.[10] But many exercised their freedom to make objective judgements, and those early days were marked by critical reporting of allied disunity and distrust.[11] Much of this centred on the supposed use of United Nations cover for what many perceived to be American international objectives.[12] In the main, they reported what they saw, and what they saw was a disorganised retreat, poor morale and lack of equipment. This was viewed by the military as alarmist reporting and, as Knightley reports, those responsible were branded traitors for 'giving aid and comfort to the enemy.' Some were banned for what one public relations officer described as failing to observe 'discretion and cooperation in the dispatch of their file' and were guilty of disclosing information that would have 'a bad moral and psychological effect' on the troops.[13]

The ban was eventually lifted, following representations in Washington. However, the offence of reporting anything that the military might interpret as having an undesirable impact on the troops was extended to any criticism of either the conduct of the war or the performance of allied troops; this was subsequently incorporated into the voluntary media guidelines.

Because of the remoteness and harsh climate and terrain of Korea, the military was able to exploit to the full the utter reliance of correspondents on the military for accommodation, rations, transport and communications. In the early days, there was no actual censorship, but the military exploited the fact that there was also no direct communication out of Korea and all copy had to be routed by military channels through Army HQ in Tokyo. This afforded an open invitation to censorship by selection and delay.[14] In contrast, at the Inchon landings on 15 September 1950, the official version was speeded on its way by a select group of American correspondents who were given passage in MacArthur's ship, personally briefed on the operation, and given direct communications to Tokyo.[15] This guaranteed that a near instant official version of the success of the landings would be disseminated, while at the same time it allowed MacArthur the option of denying communications to the media in the event of a failure.

As it happened, the Inchon landings were an outstanding success, and the subsequent advance gave the mainly American press corps the copy they needed to match the generally anti-communist leanings of their audience. In the circumstances, the Army was only too happy to provide them with everything. Then, early in November, China entered the war and struck back in massive strength. MacArthur's headquarters desperately tried to maintain its optimism, refusing even to admit to the open presence of the Chicom (Chinese communist) troops. But the North Korean and Chicom forces were overwhelming.

As the United Nations forces began to stream south again, the news dried up.[16] In a rerun of the first months of the war, media recriminations and criticisms re-emerged, with a repeat of the reprisals and denial of access by the American high command. This time, reports began to openly question the wisdom of the war and to highlight the widespread corruption within, and atrocities being carried out by, the Rhee administration. As Knightley states, the atrocities held the promise of becoming international incidents and the reports received such widespread publicity that, along with the worsening military situation, they caused a wave of disillusionment with the South Koreans and the war in general.[17] MacArthur could not afford the political risks of such negative reporting and on 21 December, imposed strict military censorship.

These new restrictions went well beyond military or operational security. It was now forbidden to report on any military activity and forbidden to make any criticism of the allied conduct of the war or any 'derogatory' comments about either troops or commanders.[18] More importantly, these unprecedented restrictions were backed up by an informal 'get on the team' attitude which appeared to find a ready response among proprietors and editors. A prime example of this editorial censorship, which may have been the result of private governmental pressure, can be found in the decision by the editors of the British *Picture Post*, to withdraw a highly critical article by James Cameron.[19] In another incident, the respected journalist, I.F. Stone, had his critical book, *The Hidden History of the Korean War*, turned down by British publishers and then by some twenty-eight American publishers before finally having it accepted.[20]

The problem was that, for the first time, the military had come up against the combination of a relatively open-minded national and international opinion, and war correspondents reporting without any limitation on the truth as they saw it. The only restriction was a self-imposed one of respect for the immediate security of operations. But the correspondents themselves retained the right to interpret what was and was not operational security.

The major worry for the military was in the uneven quality of the correspondents making the decisions.[21] On the other hand, the correspondents – both good and bad – were now faced with covering a stalemate that led eventually to extended peace negotiations. They also came up against an even tougher censorship system introduced by the new commander, General Ridgeway, following the dismissal of MacArthur, who had been in favour of breaking the nuclear and geographic limitations of the conflict.[22] Ridgeway was all too aware of the dangers of the media in a sensitive international conflict and, as a result, he introduced censorship both at source in the field and in Tokyo. He also imposed a near total blackout censorship on the peace talks at Panmunjon.[23]

It was because of this blackout that two correspondents, Winnington and the Australian, Wilfred Burchett, came into their own. They were able to provide chapter and verse on the progress of the talks from their communist sources. More importantly, Burchett and Winnington proved the official American version wrong,[24] although they later lost credibility over claims of United States use of germ warfare, based largely on admissions by United Nations prisoners of war taken under duress.[25] Beyond that alternative perspective on the war, the press corps was completely reliant on the military and had to accommodate copy to the strict levels of censorship instituted by Ridgeway. The censorship continued to the end of the actual hostilities and exists in South Korea even today, backed up by threats of violence, arrest and imprisonment, not only of the reporter but his or her sources.[26]

The war in Korea officially ended on 27 July 1953. Over one and a half million men and women had died and two and a half million were wounded or injured.[27] The financial costs were incalculable, as was the cost to the prestige of the United Nations, which was perceived thereafter in some quarters to have been little more than a tool of American ideological imperialism.[28] Until Vietnam, Korea was to remain one of the bloodiest limited conflicts in history. But while few realised it at the time, the war correspondents in Korea were breaking new ground, paving the way for a new style of post-patriotic war reporting.

Despite the incredible pressures to maintain the national commitment of World War II, and the continuing calls for them to 'get on side', for the first time journalists had to confront the challenge of independent reporting free of the trammels of patriotism. It is true that they were faced with an anti-communist crusade that had to a large extent replaced the patriotism of previous wars, especially in America. Nor should the influence of McCarthyism be underestimated. But whereas in previous wars the media had been bound by a common commitment to patriotism, in this case they were dealing with an ideology which had no prior claim on them.

In addition, correspondents were faced with the problems of reporting objectively on matters of grave importance, such as the possible use of nuclear weapons in a direct confrontation that threatened a third world war. All this took place in the face of an increasingly hostile military and disapproving governments which might have been applying covert pressure on the correspondents' employers – the newspapers and other media proprietors. Few realised it at the time, but the courageous actions of those who broke ranks and reported factually to their independent-minded audiences – also free of any restraint other than anti-communist tendencies – had broken the mould of the committed correspondent. It was not a conscious decision, more a consequence of Korea being the first of the limited wars fought in an area remote from the home nations. This was an international conflict which, for the first time, apart from the threat of escalation and possible inclusion of their sons in a draft, did not affect the welfare of people in the West, let alone their survival. And, for the first time, war correspondents were reporting to an international audience which accepted neither the call to patriotism by their governments nor the automatic right of the military to deny them information on which they might form an opinion.

Technology was also on the move. Television was now entering its second decade in America, with almost 65 per cent penetration of American homes. It was poised to make a similar impact in Western Europe.[29] But while the audience was there, without the means to bring the battlefield direct to the home viewer, television was as slow as film.

The coverage that went to air also had to run the gauntlet of self-censorship within the networks, and – quite apart from the desire of audiences to be fully informed – the networks could not go too far beyond audience expectations in other areas. Those expectations were based largely on a pride in the American military and the McCarthyist belief that America was fighting a crusade against communism. Both these concepts had been carefully fostered by what MacDonald terms the anti-communist militarisation of the screen, with military-based programs such as the Phil Silvers Show, Navy Log, Air Power, The West Point Story, Combat Sergeant and Pentagon-supported documentaries as staple fare.[30]

Ultimately it was not simply political questions which raised the level of public disquiet about Korea. Rather, it was the dissonance created by feelings of support for the national forces on the one hand, and attempts to put this into perspective with objective (and negative) information about the conflict on the other. The obvious distress felt by a public coming to terms with this inconsistency would be seen more clearly a decade or so later with American involvement in Vietnam.

In summary, because of the technical immaturity of television in Korea, film, radio and print remained pre-eminent.[31] Each of these media could point to technological gains, but in the main it was not sufficient to exploit the vivid imagery and immediacy that was later to become the hallmark of the electronic media. Each was limited by the physical censorship of transmission since there was no alternative indigenous free press or local facilities. The reporters, in turn, were almost entirely dependent on the military for access, transport and maintenance in an expeditionary war, waged in remote and difficult terrain, and in extremes of climate.

The response of the military to both the philosophical and technical changes in war reporting that were underway appeared to be one of bafflement.[32] Their thinking was based on the belief that if their governments had dispatched them to fight a war, then they were entitled to the automatic support of the media as in previous wars. If that support was not forthcoming, the military had only to exploit their monopoly of resources and impose censorship by denial, delay or through control of the means of communications. Beyond that, there is no evidence of any new policies other than the 'carrot and stick' approach as the military alternately attempted to encourage or penalise correspondents to get them 'on the team.'

Korea was the link, the indeterminate end of one era and the beginning of another. It followed on the heels of a great war of total commitment and patriotic support. But it also heralded the freedom of the correspondent to report to an audience able to make up its own mind, unencumbered by national interest, and it heralded a burgeoning new media technology, particularly television. The technological explosion in communications still lay in the future, but the philosophical changes and the challenges to the order under the old social contract were about to begin.

The French in Indochina: The First Real Test

Vietnam is about 1600 kilometres (1000 miles) long with a maximum width of 400 kilometres (250 miles), pinched in to less than 80 kilometres (50 miles) at its narrowest point on the 17th parallel. Its coastline sweeps down in a gentle arc from the Chinese border to the Gulf of Thailand. Cambodia extends southwards from the Laotian border to the west of Vietnam. In 1945, the population of Vietnam was just on 16 million. The region was a major rice producing area and was rich in tin, rubber, gold and coal. Following normal colonial patterns, the Vietnamese economy became an extension of French mercantile policies, with raw material exports being returned as finished goods to a tied market.[33]

Vietnam had been host to a plethora of independence movements since long before World War II. After the takeover by the Japanese, the various movements were re-organised into a broad-based nationalist, but communist dominated coalition named the Viet Minh, with Ho Chi Minh as its political leader. The Viet Minh soon established a formidable anti-Japanese resistance under General Giap. More importantly, it was recognised and assisted by the American Office of Strategic Services, (OSS).[34]

Following the Japanese collapse in 1945, Ho Chi Minh emerged as undisputed leader of the Viet Minh and head of a government which proclaimed its independence. In December 1946, after an initial period of negotiations with the French, who were trying to re-establish their interests, Ho Chi Minh's forces, the People's Army of Vietnam (PAVN), attacked the former colonial power and the first Indochina war was under way.[35]

Space precludes anything more than a brief outline of the military campaign, since the aim is to examine how the conflict affected the home and international audience. From the start, however, the French spread their forces too thinly and were forced onto the defensive in a costly war of attrition. By 1950, when Giap launched a successful offensive, there was public unrest at home over the mounting casualty lists. Paris was forced to contemplate withdrawal and evacuation plans were prepared.[36] However, the French managed to retrieve the situation, aided by the United States who by then had abandoned their anti-colonialist stance in favour of anti-communism.[37]

By 1953, the situation was worsening again and the French appointed General Navarre as their new commander. Unable to defeat the Viet Minh in guerrilla warfare, Navarre sought to draw Giap into a set-piece battle on Giap's own ground, and established the fortress of Dien Bien Phu in the mountainous border region of Laos and north Vietnam. Appreciating that the French were at the end of a perilously vulnerable air supply line, Giap invested the fortress using heavy artillery on a scale never before seen in the conflict and constantly eroded the French perimeter by a series of mass attacks and sapping. When the monsoons came, weather curtailed French air activity and Dien Bien Phu was lost. It was a catastrophic and decisive defeat, leading directly to the Geneva Armistice which ordered a cease-fire on 21 July 1954.[38]

From the start, the Vietnamese were aware of the need to propagandise to the home nation in France. They had a head start in that, from the turn of the century until the fall of Dien Bien Phu, many of their ranks had been fully accepted in French intellectual circles.[39] Throughout the war, there was a high level of intellectual discussion as to the wisdom of the French commitment, with leading francophone Vietnamese presenting the case with force and persuasion in the French media. They were aided by the fact that French sentiment and French education pointed inevitably to the concept of liberty and self-determination. More importantly, the Vietnamese enjoyed the support of both Moscow and Beijing, and this support was translated into identification with their cause by the strong socialist and communist parties and left-wing dominated French trade unions.

With the rise of socialism and communism in post-war France, the media divided generally on party lines. The popular press tended to be left-leaning while the more conservative publications favoured the right. Initially the media joined in support of the expeditionary forces, probably reflecting the desire of their national audience for a return to the glory days of empire. However, as the cost of what was obviously going to be a protracted war became apparent, the media reverted to political divisions.[40]

The right wing French government was fully committed to the conflict, but the left was predominantly pro-Vietnamese. Raymonde Barre stated from the communist benches of the Assembly of the French Union that:

> It can only be a question of one thing, I say not of a truce, which would be a trap, but of withdrawing the expeditionary force from Indochina, or repatriating it in order to permit the Vietnamese people to direct freely their own affairs.[41]

Barre also served notice on the French government that the Communist Party intended to do everything it could do to force this withdrawal by instigating strikes, particularly among sailors and dockyard workers.[42] This threat was carried out in Marseilles, where the railways union blacklisted trains carrying troops and equipment. Such actions were fully supported by the left wing media.[43]

The media battle was, in the main, waged in print, with the provincial newspapers and party organs playing an important role. This was because the major Paris dailies, though influential, had a limited circulation outside the capital. The most powerful, *Le Monde*, had a circulation at the time of less than half a million. Television was in its infancy; data for 1953 show only 60,000 television sets in France, the lowest number in

Europe.[44] In addition, French laws prohibit the publication of any judicial, governmental, or more importantly for our case, military information, that has not been expressly cleared for publication.[45]

The media coverage of the increasingly divided view of left and right was in itself indicative of the freedom of choice that was presented to the French citizen. And ideology was reinforced by the cost of the war and by war weariness.

In 1952, President Vincent Auriol revealed that the seven years of war had cost 1,600 million francs – twice the Marshal Plan aid designed to rejuvenate metropolitan France – and that casualties totalled more than 90,000.[46] The sheer size of the losses including, in particular, the virtual wiping out of the flower of the post-war officer corps, had an effect on public opinion. There was also growing revulsion over some of the actions of the French Army and reports of currency speculation. Again, this was reflected in the media, with the editor of an influential populist paper claiming that:

> ... the prolongation of the war in Indochina is a fatality imposed by events, one of those dramas in history which have no solution ... our policy in Indochina (has) prevented us from finding a way out of this catastrophe.[47]

But it was General Giap who best summed up the impact of this crisis of confidence and division of opinion, brought about by the citizen's freedom of choice in time of limited conflict and the newfound ability to express it. Giap observed that:

> In all likelihood, public opinion in the democracy (France) will demand an end to useless bloodshed or its legislature will insist on knowing for how long it will have to vote astronomical credits without a clear cut victory.[48]

While defeat or a drawn-out war of attrition will lessen public support, it was obvious that the French people, for any of the reasons outlined above, felt that they had the right to decide whether French involvement in Vietnam should continue. This was not a patriotic war, but a new regime of limited conflict that threatened neither the common survival nor most people's personal safety. For the first time, citizens of a Western liberal democracy could make up their minds as to whether they should obstruct the supply of men and matériel to a war they did not support, and whether they would vote for policies that went against those of the government or military. There were the expected demands by the military for the same support they had enjoyed in previous patriotic wars, but while some chose to give that support, others did not. As a result, the tocsin had been well and truly sounded for the governments and militaries of Western liberal democracies.

Algeria: The Final Warning

Stretching about 1000 kilometres (620 miles) along the northern coastline of Africa between Morocco to the west and Tunisia to the east, with a massive hinterland of some 2,200,000 square kilometres (850,000 square miles), Algeria had seemed the perfect example of an overseas department of metropolitan France. The population in 1945 was 9.5 million, of which 8.4 were Muslim Berbers. The remainder – just over 1 million – was made up of Europeans, the majority of whom were long-time French settlers known as *colons* or, more graphically, *pieds noirs*. The *pieds noirs* constituted a political and economic elite who rejected the normal French colonial concept of total acceptance of those natives who had become *civilisees*. The wealthy class of Muslims was patronised and were known locally as *Beni ouis ouis*, or 'yes men'. The remainder were held in contempt. As a result, the population was divided along racial and economic lines. In 1947, this was formalised by a statute that created two separate political constituencies, Muslim and French. The statute effectively put paid to the French promise of total integration and sowed the seeds of rebellion.

Based to a large extent on the discrimination that this division entailed, Algerian nationalism grew under the leadership of Ferhat Abbas and, from 1950 onwards, the more belligerent leadership of Ben Bella. With Tunisia and Morocco already independent, the French defeated in Vietnam and, in 1954, the coming to power in Egypt of Nasser as a new Saladin, Ben Bella had the chance he needed.

The conflict opened when, in the early hours of 1 November 1954, a series of bomb attacks was launched against French military posts throughout Algeria. The newly-formed Algerian Front for National Liberation (FLN) announced through Radio Cairo that it had launched a war of independence. The conflict was to last for seven and a half years, and cost a total of 100,000 casualties before a coalition of nationalists eventually forced Algerian independence from the French.[49]

Space again precludes other than a rough outline of the campaign but, stung by their defeat in Vietnam, the French Army contained the initial Algerian rebellion with some success. However, Algeria was to be more than a military confrontation. From the outset, the Algerians realised that their major battle would be the fight for public opinion both in France and internationally. Like the Vietnamese before them, they could count on a large number of Algerian intellectuals who were influential in left wing and communist circles in France. They also had access to radio broadcasts beamed to their largely illiterate followers from Tunisia, Cairo and Damascus.[50]

The FLN won the first round when, at the urging of the Arab world, the United Nations took Algeria 'under consideration' in September 1955.[51] World opinion was also strengthened by calls for pan-Arabism emanating from Cairo in response to extreme measures being taken against the Algerians by the French, and by the kidnapping of Ben Bella by the French secret service. At the time, Ben Bella was on a flight between Morocco and Tunisia for discussions in France with French left wing leaders. The kidnapping enraged Morocco and Tunisia as well as the French left. As had occurred in the Indochina campaign, it was well publicised in the left-leaning newspapers.[52]

Meanwhile, the French had further offended the Arab world by their participation in the abortive Suez invasion of October and November 1956. Nor did the Suez fiasco endear the French to the United States. Rather, it reinforced American views that the conflict in Algeria was one against legitimate, and more importantly, non-communist, national aspirations. Washington allowed the establishment of an Algerian Office of Information in the United States and granted visas for members of the Provisional Government of the Algerian Republic (GPRA) to attend debates at the United Nations.[53] From the media and public opinion point of view, this was a formidable victory.

But these were triumphs in the international arena. Consideration of the conduct of the war on the ground demonstrates the depth of feeling and levels of political support.

Militarily the French were very successful. Their tactics were based on the policy of 'quadrillage' which called for the garrisoning of all major population centres in an attempt to isolate the rebels. This was accompanied by offensive patrols by special forces to hunt down the individual bands. The FLN reacted by stepping up terrorism in the cities and the French responded with even more stringent controls. The security forces were given *carte blanche* in counter measures and instituted a form of security terror including individual and collective responsibility which allowed them to lay their hands on any individual within a matter of minutes.[54]

Although the Army was soon bogged down in yet another Vietnam-style war of attrition, this time the whole resources of the French forces were available. The military committed itself to the concept of *Algerie Francais*, almost as an article of faith in a strong and purified France, with success in Algeria vindicating their failures in World War II and

Vietnam.[55] This pointed to an increasingly politicised military which began to side openly with the *pieds noirs*. The *pieds noirs*, for their part, wanted a tougher line taken, while Paris was looking at the realities of an eventual rapprochement.

As the war dragged on into 1957, there was a feeling of war weariness and loss of direction. Even though the French Army was gaining the upper hand militarily, a moral victory was nowhere in sight. But Paris could not afford Algerian independence without a political backlash from the *pieds noirs* which could bring down the government. Increasingly, the country looked to General de Gaulle brooding in retirement. Then, in May 1958, General Salan, the commander in Algeria, and his generals gave an ultimatum to the government – that the Army would never consent to abandon Algeria. The ultimatum was backed by a plot for an armed military uprising spearheaded by para-troopers from Algeria. When the newly-formed government in Paris, headed by Pierre Pflimlin, proposed a negotiated settlement with the Algerian rebels on 13 May, a general strike was declared in Algiers and rioting broke out. Faced with the prospect of rebelling himself, General Salan declared himself for de Gaulle the next day.

By 28 May, de Gaulle had assumed power on the strength of his supposed support for the Army and the settlers. However, over the next few years he defused the capability of the Army and shifted his position to one of negotiation. This was opposed by the settlers who openly demonstrated in early 1960, but by then de Gaulle had the Army under control and the *pieds noirs* were effectively isolated.

In April 1961 negotiations were opened with the FLN. They were opposed by a revolt in Algiers, led by four retired generals – Salan, Challe, Jouhard and Zeller – but de Gaulle acted swiftly, aided by a general strike in favour of his stand in France and by the refusal of conscripts to obey their officers in Algeria. The revolt – and attempted coup – fizzled out. Challe and Zeller were forced to surrender while Salan, Jouhard and most of the other military officers involved went underground, into the *pied noir Organisation Armée Secrète* (OAS) which engaged in a vicious war of terrorism to press their claims. This continued until a cease-fire in Algeria was signed on 20 April 1962. On 3 July of that year, the FLN set up a provisional government and the conflict was over.[56]

As this short review of the course of the war demonstrates, the freedom of choice to pursue individual social, economic and political views, as well as supra-nationalist sentiments, was virtually limitless. It culminated in the politicisation of the army, general strikes, boycotts, terrorism in metropolitan France on a scale never seen before, and massive divisions in the home nation. Some of those divisions have proved irreconcilable, even to this day. Yet this farrago of opposition, strike and even revolt was played out within a decade of World War II, when the requirement for the citizen to support the war aims of the government and military as part of the social contract had seemed inviolate.

Again, the battle was fought out in the print and radio media, since television had still to make significant penetration into French homes. As in the Indochina campaign, television ownership in France over this period was the lowest in Europe. Further, as Merill states, the five year plans for a very slow growth of television, adopted by the National Assembly in 1955, '... reflected the government's fears that television coverage of the Algerian conflict might inflame public opinion more than the less graphic radio reports.'[57]

The French government maintained a strict but legal censorship over what was seen or heard. The Algerians were without a print outlet, other than one or two clandestine papers and leaflets, and the impact of these was limited by the illiteracy of the target audience. Radio was the major medium and the FLN was afforded access to the foreign radio services of neighbouring Arab nations sympathetic to their cause. Externally, there was no limitation, and the FLN used the media to plead their case both nationally and internationally. They took their case to any and every international forum, including the United Nations and the Arab world. Iraq and Algeria's neighbours, Tunisia and Morocco, each provided political and clandestine military support and sanctuary. In France itself, the FLN relied on sympathetic journalists and writers to produce books and pamphlets supporting their cause. They made use of figures such as Jean-Paul Sartre and church groups who were horrified at the repressive measures adopted by the French Army.[58]

But the main target of the FLN were the French liberals. Propaganda appeals attempted to convince them that Algeria was an unjust war and that the Algerians were doing no more than following French revolutionary principles. They also opened information centres in most world capitals and, as the American Operational Research Centre relates, 'Through them, propaganda literature was made available to the public, while the staffs of these offices made every attempt to establish contacts with the press and important officials and took every opportunity to expound the case for the FLN cause in speeches and debates.'[59] Within Algeria this effort was countered as much as possible by the French through their radio broadcasts on the twelve radio stations in Algiers and the French language newspapers, all of which were tightly controlled by the French Ministry of Information.[60] However, they could not stop the radio broadcasts from neighbouring Arab countries. In the face of widespread demands for independence by the Algerians, and considering the pan-Arabism that surrounded them, for the French the battle was near hopeless. As Fanon said, in the colonial context, 'truth is the property of the national cause, and cannot be denied.'[61]

Within France, it was equally impossible. Conscription and the deaths of conscripts in a war which had little meaning to the French public, were bringing the message home to ordinary people. The war was increasingly rejected by the left and the trade unions, which placed the same sort of industrial sanctions on the war effort that they had levied during the Indochina war. France had also lost the battle for legitimacy in the world forum of the United Nations. But, perhaps more importantly, the French nation was subjected to a continuing barrage of condemnation by intellectuals who appealed to France's own revolutionary backgrounds. As Jean-Paul Sartre asked, '... which side are the savages on? Where is the barbarism? ... the motor horns beat out Al-ger-ie Franc-ais, while the Europeans burn moslems alive.'[62]

There was little the government or the military could do in the face of such stunning imagery and similar calls, all of which were duly reported in the mainly print and radio media, with the exception of those of the ultra-right. The government could limit information on the conduct of the war but it could not limit the wider philosophical discussion. The truth and rightness of the argument was there for all to see and, in a Western liberal democracy such as France, freed of the imperatives of national survival, the citizen could make up his or her own mind. This ability of people to decide for themselves led eventually to a major split within the French nation and that split, in turn, led to a revolt by Algerian-based elements of the Army. It was a graphic demonstration of the changed circumstances and changed obligations arising from limited conflict.

Conclusion

Algeria was perhaps the ultimate warning. Yet the writing had been on the wall in Malaya, Indonesia, Indochina and the round of smaller post-colonial conflicts in Africa and the Middle East – in Kenya and Aden, in fact everywhere that imperialism was met by armed insurrection. Korea was too close to World War II and too imbued with the substitute patriotism of the anti-communist crusade to be a prime example, although it certainly showed the way. It can also be taken as the real harbinger of the impact of television, since America was the most advanced user of the medium at that time. The audience was there; what was lacking was the means of transmission.

In the case of Indochina, television had little or no impact due to the lack of means of transmission and the small audience. What coverage was available, was heavily censored in France. Despite this, the French people became aware, from returning soldiers and other sources, of the wider issues such as mounting casualties and the heavy cost of a war that was not going well. The sources included a carefully mounted information campaign by the Viet Minh, echoed by the left wing of French politics. More importantly, the French people made up their minds on the issues irrespective of the fact that their armed forces had been legally and properly committed to the conflict. For the first time, they exercised their freedom of choice in a matter of war freed of the constraints of either personal or national survival.

As a result, it was no surprise that, when confronted with a similar situation close to home in Algeria, those same rights were exercised to the point of a bitter national split on the issue. That division, based on the new-found freedom of choice, led to open revolt by the Army, an unprecedented terror campaign on the one side and civil disobedience and sabotage on the other. The Army was prepared to revolt in the belief that support was 'owed' to them, under the concept of a social contract based on national and personal survival. What both the government and the military failed to realise was that this concept became outdated from the moment that the first atomic bomb exploded in the American desert. But despite the warnings provided by Indochina and Algeria, no one, least of all the military, accepted this fact. It would be left to the British in Northern Ireland and the Americans in Vietnam , the first two of our detailed case studies, to bring home to Western military forces the new problem that lay in wait for them.

4

Northern Ireland: A Classic Democratic Dilemma

Northern Ireland (Ulster) is a near perfect example of a democracy attempting to contain a *protracted* limited conflict within that same working democracy. This is not to say that Northern Ireland itself can be accepted as a true Western liberal democracy. Despite continuing initiatives, Northern Ireland does not meet basic requirements such as equality before the law and regular elections. But it nevertheless remains part of the United Kingdom, and the acknowledged standards of liberal democracy, including freedom of the press and the public's right to know, can be accepted as applying in Northern Ireland as they do elsewhere within the British state.

In theory, Northern Ireland's one and a half million citizens, about two thirds of whom are Protestant, enjoy the same rights as every other citizen of the United Kingdom. They are represented in Westminster and their constitutional position as a political entity is safeguarded by Parliament: Section 1 of the Northern Ireland Constitution Act states that 'In no event will Northern Ireland, or any part of it, cease to be part of ... the United Kingdom without the consent of the majority of the people of Northern Ireland voting in a poll.'[1]

In spite of this, for some thirty years the British Army has been engaged in Northern Ireland against urban terrorism directed at forcing political separation from Westminster. During this period – known as 'the troubles' – action has been sporadic and, at times, indiscriminately bloody. However, because the standards of liberal democracy generally apply, the military have had to operate under the rule of law and with high levels of national and international attention.

Active scrutiny is provided by both local and British media which rightly see a duty to report any transgression or infringement of the rights of the citizen. At the same time, because of the random threat posed by terrorism, even private soldiers and junior non-commissioned officers in Northern Ireland are called on to make on-the-spot decisions which might develop into matters of serious political significance. This has produced a continuing tension between media and the military that goes beyond the normal levels of mutual distrust.[2] The 'enemy', in contrast, acknowledge the law only when it suits their purposes, but retain full recourse to the remedies and protection afforded by the British legal system. Further, despite the limitations imposed by the *Northern Ireland Broadcasting Ban*, they have indirect access to the local and British media and enjoy widespread international support, particularly from groups within the United States.[3]

Given the circumstances of the conflict, it is not surprising that allegations of abuse of power have figured prominently in 'the troubles.' From time to time, the issues have been canvassed by the media. However, the rule of law under which the military operates in Ulster are legitimised by specific legislation.

In the early years, the *Civil Authorities (Special Powers) Act (Amended)* provided local backing for police and military operations against terrorism and, to a lesser extent, public disorder. But full control of internal security passed to the Westminster Government when the Special Powers Act was replaced by the *Northern Ireland (Emergency Provisions) Act* in July 1973. The new Act conferred greater powers of arrest and detention against suspected terrorists, and took the contentious step of abolishing trial by jury. The Northern Ireland situation also falls within the scope of the *Prevention of Terrorism Act*.[4]

Understandably, considering the nature of the legislation, some jurists have argued that both the Special Powers Act and the Emergency Provisions Act constitute an abrogation of the rule of law. Specifically, according to these jurists, there is diminished legal accountability on the part of the security forces and, under the legislation, Northern Ireland met, and still in part meets, the definition of a police state.[5] This argument gains credence from the generally sympathetic view that the courts have taken of military actions in Ulster.[6] Despite the differing views, however, the fact is that the security forces in Northern Ireland have operated with the consent of Parliament, subject, in some cases, to voluntary acceptance of guidelines adopted by other international forums such as the European Community.[7]

This case study looks at how the government and military have responded to these limitations in their handling of the media during operations in Northern Ireland, and how they have presented the situation to a British public and local constituency which, apart from sporadic acts of terrorism, has been largely unaffected by the conflict. It is a public which expects to be extended all democratic privileges, including that of a free press, as a right. It also raises the question of how the media itself sees its responsibilities in these circumstances.

Background to the Problem

Although the problems in Ulster have their roots in the Middle Ages, the background to the present conflict rests on the imbalance between the minority (40 per cent) Catholic community and the Protestant majority created by the partition of Ireland in 1920. The Catholics have always sought unity with the Irish Republic to the south while the Protestants are determined to retain their political advantages and keep Northern Ireland within the United Kingdom.[8] The simmering unrest created by political and religious differences erupted into open conflict early in 1969 when Catholic civil rights demonstrations provoked the Royal Ulster Constabulary (RUC) into violent confrontation on the streets of Belfast. The continuing disturbances culminated in major riots in August of that year when the RUC was forced to admit they had lost control of the situation and the British Army was called in.[9] 'The troubles' had begun.

It is now widely accepted that, in the summer of 1969, the Irish Republican Army (IRA) existed as a serious force only in the files of the RUC Special Branch and in the imagination of leading Unionists (the active supporters of continuing union with Britain).[10] But with the arrival of the British Army, the organisation was rejuvenated.[11] Riots in August 1969 led to the formation of a new grouping, the Provisional IRA (PIRA), or the Provos, who were committed to a policy of increased violence and the expulsion of the British from Northern Ireland by force.[12]

The British Army, charged with the task of restoring law and order until political reform could be achieved, was originally welcomed by the population as protectors. However, by late 1970, the Army had lost the trust of the Catholic community and began to face increasing levels of street violence and urban terrorism as the Provos commenced their campaign. The withdrawal of the opposition from the Stormont, Ulster's

Parliament, in 1971 put an end to any hopes of a political settlement. The introduction of internment later that year – and the harsh treatment of the internees – completed the process of Catholic alienation.[13]

In the 1990s, the actual number of IRA activists is estimated to be no more than 200 men and women.[14] Historically, this active cadre has commanded support from a significant minority of the Catholic community; its political arm, Sinn Fein, has received 35 to 40 per cent of the Catholic vote.[15] Further, despite its small size, the IRA is one of the most potent terrorist forces in the world, accepted by British military intelligence as sophisticated, smart and patient. Between 1969 and 1996, the cost in lives was more that three thousand people killed as a direct result of the conflict.[16] The tally goes on.

The annual budget for all IRA operations remains comparatively small, no more than a few million pounds Sterling, but their equipment includes the latest high technology weaponry, including Redeye shoulder-borne surface-to-air missiles capable of deployment against incoming and outgoing domestic air traffic. The IRA accepts donations from any quarter, especially the United States where finance is channelled through the Irish-American organisation, NORAID. Although this operation is being scaled down following President Clinton's initiatives for peace in Northern Ireland, NORAID has an ongoing public relations and propaganda role. Similar support systems operate within Canada, Australia and New Zealand, but on a much smaller scale; Australian security estimates the fundraising capacity in that country at no more than A$20,000 a year. The IRA also generates local income through covert and overt means. Overt means include clubs and business activities such as the 350 vehicle IRA taxi companies – the Falls Taxis and People's Taxis. Covert activities are believed to include extortion, especially in the building industry, armed robbery, smuggling and, more recently, video piracy.[17]

On the British side, prior to the 1995 relaxation of tension, there were about 30,000 members of the security forces in Northern Ireland, of whom 11,000 were British Regular Army. The remaining 19,000 were members of the RUC and Ulster Defence Regiment (UDR), the locally recruited militia. British counter-intelligence costs alone remain around 150 million pounds Sterling annually, with a total cost of two billion pounds Sterling a year in defence expenditure and subsidies to keep Ulster afloat.[18]

The British Army is highly disciplined and very professional. Many regiments have completed two or three tours of duty in Northern Ireland. Over the years, however, the British have tried to 'Ulsterise' the conflict by placing greater reliance on the RUC and the UDR. In 1972, local units accounted for 47 per cent of the security forces while 70 per cent of fatalities were British. With 'Ulsterisation', the proportion of local unit fatalities has risen to 70 per cent.[19] The RUC and UDR undertake the bulk of sentry duty and routine patrols, standing in the drizzle checking licences and identification. It is a necessary, demanding, dangerous, but generally thankless task, which they do well.

Despite their record, however, both the RUC and UDR have been subject to charges of extremism, with allegations of 'payback' killings and harassment. Such charges are understandable as the RUC and UDR are 90 per cent Protestant, drawn from the Protestant working class which is also the recruiting ground for Protestant paramilitary forces – the Ulster Freedom Fighters (UFF) and Ulster Volunteer Force (UVF). There have been documented instances of collusion and the leaking of official information to the paramilitaries in support of the common aim.[20]

Tactically, the IRA has achieved its greatest successes through selective use of terror, taking its battle to other parts of the United Kingdom and to British installations in Europe. This has assisted the IRA to obtain media coverage calculated to weaken the British will to remain in Northern Ireland.[21] For their part, the British have had notable success in intelligence, with the use of 'supergrass' informants and very successful moles, some of whom have infiltrated the highest levels of command within the IRA.[22]

In line with IRA expectations, the British public has become increasingly exasperated with the seemingly intractable war in which they are forced to provide housing and the full range of social welfare benefits to their enemy. The media have generally followed and supported this public exasperation by airing the highly graphic propaganda incidents staged by the IRA. They have also confirmed public suspicions by dutifully reporting the shortcomings of the British operation. The British government and military have long lost any claim to 'patriotic' support for the unpopular and protracted war, and their record of truthfulness no longer affords them the benefit of the doubt.[23]

Over the years there have been repeated attempts to find a compromise enabling Catholics and Protestants to share political power. All have failed, mainly because the Protestants take the not unreasonable view that they constitute an electoral majority and should not be asked to surrender the advantages that confers on them in a democracy. Failure to find a solution has fed antagonism towards the British from both the Provos and another IRA splinter group, the Irish National Liberation Army. These, in turn, have received widespread support from the increasingly hostile Catholic community. From the other side, any suggestion of concessions has been fiercely resisted by Protestant loyalist paramilitary groups such as the Ulster Volunteer Force and the Ulster Defence Association.[24]

Some hope appeared in the Northern Ireland when, on 31 August 1994, the IRA declared a unilateral cease-fire.[25] Six weeks later the Unionists also pledged a halt to hostilities. However, after almost two years of stop-start peace negotiations, it is still not clear whether a solution is achievable.[26] A general transition to power-sharing was heralded in the Anglo-Irish Agreement of 1985, but the Unionist reaction at that time was violently hostile.[27] In the end, as Paul Foot once put it, if any settlement is seen to be to their detriment, the Protestants:

> ... would fight with far more determination, unity and military skill than the Catholic minority has ever done. The terrorism of the IRA, it is said, would be as nothing compared to the violence which would be unleashed on the Protestant side if the British decided to withdraw.[28]

The Selling of a Campaign

Given the intractable situation, the international support for the IRA ,the constitutional freedoms affording media coverage, and the political nature of the conflict, the British could have been expected to give public relations a higher priority than they did in efforts to 'sell' their presence in Northern Ireland. Initially, however, they took an amateurish approach to the task, seeing the media as an irritation instead of an important part of their overall strategy. British defence public relations got off on the wrong foot, setting a pattern of denial and bluster when confronted with problems. The policy inevitably led to distrust and suspicion and, as a result, their efforts received a generally hostile press.

While the situation in Northern Ireland is still too fluid to attempt a major media analysis of the campaign, three incidents will be critically examined in this chapter to demonstrate how the distrust between military and the media evolved in Ulster. These incidents are the Falls Curfew of 3 July 1970, the action known as 'Bloody Sunday' on 30 January 1972, and the Milltown cemetery incident of 16 March 1988. The Milltown cemetery incident led to the related killing of two British servicemen at the funeral of one of the victims a week later, followed by government demands for film footage of the event.

There were numerous similar incidents, but these three examples have been chosen because of their chronological sequence which aids comparison between evolving methods of handling the media.

The Falls Road Curfew, 1970

In April 1970, the General Officer Commanding Northern Ireland, Lieutenant General Sir Ian Freeland, announced a new 'get tough' policy in response to the worsening security situation, threatening that the Army would shoot demonstrators throwing petrol bombs. An IRA spokesman promptly issued a statement threatening to shoot British soldiers in reprisal if this occurred. Not to be outdone, the Protestant paramilitary UVF offered to shoot a Catholic in return for every British soldier shot by the IRA.[29]

In July, a joint RUC/Army raid for arms in the Lower Falls Road area gave the Army an opportunity to try out its new policy. The British found a substantial cache of arms in a house-to-house search of some 3,000 homes. Crowds gathered, insults were exchanged, and stones began to fly. The raw troops responded with teargas. By evening the streets were clouded with gas and a total of 2,000 troops were committed against an area containing approximately 30,000 Catholics. That night, in the face of increasing unrest, Freeland imposed a curfew. Ironically, as Rose reports, in the previous August Freeland had dismissed the idea of a curfew, with the remark, 'What do you do if people disobey it? Shoot them?'[30] In the event, that is exactly what the Army did and four locals were shot dead by the military.

Media eyewitnesses reported that 'hundreds and hundreds' of bullets were fired by the British in what was described as a 'one-sided pitched battle.' This was supported by the evidence of local residents. However, the official response was that only fifteen rounds had been fired. A revised official statement – quietly released much later by HQ Northern Ireland Command – admitted that 1,450 rounds of small arms and some 1,600 gas canisters had been used. Yet few within the media who had been there believed even these estimates.[31]

The curfew denied access to shops or delivery for some 30,000 people over a whole weekend. As the weekend wore on, young mothers, desperate for milk for their babies, assembled en masse and pushed their way through the cordon with perambulators. The troops gave way and shortly after the curfew was ended. Such incidents made highly charged and emotive television, as did other coverage of the extensive damage alleged to have been caused by police and troops.[32]

The result was a public relations disaster for the military. They were faced with press and radio reports – and graphic and emotive television pictures – of mothers and the elderly pointing to the damage said to have been caused by the forces of law and order. Worse was the media's loss of trust in the military. Few working journalists accepted the official accounts of the army's public relations machine. One seasoned reporter who was present discounted both the original and revised figures, saying,

> Never since then have I found myself able to take the Army's explanations about any single incident with any less than a pinch of salt.[33]

This led to resentment within the military, but the media was doing no more than its duty in reporting what was proved later as the 'unlawful' harassment of a large segment of the population whose democratic rights had been arrogated. Such reporting had a major influence on public opinion within Northern Ireland itself, where the lack of government response to the excesses of the military as documented by the media led to a belief that there was no chance of obtaining justice from the Army.[34] The reporting went national and was exploited by NORAID in America as an example of '... an army of occupation out of control.'[35]

'Bloody Sunday', 1972

The Falls Road curfew was highly symbolic, but the most significant of all incidents in Northern Ireland from a public relations and media point of view, was 'Bloody Sunday.' The incident occurred on Sunday, 30 January 1972, when British paratroopers shot dead civilians in an action which ended in national and international condemnation, increased distrust within the media, and led to charges of national deception on the part of Westminster.

The events leading to Bloody Sunday followed the normal pattern of rapid escalation, following on from incidents arising from an attempted procession and the counter-deployment of a company from a parachute regiment. In the ensuing shootout, thirteen civilians were killed, seemingly with no provocation. Another civilian later died of wounds. None of those killed were members of the IRA. As de Paor puts it, this was no flash of imperial rage; it was a restrained and calculated response – '... a nicely measured whiff of grapeshot.'[36]

At first, the military attempted to deny the action despite television, radio and eyewitness reports by the media. The denials were steadfastly maintained even though some of the working media had actually sighted the bodies, and the type and number of gunshot wounds they bore.[37] The military was also reported to have attempted to place arms alongside, or with, the bodies.[38]

A Royal Commission, headed by Chief Justice Lord Widgery, was immediately set up by Parliament to investigate Bloody Sunday.[39]

However, the interpretation of his terms of reference favoured the Army and reduced the credibility of the report. As an example, the Commission's basically approving assessment of the conduct of the paratroopers is difficult to accept given the weight of eyewitness reports.[40] Widgery is also said to have given undue credence to Army sources and to have distrusted all others.[41]

According to Winchester, the report was little more than a 'whitewash', but the selective leaking by Defence of quotes favourable to the Army turned the media stance into a generally laudatory and uncritical acceptance of the report after the event. This pre-emptive leaking also blunted any critical examination of the more contentious recommendations and findings. As Winchester put it:

> Those who read the front pages on Wednesday morning would have to have been very short sighted indeed to have missed the results of the PR work. 'Widgery Clears Army', they shrieked in unison, and a relieved British public read no more. Bloody Sunday, thanks to the propaganda merchants and half a dozen lazy hacks, was now a closed book and the Irish fully to blame.[42]

According to Winchester, at a later press conference in London only 'accredited defence correspondents' were permitted entry. Not one of them had been present at the incident, save for one elderly retired brigadier who had missed the entire story. In a manner which would soon find favour with other government and military officials intent on managing media analysis of incidents in limited conflict, requests to attend by those who might have proved an embarrassment because of their knowledge, were firmly denied.[43] It was widely agreed at the time that the observed actions of the military constituted the criminal offences of assault or manslaughter, if not murder. Yet no action was taken against those involved.

Apart from the deceitful handling of the incident by defence public relations, both before and after the report, the government's handling of the media highlights the problem of what McKinley calls the 'manufacture of consent'. This is the propaganda function which, he argues, the media fulfils on behalf of popular government.[44] It is what Herman and Chomsky have described as a 'guided market system', with the guidance provided primarily by the government and its agents.[45] McKinley echoes Winchester in summarising the problem presented by this concept of 'manufactured consent' as it applied to the Widgery Report. According to McKinley:

> ... to the extent that deformations, myths and silences operate at the level of popular belief (and disbelief) government remains

above accountability and responsibility; the state, as the repository of the right and resources to legal violence, remains unchallenged, and the governed remain not only ignorant but also incapable of giving voice to an informed demand and consent.[46]

The lesson to be learned from this incident is in the formal links between government and military in their attempts to first deny, then marginalise, and finally 'bury' negative reporting which they have no other means of controlling. This is accomplished by filtering information through official systems. A prime example can be found in the court challenge to the Special Powers Act mounted by two members of the Stormont. Their appeal before the Northern Ireland High Court held that '... in purporting to confer powers on the British Army, the regulation sought to achieve a lawful object by unlawful means.'[47] The decision raised doubts as to the legality of the standing of the British Forces in Ireland. But before the media could report the findings of the High Court's decision, the British Parliament sat late into the night to pass retrospective legislation that indemnified and legalised every action by the British forces over the previous three years.[48] This action was undertaken with no prior public warning, with no press releases and, it would appear, with as little delay as possible. The aim was to render the judgement irrelevant in terms of it being relayed to the peoples of Northern Ireland and the rest of the United Kingdom, or America and the rest of the world.[49]

The Milltown Cemetery Killings and Freedom of the Press

The series of killings that led to the televised death of two British soldiers caught up in an IRA funeral in late March 1988, began with the shooting of three IRA terrorists in Gibraltar by the British Special Air Service (SAS) earlier that month. In an action which remains contentious, the three men – Farrel, McCann, and Savage – were allegedly shot dead without warning; one was reportedly killed as he lay wounded. The defence offered by the seven SAS troopers was that, according to their intelligence, the men were armed and carried remote detonators for a car bomb they had just planted.[50]

The bodies of the three were flown back to Ireland and driven from Dublin to Northern Ireland with their coffins draped in the Irish flag. A piper lamented the cortege and there was a following convoy of cars for more than a mile.[51] The flags were removed by the RUC at the border.

It was against this background that the funeral, on 17 March, at the Milltown cemetery in Roman Catholic West Belfast, attracted a crowd of more than 10,000 mourners. As the last of the three coffins was lowered into the ground, a gunman, later identified as a member of a splinter Protestant loyalist group, threw blast grenades and opened fire with an automatic weapon. Three men were killed and seventy other people wounded, two of them seriously.[52] Despite the presence of an RUC van, the event was largely unpoliced by either the RUC or Army, though there was discreet surveillance. The assailant was chased and severely beaten by young men at the funeral. He was then rescued by the RUC, who took him into custody.

Two of the victims were later buried amid rioting and disturbances in Catholic West Belfast. But on 20 March, as crowds gathered for the burial of the third victim, Kevin Brady, two British soldiers, Corporals Derek Wood and David Howes, inadvertently drove their car through the mourners against the drift of the cortege. In their attempts to get through, they drove on the pavement with their lights on and horn blaring.[53] Initially, there were indications that they might have formed part of a surveillance team. Later information showed that they were travelling from a routine maintenance task and, though warned to avoid the area, had chosen to take that route for convenience. The men were dragged from their car, savagely beaten, taken behind a wall and shot at least twelve times.

It could be argued that these deaths were just another example of the back-to-back killings that had seen eight dead and seventy injured in that single week. However, what singled out the killings at Milltown Cemetery and of the British soldiers in West Belfast was that they were televised, with the two incidents being beamed out live on the days they happened.[54]

Individual violent incidents had been televised before, but never had there been major coverage of such immediate and emotional events as these. The cameras had captured the stark terror and reaction of the crowd, and even the actual moment of death. These factors increased the importance of the events from a public relations and media point of view. They took the conflict right into the national and international public domain, alerting hitherto uncommitted viewers to the realities of the conflict. This might have been welcomed by the security forces, in that it showed terrorism and raw sectarian violence at its worst. But it also brought home to the British television audience the depth of feeling of the Catholics and their reaction to living under what some could interpret as a repressive regime.[55]

However, what was to be even more important was that the television cameras had recorded the faces of those involved in the killings.

Alarmed by the coverage and aware of the intelligence value of the television footage of the events, the British Government moved to exert unprecedented control over the media. The transmitted coverage had already been recorded but the British Broadcasting Corporation (BBC) and Independent Television Network (ITN) were forced also to hand over untransmitted video film of the incident.[56] The BBC film was handed over by the Corporation's local news editor, John Conway, only on the threat of arrest under the Prevention of Terrorism Act. Under this Act, it is a criminal offence to fail to give information to police which might assist in securing the arrest or conviction of a person involved in a terrorist offence. The Controller of BBC Northern Ireland, Dr Colin Morris, who handed over the tapes after consulting London, recalls the occasion:

> About 6.30 pm, two senior detectives appeared in my office and announced that they had reason to believe we were in possession of material relevant to murder. They said they required me to deliver it to them otherwise John Conway would be liable to arrest under the Prevention of Terrorism Act. They then read out the relevant sections.[57]

The BBC handed over 49 seconds of tape and ITN some 12 minutes, including the 75 seconds of coverage which showed the actual attack on the car driven by the two British soldiers. In handing over the material, the Director General of the BBC, Michael Checkland, observed that, 'The BBC has never set itself above the law; in dealing with this matter we have been concerned with the difficult and dangerous position of our crews in Northern Ireland.' A spokesman for ITN said that, 'The principle of withholding our untransmitted material remains important to us, but ITN's policy is to obey the law.'[58] Both the demand to hand over the film and the decision to give it were the subject of widespread debate. In Parliament, the Labour member for Wokington, Mr Dale Campbell-Savours, tabled a motion signed by some thirty opposition members opposing the decision. On the same day, Mr James Kilfedder, the popular Unionist Member of Parliament for South Down, congratulated the media on its cooperation, on behalf of the people of the United Kingdom, who he said were 'appalled' by the crime.[59]

However, the demand to hand over the television footage raises the question of impartiality, objectivity, and the ability of the media to do its job of informing the public. It questions whether the media can be called to account as an agent of the law in time of perceived need. It also raises the question of the acceptance of the media as an outlet for any opposition force which, while being tagged as 'terrorists', might be seen by parts of a wider audience as 'freedom fighters'. Beyond these ethical issues, there remains the practical issue of whether the media might not, in future, be limited in its access to coverage of any individual, group or organisation that might be perceived as illegal. None of these arguments were accepted by the government at the time, nor was there any sustained or organised opposition presented by the media. But while the national media holds an undoubted duty to obey the law, there is still the issue of where the foreign media stand. This question was not tested, since there is no evidence of any demand for film being placed on the American and European media who were also present. Nevertheless, the situation highlights the unresolved issue of the legal and moral obligations and limitations on third-party nationals covering such conflicts.

The IRA Public Relations Machine

Terrorism, as the saying goes, feeds on publicity, and the British government has been acutely aware of the value to the IRA of their formidable propaganda machine. However, while coverage of the IRA has long been restricted in the Republic of Ireland, until 1988 there were few restrictions in the United Kingdom. There was, instead, a longstanding 'closeness' in perspectives between the BBC and the British government which showed through in presentation of events in Northern Ireland. In November 1973, the Governor of the BBC, Lord Hill, responded to pressure over television coverage of the IRA in a letter to the Home Secretary, stating that 'The BBC has a duty to be impartial no less than the rest of the United Kingdom, but as between the British Army and the gunmen, the BBC is not, and cannot be impartial.'[60] This attitude caused widespread concern within the BBC where staff regarded it as self-censorship. Hill's response was that it was necessary in order to avoid imposed censorship and the resultant loss of independence. The end result was an unspoken agreement that both sides could be represented.[61]

The IRA fully exploited this opportunity. They appreciated the dramatic news value of comment from clandestine sources, of favoured journalists being received in safe houses, and the impact of interviewees being backlit or electronically shaded with a disguised voice. The IRA has also demonstrated skill in providing credible 'talent' for any incident. As many journalists, observers and politicians new to Ulster were to discover, they were natural propagandists.[62] Tugwell points to a pattern of exploiting the media in sustained campaigns such as attempting to discredit the RUC and UDR, painting the SAS as operating outside the law, and suggesting the existence of an official shoot-to-kill policy. Incidents of security brutality have all too often been recorded on television by waiting crews whom the security forces complain have been tipped off. Similarly, as Hooper reports, in July 1974 an analysis of sixty bomb explosions showed that over 80 per cent were timed to obtain maximum coverage on television news.[63] More negative actions by the IRA, such as 'kneecapping' or any of the other forms of IRA retribution, are kept private in an effort to protect their own image.[64]

The IRA's continuing use of the media to publicise their cause also aimed at the international press. The primary target has been the United States, in order to sway Irish American opinion and boost NORAID fundraising activities. The effectiveness of these activities was demonstrated in 1985 when Congress rejected an agreement between President Reagan and British Prime Minister Thatcher for a supplementary clause to the extradition treaty between the two nations, to cover terrorists. The reason was fear of a backlash from the large Irish American vote.[65]

At the local level, the IRA has developed its media advantage by cultivating links with news outlets. Hooper, a Royal Marine and a veteran of Northern Ireland, suggests that whoever gets in first usually wins the media battle. The first statement carries the bigger impact and is seldom lessened by any counter-claim, no matter how inaccurate the first report may be.[66] It was partly for this reason that, in October 1988, Prime Minister Thatcher moved to limit debate on Ulster by banning eleven groups, from both sides of the conflict, from making direct appearances on television or radio. The reason, was to cut off what she termed the 'oxygen of publicity.'[67] In introducing the legislation, Home Secretary Douglas Hurd, furthered this theme by claiming that terrorists drew support and sustenance from having access to radio and television, and that this was the only way to curb their power.[68] The Chairman of the BBC, Marmaduke Hussey, responded that the ban set a dangerous precedent and would prevent a full and balanced coverage of Northern Ireland. The National Union of Journalists accused the government of embracing the same standards as South Africa and said that in attempting to cut off the 'oxygen of publicity' from the terrorists, the government risked cutting the oxygen of democracy, the free flow of information and views. Labour Party Home Affairs spokesman Roy Hatterseley described the ban as 'repressive and ridiculous', while the leader of the Democrats in Westminster, Paddy Ashdown, declared it to be 'counterproductive.'[69]

Despite the outcry and the use of actors to voice over statements by representatives of banned organisations, the government effectively closed off the easiest avenue of information from the extremists to

Northern Ireland and the United Kingdom. More importantly, it also stopped the passage of that information on exchange to other international networks, especially North America. One of the reasons for the ban, apart from the need to limit international opprobrium, may have been that the British government sensed that British public opinion was wavering in the face of the success of the IRA in extending the conflict into a protracted war. Comparative polls taken in 1984 and 1988 showed that far more Britons wanted to withdraw British troops than wanted them to stay, and the majority did not think that Northern Ireland should remain part of the United Kingdom. There was also a marked decline of 8 per cent of those in favour of spending more money to secure Ulster, with only 6 per cent advocating an increase.[70]

The ban was not applied to non-British crews or reporters and it seems likely that, in any case, its efficacy would have been limited by the extension of the conflict over time. If a conflict is conducted within the rule of law, an opposing force, no matter how illegal or proscribed, not only has guaranteed access to the courts and the media on capture or surrender, but can still manipulate and exploit a 'once removed' access to the press through the popular support that is evidenced by their ability to continue the fight.

Conclusion

Northern Ireland is a classic case of limited conflict being conducted within the confines of the rule of law, with regard for the need to allow the majority of the population to function freely and maintain democratic values, procedures and institutions. One of the most important of those institutions remains the media.

It can be argued that, despite the evidence of patriotic bias shown by Lord Hill in commenting that the BBC would, of necessity, side with the security forces, the media in Northern Ireland generally met its obligations of impartiality and objectivity in reporting events as it saw them. This was anathema to the government and security forces, who realised that they were locked in a battle for public opinion in the face of an enemy campaign to wear down the British will to win by making the conflict a protracted war. The end result of this thinking was the banning of extremist organisations from the air waves – in itself an act which could be interpreted as a victory for the IRA because it diminished the rule of law.

The British military and government in Northern Ireland operated under the outdated social contract delusion that, because troops were deployed on government instructions, they were automatically entitled to the full support of the country and its media. The military in particular seemed to think that to report something was to condone it. On the other hand, the media, while distrustful of the military, was open to manipulation and IRA propaganda. Under these circumstances, it takes time to develop a corps of experienced correspondents who are capable of understanding the complexity of the military and political situations. Even so, despite the growing expertise, the competitive and transient nature of the media often left it open to charges of sensationalism and bad taste, and some saw it as having a malignant rather than a restraining effect on public order.

Limiting analysis to the incidents discussed in this case study, the evidence presented points to a number of conclusions. First, on Bloody Sunday and in the Falls Road incident, the British army deceived or, at best, misled the media. In the case of the Widgery Report findings (which in themselves demonstrate a degree of bias) the government used every means at its disposal to manipulate the media to defuse the situation. Second, in passing retrospective legislation the government was prepared to use its legislative authority to legitimise actions which the Courts had ruled to be illegal. In acting as it did, the government, despite the paramountcy of Parliament, denied the public's right to know by killing the story in the media. Third, the government was prepared to use its legal powers to implicate the media in the conflict by the successful demand for the handing over of television footage of the Milltown cemetery killings, and to use its reserve powers to ban proscribed organisations from access to the media in Northern Ireland. Against this, the case study shows that public support for the military in such situations will erode in the face of a protracted conflict where there is little prospect of success. This erosion of support and confidence may lead to calls for the provision of more information and an acceptance of increasing criticism in the media. In turn, the longer the conflict and the greater the evidence of lack of success, the more emboldened the media will become to meet this audience requirement.

There is also evidence that, when faced with legitimate media scrutiny, the military and the government will resort to the full armoury of denial, misinformation and classification in order to avoid that scrutiny. This can be expected to increase, the worse the security situation becomes and the longer the conflict drags on. The dilemma was summed up in an editorial in the London *Times* following the publication in 1976 of what became known as 'The Army Documents', a series of criticisms of the media by an exasperated military. The editorial said in part:

In conditions of near civil war, the Army are engaged in a conflict that is both military and psychological. Because they are fighting urban terrorists, who are pursuing their political ends without scruple or regard for the democratic wishes of the people in either part of Ireland and in the process have put civilised life in jeopardy in Northern Ireland and elsewhere in the United Kingdom, there is an unqualified national interest in the Army's success in this struggle. Yet that success cannot be obtained without the sustained support of public opinion. So the security authorities are engaged in a propaganda war which it is in the national interest to win.

The press, however, while sharing in the general national interest, have different responsibilities. A newspaper that is realistic will accept that the Army must wage a propaganda war. But a newspaper which retains its principles will have no part itself in the conduct of that war. Its task is to see that its readers are informed as fully and clearly as possible. That includes not merely the events on the ground, but the nature of the conflict, political attitudes on both sides, the relationship of the IRA to the local community and changing strength of the organisation itself. The more complete and accurate the picture, the more adequately the task is performed.[71]

The last word however, should perhaps go to a soldier, a battalion commander, who served two tours in Northern Ireland and who, when writing on Bloody Sunday, complained that the immediacy of what in that case was the actual and visual truth, led the world to believe that the troops behaved wrongly. This sort of situation, he said 'ignores the reality of a counter insurgency campaign, and ... if armies are not prepared to state the government's case on television, no one else will do so, and the rebels will win a propaganda victory by default... in many cases, this means that the soldier will have to lie in order to conceal an unpalatable truth.'[72] The troubling conclusion that his comments and the evidence in this case study point to is that lies, in one form or another, remain the only real weapon available to governments in similar urban limited conflicts, operating under the rule of law and subject to media scrutiny.

5

Vietnam:
Deception on a National Scale

Vietnam was the first real 'television' war – the first conflict where, apart from the Dominican Republic intervention in 1965, the military found themselves attempting to control a media which was not fully supportive of their country's involvement.[1] It was also the first 'open' limited conflict, where the full weight of the modern media was deployed without restriction.

For the first time, the national media saw a duty to cater to those in opposition to the conflict. The war was waged in a remote area and, apart from concerns with conscription, did not pose a direct threat to the citizen or the state. The war is also a prime example of the government and military holding outdated expectations of popular support under the social contract. The fact that the people were afforded the luxury of making up their minds on the merits of the conflict, with many finding the official reasons wanting, was something for which the government was not prepared. The military was even more unprepared since, up until then, the tradition had been one of winning popular wars as an extension of the people.[2]

The Vietnam war is a classic example of a limited conflict in that it was localised and operated within strict weaponry and geographical limitations; yet it held regional and global security implications. Above all, it was a politico-military confrontation between competing principles and ideologies. This restricted the Americans to maintaining the conceit that they were invited allies in Vietnam. It meant that they were unable to impose any limitations on media coverage as the war was technically being waged by the Vietnamese. The Americans were also faced with the contradiction that limiting the freedom of the media would have been at odds with their declared aim of restoring democracy to Vietnam.[3] But despite the warnings that had been sounded in the round of post-World War II struggles for self determination and in Korea, the American military went into Indochina with little thought for the problems of controlling the media.[4]

For the purposes of this study, Vietnam takes on added importance in that the military build-up period, from the late 1950s to the mid-1960s, coincided with saturation penetration of television into homes in the United States. At the same time, the growing mass audience was served by one of the most sophisticated television news gathering network systems in the world.[5]

As might have been expected, from such a patriotic nation, the American media in Vietnam started out generally supportive of their military. That support gradually lessened, however, in the face of over-optimistic official statements on the progress of the war – statements which contradicted what reporters in the field could see for themselves. And the media could have this uncensored alternative information on television screens in America within twelve hours.[6] As a result, many of the journalists providing television coverage, together with their equally dedicated partners in radio and print, saw themselves playing a valid role in exposing the truth behind what they were privileged to see as little less than a national deception.

A popular argument is that the media were directly responsible for the loss of political and military will to continue the war in Vietnam. However, as this case study demonstrates, while the media played an important part in educating the home nation to the realities of the situation, they reflected public opinion rather than formed it. The real reasons for the American loss of will in Vietnam lay more with war weariness in the face of a protracted and unsuccessful campaign, and disillusionment in the face of government disinformation, denial and deception. As examples, this case study discusses the Gulf of Tonkin incident, the Tet offensive, and the concept of the 'Vietnamisation' of the war. These incidents and strategies have been selected because of their chronological sequence which allows comparisons between the events, the media response and levels of public support. More importantly for this study, the incidents demonstrate the high levels of deception that emerged as the principal form of response by the United States government and military in the face of their lack of control over the media. Each incident also demonstrates that the promise of success could not be sustained in the face of a media which presented credible evidence to the contrary.

Background to the Campaign

The first Indochina War ended with the Geneva Accords in 1954. The Accords were the direct outcome of the decisive defeat inflicted on the French by the communist/nationalist Viet Minh at Dien Bien Phu. The agreement called for the division of the country by a de-militarised zone at the 17th parallel. It allowed for a cease-fire and regrouping of forces and population, and stipulated that unifying elections should be held within two years.

Although the wider international needs of the great powers to a large extent robbed the Viet Minh of the fruits of their military victory in this settlement, they remained confident that they would win out eventually over the puppet Bao Dai government set in place by the French in Saigon. But, with the advent of the American-backed Ngo Dinh Diem as President of South Vietnam in 1955, the situation changed. In 1956, Diem repudiated the elections called for under the Accords and the Viet Minh resumed military efforts through their southern front, the Viet Cong. American covert military aid was expanded to arm Diem's forces and economic credits were given to shore up the economy.

The Gulf of Tonkin incident in 1964 gave the Americans the excuse they needed for more direct involvement in Vietnam. In this incident it was alleged that the North Vietnamese fired on American warships in an open act of belligerence. The United States took the opportunity to commence a major military build-up that eventually saw American troop levels reach a peak of over half a million as they attempted to contain the matching escalation of Chinese and Soviet backed North Vietnamese (PAVN) main forces that were being infiltrated into South Vietnam. The result was a stalemate situation in which the air and firepower of the United States controlled the open coastal areas while the Viet Cong and PAVN held the mountainous hinterland.

This stalemate continued until January 1968, when the North embarked on a political and military adventure designed to exploit Vietnam's major holiday period, the Tet celebrations. The offensive was a costly defeat for Hanoi as the expected popular uprising failed to materialise and the communists took heavy losses. Nevertheless, it achieved its major aim of underlining the impotence of the Americans.

Largely because of the way it was presented by the media, the Tet offensive had a profound effect on world and United States public opinion, and it paved the way for an eventual negotiated settlement as surely as had events at Dien Bien Phu some thirteen years earlier.

After Tet, the United States continued their campaign of aerial bombardment, aimed at improving their bargaining position at the ensuing peace talks. At the same time, they began to wind down their forces under the concept of 'Vietnamisation'. This was a cynical policy based on the presumption that the smaller, under-equipped and under-trained Vietnamese forces could succeed where the massive financial resources and might of the United States military had failed. Following a peace agreement in January 1973, and using Vietnamisation as the rationale, the United States eventually withdrew completely. The South Vietnamese government was left to fight on with failing morale until they were rolled up from the central highlands and decisively defeated eighteen months later.[7]

Wholesale Deception: The Gulf of Tonkin Incident

The public relations battle was fought on almost every front and at every level during the Vietnam war. But everything centred on the ability of the media and, in particular, television, to provide an immediate and uncensored coverage of the conflict. The Americans had no policy or machinery in place to handle the media, even when Vietnam became news with the beginnings of the deployment of mass forces in 1965.[8] At that stage, Vietnam was still viewed by the American public as little more than a small part in the crusade to contain communism. It was perhaps this attitude that allowed the government to manipulate the media into accepting the patently manufactured Gulf of Tonkin incident of July 1964 – the incident which was used as the pretext for the first round of United States military escalation.

By the beginning of 1963 it was becoming evident that formed units of the PAVN were being introduced into the South by Hanoi. At a conference in Hawaii in June of that year, it was agreed that there was a need for escalation of the covert presence to match this growing incursion if the weak South Vietnamese regime was not to collapse.[9] However, at the time the American military effort was restricted to advisers and air and logistic support. The limited offensive capability which existed was under the control of the Central Intelligence Agency (CIA).

Escalation commenced with the deployment of the CIA tasked Special Observation Group (SOG) in February 1964. This was made up of

United States special forces, CIA case officers and Vietnamese mercenaries. Codenamed OPLAN 34A, the role of this force was to mount diversionary raids into North Vietnam (DRV). The incursions into the North were accompanied by a similar Naval program called DESOTO patrols which ran electronic intelligence missions in the Gulf of Tonkin.[10] But the escalation clearly required some form of Congressional resolution, as had been applied in Cuba and Formosa (later Taiwan).[11] And there needed to be a reason for the resolution.

On 31 July, the USS Maddox was sent on a DESOTO patrol into the Gulf. There is little doubt that its mission was to draw DRV boats away from OPLAN 34A activities. The available evidence shows that Hanoi was forewarned and the Maddox came under attack. This led to the so-called Gulf of Tonkin incident on 2 August,[12] and formed the basis for what had obviously been the long-prepared Tonkin Gulf Resolution. The resolution authorised the President to, 'take all necessary steps, including the use of armed force, to aid any South East Asian state.'[13] US Under Secretary of State, George Ball, later described the DESOTO missions as serving 'primarily for provocation', and there can be no doubt that the mission of the Maddox was designed to provide the rationale for a formal approval by Congress of a foregone decision. Three years later, Senator Fulbright expressed his regrets: 'Imagine, we spent all of an hour and forty minutes on that resolution. A disaster; a tragic mistake.'[14] Given the weight of evidence now available, there is no doubt that Congress and the people were deceived. As Kolko puts it:

> The Administration had in fact lied to Congress regarding the details of the Tonkin Affair, obscuring the political fact that the policy had been drawn up much earlier and had been predetermined by its responses. Above all, the White House claimed that it had been provoked, when in reality it was the provoker.[15]

The uncritical support President Johnson received from Congress was matched by that of the media. The resolution was supported by three of America's largest and most influential newspapers, whose editorials were inserted in the Congressional record as part of the argument. The *Washington Post* editorial read in part that:

> President Johnson has earned the gratitude of the free world for his careful and effective handling of the Vietnam crisis. The paramount need was to show the North Vietnamese aggressors their self defeating folly in ignoring an unequivocal American warning and again attacking the American Navy on the high seas.[16]

In similar fashion, the *New York Times* demonstrated just how far the media had been deceived by the administration's actions and intentions when it said that 'we still want no wider war.'[17] The *Philadelphia Inquirer* rallied public support for Johnson, calling the nation to stand firm and united in support of the President '... at this crucial juncture in the history of mankind, in the face of a treacherous foe.'[18] For his part, Johnson delayed immediate action on the escalation while he campaigned for re-election on a peace ticket.[19]

The success of this first instance of national deception set the pattern for continued deception over American aims and policies in Vietnam. It was not until June 1965 that the US military revealed the scale of the US Marine Corps combat role in Vietnam, and then its admissions were only in response to heavy losses that could no longer be concealed.[20] This policy of denial and deception might have been sustainable if it had met with success, but the administration attempted to maintain its fictions in the face of an increasingly distrustful media and a nation facing a protracted war.[21] This created a credibility gap which was to grow until the discrepancies between what was being claimed and what was being reported led to a shift, from Congressional and popular support for the war, to outright opposition.

The Erosion of Public Support

The end result of this credibility gap was the emergence of a small but crucial sector of the community who, as Kolko puts it, 'publicly recognised the guile and began to erode the national consensus on foreign policy.'[22] Loss of faith in the government and the conduct of the war became evident initially within the university elite. The first teach-in at the University of Michigan attracted 30,000 students. The idea rapidly spread to other campuses as students attempted to educate the wider public to see that the war was irrational and immoral.[23] Slowly, because of the obvious cost of the conflict in both resources and lives, the protest movement spread into the general community, aided by the penetration of the media, particularly television.[24]

By the end of 1967, more Americans opposed the decision to deploy troops in Vietnam than supported it. This trend was to continue until the end of the war in 1975, when opposition outweighed support by almost two to one.

One of the questions pollsters asked most frequently during the Vietnam war was, 'In view of the developments since we entered the fighting in Vietnam, do you think that the United States made a mistake in sending troops to fight in Vietnam?' In August 1965 as America was rapidly increasing its involvement in the war, 61 per cent said 'no' and 24 per cent said 'yes.' For the next two years between 48 and 59 per cent continued to believe that the United States had not erred in entering the fighting in Vietnam.[25] When the same question was asked in late 1967, the respondents who answered 'not a mistake' were more numerous than the respondents who answered 'mistake', but only by a margin of 46 percent to 45 per cent. By March 1968, in the wake of the Tet offensive, the percentage answering 'mistake' had grown to 49, while the percentage answering 'not a mistake' had dropped to 41 per cent. By August 1968, only 35 per cent believed that American involvement in Vietnam had not been a mistake.[26]

The problem was that the government and the military failed to educate the public into the realities of a protracted limited conflict. Instead, they relied upon the outdated concept of public support for any external conflict. In relation to Vietnam, such support was expected because the war formed part of the anti-communist crusade then being waged by America. What the United States government and military failed to realise was that, given the opportunity to make up their own minds, at no cost to their immediate security or the survival of the nation, the American people took advantage of the new high technology media to avail themselves of enough independent information to decide the case on its merits rather than on any concept of 'duty' to the state.

Retail Deception: The Media and the Masses

It was much the same in-country in Vietnam. The ever growing demand for official information was met by a formalised and generally ill-informed Joint United States Public Affairs Office (JUSPAO) manned by 'professional' briefers backed up with a formidable array of slides, backdrops and other visual aids. The only thing missing was the truth. This was because the military had to follow the policy gyrations of the government in Washington in providing the rationale for escalation, vindication for a generally misplaced trust in the fighting abilities of the Vietnamese Army, and justification for the constant coups and leadership changes in South Vietnam. They did so by producing 'evidence' for a success that patently was not there.[27]

Since there was no effective censorship beyond voluntary acceptance of the needs of operational security, the only way the military could influence the media was by presenting its own official version of events. The line put forward by military public affairs on the ground was one of unalloyed optimism and an ever-improving military situation. The problem was that the media could – and did – easily disprove the official line simply by going into the field for a few hours. The nonsensical claims made by the military led to an outright contempt for the official public relations handouts and the nightly briefings at JUSPAO, fondly known as the 'five o'clock follies.' Reporters who had only that day come in from the field were able to deride the 'body count' tally that JUSPAO used as the measure of success, and could debunk the official version of events on the basis of having seen and recorded the true situation for themselves.[28] This coverage, made all the more newsworthy when accompanied by the official denial, was beamed into homes in the United States and elsewhere around the world within hours. Because of its immediacy and visual credibility, it had a major effect on public opinion, especially with a people who were becoming increasingly cynical about the likely end result in a clearly unsuccessful and protracted war.[29]

In 1962, when asked who they would trust in the event of conflicting evidence in the press and television, 48 per cent of the Americans polled opted for television and only 21 per cent for newspapers.[30] A similar survey five years later showed that the American public overwhelmingly relied on television over newspapers.[31] Such figures led Hofstetter and Moore to argue that the initial television coverage of the conflict had conditioned the population to war and encouraged support for the armed forces. In their 1972 study, they found that 69 per cent of those who watched television news expressed a high regard for the military as opposed to 59 per cent who favoured other news sources. There was a similar response in favour of greater defence spending.[32] But support for the military did not necessarily equate with support for the war.

Although its images were compressed because of the limitations of the electronic media, the television coverage of Vietnam showed no major battles with which the home audience might identify. Instead, it reflected the continuous and seemingly inconclusive actions that typified Vietnam until the major battles of Tet. Thayer makes the point that, with the exception of the small group of younger journalists working in Vietnam who took issue with the Diem regime rather than with American foreign policy, the overall trend in reporting up until the mid-1960s was generally supportive of the administration's line.[33] Nevertheless, he believes that popular support waned in direct relation to the rise in casualties, with total support dropping by 15 per cent when casualties rose by a factor of ten from 1,000 to 10,000. This response, Thayer claims, was regardless of whether the war was going well or not, with the same pattern having been observed in Korea.[34] In both cases, the media was the intermediary, and in Vietnam it was the early reporters such as David Halberstam of the

New York Times and Malcolm Brown of Associated Press who laid the groundwork for the continuing negative images that were to follow. Their reports led General Westmoreland, the US Field Commander to angrily state in his memoirs that:

> Finding fault was one way to achieve the sensational, and finding fault with an oriental regime with little background in or respect for Western style democracy was easy ... When their peers back home rewarded two of them with a shared Pulitzer prize (Brown and Halberstam), the pattern for those who followed was set ... the more criticisms and the more negativism, the greater possibility of recognition and reward.[35]

Despite these bad beginnings, there was no actual censorship imposed on the media in Vietnam. To have done so would have been to negate the American pretence of working through the Vietnamese. But apart from a small local press which was under tight control, few foreigners bothered to get a Vietnamese press pass. American accreditation was given '... within the bounds of operational requirements and military security.'[36] Beyond that was a set of voluntary guidelines covering some fifteen areas concerning troop movements, equipment and locations.[37]

The size of the press corps was staggering. At any one time there were upwards of 1,000 accredited journalists in the country. They ranged from seasoned reporters to representatives from college newspapers. All that a journalist from a recognised media outlet required for accreditation was a letter from the editor. In the case of freelance reporters, two letters typed on official stationery identified the applicant as a potential contributor and would secure accreditation. This entitled the journalist to transport and accommodation on an 'as available' basis under a Category 3 priority; this put him or her roughly on a par with troops returning from leave or going on rest and recreation.[38]

In reality, correspondents became adept at hitching rides and, in many cases, were adopted by the units with whom they shared the same dangers. Generally this worked well, although there could be some hostility from troops who pointed to the fact that the media had the option to pick and choose the levels and duration of action they covered – the media could retreat to the safety of the seventh floor bar at the Caravelle Hotel in Saigon, while the troops had to remain in the field. Many soldiers also resented the media's intrusion into their grief or the filming of their dead or wounded.[39] Others, especially at senior levels, were hostile in view of what they saw as the media's betrayal of their efforts, feeling that the media always took a critical viewpoint.[40]

There were charges, too, that the television crews created their own
news and that the mere presence of cameras encouraged a sense of the
dramatic among the troops. In 1967, one journalist saw US Marines
acting in a 'John Wayne' manner before the camera at Khe Sanh in
northern South Vietnam. On another occasion, during the Buddhist riots
in 1962, American and Japanese television crews actively encouraged
children to climb the wall of a police compound. The crews obtained
vivid television images of the mob which followed and stormed the
District Chief's compound in Danang. Such behaviour on the part of
journalists may have been due to the fact that as the war progressed,
home based news editors were demanding more and more combat and
action footage at the expense of a longer-term analytical view.[41]

It was this sort of coverage that led General Westmoreland to charge
that the majority of the coverage was:

> ... almost exclusively violent, miserable or controversial; guns
> firing, men falling, helicopters crashing, buildings toppling, huts
> burning, refugees fleeing, women wailing. A shot of a single
> building in ruins could give the impression of an entire town
> destroyed. The propensity of the cameramen at Khe Sanh to pose
> their commentators before a wrecked C-130 and deliver reports in
> a tone of voice suggesting doomsday was all too common. Only
> scant attention was paid to pacification, civic action, medical
> assistance, the way life went on in a generally normal way for most
> of the people most of the time.[42]

Westmoreland was also critical of the American media for its
willingness to give Hanoi the benefit of the doubt, or at least the benefit
of a lack of critical examination as opposed to the growing hostility and
critical attitude the media took towards its own military:

> An adversary relationship evolved between the media and all
> parties associated with the war, except, ironically, the enemy.
> Hanoi was able to cultivate the fiction that there were no North
> Vietnamese troops in the South and that the war was basically a
> people's revolution and that it was an illegal and immoral war. It is
> astonishing that great numbers of our citizens and many
> representatives of the news media were taken in by Hanoi's
> propaganda ... There were no TV cameras behind enemy lines. All
> news from North Vietnam was propaganda to serve their purposes.
> And serve it did. There was no other news from the camp of the
> enemy. 'If a mighty oak falls unobserved in a mighty forest,' the
> saying goes, 'it neither exists nor falls'. It apparently never
> occurred to the media that they were being used by our enemies.[43]

Westmoreland's views were endorsed by Kenneth Granville, a former Communist, who wrote:

> Its (the international communist apparatus) image makers promoted the Viet Cong as Robin Hoods delivering the poor from the robber barons of Saigon, burying beneath this fantasy the truth that the National Liberation Front was the tool of the Hanoi politburo.[44]

Yet as angry and betrayed as the military felt at what they saw as a hostile press duped by a Hanoi-directed peace movement, there was simply no way of reversing the trend nor of cutting off the means of communication. From 1962 onwards, these trends grew increasingly sophisticated, with direct telephone and teletype links, and some radio telephone and wireless. In addition, there were constant couriers who could have film or video shipped back to the United States through Singapore in less than a day. And given the privileges of American society and its guarantees of freedom of speech, there was no way that that film could be censored once it arrived home. Nor would the public have stood for any form of censorship even if it had been feasible. The newfound technical autonomy of this independent-minded media even denied the military the weapons of limited access or delay in transmission. The only answer in the battle for the public mind lay in ever stronger official denials and promises of success. These denials and promises increasingly proved to be false.[45]

Media coverage for American allies involved in Vietnam took a similar course. Australian reporting was universally favourable to the troops, even during the height of the anti-war demonstrations from 1969 onwards. To be fair, though, the Australian media largely limited its interest to the area of Australian operations. No one beyond Wilfred Burchett questioned the conduct of Australian troops other than in two isolated incidents, one involving the field punishment of a soldier and the other when the Army attempted a clumsy cover-up of the torture of a young girl Viet Cong suspect.[46]

Control of the Australian media was not difficult because of the degree of self-censorship exercised. Australia was, after all, in Vietnam in pursuit of the easily identifiable and widely-accepted objectives of forward defence and the containment of communism. The Australians were well disciplined and very professional. Australian journalists took pride in the preference expressed by some of their American colleagues for working with the Australian Task Force.[47] As a result, although there was sharp political debate on the commitment and overall conduct of the war, Australian reporting was generally favourable to the troops. Even when the Australian media followed their American counterparts in catering to the increasingly strident anti-war movements at home, as they saw for themselves the truth of the war, the 'diggers', almost half of whom were conscripts, were never to blame.[48]

The Tet Offensive

Just before dawn on 31 January 1968, with the Vietnamese Army virtually stood down for the country's most important annual holiday, a taxi drew up outside the United States Embassy in Saigon. A Viet Cong commando jumped out and opened fire. The Tet Offensive was underway.

There had been adequate early intelligence of the event, pieced together by a small but highly classified group in Saigon. The analysis provided by this group was extremely accurate, down to an assessment of the exact time and date of the attack and the prediction that up to six PAVN divisions would be deployed against targets throughout the length and breadth of the country. But both the US State Department and the Australian Department off Foreign Affairs chose to deny the evidence.[49]

The rationale behind the attack, which intelligence had foreshadowed, was that the PAVN had to break the stalemate under which they controlled the interior but lacked the force to take on the firepower and air superiority of the allied forces on the open coastal strip. Morale would suffer if forces kept pouring in and sacrifices continued to be made by the North Vietnamese population without some decisive victory. Since the North could not take on the allies in open battle at that stage or in the foreseeable future, the answer lay in a major political and military adventure designed to break the American will to continue. The American High Command accepted these warnings and they were passed on by Westmoreland and the United States Chairman of the Joint Chiefs of Staff Committee. President Johnson, however, refuted the advice within the week. There was no way he could allow the great deception of an ever bright optimism to be undermined by accepting such negative intelligence.

The impact of the attack outside the United States Embassy was the beginning of the end for the American involvement in Vietnam. Saigon and the old imperial capital of Hue were only two of the hundreds of towns attacked throughout the country by an initial wave of some 80,000 PAVN and local Viet Cong. The result was a devastating defeat for the enemy, but it became a massive psychological victory for them – a victory which many saw as aided by the media:

The general effect of the news media's commentary coverage of Tet in February and March 1968, was a distortion of reality, through sins of omission and commission, on a scale that helped spur major repercussions in US domestic politics, if not in foreign policy. For a number of military men in Vietnam during the Tet offensive, it must have been ironic to win a military victory, have it reported by American journalists as a defeat, and have those reports accepted as fact by many Americans.[50]

General Westmoreland put it more strongly, claiming that:

> ... voluminous, lurid and distorted newspaper and particularly television reporting of the Tet offensive, had transformed a devastating Communist military defeat into a 'psychological victory'.[51]

Peter Braestrup, who covered the war for the *Washington Post*, levelled the same charges as Westmoreland, in his book, *The Big Story*, stating that in describing and interpreting the events of Tet, 'crisis journalism had rarely veered so widely from reality.' But, to be fair, the media was put in the position of having to balance the evidence of their eyes against the false sense of security and optimism constantly peddled by the military and the administration. These were based on illusory reports of North Vietnamese and Viet Cong casualties, infiltration, recruitment and morale, all of which tended to downgrade the image of the enemy.[52]   Irrespective of the defeat inflicted on the enemy, Tet demonstrated the absurdity of the earlier official line. The military, however, was left with an absolute sense of betrayal made all the worse by the fact that, as Westmoreland charged, the media would not even admit to any error when the true facts came to light: 'The sad thing is that those controlling media policies did not have the sophistication, the integrity or the courage to admit their error.'[53] It was a fact broadly recognised several weeks after the initial event.

It would have done no good if the media had apologised. The crisis had passed, the floodgates had been opened.

As Kolko states, the Tet Offensive caused public opposition to rise sharply. By the summer of 1968 Americans believed, by a majority of two to one, that the deployment into Vietnam had been an error.[54] The conventional wisdom is that the Tet coverage, and television pictures of the battles of Khe Sanh that followed, were the last straw for the American public. There is little doubt that these actions played an important part in strengthening opposition to the war, but it is apparent that the tide of public opinion had already turned. All the media did was confirm the widespread public view held well before Tet, that the people had been the victims of a massive deception – wholesale in the political arena and retail from the field.

As Hallin remarked, the impact of Tet on public opinion was, 'more complex and less dramatic, though certainly not insignificant, than generally supposed.' Tet was less a turning point than a crossover point, a moment where trends that have been in motion for some time reach balance and began to tip the other way.[55]

Vietnamisation : The Ultimate Deception

If Tet had exposed the long years of official deception, the next makeshift policy of 'Vietnamisation' was to emerge as the ultimate in cynical self-delusion and public relations image making. Under this concept, the world was asked to believe that what could not be done by the mightiest military power on earth could be achieved by a lesser, weak and demoralised South Vietnamese Army (ARVN) in the face of a post-Tet enemy who sensed a loss of American will to win and who scented victory.

The myth that the South Vietnamese Army was the major military power, with the United States military in direct support, had always been a cornerstone policy position for American involvement in Vietnam. This myth was rapidly stripped away after 1965, but the Vietnamese still had a major role to play in manning the static defences throughout the country while the Americans provided manoeuvre forces. By 1973, the Vietnamese had 1.1 million men under arms, just on half of all males between 18 and 35 years of age. The South Vietnamese armed forces had also been almost completely re-equipped with a formidable line up of high technology weaponry, including 657 of the latest helicopters and 740 front line combat aircraft. But South Vietnam lacked the technical resources to maintain such a capability. And, after Tet, morale within the South Vietnamese ranks was understandably low, with high levels of desertion and corruption on a grand scale.[56]

It was against this background of a weak and generally ineffective South Vietnamese Armed Forces that, in late 1969 and early 1970, the Nixon administration came up with the concept of Vietnamisation – a policy designed solely to provide the rationale and cover for an American-negotiated withdrawal.[57]

The opportunity to demonstrate this supposed new-found self reliance on the part of the Vietnamese came in March and April the next year, when Prince Sihanouk of Cambodia was overthrown by the pro-American Lon Nol regime. One purpose of the American-engineered coup was to mount a military effort from within Cambodia to expel the North Vietnamese forces and their major Central Office for South Vietnam HQ (COSVN), from the Bec-du-Canard area in the Vietnamese-Cambodian, Transbassac border region. As part of that aim, 'newly transformed' ARVN forces were helicoptered into Cambodia with the task of destroying the COSVN HQ. Aided by massive American air and artillery support over favourable open terrain, the Vietnamese initially enjoyed some limited success which was put forward as evidence of viability of the concept. The next test, code-named LAMSON 719, aimed to attack and deny the enemy the southern end of the Ho Chi Minh supply trail in southern Laos and northern Cambodia. But this operation resulted in a disastrous rout. As Kolko reports, 'Lam Son 719 disclosed the inability of the ARVN to coordinate a major campaign and use superior firepower rationally. Journalists repeatedly reinforced the argument that the ARVN could never replace, much less improve, on American soldiers.'[58]

The working media, who were well aware of the true state of the ARVN, were generally aghast at the concept of Vietnamisation and horrified at the beating that lay in wait for the Vietnamese. As one correspondent wrote at the time:

> To invite the South Vietnamese to the equivalent of a military picnic in Cambodia was one thing, but to expect them to take on the North in its home ground was quite another. The more so when the target area was of vital importance to Hanoi's eventual war aims ... the results were obvious before they started. They quickly bogged down just over the border and the US had to resort to leapfrogging whole units out by helicopter.[59]

Despite the crescendo of warnings, LAMSOM 719 destroyed once and for all the myth that the Vietnamese could take over the mobile role and highlighted the nonsense that they could cover the withdrawal of major United States troop units. That truth was revealed to the world through the offices of the by now combat-hardened and generally critical media in Vietnam, especially through the graphic television images such as those of Vietnamese troops hanging on to the skids of departing helicopters.[60]

There is little doubt that the Pentagon and the field commanders in Vietnam knew exactly the confidence trick that Vietnamisation was. And the American administration knew that the concept had to become a public relations success if they were to be able to continue withdrawing American forces. As a result, the United States government embarked on a campaign to refute media pessimism in a major public relations effort. As Kolko reports:

Praise for Thieu's military achievements came largely from Pentagon press efforts and of course from Laird (US Secretary for Defence) himself who even in June 1972, after the ARVN's debacle in Laos and in face of the PAVN's April 1972 offensive maintained that Thieu's forces had 'performed adequately.'[61]

But by then, the full measure of the government deception had been well and truly exposed, if not by the media then by the returning American soldiers.

The scope of this chapter does not allow us to follow the full extent of deception that the United States administration engaged in with the war in Vietnam. It includes the fostering of false optimism over the pacification program and the failure of civil defence, strategic hamlets and local defence programs. These deceptions were maintained right up until the fall of Saigon. Other examples are the Chieu Hoi, 'open arms' surrender program (which ended up being used by the enemy for espionage purposes), the air war and the bombing pauses, the aid program, cultural and economic initiatives, the attempts at industrialisation, cross-border operations, and the abortive Montagnard operations. Without exception, they all failed and without exception they were exposed by the media. But without exception the fiction of success was maintained to the end. Only when the American public was confronted with the realities of the March 1975 offensive by the North and the military debacle that followed, culminating in the occupation of Saigon, did the pretence stop.[62]

Conclusion

The overriding conclusion emerging from an examination of Vietnam is that in limited conflicts, where the media is free to report the truth as it sees it, where that truth is perceived by the public as accurate and where the public are free to make up their minds unconstrained by considerations of personal or national survival, the government and the military are virtually powerless. In Vietnam, the well documented loss of popular support in the face of what became a protracted and increasingly unpopular war, while led by the media, was largely due to the exercise of the people's freedom to decide matters of national security and foreign policy on their merits. This came as a shock to the government and military who entered the conflict still relying on an outdated social contract that promised the same automatic support for the national war aims in Vietnam that had been given so freely in the past.

Censorship, the right to censor, and the question of whether the government had the means to technically censor information, becomes irrelevant in the special circumstances surrounding Vietnam. As this case shows, the American government could not impose censorship because the United States was technically only an ally fighting at the invitation of the sovereign state of South Vietnam. To have exercised a right to censor would have been to lessen the standing of the South Vietnamese government and deny the very democratic freedoms the Americans had been invited in ostensibly to protect. Nor yet could the Americans impose censorship in their home country, because of the limited nature of the conflict which posed no threat to the United States itself, and because of the constitutional guarantees safeguarding a free press. They were also limited in the use of classification and in withholding access. And they had no control whatsoever over the means of communication.

Deprived of censorship, the only weapons that the government had at its disposal were persuasion, and when that failed, deception was used in their attempts to implement a secret agenda. This was evidenced in the Gulf of Tonkin incident, where the facts were distorted to provide a rationale for escalation, in the continuing deception over progress and success that was exposed during the Tet offensive, and in the official self-delusion over Vietnamisation. It was the public rejection of these deceptions that led to the eventual loss of popular support. The role of the media was certainly important, but, as the chronology of events and tide of opinion demonstrates, it followed and moulded public opinion rather than formed it.

In hindsight, containing the press and managing perceptions of the war was an almost impossible task for a democracy such as America, which had one of the most unrestricted media in the world. Yet, in the face of an active press and constitutionally guaranteed media freedoms, the administration attempted to limit and manipulate coverage of a wide range of lost causes. These included a secret and engineered foreign policy, a record of continuing military failure, a decisive political and psychological defeat in the Tet Offensive, a disintegrating South Vietnamese army, a secret conventional bombing war on a scale never seen before, and a withdrawal and disengagement that did not make military sense. To make matters worse, it was attempted against a background of racial, economic and political dissent within the United States itself.

At the beginning of the war, the main elements in American policy moved in a direction that represented the greatest perceived good – the containment of Chinese and Soviet ambitions in southeast Asia by taking a stand in South Vietnam. Although prone at times to believe the worst of officialdom, the American news media both reflected and reinforced that trend, replaying official statements on the value of the war and supporting the soldier in the field, if not always his generals. With time, under the influence of many deaths and contradictions, directions changed. Significant portions of the leadership in American society moved to repudiate the earlier decision. Cuing to that trend, the press followed suit, but the government and military lacked the ability to respond. As Hammond sums it up:

> Locked into retrieving whatever national face they could, those most emotionally tied to the failed policy fixed their anger upon the news media, the most visible exponent of the society that appeared to have rejected them. The recriminations that we see today became the inevitable result.[63]

The effect of this failure was to play a large part in the eventual defeat and humiliation of American arms and the downfall of a president. But, most important for this study is the fact that failure to control the media also served as a stern warning to those responsible for the future conduct of military operations in the field. It led to a deep distrust of – and in some cases contempt for – the media by the military that was to colour its judgement in future handling of war reporting. It is a resentment that has long been evident to those who have attempted to open any dialogue on the subject with the military. As Trainor reports, this attitude, stemming from the Vietnam experience, persists in service academies and military schools to the present day:

> At first they are polite, respectful, prefacing each question with 'sir', but when faced with their own prejudices, the veneer of civility evaporates, hostility surfaces and the questions give way to a frenzy of accusations. No these aren't journalists asking the questions. They are young officers and cadets ... carrying as part of their baggage a loathing for the press.[64]

It is an attitude that is common in the military academies of the Western world. It is an attitude that has led to a determination among the military forces of the West and, indeed, the communist bloc countries, to pursue the secret agenda that never again should the press, and above all, television, be given unlimited or uncontrolled access to cover a conflict. Better still, the media should not be given any access at all.

6

The Falklands Conflict:
A Policy of Media
Manipulation

The Vietnam experience shook defence forces all around the world, especially in Western democracies where the military were quick to appreciate the importance and impact of public opinion on operations. As a result, measures were taken to ensure that never again would the media enjoy the same degree of influence over the conduct and outcome of a conflict.

The common thread running through early proposals for media management was a policy of control through cooperation. In the absence of any major conflict, however, these plans were limited to little more than the establishment of formal links between the military and media at editor level. The Vietnam war was also widely appreciated as a 'one off' conflict – a unique set of circumstances not likely to be repeated. In this environment the immediate post-war concern over the role of the media soon dissipated, with the issue of media-military relations relegated to the staff colleges and given low levels of priority in defence planning.

There the matter rested, as little more than an academic curiosity, until that complacency was disturbed, in 1982, by the outbreak of the Falklands conflict.

In mounting the Falklands campaign, the British military and, significantly, the government were quick to grasp the importance of securing public support for the war. Interest in the issue of media management was revived. However, despite the early appreciation of the problem, media policy was, in the main, developed on the run by both the military and government. Cooperation was largely forgotten as the military exploited to the full the control which the remoteness of the conflict afforded them. At the same time, the government used every available means to manipulate the media in support of its war aims.

The Falklands conflict is the perfect example of an 'expeditionary' campaign. It also provides clear insights into a government and military relying on outdated expectations of the citizen's duty to support the political ambitions of a state engaged in a limited conflict. As the campaign developed, these expectations were bolstered by a government-contrived nineteenth century jingoism, eagerly taken up by some sections of the media in catering to the general mood of their audience. Behind the scenes, however, the penalties and pressures imposed by the government in support of its war aims were based on state-of-the-art political agenda-setting and public relations. Tactics employed included the use of deception, misinformation, disinformation, and media manipulation through denial of access, control of communications and politically based censorship.

Four aspects of the Falklands campaign will be examined in this case study. The first is the way the military exercised control through its monopoly of access to transport and communications, exploiting to the maximum the advantages inherent in a true expeditionary campaign. Second is the government's management of the media to secure the political aims of enlisting national and international support, and its acceptance of the use of censorship, deception, disinformation and misinformation in pursuit of those aims. The third matter for attention is the 'win at all costs' attitude displayed by the politicised military. This saw the media enlisted as yet another weapon of war, with little or no appreciation of wider issues, such as the democratic need for the public to be informed. Finally, the case looks at the unpreparedness, acquiescence and lack of cohesion of the British media in challenging the exploitation and manipulation practised by the government.

The short duration of the Falklands conflict and its successful outcome are limiting factors which must be taken into account in this discussion. Despite some setbacks, the rapid sequence of events leading to victory did not allow time for any serious re-consideration of the wider democratic issues or for more thoughtful military analysis to develop. These would come later in a Parliamentary inquiry. Another limitation –

important for the thesis being developed – was that the war was concluded before the media had time to deploy the new technology communications systems which would have tested the theory that governments no longer have the capability to impose censorship.

Background to the Campaign

The Falkland Islands lie some 500 kilometres (approximately 300 miles) to the East of Argentina – well within combat air range. Their ownership has long been disputed by the United Kingdom (Britain), which controls them, and Argentina, which sees them as a natural adjunct to Argentinian territory. Negotiations had begun in 1982 for some form of lease-back arrangement from Britain in return for recognition of Argentinian sovereignty, but the talks failed in the face of objections from the local inhabitants who regarded themselves as British and part of the British Commonwealth. Subsequently, on 2 April 1982, the Argentinians brought the issue to a head by invading and taking possession of the Islands – possibly in an attempt to distract Argentinian public opinion from internal economic problems.

However, the Argentinians were not prepared for the speed and determination of the British response. Britain mobilised extensive support from her European Union (then EEC) partners and gained tacit approval and support for the response from the United States. On 5 April, Britain dispatched an amphibious force to retake the islands.

The campaign was a classic example of limited conflict. Britain announced an 'Exclusion Zone' around the Falklands and prepared to wage war within that zone. For political as well as military reasons, action against the Argentinian mainland was not an option. The British forces' Rules of Engagement were heavily circumscribed and some units – such as the nuclear submarines patrolling the area – remained under the control of superior headquarters in Britain rather than the Taskforce Commander.

Within the area of activity, the biggest problem confronting Britain was in the deployment and maintenance of her forces at the end of a 12,000 kilometre (7,500 mile) supply line, against enemy forces deploying weaponry comparable (and in some cases identical) to that possessed by the British. The Argentinian Navy posed a substantial threat but, early in the campaign, lost one of its principal surface vessels, the cruiser *General Belgrano*, to a British nuclear submarine. With this, Argentina was effectively deterred from further naval operations. Another problem was that the carrier-borne Harrier VSTOL aircraft had to hold off the full weight of the Argentinian Air Force operating on short interior lines of communications. Britain was fortunate in that the Harriers proved up to the task. Although the Argentinian pilots pressed home their attacks with great determination and scored some notable successes, they were unable to stop the British from taking the lesser South Atlantic island of South Georgia and then establishing a beachhead on the main East Falkland Island on 21 May.

Once ashore, the better trained British regular forces defeated the Argentinian land forces in a three week land campaign that carried them the full length of East Falkland Island. The principal town of Port Stanley surrendered on 14 June, leaving the British in absolute command of the islands. Following the surrender, the Argentinian President, General Galtieri was forced to resign.

Britain has since built up the Falklands into a fortress. A regular garrison is maintained there and costly airport facilities have been built to facilitate rapid reinforcement by air.

Despite its short duration, however, the outcome of the Falklands war was a close run thing. The British land force commander, General Sir Jeremy Moore, later admitted that he was almost at the end of his logistical tether when the surrender took place. Though better trained and enjoying better morale, the British troops were near exhaustion, and only recently has it been revealed that the United States was providing Britain with emergency at-sea replenishment of missiles and other first-line requirements, while France provided information on the Exocet missile.[1] Though much has been made of the fact that the eventual British success reinforced the rule of international law and serves as a useful precedent, in reality the campaign made economic nonsense. It was based more on political imperatives backed up by a nostalgic and neo-imperialistic jingoism than anything else. The conflict also carried with it a high level of political and military risk.[2]

The Search for Legitimacy

Britain did not formally declare war on Argentina but rested her case on Article 51 of the United Nations Charter. The Article gives member nations the right to defend themselves and, in the circumstances, that right was confirmed; Britain's actions were backed by United Nations Security Council Resolution 502, which demanded the withdrawal of Argentinian forces.[3]

While the lack of any formal declaration of war was based on sound financial and political factors, one of its consequences was that it denied the British government emergency powers to formally control the media. This was accepted with equanimity by the government and the military because, as it has been observed, 'the crisis was never going to jeopardise the security of the United Kingdom in a way that would persuade the media, or probably the country to accept the abrogation of the democratic rights of free speech.'[4] It was perhaps in recognition of this and the geographical remoteness of the campaign that the government saw early the importance of public relations in rallying national and, to a lesser extent, international support. This need for public approval – and for the campaign to be viewed as a 'just' war – had its genesis in the Emergency Parliamentary Debate on 3 April 1982, which was called in response to the Argentinian invasion. It was, as Foster puts it, little more than a rousing patriotic chorus designed to prove that the British lion could still bite back.[5]

Prime Minister Margaret Thatcher's successfully orchestrated effort to gain near unanimous parliamentary approval for her bellicosity as a fight between good and evil, and a symbol of national resurgence, was quickly taken up by sections of the media. The London *Times* labelled the Argentinian invasion as '... an incontrovertibly evil act.'[6] The *Sun, Star, Express* and *Mail* damned opponents of the war as appeasers, fainthearts and traitors.[7] A *Sun* reporter allegedly '... scrawled 'Up yours Galtieri' on the side of a British missile, and wrote next day that it had been sent on behalf of the *Sun's* readers'; the paper also ran competitions for abusive jokes about Argentinians.[8] Such attitudes led the opposition leader, Michael Foot, to ask the Prime Minister in the House whether she was prepared to reprove the attitude of some newspapers that supported 'the hysterical bloodlust' which he claimed disgraced British journalism. Thatcher pointedly refused to do so. Foster makes the pertinent point that to have acted would have been to silence some of the most effective supporters of government policy.[9]

It was against this combination of a government committed to rallying and maintaining national and international opinion, and a generally supportive press fostering a chauvinistic fervour that would brook no opposition, that the media had to come to terms with the military. To make matters worse, it had to come to terms with a military which held the whip hand because of the expeditionary nature of the conflict, which would unfold in a remote and inhospitable area. This afforded the military a near-monopoly on support and communications. The media, faced with the lack of any indigenous media or media infrastructure of the kind it could normally expect to find in most parts of the world, and lacking any pre-arranged contingency plan or even dedicated specialist defence writers, was quite unprepared to meet the physical, professional or ethical challenges that would be placed before its journalists.

It can be argued that the media never recovered from this initial disadvantage, which allowed it to be manipulated by the deliberate policy of misinformation and censorship adopted by both the Ministry of Defence (MoD) and the government. It was a media management approach, which, according to General Moore, '... at least appeared to have had a positive effect on the outcome of the conflict.'[10] Another problem for the media was that the conflict itself was concluded quickly; the whole period of operations lasted only some six and a half weeks, with the land operations running for twenty-five days. The operation was also put together and implemented in a matter of days. This presented obvious difficulties to the military, but they were organised and prepared for such emergencies and the short duration of the conflict worked in their favour. The media on the other hand was not organised, nor was there any prepared plan to exploit such a situation.

In contrast with the military and government, who enjoyed and benefited from the momentum of success as the conflict moved to its close, the media suffered from lack of time in which to bring the full arsenal of critical coverage to bear. The media was also faced with a public that grew increasingly hostile to negative or even analytical reporting, the nearer their forces drew to victory.

The Despatch of the Media

Preparations for the despatch of media with the British forces began on 31 March, when the public relations branch of the MoD queried the Service Chiefs about what press attendance would be acceptable. The blunt answer was, 'None!' As the Chief of Defence Staff, Admiral of the Fleet, Sir Terence Lewin, later told the House of Commons Select Committee on Defence:

> The first concern to us was military, and here there was the paramount importance of not making public any information which would prejudice future operations, prejudice the lives of our people – and indeed, to perhaps a lesser extent, there was a need to protect the next of kin of our people.[11]

The Service Chiefs were quickly overruled by the government, who recognised that since they could not control the media they had best accommodate them. As a result, the initial policy of excluding the press was changed to one of accepting six, and later ten, correspondents.

Initially the plan was to fly the media direct to the island of Ascension, but this was vetoed on the grounds that they would have reported the paucity of anti-air defences there. Instead, they were taken on board the Task Force. This left the Ministry with only twenty-four hours in which to select and organise the media before the fleet sailed. Guidelines were already in place for such an eventuality, in a May 1981 instruction entitled *The Administration of Public Relations in Times of Tension or War*. The paper set out detailed plans for a balanced team of twelve media representatives to be based on the pooling of technical facilities. But, in the confusion, it seems these plans were forgotten.

There was also the potential for problems within the MoD itself. The acting head of Defence public relations at the time was Ian McDonald, a career public servant with no previous experience in the field of public relations. He was subject to interference from the Prime Minister's press secretary, Bernard Ingham (later Sir Bernard Ingham), who was much more alert to the government's requirements for a positive press. McDonald's solution to the problem of who and how many media representatives should go, was to simply pass the responsibility back to the media in the shape of the Newspaper Publishers Association (NPA).[12]

When confronted with demands for inclusion from every section of the media, the NPA opted for one pooled television crew, one communications engineer, and two television journalists – one from the BBC and one from the commercial channel, ITN. This resulted in an immediate round of lobbying at the highest level from those who had been disappointed. The result was that the number was again increased, first to fifteen and eventually to twenty eight representatives including press photographers. These were deployed in two stages, the first in *HMS Hermes* and *HMS Invincible*, the second, four days later in *HMS Canberra*.[13]

In the meantime, in the few hours preceding the departure of the first units, the MoD refused to answer any queries on the basis of a policy, arrived at by McDonald, that to give out *any* information before the sailing of the Task Force would be to aid the enemy.[14] For the members of the Task Force, the only directive for handling the media came in the form of a Navy signal sent to all ships on 2 April. This appointed the Deputy Fleet Public Relations Officer as principal adviser on all naval matters and stated the importance of public support.[15] But these guidelines appear to have had little or no effect. To the Navy, this was new territory; it quickly became obvious that the Service was hostile to the correspondents and that neither side knew how control should be exercised.[16]

As an example of this hostility, Admiral Sir Sandy Woodward, the then Commander of the South Atlantic Task Force, reports that the official policy was 'Co-operation yes; information, no.' As far as Woodward was concerned, the media barely rated acknowledgment. It was only after a series of embarrassing gaffes that reverberated all the way up to the Cabinet room, that he later saw the media as '... one of my biggest problems.' The end result, according to Woodward, was a mindset that said 'Say and do whatever you have to to win.'[17] It was a mindset that appeared to permeate the whole of the Navy.

The application of this policy was left to the 'minders' – public relations men in uniform who, in general, were perceived by the press as failed members of the journalistic profession. A recurrent theme, running through each case study in which such appointments are noted, is that such minders are seen as neither soldiers nor first-line journalists. In the Falklands, as elsewhere, they were never fully accepted or trusted by either profession.

Given this situation, it was inevitable that the minders should be caught up in the cross-fire between the military and the media. In some circumstances, however, they were themselves the source of conflict and their performance has been heavily criticised in almost every recollection of the campaign.

To be fair, they had a difficult task. They were selected and deployed with the same speed as the media, and many of them lacked the qualifications, experience, and – certainly – the rank to handle their task effectively.[18] They were also prone to being sidelined by the media in the understandable urge to get whatever information there was from the most senior commander present. Against this, there were tensions within the media contingent itself, with some proving to be unequal to the task either by temperament or training.[19]

Another problem was that no foreign press was included, a decision that would later raise charges of propaganda management by the British.[20] In a memorandum to the House of Commons Defence Committee dated 20 July 1982, the Foreign Press Association not only complained about the exclusion of their members and the lack of briefings, but pointed out that the Foreign Office News Department had been unhelpful in mediating with the MoD on behalf of its members.[21] The upshot of their exclusion was, of course, paid for in a lack of credibility.

Problems of Communication

The most immediate problem for those correspondents embarked with the first fleet was that of communications. They were told that all voice communications for radio had to be through the MARISAT (now INMARSAT) system which was carried on only one of the ships. This was because the signatories to the international agreement covering MARISAT – one of which was Argentina – restricted it to non-combatant vessels. Access to this single transmission point necessitated a hazardous and time consuming ship-to-ship transfer. Although it was later discovered that acceptable radio voice levels could have been carried through the combat ship systems, the extra effort to use MARISAT was a small price to pay since the system provided a direct link to newsrooms without having to be channelled through the MoD.[22] This was a matter of some concern to the minders who were reported to have been poised to 'pull the plug' in the event of any unguarded voice traffic which they perceived as being in breach of security.

Print went out using normal shipborne radio teletype traffic. However, after what the Navy saw as over-use of the system, with three journalists on board *HMS Hermes* alleged to have generated 40 per cent of the entire outgoing traffic, and others accounting for 30 per cent on *Invincible*, journalists were restricted to access only during low traffic times. In some cases this resulted in missed deadlines.[23] Television communications *could* have been sent using the commercial systems taken on board by the television team. It would have been difficult and restricted to military satellite downtime. It may also have required a partial shutdown of the vessel's electronic systems or some form of electronic shielding, but it could have been done. The Navy, however, made sure that this was never attempted. Consequently the average time delay for television transmission from the campaign was an astonishing eight to ten days.[24] The lack of effort to ensure more timely television transmission was later acknowledged as worth the lack of coverage achieved. As Minister for Defence, Sir John Nott, observed:

> I do not think television would have made our operations any easier to conduct, and after all we were trying to win a war...We intended that television should go and there were technical problems that could not be overcome.[25]

There was a limited access to the American Defense Systems Communications System, DSCS or DISCUS satellite through the on-board military SCOT system; the DISCUS satellite holds a geo-stationary position above the equator. An examination was also made of the use of the ageing British military SKYNET satellite which, along with the DISCUS, could have taken the heavy drive needed for satisfactory television pictures.[26] In the event, television footage was airlifted to the mainland of South America and then uplifted through commercial satellite. This meant that, in much the same manner as access to radio telecommunications was controlled by the Navy at their discretion, so too was the airlift capability for television footage to South American ground stations in their hands.

There are, it must be said, considerable difficulties in passing the broad band signal required for television through the narrow band used by satellites for mainly voice communications. In addition, the use of SKYNET in the early stages of the deployment would have necessitated a detour of some hundreds of miles to position a ship within the satellite footprint.[27] Understandably, this was rejected on operational grounds. Although the American system could easily have been exploited, later unconfirmed reports indicate that approaches to the American authorities were made only at very low levels. This led to a widespread suspicion in media circles that the Americans and British had come to a tacit arrangement not to facilitate transmission. If the conflict had continued, the networks might well have considered flying in a ground station capable of linking into the commercial INTELSAT whose footprint covered the Falklands.

To sum up, the low latitudes in which the force operated were not well served by commercial satellite cover, and the cover became technically worse the further south the fleet sailed. The Task Force also afforded media communications a low priority classification. There is little doubt that much of the problem rested with an uncooperative Navy, but there is equally little doubt that something could have been done about the problems. In the face of all of these difficulties – technical and man made – and before the use of the Special Air Service operational satellite links had been fully explored, the television technicians gave up and were flown home.[28]

The end result was that it took twenty-three days for pictures of the *Sheffield* incident to return home, sixteen days for coverage of the Goose Green casualties and the Bluff Cove attacks, and eleven days for the surrender.[29] Consequently, there was never any 'live' or real-time television coverage of the conflict. Many within the British media saw this as evidence of government and military unwillingness to allow any negative reporting to undermine public support for the campaign.[30] The allegation was, of course, repudiated by Defence. Their claim was that tests had shown that the 'tilting' available military satellites at the extreme edge of their range, to produce the spot beam needed for the heavy drive television transmission, would have given pictures of unacceptable quality. They also claimed that to have employed the satellites for this purpose could have jeopardised the already tenuous military communications.[31]

Another area of communications concern was that of still-photography. Only two press photographers were accredited to the Task Force, one with the aircraft carriers and the second in the later deployment. On the voyage south, neither was equipped with the wire machines which are the standard transmission tool of their trade and, as a result, film had to be sent back by ship. On arrival, film was sent by wire from the *Canberra*.

When combined with the seeming reluctance to allow immediate television coverage, this lack of pictorial coverage of the initial stages of the conflict has given rise to further claims of 'indirect' or discretionary censorship. Certainly the end product showed a priority for 'beneficial' as opposed to contentious photographs being released by the MoD. This problem worsened once the landing had been effected. As Mercer, Mungham and Williams point out:

> A photograph of *Antelope* exploding was delayed for several days on the pretext that the explosion was caused by the detonation of an unexploded bomb. This was taken by Martin Cleaver (Press Association) who was not allowed to go ashore until twelve days after the landing. One consequence of this was a conspicuous absence of pictures of injured or dead.[32]

The charges of deliberate delays to coverage have never been satisfactorily addressed, but Robert Harris summed up the reality with his observation that:

> The situation was only marginally worse than during the Crimea. In 1854, the charge of the Light Brigade was graphically described in the *Times* (of London) twenty days after it took place. In 1982, some TV file took as long as twenty three days to get back to London. The first still photo did not arrive until 19 May – three weeks after the event, and even then it was a blatant propaganda shot, showing the Union Jack being unfurled over South Georgia.[33]

Censorship and Political Pressure

The first taste of the indirect censorship that was to overshadow media coverage of the Falklands conflict, came when the on-board correspondents were denied access to Ascension Island on the way to the war zone. In later evidence given on the conduct of the campaign, Admiral John Fieldhouse indicated that this decision was taken because journalists could have used the commercial radio-telephone service to report the vulnerability of the island and reveal classified American activities conducted there. This pointed the way to the introduction of a range of more insidious indirect censorship measures including restricted access, lack of transport, 'care for the safety of the correspondents', and – most telling – delay in the transmission of information.

Such measures exploited to the full the advantages of an expeditionary force in which the media contingent was totally dependent on the military. However, the relationship faced a major test when Britain suffered the loss of *HMS Sheffield* on 4 May. There was the real risk of a public opinion backlash, with no time to condition the home nation to the reverse of fortunes, especially considering the carefully controlled, optimistic reporting that had been fed to the public.[34] And so the news was contained. Journalists accompanying the Task Force were fully aware of what was happening, but they were denied both helicopter transport to film the event and communications to relay the news back to London. A television crew was eventually given helicopter support to film the stricken vessel, but only after the damage had been contained and the fires put out, and only on condition that the film was made available to the Navy.[35]

Thus, by exploiting the advantages of its monopoly over communications, the government was able to keep news of the sinking secret until it had decided how to handle the problem. Once the timing had been agreed for an announcement in parliament, Ian McDonald, acting as the MoD spokesperson, was permitted to break into normal television programming, using the same style and settings as a newsreader, and deliver the report direct. This style of 'live' reporting, which generally coincided with the nine o'clock news and was strongly reminiscent of World War II announcements, set the pattern for similar statements by the government throughout the Falklands campaign. Apart from reinforcing the sense of a nation at war, it had the effect of giving the government spokesperson the authority and position of an independent correspondent. This image was naturally resented by producers responsible for regular news programming.[36] It led to later charges by the BBC that the government had '... come very close to the management and manipulation of the news.'[37]

The government also exploited control over background information and daily briefings at home to consolidate its position, doling out selected news of the fighting and shaping presentations to suit government policy. Press conferences were restricted to terse statements, or restricted and unattributable question and answer sessions from which television was excluded. What went to television was given either direct, as a live communique to the public, or under lights, as a planned and pre-packaged segment that left no room for editing or comment. Presentation of the government view was aided by the lack of actual footage around which the pictorial element of stories could have been built.[38] And, as Pilger writes, censorship by exclusion was another factor was another factor in the media management:

> In 1982 a plan put forward by Peru for a negotiated settlement between Britain and Argentina came close to success. How close the public never knew. On 13 May 1982 Edward Heath told ITN the Argentines had requested three minor amendments to the peace plan. They were so minor, said Heath, that they could not possibly be rejected. But Margaret Thatcher rejected them out of hand; and that brief interview with Heath was the only occasion on television news that reference was made to the British government's having a case to answer. Thereafter the story died and the invasion went ahead.[39]

The lack of video footage only served to heighten the concerns of some sections of the media that the government's approach to news 'packaging' amounted to media manipulation. One result was a tendency to fill the vacuum by using American or Argentinian television coverage. This move caused alarm in government circles when it became apparent that the Argentinian coverage – after an uncertain start in which the junta attempted to sell propaganda – was both credible and accurate. In the absence of British footage, then, Argentinian coverage soon became a feature of most reports and background analysis, as some sections of the London-based media sought to find out exactly what was going on and to provide a balanced point of view. The choice was summed up by the editor of the *Sunday People*, who observed that the lack of fast and accurate information from the British side '... resulted in a greater dependence on unofficial sources of information, including Buenos Aires.' This view captured the growing feeling that, whatever else was happening, Britain was losing the war of words and pictures.[40]

The increasing use of overseas footage came to a head when Peter Snow, a commentator on the British current affairs program *Newsnight*, questioned the veracity of British official reports, and the BBC's *Panorama* current affairs program, presented by Robert Kee, aired a segment that put not only the Argentinian point of view, but also the views of the anti-war movement.[41]

This journalistically commendable objectivity brought howls of outrage from the government and those who felt that the BBC, in particular, should be reporting only the British point of view. As Prime Minister Thatcher put it in parliament, on 6 May:

> ... many people are very concerned indeed that the case for our British forces is not being put fully and effectively. I understand that there are times when it seems that we and the Argentinians are being treated almost as equals and almost on a neutral basis.[42]

It was, it seems, acceptable to take government communiques uncritically, but verging on treason to consider alternative information from the other side. Kee and Snow were both labelled traitors – Snow in the *Sun*, the morning after his broadcast, and Kee two days later in the House of Commons.[43]

Nevertheless, the BBC fought back, arguing that truth should not become a casualty of government policy or be manipulated to maintain a high level of political support for the war. It was not, argued Alistair Milne, the director general-designate of the BBC, 'total war'; rather it was a very questionable limited conflict with doubtful aims. The suggestion that the BBC were traitors, Milne said, was outrageous.[44] Milne held this line before the ruling Conservative Party's Parliamentary Media Committee, while undergoing what has been described as little better than a 'public school ragging'.[45] Feelings ran so high that one member of parliament who had supported the BBC was later abused by a group of Conservative MPs as a '... disgrace to your school, your regiment and your country.'[46]

Happily, the majority of the print media supported the BBC in its stand. But political pressure eventually caused a backdown within the ranks of the BBC itself. Foster has described how, the morning after the *Panorama* segment went to air, the head of the BBC reminded editors and producers, at a news and current affairs meeting that,

> ... the BBC was the *BRITISH* Broadcasting Corporation. It was by then clear that a large section of the public shared this view and the corporate head believed it was an unnecessary irritation to stick with a detached style of reporting.[47]

That part of the press which had deliberately embarked on a near hysterical policy of jingoism also took up cudgels on behalf of Prime Minister Thatcher, with one headline referring to 'traitors at the BEEB.'[48] The headline could be seen as a response to Mrs Thatcher's urgings, in her role as 'war leader', for the nation to make its feelings known over what she inferred was irresponsible reporting reflecting a lack of patriotism. The connection was both real and apparent. The jingoism 'from the cheaper sections of the press', General Moore observed later, was 'reinforced and fitted in with a strong lead by a powerful personality in Downing Street.'[49]

The Prime Minister's attitude, however, while reflected by a vocal minority, appears to have been somewhat out of step with the bulk of the public she was trying to manipulate. Despite appeals to patriotism, polls conducted by the BBC itself on 10 May reported that 81 per cent of those surveyed thought that the BBC had behaved in a responsible manner in its coverage of the Falklands conflict. Only 14 per cent expressed a contrary opinion. More important, 81 per cent believed that the BBC, '... should pursue its traditional policy of reflecting the full range of opinions', as opposed to 10 per cent who felt otherwise. On the question of who was doing the better job of reporting the conflict, ITN, the commercial television broadcaster, received the highest approval rating with 40 per cent of respondents assessing ITN's coverage as 'very good', as opposed to 36 per cent for BBC TV, and 32 per cent for BBC Radio. The majority, however, felt that the three media outlets were nearly equal in doing a 'fairly good job', with BBC TV at 51 per cent, ITN at 52 per cent and BBC Radio at 57 per cent.[50] A Gallup poll conducted around the same time by the *Daily Telegraph* newspaper reported that 62 per cent of those surveyed supported the BBC. More importantly from a political point of view, a high 57 per cent of Conservative voters supported what was in effect an appeal for the freedom of the press in limited conflict. This was only a few percentage points under the average 65 per cent rating by Labour, Liberal and Social Democratic Party supporters who responded.[51]

In the field of operations, censorship was the main source of irritation. However, as events in the home nation demonstrate, both censorship and political pressure impacted on the ultimate presentation of the conflict. Although MacDonald was anxious to limit censorship to the needs of operational security, what eventuated was an uncoordinated two tier effort – the first tier manned by relatively junior officers in military units and on ships, and the second tier, often irrationally opposed to media coverage, 'vetting' reports back in London. This was in spite of the fact that the accredited journalists were mostly pro-British. It was unlikely that any of them would have knowingly put British lives at stake and they were, in any case, under the self-imposed constraint of reporting for a media which generally expected a patriotic stance. Even though some had refused to sign the Official Secrets Act (a condition which was waived as a pre-requisite to accreditation), all of them were required to subscribe to a ten point instruction issued by the MoD on 8 April 1982. The guidelines embargoed the following subjects:

1 Operational plans which would enable a potential enemy to deduce details of intentions.
2 Speculation on possible courses of action.
3 State of readiness and detailed operational capability of individual units or formations.
4 Location, employment and operational movement of individual units or formations, particularly specialist units.
5 Particulars of current tactics and techniques.
6 Operational capabilities of all types of equipment.
7 Stocks of equipment and other details of logistics.
8 Information about intelligence on Argentinian dispositions or capabilities.
9 Communications.
10 Equipment or other defects.[52]

The operational security that these guidelines were designed to protect was later spelled out to parliament by the First Sea Lord, Admiral Sir Henry Leach, who defined it as, 'information which if released or is released at a certain time, in the military judgement, prejudices the operation.' To this Leach added the rights of next of kin of casualties.[53]

The problem with both of these concepts is that they are as long as a piece of string. If properly handled, the generally positive attitude of the journalists, their own appreciation of security needs, plus the 'bonding' that inevitably occurs when correspondents become attached to a unit, should have ensured a positive press.[54] This would have been balanced by the ever present pressure of competition, but overall, the combination of guidelines, pre-disposition and a campaign which appeared to be headed towards success should have resulted in few problems. As it turned out, the overwhelming weight of evidence given to the later inquiry condemned the military and the MoD for their 'manipulative censorship', with the strongest criticisms levelled at the minders in the field and the second tier vetting reports back at Whitehall. The attitude of the media is summed up in a memorandum from the *News of the World* newspaper group to the Defence Committee, which asked:

> Did the Ministry of Defence REALLY want this war covered? That is the question that must be asked... why the MoD did not lay down sensible censorship regulations with the help of media experts conscious of the national interest. As it was, the whole operation was a shambles from the media point of view and the

figleaf of 'national interest' was used to cover the errors, omissions, muddle and lack of information.[55]

In all, some seventeen Task Force correspondents gave evidence to the parliamentary inquiry. The majority roundly condemned the handling of the media and official censorship. Max Hastings, probably the most experienced of the journalists stated that the officials responsible:

... lacked knowledge either of media needs or of military affairs, and failed to gain the respect or trust of either the correspondents or, more important, of the senior officers of the Task Force. Their only contribution to the reporting of the war was to rigorously enforce increasingly erratic restrictions on outgoing news.[56]

According to the *Daily Express*, favoured defence and political correspondents in London were given details of stories from dispatches sent by correspondents in the field that had been censored or withheld.[57] Similar evidence given to the Parliamentary Media Committee points to example after example of inconsistent censorship at the front by junior officers who deleted items that had previously been passed. In some cases, it was claimed, they imposed their own grammar and style on pieces written by professional journalists. According to one report, 'they appeared to have stifled any suggestion that the campaign was doing anything but rolling on inexorably towards Victory.'[58]

Tony Snow, the *Sun's* correspondent, summed up the general feeling against the 'minder-censors', describing them as slow and unable to accept the urgency of journalism. They were, he said, inefficient, lazy and dishonest. Snow further accused them of 'censoring by delay.'[59] Peter Archer of Press Association, on board *HMS Hermes*, accused the minders of inconsistency and of censorship by 'losing' material; a story that had been grudgingly censored was misplaced and only found again when Archer took his complaint to the captain of the vessel to which he was attached. Archer, as a journalist, documented the complaint of a 'complete blackout' on news when the *Sheffield* was hit by an Exocet, when two Sea Harriers were lost, and when *HMS Glasgow* was bombed.[60]

There was some improvement in the situation once correspondents were ashore with more experienced and accommodating Army personnel. As General Moore put it, 'our small press corps would have said, almost to a man, many of them have, that they would always have sought out my public relations officer where they could.'[61] But, despite these improved relations, much the same attitudes prevailed. Both direct and indirect censorship of copy traversing the military communications system continued, until reports were received at the second tier of vetting back in

London; and it appears to have been in this second tier that political pressure was introduced.

Second tier censorship was carried out originally by untrained junior service officers. However, because of the increased workload, civilian information officers were brought in. Task Force censors apparently were not informed of this change. It was significant because of the evidence of politics intruding into the second tier. A memorandum from the London *Times* to the Defence Committee charged that '... it became evident that material was removed (from copy) at a later date, either with the Task Force before transmission or on receipt at the Ministry in London.'[62] Bernard Ingham, the Prime Minister's press secretary, who took over the coordination of the flow of information in London, said that this was because they had to be '... much more keenly aware of the political dimension.'[63] Despite denials to the contrary, the suspicion remains that information policy was closely controlled through the Prime Minister's office, and that the Whitehall vetting group was part of that control.

Disinformation and Deception

Deception is a necessary and vital part of war planning, and few would disapprove of the masterly games aimed at avoiding casualties which were played out, for example, in World War II.[64] But the Falklands was a limited war, with no such national imperatives, and the evidence points to information being withheld, if not suppressed, for political reasons. As Sir Frank Cooper, the permanent Under Secretary for Defence made plain to the House of Commons Defence Committee, 'we did not tell a lie, but we did not tell the whole truth.'[65] It was an attitude echoed by the military who saw their first duty as winning the war, whatever the means. That the military approach complemented the government's priorities of enlisting and maintaining national and international support came as a bonus.

Even General Moore, a soldier with a keen sense of democratic duty, stated quite openly that he accepted the 'positive' use of media coverage for the purpose of deception to aid operations.[66] This operational level deception – along with less savoury examples emanating from London, such as the denial of the strafing of survivors from an Argentinian electronic surveillance vessel – obviously bore the imprimatur of the service chiefs. When Admiral Lewin was queried about a Royal United Services Institute lecture given by him in July 1982, where he was reported to have said that the press were fed misinformation during the Falklands war, he replied that, '... they (the press) were most helpful to our plans.' In further evidence before the parliamentary inquiry, Lewin stated:

> I do not see it as deceiving the press or the public: I see it as deceiving the enemy. What I am trying to do is win. Anything I can do to help me win is fair as far as I am concerned. And I would have thought that was what the Government and the public and the media would want too, provided the outcome was the one we were after.[67]

The government was already employing this tactic before the Falklands was invaded. A prime example of misinformation and deception by lack of comment or denial came on 29 March, when the media was allowed to believe that the submarine *HMS Superb* had been deployed. This was not the case, but the rumour was neither confirmed nor denied. As Ian McDonald put it in later evidence:

> The media error over Superb was extremely helpful to us, but I gave precise instructions to my staff that they were never to say anything other than 'as you know, we never discuss the position of nuclear submarines.[68]

The media was to blame for the speculation, but the public as well as the enemy was deceived. Another, more politically suspect incident was the suppression of the news that two Special Air Service helicopters had crashed during surveillance operations in South Georgia. This information, which might have had some immediate operational value, was not acknowledged until it was revealed by a serviceman writing home.[69] Another, more serious, example was the official statement by the MoD on 24 April that '... the task force had not landed anywhere.' The next day, this was qualified by the exactitude that the statement had referred only to the *main* (emphasis added) Task Force.[70]

In contrast, disinformation was employed in the exaggerated reports of the success of the RAF Vulcan bomber attacks against the Argentinian-held air field at Port Stanley. The public had been led to believe that the airfield had been put out of action. In later evidence, the MoD claimed that this merely reflected its understanding of the situation at the time.[71] Given the importance of the raid, the close departmental liaison instituted by the Prime Minister's press secretary, and the availability of what would have been near real-time air photographic evidence, it is difficult to accept this statement.

The Department can also be accused of misinformation over the Vulcan raids, in that it did nothing to correct the computer graphics used on television showing a bombing line down the length of the runway. In fact, the government was well aware that the RAF had chosen to bomb across the runway because of problems of accuracy. In the event, both tactics misfired and the government was forced to announce additional raids which were seen as being needed to finalise the job. At the same time the Argentinians released footage showing the airstrip in actual use. The government's discomfiture increased with comments from field units surprised at the appearance of Argentinian air cover flying out of a supposedly disabled airbase.[72] There can be no excuse for official misinformation which deceives one's own forces.

The most notorious case of disinformation, however, was that of the sinking of the Argentinian battle cruiser, *General Belgrano*. The impact of its sinking with the loss of 368 lives was quickly overtaken in news value by the loss of the *Sheffield*, and there was little British media analysis of the *Belgrano* action. Nevertheless, dispute continues over when the *Belgrano* was first sighted, who gave the order to attack, whether the action was legal, when and what changes were made to the rules of engagement, and to what extent Prime Minister Thatcher was involved in the decision making process. As the authors of the definitive on the media in the Falklands, *The Fog of War*, point out, the government has since admitted that it created some confusion with inconsistent and inaccurate statements. Nevertheless, the gravamen of the case rests on official statements that the *Belgrano* and her accompanying destroyer screen was moving to attack elements of the British task force.[73] In fact, the *Belgrano* group was sailing away from the Task Force when the Royal Navy deemed it an opportune time to destroy the Argentinian's main surface deterrent. However, instead of telling the truth, the government prevaricated, and both the media and the people, as well as parliament, were misled.[74]

The other area of possible disinformation still in contention was the clear statement by Sir Frank Cooper, the Permanent Under Secretary for Defence, at a background briefing to defence correspondents on 20 May, and to a group of editors the next day, in which he firmly discounted the possibility of a major landing in the Falklands, saying that a full scale invasion was unlikely. Instead he suggested a war of attrition would probably take place. Yet the invasion was underway at the time that he was speaking.[75] Another media source confirmed that:

> Sir Frank Cooper and other senior Ministry of Defence Officials indicated in an off-the-record briefing to defence correspondents that there would be hit-and-run raids of the Pebble Island-style before any full scale invasion of the Falklands. The next day, 3000 men went ashore in Port San Carlos.[76]

These are only some of the Falklands conflict examples of misinformation, disinformation and deception that can be backed up by evidence. It seems reasonable to assume that the attitude within the military and government that allowed these instances to be perpetrated would have opened the way for many other such actions. This has led to a strong suspicion among many of the media involved, that the known and proven instances were merely the tip of the iceberg.[77] Yet, despite this record of knowing deception and exploitation of the media, Admiral Woodward was later to echo the familiar complaint that '... the Press did not see itself as being on 'our' side at all.' He also followed the familiar pattern of accusing the media of providing information to the enemy, with the startling, and still unproven claim that 'The Argentinian generals and admirals admitted after the war that they gained ninety per cent of all their intelligence about our activities from the British Press.'[78]

The coverage of the Falklands also highlighted a lesson that was underlined in the later Gulf conflict. This is the role of retired military officers – the armchair critics – who can often short circuit the system and second-guess the establishment drawing on a combination of their own experience, map studies, and a detailed knowledge of order of battle, ranges, and capabilities. In the case of the Falklands, a group of retired military officers was hired by the media to act as commentators. These individuals were employed mainly by television to fill out the lack of footage, and some of them proved to be very accurate. Their assessments were based on freely available information and their own background knowledge, which together transcended both security classifications and censorship.[79]

When questioned on this aspect of the media campaign by the House of Commons Defence Committee, Admiral Sir Henry Leach admitted, that, along with others of his colleagues, he was concerned at this use of retired officers. It was, he said '... potentially if not actually highly prejudicial to the success of the operation.' Yet, when pressed further, he admitted that the MoD had actually considered setting up its own panel of recently retired service officers and making them available to the media. These men could be briefed and '... would be on their guard accordingly to stop indiscriminate speculation.'[80] This raises a double standard and the possibility of another avenue for manipulating the media that will be developed in future conflicts. 'Expert' analyses could be provided by selected officers, who may or may not have had their affiliations and instructions revealed to the media, and who might not be prepared to make the sort of predictions that the Ministry found so troubling in the Falklands.

Conclusion

The result of all this manipulation, misinformation and censorship was the creation of a completely false picture of events at the front. It confused and baffled the public, and cost Britain a measure of international credibility. Without doubt, the responsibility for this rests with the government's politically oriented 'coordination' of what Bernard Ingham termed the information war, and with MoD Public Relations. But while the British government may have achieved its short-term political aims (and some limited operational gains) they lost Ingham's information battle well before the end of the shooting war; and long before that, they had lost the trust and respect of the accredited correspondents and the home media. They had also lost the trust of the international media. The American media had discounted British coverage as a reliable source of news as early as the beginning of May.[81]

The major fact in assessing this war against the premises and questions outlined in Chapter 1, is that this was an atypical conflict, the last of the 'colonial' style expeditionary campaigns to be fought at the ends of the earth in media terms, of short duration, and finalised with great speed. It was also successful, a factor which limited detailed analysis. The short duration of the campaign and the absolute military monopoly on communications precluded any test of whether the military or government could have imposed censorship in the face of the new high technology global media. It was all over before the media could set up alternative means of communication.

Where the major lessons emerge is in the speed and willingness with which the government and military exercised the full range of direct and indirect control of the information flow by every means at their disposal. Another lesson to emerge is in the way in which the military exploited to the full its monopoly on access, transport and communications, and instituted a censorship system that went well beyond the valid needs of operational security. The condemnation of the performance of the military in their dealings with the media by the House of Commons Defence Committee, pointed to the conclusion that the media was the major loser in a cooperative scheme based on the concept of operational security. But, from the evidence of the Falklands campaign, it could be expected that the military in future would use any 'emergency' situation to abrogate their side of the bargain with the media and exploit to the full whatever advantages they might hold.

Finally, the Falklands saw the beginnings of the process of 'demonisation' of the enemy in a modern conflict. In this case, the whole of the Argentinian nation, as well as their leader, General Galtieri, was held up to ridicule and hate. Demonisation was a useful tactic from the British government perspective, because the war was aimed at winning out over the enemy nation. In future limited conflicts it would be more usual to find the population carefully separated from their leaders to legitimise a subsequent 'liberation'.

The media acquiesced in all the government's measures in responding to the invasion of the Falklands. It was only the quality media, such as the BBC, that questioned the conflict. The popular press in its search for circulation closely followed the pattern of jingoistic patriotism fostered by the government.

In summary, the Falklands conflict was a unique campaign. It was the first of the new style of post-nuclear limited conflicts to be fought by regular forces as part of an expeditionary force in remote and inhospitable terrain. It is difficult to imagine circumstances in which such a classic expeditionary conflict might be repeated. As a result, it is difficult to draw any firm conclusions from which to construct a model of media management for a similar campaign, although the evidence points to deliberate government and military exploitation of the advantages of a monopoly of communications to limit media coverage and institute the full range of misinformation, disinformation and deception. From a media viewpoint, however, all was not lost. The Falklands had one value in that it highlighted the need for a critical examination of the problems posed by this new style of conflict. As Sir Frank Cooper expressed it:

> Nobody had thought about this in anything like the depth that needs to be done to try and find the answers to difficult questions. Indeed, there are no simple or short answers to any of these issues. These are major and fundamental questions which will have a bigger impact on any kind of warfare than we have ever supposed to be the case.[82]

These were prophetic words and they stirred the military forces of Western democracies to prepare themselves. The Falklands experience led to the formulation of new standardised policies aimed at limiting the media – policies which would be put into practice next by the American military, as will be seen in the case study of Grenada.

7

Grenada:
An Emerging Pattern of Control

While the media debacle of Vietnam sounded an alarm for the defence forces of many Western democracies, there was a dichotomy of thinking on the implications of the Vietnam experience. One school of thought held that the position of Vietnam, as the definitive Cold War conflict, created such a unique set of circumstances as to make it an aberration that could be largely ignored. Others took a more general lesson from the experience and argued that a major effort should be made to educate and harness the media in order to prevent any recurrence of an unrestrained media on the battlefield.

The Falklands conflict revisited these arguments and refocused thinking on media control in limited conflict. The lessons learned from the British manipulation of the media to enlist popular support both at home and abroad were quickly appreciated. So too was the importance of establishing broad legitimacy and the need to control the media if national and international support was to be maintained in the absence of either a direct threat to national survival or a strong case for intervention.

Because of this, the major significance of the Grenadan operation lies in the fact that it was the first opportunity for the United States military to put into practice the lessons learned from Britain in the Falklands, and to institute similar policies of media exclusion and containment. The American intervention in Grenada in October 1983 was in some ways reminiscent of the Falklands. It was an expeditionary campaign fought by regular forces, in a relatively remote area which lacked any major media infrastructure. In the same way that the British had approached the Falklands conflict, the campaign was marked by secrecy of planning, the absence of any public information annexe in the operational plan, deliberate initial exclusion of the media, and the manipulation and management of news. Of even greater importance, however, was the fact that, for the first time, the military was given a completely free hand in the control of the media – even when decisions impinged on political areas.[1] The effect of this was to exclude the American and world media from operational planning and the initial assault on Grenada, and to subject the media to a systematic policy of constraint and manipulation designed to avoid military or political embarrassment, especially in the first few vulnerable days of the operation.

But Grenada also established the precedent for formal complaints and public condemnation of such practices in the United States. As in the case of the Falklands, despite an overwhelming initial public approval of the government's actions, these complaints led to the later establishment of a major (albeit limited) fact-finding commission into the handling of the media during the campaign.

Background to the Campaign

Grenada is a small Caribbean island lying approximately 100 kilometres (62.5 miles) north of Trinidad, off the coast of Venezuela. It is the second in the chain of islands that sweep upwards in an arc north and north west from the coast of Venezuela, through Haiti and the Dominican Republic, Cuba and the Bahamas, to Florida. Grenada is about 340 square kilometres (133 square miles) in area, with a population in 1978 of around 97,000. The island was discovered by Colombus on his third voyage in 1498. It was taken by the French in 1651, then by the English in 1762, and again by the French in 1779. Finally, in 1782, Grenada was retaken by the English, who retained it until it was granted full independence in 1974, after which the island nation remained within the Commonwealth.[2]

On 13 March 1979, the repressive and unpopular, but strongly anti-communist prime minister, Sir Eric Geary, was overthrown in a bloodless coup by the New Jewel Movement (NJM) headed by Maurice Bishop. Apart from being a popular reaction against Geary's increasing mystical, sexual and political eccentricities, the coup was spurred on by the knowledge that, before leaving Grenada to put a case to the United Nations for a study of Unidentified Flying Objects, Geary had ordered the 'liquidation' of the NJM leadership.[3] In that same year, Cuban engineers were invited to construct a 10,000 foot (approximately 3,000 metres) runway at Point Salines at the southern end of the island.

Since Grenada had no airforce of its own, this development was interpreted by Washington as a prelude to Soviet-backed Cuban plans to militarise the island. The indicators were there in as much as newly-installed Prime Minister Bishop had approved of the initiative and had established close relations with the Soviet Union and Cuba. But he was still considered to be too moderate by some elements within the Central Committee of the NJM. Subsequently, on 12 October 1983, Deputy Prime Minister Bernard Coard moved to oust Bishop on the grounds of 'bourgeois deviationism' and of moving too slowly to restructure Grenadan society.[4]

Bishop was placed under house arrest on 14 October. Five days later, on 19 October, he was executed along with other members of his cabinet. The People's Revolutionary Army (PRA) then announced the dissolution of the government and the formation of a sixteen member Revolutionary Military Council (RMC) headed by General Hudson Austin.

The Quest for Legitimacy

On 21 October, supposedly alarmed over the course of events in Grenada, the member nations of the Organisation of Eastern Caribbean States, (OECS) met in emergency session. This regional grouping – made up of Antigua, Dominica, St Lucia, St Kitts-Nevis, Monserrat, and St Vincent and the Grenadines – called upon the United States and other regional powers to intervene under the terms of the defence provisions in Article 8 of the OECS Treaty.[5] The aim of this call, the OECS said, was to restore law and order, after which 'non-Caribbean forces will be invited to withdraw from Grenada.'[6]

Barbados, Jamaica and the United States responded, the United States participating as a regional power and Barbados and Jamaica through their membership of the Caribbean Community (CARICOM). The military response was billed as local Caribbean States 'supplemented' by United States forces.[7]

American action was immediate. In a letter to Congress sent in order to meet the requirements of the United States *War Powers Resolution Act*, President Reagan stated:

Today at 5.00 AM Eastern Daylight Time, approximately 1,900 United States Army and United States Marine Corps personnel began landing in Grenada. They were supported by elements of the United States Navy and United States Air Force. Members of the OECS along with Jamaica and Barbados are providing approximately 300 personnel.[8]

However, in the event, none of the Caribbean contingents saw combat; the invasion was entirely an American operation.

At a press conference that same day, held jointly with Mrs Eugenia Charles, the Prime Minister of Dominica and Chair of the OECS, President Reagan explained the reasons for the deployment as:

Firstly, and of overriding importance, to protect innocent lives, including up to 1,000 Americans whose personal safety is of course my paramount concern. Second, to forestall further chaos. And third, to assist in the restoration of conditions of law and order and of governmental institutions to the island of Grenada where a brutal group of leftist thugs violently seized power, killing the Prime Minister, three Cabinet Ministers, two labour leaders and other civilians including children.[9]

According to President Reagan, the prime reason was the protection of American civilians. Yet, the RMC had already given a positive answer, on 23 October, to a request from the United States Embassy in Barbados for assurances over the well-being and safety of United States citizens.[10] Apparently having been forewarned of possible military action, the RMC went even further and responded immediately with a diplomatic note to the United States and the United Nations restating its commitment to guaranteeing the safety of American citizens and reaffirming its intention not to use force against any other state. It also warned that it would view any invasion of Grenada, whether based on the decision of CARICOM governments or by any other government as '... a rude violation of Grenada's sovereignty and of international law.'[11]

The record of Grenadan assurances raises the question of the validity of the American claim that its citizens were in danger. It also raises the question of whether the military action was pre-planned, before the intervention was announced. It is known that there was disagreement within CARICOM over what sort of response should be made to the OECS nations' request. According to Davidson, CARICOM decisions have to be unanimous, yet at the 22–23 October meeting in Port of Spain called to debate the issue, the majority were opposed to a military solution or any external involvement. The consensus was that sanctions or other measures short of military intervention should be pursued. Despite this clear direction, two CARICOM nations took part in the commitment and CARICOM was quoted by the United States as having legitimised the action.[12]

There is further evidence that Barbados was engaged in preparations for military action as early as 21 October and that Prime Minister John Adams had issued a verbal invitation to the British Government, through the local High Commission, to participate. This could have alerted the RMC to the possibility of armed intervention and precipitated their re-assurances over the safety of American nationals – a concern which they would have readily appreciated as a *causus belli* to the United States. Certainly, Cuba was aware of the course being taken and sent a message to Washington urging the United States to refrain from military action.

But all these actions may have indicated simply that matters were coming to a head. There is evidence that the Grenadan government was wary of the potential for military intervention as early as March 1983, when it made appeals to United Nations and the Non-Aligned Movement to head off a possible American invasion.[13]

On the morning of Tuesday 25 October, when the Americans launched Operation Urgent Fury, the action was immediately challenged in the United Nations. Guyana, Nicaragua and Zimbabwe sponsored a resolution before the Security Council condemning the invasion. The United States Ambassador to the United Nations, Mrs Jean Kirkpatrick, responded by accusing the new regime of murder and again emphasised the issue of the safety of her country's nationals. Ambassador Kirkpatrick stated that in the circumstances

> ... it was fully reasonable for the United States to conclude that these madmen might decide at any moment to hold hostage the 1,000 American citizens on that island.'[14]

Later, in a similar speech to the General Assembly, Ambassador Kirkpatrick, produced evidence of 'secret agreements' between Grenada and North Korea, Cuba and the Soviet Union for military training and the delivery, free of charge, of what she described as '... millions of dollars worth of military supplies.'[15] On the same day, the US Deputy Secretary for State revealed that the Governor-General of Grenada, Sir Paul Scoon, had appealed to the OECS and other regional states to restore order on the island.[16]

This interpretation of Sir Paul Scoon's right or authority to extend such an invitation, and the question of whether he actually made the request, will be long debated. His appeal was to be used by the Americans as evidence that the invasion had been mounted in response to a request from a properly constituted authority, although London or his duties to the Crown were never mentioned.[17]

While the legitimacy of calls for intervention is debatable – involving the Governor-General of Grenada and CARICOM – the rescue of American nationals as a rationale for the invasion is also suspect. As indicated earlier, the RMC had provided firm assurances of the safety of the 1,000 or so United States nationals, the majority of whom attended a medical school on the island. Most had no desire to leave the island and saw no threat to their safety. A poll conducted by Dr Charles Modicus, the Chancellor of the medical school, suggested that only 10 per cent wanted to leave.[18] There was no evidence of any immediate threat to their safety. In the end, the Americans were the only nationals evacuated and no action was taken by any other nation with respect to its citizens. This included the large British contingent which remained following an inspection of the situation by the British High Commission in Barbados.

World reaction to the invasion was not long in coming. The draft resolution presented to the United Nations Security Council not only condemned the intervention, but called for an immediate cease-fire and the withdrawal of the invading forces under the terms of Article 2 (4) of the United Nations Charter. This article states that all members should refrain from the threat of force against another member country.[19] The resolution was strongly denounced by Ambassador Kirkpatrick on the floor of the house, but was passed on a call of 108 nations for, 9 against and 27 abstentions. The debate revealed a strong belief that there was no direct threat to the security of any of the nations taking part in the invasion and that the intervention went directly against the stated aims of the United Nations. The Communist News Agency, Tass, predictably condemned the invasion as an 'act of open banditry.'[20] It was not alone.

Substantial criticism emerged from the United States' closest allies. Britain remained equivocal, despite the fact that a Commonwealth country was being invaded. The British stance possibly owed something to Prime Minister Thatcher's debt to Reagan during the Falklands. But France, Belgium and Germany strongly condemned the invasion with Italy rejecting it as a 'grave violation of international law.' In Australia, Foreign Minister Bill Hayden, said that Australia '... would be uneasy and discomfited if the US action proved to be an external solution to an internal problem.'[21] The only states which voted against the Resolution as a whole, apart from the United States and its Caribbean allies, were El Salvador and Israel.

The international judgement was unequivocal: the United States, it was felt, had violated international law proscribing interference in the affairs of a sovereign state. There appeared to be no credible threat to US citizens, and no armed threat to any nation which might have afforded the right of self defence under Article 51 of the United Nations Charter. Nor yet could the United States characterise the deployment as a peace-keeping force within the Charter, since the request from the OECS had not been registered with the United Nations and the CARICOM endorsement appeared to be wanting. In view of these factors, it is difficult not to agree with Davidson's conclusion that the United States had no compelling reasons to justify its actions and that '... the legitimacy of the intervention under international law, must clearly be open to doubt.'[22] The only official response from Washington was to emphasise to the local and international media the plight of American nationals.[23]

The Military Campaign

The actual military campaign was fairly simple. In the early hours of 25 October, a task force under the immediate command of Vice Admiral Joseph Metcalf III, consisting of some 2,000 US Marine Corps and Army special forces, invaded Grenada. They were supported by strong naval and air elements. The initial landings brushed aside the 1,200 man Grenadan defence force, who melted back into the civilian community.[24] However, the Americans met with stiffer resistance than had been anticipated from the estimated 600 Cuban construction workers, who put up a formidable defence of what the United States claimed was a new military airfield. Because of this, the initial force was reinforced with a further 5,000 paratroopers of the 82nd Airborne Division and 500 Rangers. The main targets were the capital, St George, and the two airports, Pearls on the eastern side of the island, and Salines at the extreme southern tip. Despite White House suggestions to the contrary, St George and Pearls airport were taken quickly and easily. It was only at the Salines airport that the Americans met significant resistance. By the evening of 27 October, Admiral Wesley McDonald, the overall commander, reported that 'all major military objectives' had been secured, though he admitted later that 'scattered pockets of resistance' remained.[25]

Apart from the normal problems of coordination, which mainly affected the Special Forces and Ranger units, the operation went relatively smoothly.[26] The American losses came to 11 killed and 67 wounded. A total of 599 United States nationals and 121 third party nationals were evacuated in seventeen flights, on the strength of information which purported to show that the PRA had contingency plans to hold the US citizens hostage.[27] In fact, none of the Americans was harmed in any way, despite the close proximity of the medical school to the area in which the Cubans were based.

On 3 November, President Reagan brought the campaign to a close with the announcement that

... Secretary of Defence Caspar Weinberger called to inform me that hostilities in Grenada have ended and that he instructed our military commanders to begin withdrawing their forces within a few days.'[28]

The details of the Grenadan and Cuban casualties have never been released and so far there has been no official unclassified evaluation of the campaign.[29] What has been made clear, however, is that the Cuban presence was vastly overrated. In a speech in Havana, on 14 November 1983, Castro claimed that:

When the US Government spokesmen asserted that there were from 1,000 to 1,500 Cubans in Grenada at the time of the invasion and that hundreds of them were still fighting in the mountains, Cuba published the exact number of Cuban citizens who were in Grenada on the day of the invasion – 784, including diplomatic personnel with their children and other relatives.[30]

Castro also claimed that nearly 50 per cent of the estimated 500 construction workers were over the age of 50 and that, far from being armed, weapons had not been distributed at the time of the attack. He also refuted the claim that the airfield was a military base. He pointed to the 'English capitalist' construction firm in charge of the project as evidence that it was nothing more than a normal airfield and that the workers were civilians.[31]

Secrecy of Planning and the Exclusion of the Media

According to the tactical commander, Admiral Metcalf, Operation Urgent Fury was a success despite the fact that 'It was put together in hours... with a command structure that was invented on the spot.'[32] But Metcalf's claims appear to have been contradicted in testimony before Congress by the overall commander, Admiral McDonald; it seems that planning had been underway for some time. According to Admiral McDonald, the United States

> ... started preliminary planning for the evacuation of US citizens after Prime Minister Bishop was arrested on 13 October 1983; detailed planning, however, did not commence until after he was killed on 19 October.[33]

At a Washington press conference held on 25 October, President Reagan stated that the request for assistance had been received on 23 October. This was later revised by US Secretary of State, George Schultz, to 2.45 on the morning of 22 October.[34] Yet Prime Minister Adams of Barbados claimed that he was approached by the United States on 15 October.[35] Admiral McDonald stated that detailed planning started on 19 October, and the Task Force was diverted to Grenada the next day. Metcalf claimed to have been notified 39 hours before the landing, at 5am on 25 October, which suggests that the decision to invade would have been taken in Washington sometime before mid-afternoon on 23 October.[36]

As with the legality of the action, the issue of when planning for the operation began will long be debated. Nevertheless the discrepancies demonstrate that immediate planning for the specific operation was underway at least a week before its actual launch. During that time, there was no press participation, even on an informal basis. As a result, it is difficult not to conclude that a conscious decision was taken to exclude the media.

The reason for the decision to exclude the media, according to US Defense Secretary, Caspar Weinberger, was that the Chiefs of Staff, concluded that they were

> ... not able to guarantee any kind of safety to anyone. We just didn't have the conditions under which we would be able to detach enough people to protect all of the newsmen, cameramen, gripmen and all that.[37]

Such a decision could only be welcomed by Metcalf, who observed that:

> The lapse of time between notification that I was to lead the Grenada operation to the first landing of troops was 39 hours. In this brief period before combat, the only consideration I gave to the media occurred at about six hours into the thirty nine. A Lieutenant Commander, a CINCLANT (Commander-in-Chief Atlantic) public affairs officer (PAO) came to me and said, '... there will be no press, do you have any problems with this?' I said

I did not. My answer came from attention to urgent operational matters rather than a thought out position on the press. Was this formulation of media policy by acquisition or did I have an option? I suspect the policy was de facto, but the truth is I do not know.[38]

The decision to exclude the press was taken in Washington and resulted in an effective news blackout. At no time was any section of the media taken into the confidence of the military. Even the White House press secretary, Larry Speakes, was kept in the dark and was reported to have been furious when he eventually learned about the operation. In a memo to White House Chief of Staff, Michael Deaver, and Counsellor to the President, Edwin Meese, Speakes complained that he had been misled and had misrepresented the situation to the media because he had not been informed of the action until the invasion was underway. He was reported as saying that the credibility of the Reagan administration was at stake over the deception practiced on the press.[39] Speakes later backed away from this extreme position and, in a subsequent press release, stated that the policy of the White House was always to tell the truth. He admitted, however, that his original denials 'could have caused confusion.'[40]

The issue of the media came to a head when three American and one British journalist chartered a fishing boat and landed on the island. They were promptly picked up by the military and transported offshore to the *USS Guam*, Metcalf's flagship, where their film and notes were confiscated. They were held incommunicado for 24 hours during which time the State Department issued a release saying they were safe at a hotel in St George.[41]

A further six reporters were intercepted later, trying to land on the island, and removed to the *Guam*. According to Edward Cody of the *Washington Post*, who was one of the party, they were denied access to communications, guarded and watched even while they slept.[42] Metcalf makes no mention of this incident but, according to the *Washington Post*:

> He deliberately held them aboard his flagship the carrier *USS Guam*, for 18 hours to prevent them from filing first hand accounts of the invasion. The task force commander said that he had been 'following orders' from Washington in holding the reporters, but he did not specify who had given the orders.[43]

Metcalf, however, relates his own version of a media encounter which leaves several questions unanswered:

The first on-scene 'media event' occurred in mid-morning of the first day when an enterprising stringer representing the *Washington Post* appeared on the flagship, demanding that we relay his copy to the paper. He was advised that no immediate press coverage of the operation was permitted... My PAO escorted him below.[44]

No mention is made of how a reporter arrived on board a warship which was presumably steaming at speed in a defensive pattern, nor yet of what was meant by being 'escorted below.' Schwarzkopf denies that they were held incommunicado, stating that, 'they spent the rest of the afternoon in the officers' wardroom drinking coffee and eating sweet rolls.'[45] According to Metcalf, however, when the incident became known in Washington, the Pentagon demanded an explanation for the reporter's presence. The 'no press policy' was re-affirmed and Metcalf was admonished for having allowed the reporter on board. According to Metcalf, within two hours the same Pentagon officials were asking how many reporters he could handle, suggesting a total of 400. His reply was that he could not possibly handle such a number, which worked out at around one for every eighteen combat troops on the island. Metcalf went on to state: '... no further assistance or guidance was offered. It was then clear to me that the responsibility for press access had shifted.'[46]

Metcalf claims that, on the second day, he was again petitioned by Washington to allow media on the island. Once again, he refused on the grounds that combat was still taking place around the airstrip at Salines, that St George was not secure, and that the students had not been rescued. Metcalf states that it was at this time that he became aware of reporters attempting to land by fishing vessels and speedboats. It was then, on the afternoon of the second day of the invasion, that he instituted what he termed '... an exclusion zone around Grenada enforced by destroyers and aircraft.' This was later termed a 'quarantine.'[47] It would have been during this phase that the four reporters were detained. On the third day he accepted the first press pool, which he described as 'excellent and professional.' This press pool increased to fifty on the following day, the fifth day of operations.

When St George and Point Salines were secure, Metcalf granted free access to the island, the populace and the troops. The number of press who visited the island was then limited only by the availability of aircraft to ferry them from Barbados.[48] The press contingent eventually rose to 325, but by that time the fighting was over and there was nothing to report except the fact that they had not been able to report.

The final word, however, might go to Schwarzkopf, who admits in his autobiography that the decision to deny the media access was deliberate.

In later reference to events at a joint planning meeting at Atlantic Command, Schwarzkopf stated:

> As the meeting closed, somebody raised the question of the press. We agreed that we would open Grenada to reporters at 5 o'clock the next afternoon, because by then Grenada would be ours.

The Handling of the Media

The handling of the media was a source of immediate concern, and the complaints that poured in were highly condemnatory of the military. Michael Luongo of *Time* magazine, in company with three other photojournalists, was arrested while photographing US military aircraft; they were stripped naked and their film was confiscated before they were released.[49] A senior media manager, responding to Weinberger's rationale for the restrictions imposed on those who were eventually allowed in, stated:

> I've never seen such a mad dog and pony show before. I just think that the goddamn thing is such a flagrant manipulation of the press. They keep talking about how they're concerned about our safety, which I find truly touching.[50]

As with the Falklands, in the absence of reports from the field the American media was forced to turn elsewhere. It immediately tapped into information provided by Radio Havana, which was presenting the invasion as an act of piracy. The media also turned to amateur radio operators within the region and on Grenada itself. These efforts were immediately countered by military jamming, tighter frequency control of combat communications, and action by the United States Federal Communications Commission. The Commission declared some operators to be using unauthorised frequencies and put them off air.

The media management strategy, then, began with a policy of denial of information. But this, when the official pool of three networks was flown into Grenada by military aircraft on the third day, soon changed to a policy of manipulation.

The networks had agreed to have their footage checked by the military in order to at least get some independent footage back in time for their evening news deadlines in the United States. The return flight was scheduled to leave at 5 pm for Barbados, where there was a ground station that could relay the pictures back in time for the evening news. But, in an episode reminiscent of the Falklands, the return aircraft was still on the runway at Grenada at 8 pm, held up by 'excessive traffic.'

This delay allowed the President to make his planned announcement on all networks before any independent footage could be released. What was shown around the world that night, in support of Reagan's statement, was military footage showing the evacuation of young American students making the 'V' sign and smiling at the cameras as they walked up the ramp of the 'rescue' aircraft.[51]

NBC Anchorman Tom Brokaw's closing comment on air that night was that he thought the administration's actions were 'ominous and suspect.' All of the networks stated quite clearly that the footage was censored film, and graphics carrying this message was superimposed on every frame. In introducing the defence footage, Brokaw emphasised that the coverage had been 'tightly controlled', while NBC analyst Marvin Kalb openly accused the Reagan administration of 'news management.' Dan Rather of CBS told viewers that the film they had just seen had been 'shot by the Army and censored by the Army.' Howard Stringer, executive producer of the CBS evening news, said that 'it makes one anxious, suspicious and a touch sceptical about the administration's attitude towards the press coverage of the invasion.'[52] Robert Fry of the ABC's *World News Tonight*, went even further, stating that 'we are very concerned about the control, to use a polite word, that the administration has decided to exert on the coverage of the invasion. The concept of the freedom of the press in this situation has not been adhered to. We have been totally blacked out.'[53]

Protests were later lodged with the White House from almost every major media outlet in the country. In a letter to Secretary of Defense Weinberger, the President of CBS, Mr M. Joyce, remonstrated:

> I would like to protest the attitude expressed by your public affairs office that we learned lessons from the British in the Falklands. This is the United States, not Britain.'[54]

The Managing Editor of the *Washington Post*, Howard Simons, was quoted in the *New York Times* as saying,

> I'm screaming about it because writing letters takes too long. I think a secret war like a secret government is antithetical to an open society. It's absolutely outrageous.'[55]

Seymour Topping, Managing Editor of the *New York Times* and a man dedicated to the freedom of the press, strongly protested the bans:

> ... disturbed by the paucity of details about the operation released by the Pentagon at a time when the American people require all the facts to make judgements about the actions of the Government.[56]

The censored footage that did go to air was dismissed by the networks as 'garbage' and anecdotal evidence suggests that it was professional news staff's concerns with the quality of the footage, as well as journalistic outrage, that led to CBS imposing the graphic 'cleared by Defense Department' over the image.[57]

But the government had won. The government, and the government alone, had control over the media during the critical period in which military decisions were made. It was a lovely war from the public information point of view. This was the first time in modern media history that the full might and technical capability of the media could have been deployed, yet the images were of a war that had been fought without dead bodies, without fighting or blood, and without suffering or civilian casualties. Only a guaranteed showing of success and an emotive pictorial rationale of the reasons the United States went to war appeared on the television screens of America and the world.

To make matters worse, early polls indicated that the majority of Americans supported the restrictions. According to CNN news director Daniel Schorr, 80 per cent of the logged calls to his network in response to the warnings that the footage of Grenada had been censored by the military, supported the Pentagon restrictions. The minute that CBS News went to air with its 'censored' graphics, the switchboard lit up with calls, many of them charging the network with being 'unpatriotic.'[58] This strengthened the hand of an unrepentant government bureaucracy, with White House Chief of Staff, James A. Baker, commenting on the news blackout that '... a large majority of Americans support it.' A Pentagon spokesman put it more bluntly in answer to a reporter's question: 'I guess most people don't think I have to tell you a damn thing.'[59]

The findings of a more formal poll commissioned by the *Washington Post*, and the ABC Television Network, over the period 3–7 November 1983, tell a different story. This survey found that, when asked the question 'Would you say that the United States Government had tried to control news reports out of Grenada more than it should or not?', 48 per cent of those polled said 'yes', 38 per cent said 'no', and 15 per cent had no opinion. A limited review of United States editorials and articles at the time shows a concern with access to information that increased as the administration retreated from some of its earlier claims, and as it became clear that the military had taken more of a bloody nose than had been reported.[60]

On the political front, however, it had been a public relations triumph. According to a Gallup poll taken before the invasion, the President's approval rating stood at 46 per cent, against 37 per cent believing he did not handle his job well. Coming on top of those figures, the loss of 225

Marines in the Lebanon bombing incident – which occurred at the same time as the Grenada invasion – could well have produced disastrous figures with dire political effect. That the full impact of the Lebanon incident had a tendency to become lost in the invasion coverage may not have been coincidental since, on 26–27 October, a further Gallup poll showed Reagan's approval rating rising to 48 per cent. After the (apparently) successful Grenadan campaign, his approval rating rose to 53 per cent, while those registering disapproval fell to 31 per cent. It was the beginning of what Caeser describes as 'the restoration' in his graph of Reagan's approval ratings, which show a steady take off from October 1983.[61]

Metcalf has admitted that relations between the military and the media at the time of Grenada had deteriorated to 'an appalling state.'[62] It is his belief that the 'no press' policy just happened as a logical extension of the tight security that covered the early planning and diversion of the amphibious force and carrier battle group to the Caribbean.[63] Metcalf has also complained that the news blackout led to the issue of the 'right to report', rather than the conflict, becoming the story. As a result, he has observed, 'the outpouring of gratitude by the people of Grenada for the United States and her soldiers was not one of the lasting impressions the public had of Grenada.'[64]

Democracy at Work: The Sidle Report

It was against this background of resentment within the military and formal complaints from the media, that the chairman of the Joint Chiefs of Staff, General John W. Vesey, the man who had approved the news blackout, announced plans for a panel of military officers and journalists who would review media-military relations in conflict situations. The task was given to a retired officer, Major General Winant Sidle.

The review's terms of reference called for recommendations on how to conduct military operations 'in a manner that safeguards the lives of our military and protects the security of the operation while keeping the American public informed through the media.' The problem was, however, that while the terms of reference asked for recommendations on *future* operations, it specifically did not include an examination of the Grenadan campaign. Sidle recognised this, and in the covering letter to General Vesey which accompanied his final report, he argued:

> The American people must be informed about United States military operations and this information can best be provided through both the news media and the government. Therefore the

panel believes it is essential that the US news media cover US military operations to the maximum degree consistent with the mission security and the safety of the US forces.[65]

Sidle went on to make the explicit point that, while the panel had not been asked to cover Grenada, 'had our recommendations been 'in place' at the time of Grenada, there might have been no need to create our panel.' At the same time, he said, 'reporters and editors alike must exercise responsibility in covering military operations.'[66] One senior media witness was quoted as saying:

> The media must cover military operations comprehensively, intelligently and objectively. The American people deserve news coverage of this quality and nothing less. It goes without saying of course that the military also has a concurrent responsibility, that of making it possible for the media to provide such coverage.[67]

The Sidle Report contained eight recommendations. The first was that public affairs planning for military operations should be conducted concurrently with operational planning. This should be achieved by reviewing all planning documents and by directing all CINC (Commander-in-Chief) planners to include public information in their plans. The Assistant Secretary of Defense responsible for public affairs should be informed of any operations at the earliest possible time and should oversight a public affairs cell in all planning groups to ensure adequate public affairs coverage. The second recommendation called for the implementation of a pool system where this was the only way of accommodating the media. However, it recommended that pools should be used for the minimum possible period before reverting to full coverage.

The third and fourth recommendations were for the establishment of a continuously updated and accredited pool for use in time of crisis. Control of this pool, the report stated, should be exercised by media acceptance of voluntary guidelines; these should be as few as possible, with violation resulting in loss of accreditation. The next two recommendations covered the kitting and field support of correspondents, and the provision of suitably qualified escorts whose task would be to assist the media in covering operations adequately. The military should also provide adequate, and if necessary, dedicated, communications for the media. The seventh recommendation called for the provision of intra-, and inter-theatre, transportation for the media.

It was the final recommendation, however, which potentially paved the way for better relations between the media and the military. This recommendation called for a program of consultation between top military and media management, for the fostering of the issue in military schools and academies, and for military officers to visit media establishments and news organisations. It also called for working meetings with representatives of the media to explore the special problems of operational security when there might be '... real or near real-time media coverage of the battlefield.'[68]

No one could quibble with the tenor of the report, especially the far sighted recommendation dealing with real-time audiovisual coverage of the battle. But in the final analysis, it all boils down to the military interpretation of 'operational security' and the over-riding political imperatives which brought forth the Sidle Report. At a later briefing, Defense Secretary Weinberger was unrepentant over his Department's handling of the media during the Grenada campaign. But he accepted the recommendations of the report, including the setting up of a pool system. He also promised that such a pool would be tested in trial call-outs in order to ensure their responsibility in maintaining security and to convince them that every call-out would not be an actual event. Since then, a rotating pool has been established, operating under the control of a Media Advisory Committee (MAC) made up of eminent journalists charged with ensuring maximum press coverage consistent with security.[69]

Conclusion

There can be no doubt that Grenada was an extreme example of a 'closed' expeditionary force. From a media viewpoint, the most significant aspect of the operation was that the military was given absolute control over the political as well as the military handling of the media. Given the furore that followed, it is doubtful if such arrangements will ever be adopted so freely again. But control of the media remains an issue.

The extreme measures taken by the military in Grenada led to the Sidle Report, and resulted in a set of rules which should have militated against such outright exclusionary policies ever being put into effect again. But after the humiliation of Vietnam, there is little doubt that the United States military was elated with their success in containing the media, and equally little doubt that this success formed the basis of the round of sophisticated public relations policies that followed from shared experience within the ABCA (America Britain Canada Australia) military forces. As Panama and, later, the Gulf conflicts were to demonstrate, no matter how strict were safeguards such as those contained in the Sidle

Report, they could be over-ridden, in the heat of a deployment, with decisions favouring a secret agenda of excluding media scrutiny of the first few days of operations.

Another alarming feature that emerged from Grenada was control of the news by the military through the release of carefully selected still photographs and pre-edited footage shot by military cameramen and women. Several thousand feet of this videotape footage was made available to the American and international media in the absence of independent coverage. As could be expected, the footage presented a favourable image of the military and the conduct of the operation. It also met political imperatives, as with the carefully timed release of film of the evacuation of the medical students. Much the same situation was seen with still photography. Carefully selected and censored shots of the campaign taken by military personnel were released to the global media in order to gain the most favourable political and military impact. A prime example was the widespread circulation of stills showing 'multinational' troops in action, when in reality none of the Caribbean contingents saw combat.

Most alarming, however, was the initial popular support for the government's actions and the political capital reaped by President Reagan from his tough stand. While there was evidence of a change of heart on the specific question of manipulation of the media as more considered assessments began to emerge in the wake of the campaign, the political benefits that stemmed from the initial government and military-controlled images from the battlefield were not diminished.

The final lesson to be learned from Grenada was that, given the advantages of a relatively remote theatre of operations, lack of a strong local media infrastructure, use of regular forces, and the right political imperative, such as the need to restore public confidence, the media *could* be successfully excluded. The military now recognised this. But the exclusion and monopoly of information could only be sustained for a limited time, and then only on the basis of success.

Ultimately, Grenada paved the way for greater control, while providing machinery in the shape of pooling and voluntary cooperation to provide the necessary cover. The operation pointed the way to a new pattern of media management suited to the type of 'closed' expeditionary limited conflict that facilitates media control.

In Grenada, the first of these factors was the secrecy in planning and exclusion of the media from any contingency or detailed plans. In conjunction with this, a popular 'cause' was selected, in the absence of any definable personality or 'enemy' who did not pose a threat to the welfare of the citizen or the state.

Before action was commenced, legitimacy was sought through national, regional and international forums. The media was exploited in pursuit of this aim. However, the media was then excluded from coverage of the initial assault. Tightly controlled and limited pool coverage was permitted once the situation was deemed to be secure. In conjunction with this policy, the media was provided with censored and pre-digested favourable footage or copy designed to further the cause of the action and maintain popular support. The military implemented censorship, restrictions on access, limitations on transport, strict escorting, and control of the means of transmission when the media was eventually allowed into what was judged to be a 'stable' and secure situation.

In our next case study, of the invasion of Panama, we examine the application of these common measures and attitudes in practice. If Grenada was a learning experience, the lesson learned, from the perspective of a free society, was the wrong one. In Panama the measured recommendations of the Sidle Report were simply thrown out the window in yet another application of a politically-inspired and military-applied policy of initial absolute exclusion, and then containment of the media.

8

Panama:
A Deliberate Policy of
Exclusion

The United States military revised and refined the lessons of the Falklands during the Grenadan campaign, and the tight control of the press which they achieved led to strong representations from the American media following that conflict. The backlash brought home to America's politicians the need to enlist national and international support when embarking on such operations. The result was the setting up of the Sidle Report.

The Sidle Report, which leaned towards media privilege and the public's right to know, recommended closer links between the media and the military. Most of its recommendations were implemented, and the new pool system that stemmed from the report was generally considered to be equitable and workable. In the post-Grenadan period, this fostered the belief that, while the military had honed its policies of call out, access and control, the new spirit of cooperation and openness which had been endorsed by Washington now enabled a balance to be achieved between the legitimate needs of operational security and the duty of the media to keep the public informed.

What was not appreciated was that politicians and the military were still determined to exploit as far as possible their advantages of secrecy, transport and access, and would demonstrate this in Panama, in yet another 'one off' Falklands-style intervention .

Panama can be classified as a 'closed' and semi-expeditionary limited conflict. The United States military held all the advantages of timing and secrecy in planning. They also had the benefit of restricted access in that the intervention took place in a relatively isolated and lesser developed nation.[1] Playing on these advantages, the military and government made a deliberate choice to exclude the media, at least until the situation had been consolidated. This allowed the military to control the flow of information until they judged the situation to be favourable enough to allow the media access; in theory, the media would then provide independent coverage giving credibility to the military's success.

In the case of Panama, the decision to exclude the media was taken at the highest political and military levels, and with deliberate disregard for the recommendations of the Sidle Report. It was a calculated decision, based on the perceived need to avoid *any* evidence of lack of success, or coverage of the normal difficulties that can be expected in the opening phase of any campaign.[2]

Such thinking is based on the observation that the first image from the conflict, even if it is later revised or found to be wrong, gives the government and military an advantage in the quest for credibility and legitimacy. Because of this, the approach taken in Panama involved a strategy of orchestrating newsworthy images to bolster public support and off-set the adverse effects of excluding the media from preparation and the early stages of the campaign.

In an echo of Grenada, the Panamanian operation was marked by secrecy of planning, initial political and military decisions to exclude the media, and subsequent restrictions on media deployments. But, where the Grenadan intervention had been justified as a response to a request from CARICOM members, Panama was shaped around the 'demonisation' of the country's leader, General Manual Noriega, and his regime, to produce the images which were the key to exploiting the media in the American government's bid for legitimacy. These images were also used to enlist United Nations and international support.

This case study looks at the initial political and military rewards that flowed from the strategy adopted, and the high levels of public patriotic support for the deployment that stemmed from the manipulated and uncritical media coverage. It also examines the reaction and role of the media once restrictions were lifted and opportunities presented for more critical and revealing analysis.

Background to the Campaign

The tiny country of Panama spans the narrowest part of the land bridge that links North and South America. It has a population of just over 2.2 million and is a vital strategic crossroads, crucial to American defence and Western interests in general. Panama was visited by Spanish explorers in 1502, following which it developed as a Spanish colony. In 1821 it proclaimed its independence from Spain and, within a few months, voluntarily joined the Colombian Union. In succeeding years, however, remoteness from Colombia kept thoughts of full independence alive and Panama enjoyed brief periods of autonomy and self-declared independence. In this it was encouraged by the United States which saw advantages to itself, initially in the construction of the Panama Railroad in the 1850s, and later in the bid to construct a canal across the Panamanian isthmus. The canal issue was to become central to Panamanian politics.

Access across the isthmus was considered to be of such strategic importance to the United States that, by the end of the 1800s, the area was regarded as essentially United States coastline. Consequently, when difficulties were encountered over the construction of the canal, Washington was moved to back a revolution which saw Panama secede from the Colombian Union in 1903. In return, the United States gained the right to complete the canal project which had commenced, but failed, under French management. It also gained concessions from Panama, under the Panama Canal Treaty, which granted the United States an area of 1,300 square kilometres (about 500 square miles) (later to be known as the Canal Zone) in perpetuity and yielded substantial sovereign rights to American control.

Following the completion of the project in 1914, the commercial and strategic value of the canal was quickly confirmed by the growth in trade on the Panama route. Even now, there remains a strong belief that the Panama Canal is critical to United States trade interests as well as to its defence. In 1988, the last full year of normal operations before the invtervention, over 12,000 ships carrying nearly 150 million tonnes of goods and materials passed through the canal.[3]

Because of its stake in the 82 kilometre (51 mile) waterway, the United States immediately set about securing Panama as a client state.[4] It built up its defence infrastructure in the Canal Zone and it tightened its grip on the country's politics. In 1941, shortly after American entry into World War II, pursuit of these interests led the United States to encourage the overthrow of the democratically elected Panamanian president, Arnulfo Arias, in a military coup.

Arias was a populist, anti-militarist politician who, at the time, had opposed committing the large Panamanian-registered shipping fleet to the American war effort. The coup heralded the beginnings of a long and troubled period in which Arias' followers made constant calls to repudiate the Panama Canal Treaty and claim Panamanian nationhood.

Arias was returned to the presidency in 1951, to be deposed again by a military coup. The troubles continued with severe disturbances in January 1964 culminating in violent anti-American protests which left twenty-three Panamanians and three United States servicemen dead. In 1968, Arias won the presidency a third time and just as quickly lost it. The 1968 coup was led by General Omar Torrijos, who would rule Panama for the next thirteen years.[5]

With the issue of Panamanian sovereignty clearly on the agenda, the 1968 coup at least afforded an opportunity to resolve the issue on terms acceptable to the United States. In 1977, an agreement was reached promising return of the canal to Panama by 1999. In accordance with that agreement, control of the Canal Zone was to be progressively handed over to Panama with the United States retaining only the fourteen-base Southern Command HQ which was its centre for operations throughout Central America.[6] In 1981, however, Torrijos was killed in an aircrash. After a brief power struggle, General Manuel Noriega, the Army's intelligence chief who had 'come up through the ranks', became the new military commander. Two years later, he took over as unofficial head of government.

One of Noriega's first actions on taking over Panama was to prepare the country for presidential elections in 1984 – its first democratic elections in sixteen years. Noriega chose his candidate, Nicholas Barletta, on the basis of his presumed acceptability to Washington and his favourable attitude towards the military. The choice was important, as Noriega did not intend that Barletta should lose. But he could only secure a win for Barletta by fraud. Subsequent investigations suggested that a fair vote count would have given a fourth victory to Arias – arguably the most popular man in Panama.[7] In the end, far from consolidating Noriega's hold on power, the problems created by the election made it clear that Noriega's position – without American support – was far from certain.

By the end of 1985, Barletta had been forced to resign – a victim of his own efforts to set up an investigation into a political killing which pointed to military involvement, and of a subsequent failed military plot against Noriega. The plot had been masterminded by Noriega's second-in-command, Colonel Roberto Diaz Herrera.[8] However, as Kempe points out, at the time of Barletta's resignation:

What Barletta didn't know, even as president, was that Noriega had been quietly providing the CIA with enough help in its Nicaraguan war to ensure his protection by some of Washington's most influential power brokers... The (US) intelligence community felt that the loss of a president, who had been elected through fraudulent means anyway, was far less dangerous to them than a Diaz Herrera dictatorship – which might have undermined their private Contra war.[9]

Diaz Herrera would go on, in 1987, to accuse Noriega of corruption, electoral fraud, and the assassination of General Torrijos in connivance with the Central Intelligence Agency (CIA); Herrera also began to focus attention on Noriega's activities as a long-time agent of influence for the CIA.

This pulls American conduct towards Panama sharply into perspective. Noriega had initially been seen as a major asset by the United States, despite his obvious corruption and involvement in drug running, which extended to active support for the massive Columbian drug trade. It says little for Washington that Noriega's failings were known even during the Nixon era, yet he was tolerated, and even encouraged, as long as he was attentive to the interests of the United States.

In the long run, however, even American support would not be enough. Herrera's 1987 allegations sparked widespread demonstrations against Noriega in Panama City. These were controlled by tight security measures. Then, in February 1988, because of his other activities, Noriega was indicted under drug trafficking and racketeering laws by the United States Department of Justice. Later that month, a former advisor to Noriega, Jose Blandon, accused the General of a wide range of crimes, fuelling more anti-Noriega sentiment and prompting a general strike. Amid a wave of protest, President Eric Artruro Delvalle, whom Noriega had appointed as Barletta's replacement, tried to dismiss Noriega from his post as head of the Panamanian Defense Forces; instead, Noriega dismissed the President.[10]

Noriega's indictment caused consternation in Washington. According to US Secretary of State, George Schultz, the General was indicted '... without adequate consultation with the State Department or, as far as (he) could learn, with the White House.'[11] But, clearly, Noriega and Washington were coming to a parting of the ways. In March, a coup attempt failed, and Noriega imposed a 'state of urgency'. Washington began to press openly for Noriega's removal and raised the stakes. It continued to recognise Delvalle as president and backed its decision by freezing $375 million of Panamanian funds and assets in the United

States. It also imposed economic sanctions, including withholding US$86.5 million in fees collected by the Panama Canal Commission.[12] But it failed to convert Panamanian dissatisfaction into decisive pressure on Noriega, in pursuit of American objectives; Secretary of State Schultz would later observe that 'Through internal argument and inaction, our moment had passed.'[13]

Noriega held power and went on to conduct new presidential elections in 1989. Guillermo Endara, who ran for the Civic Opposition Democratic Alliance, is believed to have easily won with a 3 to 1 majority, despite widespread fraud and intimidation. Noriega's candidate, Carlos Duque, suffered a humiliating defeat. Former United States President Jimmy Carter, who had been the architect of the Treaty promising the return of the Canal, described the situation as that of a 'military dictatorship ... taking the election by fraud.'[14] Noriega responded to these criticisms and the subsequent widespread rioting by having the results annulled, claiming that Endara was simply a front for American ambitions to resume control of Panama and the Canal.[15]

America's history of direct interference in Panamanian affairs was well known. But in this, his first test of international diplomacy, President George Bush was initially reluctant to react to Noriega's defiance because of possible charges of a reversion to previous American tactics of bullying its smaller Central American neighbours. His response was to make a statement from the White House, in which he outlined a 'combination of threats and enticements' to ease out Noriega.[16] The enticements appear to have involved political asylum in Spain with a guarantee against extradition. When Noriega declined, the threats were not long in coming.

In early May, President Bush reinforced the existing 10,300 combat troops already in Panama, recalled the American ambassador, ordered the evacuation of military dependants to the United States or to the security of the American bases in Panama, requested businesses to withdraw dependants, and extended the economic sanctions already in place. He also enforced the terms of the Treaty which gave American forces the right of free movement within the Canal Zone and the right to defend it.[17] In addition, the President called on other Latin American nations to condemn Noriega's actions. President Carlos Andres Perez of Venezuela took up the call, describing the nullification of the elections as '... even worse than the actual fraud of the election itself.'[18] Other member states followed his lead, but Chile, Peru, and, more importantly, Mexico, qualified their support by expressing concern over '... any form of foreign interference in Panama or any other country.'[19]

President Bush, well aware of this sentiment, remained anxious to avoid direct confrontation. The military, too, appeared reluctant to act. The Chairman of the Joint Chiefs of Staff, Admiral William Crowe, warned Congress of the possible cost in lives.[20] His caution was echoed by the Director of the non-government Council on Hemispheric Affairs and long-time regional observer, Laurence Birns, who summed up the feelings of those who opposed use of force by asking 'since when has a dictator staging fraudulent elections in Central America ever been grounds in the past for sending in US troops?'[21]

The Organization of American States (OAS) also urged restraint, citing its Charter which supports the principle of non-intervention in the internal affairs of member states.[22] The former Chief of the Naval Staff, Admiral Elmo Zumwalt, warned Congress that the Canal was easy to damage but difficult to defend; Noriega, Zumwalt said, could close the Panama Canal as easily as did Nasser the Suez Canal in Egypt.[23] And Noriega himself was not without friends. His well-equipped 15,000 man army remained loyal and he had the declared support of Cuba and Libya's Colonel Gaddafi. To have moved against him, it was argued, would have been to have invited a wave of anti-American sentiment.

Noriega responded by playing the 'American bully' card for all it was worth. He declared Panama to be in 'a state of war' with the United States and formally declared himself 'Chief of the Government.'[24] President Bush continued to exercise restraint, despite an increased level of harassment of off-duty American servicemen. But, behind the scenes, America's newly appointed Chief of the Joint Chiefs of Staff, General Colin Powell strengthened Southern Command by replacing General Frederick Woerner, who was seen to be too weak, with the more active General Max (Mad Max) Thurman.[25]

In October, dissidents in the Panamanian Defence Force approached the CIA with offers of a coup against Noriega. The offer was poorly handled – so poorly in fact that it led Senator Jesse Helms to describe the administration, in the House, as 'a bunch of keystone cops.' Helms made the point that, after this incident, no member of the Panamanian defence forces could be expected to act against Noriega; American editorials compared it to the Carter's Iran hostage rescue or Kennedy's fiasco at the Bay of Pigs.[26] Then, on 19 December, an American serviceman was shot and his wife was subjected to sexual harassment. It was the perfect political excuse for punitive action. In the early hours of 20 December, paratroopers of the 82nd Airborne Division and troopers of the 7th Light Division were unleashed in the first wave of Operation Just Cause, the biggest United States military operation since the Vietnam War.[27]

Secret Planning and The Exclusion of the Media

Contingency plans for a possible intervention into Panama, codenamed 'Elaborate Maze', had been in existence for many years. In April 1988 new contingency plans for differing levels of intervention were drawn up under the codename 'Prayer Book'. Prayer Book incorporated an offensive component, codenamed 'Blue Spoon', and a non-combatant evacuation operation, codenamed 'Klondike Key', for the removal of the many United States citizens in the area.[28]

In August 1989, following the arrival in Panama of the new Commander-in-Chief (CINC) Southern Command, General Thurman, these plans were all reviewed and Blue Spoon was placed under the operational control of General Carl Steiner, the commander of the mobile 18th Corps at Fort Bragg.[29] On 30 October 1989, it became operations order 1–90; 'in country' rehearsals which had been underway since September were stepped up, and General Steiner and his staff set up in HQ Southern Command two days before the operation – which had been renamed 'Just Cause' – commenced.[30]

While the need for operational security and secrecy of contingency plans is understandable, *at no time, was the media advised of these developments.* Not even the Pentagon press pool was advised, even though its members had pledged to maintain operational security and had demonstrated their ability to do so during 'callouts' in Honduras in 1985 and 1988, and during the naval blockade of the Gulf.[31] The official Pentagon response – maintained until Woodward revealed otherwise – was that a Pentagon official had not brought forward plans for the media pool to accompany the first wave.[32] According to General Patrick Brady, the Army's Chief of Public Affairs up until May 1990, it was just an unfortunate slip:

> ... for reasons that are not readily understandable, the decision to send the pool was made too late, and as a result, it got to Panama late and there was little support once it did get there.[33]

More revealing, perhaps, was Brady's statement, at the same time, that television should, in any case, not be allowed on the battlefield until the situation was secure.

The exclusion of the media from Operation Just Cause led to a delay that meant that the twelve reporter and television crew pool could not be activated until the military was ready. Even then, they were forced to sit out a twenty-four hour wait at the Howard Air Force Base some 40 kilometres (25 miles) from Panama City.[34] It had all gone according to plan. The reality, according to Woodward, was that Secretary of Defense Dick Cheney decided on 18 December that he:

> ... would not have Pete Williams (Defense public relations) notify the media pool ... until after the evening television news shows the next night. This would be six hours before H Hour, making it impossible for reporters to make it to Panama in time for the start of Just Cause.[35]

This has since been confirmed by Cheney who, in a response to a later review of the handling of the media in Panama, stated unequivocally that:

> ... I specifically was the one who made the decision about whether or not to notify the pool and under what conditions and with how much lead time. That was my responsibility, and I accept whatever criticism goes with it ... But I will say that as long as I am in the job, it's a decision I'm going to make on a case by case basis.[36]

Early the next day, the military compounded this political decision when General Powell informed his public affairs chief, Colonel Bill Smullen, of the decision to invade, but swore him to secrecy.[37] This was in direct contravention of the spirit and recommendations of the Sidle Report.[38] The decision also went against defence policy, formulated less than eighteen months previously, which clearly stated that in peacetime contingency operations 'public affairs staff principals must be involved in the earliest planning stage of (the) operations.'[39]

Public affairs staff officers might well have been involved in the planning, but there was no implementation of any plans for media coverage. Instead, the planning seems to have been aimed at continuing containment of the media. The military closed the only secure point of entry, Howard Air Force Base, to all charter traffic, and no journalists were admitted to the declared military theatre of operations by land, sea or air. Some three hundred journalists who flew to Panama to cover the event in the pre-Christmas weekend were stranded at Panama City airport after being ordered to return either to the United States or a third country.[40] As Boswell put it:

> No journalists were taken in until the fighting was completed and those who made it by boat were too late to see combat ... the Pentagon, by controlling the flow of television news (gave) the impression before Christmas that the war was over on the first day and only mopping up operations remained.[41]

This was from a military and government that had endorsed Sidle's overriding principle that, 'American journalists, print and broadcast, with their professional equipment, should be present at US military operations ... permitting independent reporting to the citizens of our free and open society to whom our Government is ultimately accountable.'[42] Instead, once they were allowed in, the media were restrained by a dusk-to-dawn curfew, and by an inability to travel around the country. The media soon found an uncontrolled means of access through Costa Rica but, no matter what the point of entry, access to the actual area of operations, where the truth was to be found, remained tightly controlled. Only 'positive' news was encouraged, with defence public relations refusing to give out casualty figures on either side. Instead, it highlighted the 'warm' welcome given to the American forces by the Panamanian population.[43]

The casualties and damage inflicted on Panama City itself were euphemistically termed 'collateral damage' by the military public relations machine, to soften the impact of the fighting on public opinion. These casualties and damage were also consistently under-represented. In his scathing report on the handling of the media, Hoffman, who had been a principal Deputy Assistant Secretary of Defence for public affairs accused the military of '... mishandling news coverage of the operation from start to finish.'[44]

The evidence, particularly that of Woodward, and Cheney's own admissions, support Hoffman's view. There was a deliberate policy of exclusion, containment and manipulation designed to thwart critical analysis during the crucial initial period of the invasion. News was not actively censored, but passively censored by ensuring lack of access and delay.

The most important lesson to be learned from this was that the Defense Department had repudiated its own cooperative media system and that there had been collusion between the military and the administration in doing so.

The Demonisation of Noriega

The apparently quick and decisive nature of the Operation Just Cause earned generally uncritical public support. Much of this support, however, rested on the demonisation of Noriega, since it was difficult to target either the Panamanian people or the opposition, both of whom were to be portrayed as jubilant at their 'rescue' and needing to be 'rehabilitated' once the conflict was over.

In both the lead up to the invasion and after, the United States administration was at pains to use the media to paint Noriega in the blackest terms in order to achieve the public consensus and support so necessary for limited conflict.[45] Noriega was portrayed as a drug dealer on a massive scale, providing military and government protection for the growing, processing, and more importantly, transportation of drugs into the United States. In addition, he was accused of being a sexual deviant, a child molester, a murderer and a torturer. At the same time, he was likened to a 'demented Adolf Hitler', and said to be into '... devil worship, satanism and magic.' He was also rumoured to be suffering from a serious social disease because of his debauched lifestyle; one American newspaper suggested he was suffering from AIDS. These themes were taken up when Noriega's HQ was taken, with newsmen being invited in to see what was presented: an alleged 50 kilograms of cocaine, an opulent lifestyle and sex aids.[46]

Much of this may have been true, but there is no evidence for any of it other than the United States Supreme Court decisions on drug trafficking. The fact that Noriega was singled out for such treatment, however, demonstrates the need for the demonisation of the enemy in this type of conflict, as a necessary tool in enlisting public support. That the strategy worked was evidenced by American news bulletins which described Noriega as a

> ... narco-terrorist (belonging to) ... a special fraternity of international villains – men like Gaddafi, Idi Amin and the Ayatollah Khomeini – whom Americans just love to hate.[47]

The *New York Daily News* ran its own 'wanted' poster of Noriega and the *New York Post* asked 'Where's the Rat?' on its front page. The local Panamanian newspapers, generally believed to be influenced if not actually controlled by American intelligence services, went further. One newspaper carried a half page picture of the General as a horned devil flying over the city, with the headline reading, 'Will the Diplomatic Exorcism Work?'[48] In Australia, the headline in one paper ran, 'Noriega, Drug Despot.'[49] To complete the picture, the United States put a US$1 million bounty on Noriega's head, dead or alive.[50]

The success of the strategy was shown in instant opinion polls carried out by television and radio stations, which registered between 70 and 90 per cent support for President Bush.[51] Commentators and leaders from a wide spectrum of opinion praised Bush for deploying troops to save American lives, preserve treaty rights, and hunt down such a notorious drug dealer and enemy of democracy. The *Washington Post* summed up this perception by declaring in an editorial that 'The President did the right thing.'[52]

Congress was equally quick to offer bi-partisan support.[53] The Democratic (opposition) Senate Leader, George Mitchell, stated that '...

the action was made necessary by the reckless actions of Noriega'[54] while the Democrat Speaker of the House, Thomas Foley – who expressed some initial concerns about the deployment – backed the President's actions, saying '... when American troops are in the field and casualties are being taken ... it's not the appropriate time for a lot of complicated debate.'[55] Senate Republican leader, Robert Dole, simply stated that the President had done 'the right thing.'[56] Only Senator Edward Kennedy and Representative Donald Edwards, both Democrats, expressed concern. Beyond that, Congress was caught up in a patriotic response to a carefully sanitised, successful deployment, portrayed as producing few casualties and presented without the benefit of critical media analysis.

Significantly, the appeal to patriotism at all levels was linked to the demonisation of Noriega, which was, in turn, facilitated by secrecy in planning and the exclusion of the media. This creation of a convenient 'demonic' personal enemy is fast becoming a preferred strategy in building support for limited conflicts.

The Media in the Battle for Legitimacy

In addition to its emotional and manipulative appeals for support based on the demonisation of Noriega, the United States set out a legal basis for its invasion of Panama. The argument rested on the invocation of America's right to self defence under Articles 2 and 51 of the United Nations Charter. Terry also cites bases for the action under the Charter of the OAS, the Inter American Treaty of Reciprocal Assistance (The Rio Treaty), the 1977 Panama Canal Treaty, and the 1984 criteria for intervention set out by the former Secretary of Defense, Caspar Weinberger.[57]

Beyond the provisions of the United Nations Charter, the official argument rested on the need to protect American lives, the obligation to defend the integrity of the Panama Canal, and the fact that General Noriega had declared that a 'state of war' existed between the two countries. The declaration of war, however, was never formally delivered by Panama nor acknowledged or ratified by the United States.[58] Further legal argument was based on the ruling by the Justice Department that United States law enforcement officers could arrest a fugitive from American justice in another country without obtaining that country's permission and that limitations on the use of the military under the Posse Comitatus Act did not exist outside the United States.[59] These opinions provided the United States with the argument it needed for the extradition of Noriega, despite the fact that no right to the exercise of police powers within another nation's borders exists in international law. Indeed, to do so would be to abrogate the rights of sovereign states.[60]

These objections notwithstanding, there are precedents for the use of force to protect citizens in other countries, such as the Israeli Entebbe raid and the abortive raid to free hostages in Tehran. But a member taking these arguments to the United Nations has to meet the test of Article 2 (4) of the United Nations Charter, which specifically prohibits the use of force against the territorial integrity or political independence of any state.

It was against this background that President Bush had to muster national and international support to legitimise what was seen by many to be an act of outright aggression. The United Nations was the first target, next were major allies such as France and Britain, and friendly states such as Australia. A major tool here, in addition to government-to-government lobbying and diplomacy, was the media. The United States exploited to the full its overseas information systems in order to construct the background necessary to allow individual governments to take up a supporting position.[61] The official information releases were supported by individual briefings for selected journalists.

This use of the media probably influenced Britain and France in their veto of the United Nations General Assembly denunciation of the American action, following a resolution introduced by the Non-Aligned Movement. The resolution strongly deplored the intervention in Panama by the United States which, it said, '... constituted a flagrant violation of international law ...' as well as Panama's independence, sovereignty and territorial integrity.[62] A similar resolution was passed by the General Assembly four days later. But the veto, and the abstention of other American allies who had been enlisted in the search for international legitimacy, effectively silenced the United Nations.[63]

The Australian experience is typical of media manipulation to secure popular political support.

An Australian Foreign Affairs Ministerial Brief, dated 18 December 1989, stated that the government strongly supported a peaceful and constitutional solution to the Panamanian problem, and called for a policy of restraint by both Panama and the United States.[64] This brief was changed three days later, on 21 December, the day after the invasion, in line with support for the American action shown by Australian Prime Minister, Bob Hawke. The abrupt change in policy followed a direct call from President Bush to the Prime Minister, requesting support in the United Nations and explaining the rationale behind the invasion. In light of the government documents, the change occurred without reference either to ministerial or departmental advice to the Prime Minister. The subsequent instruction to the Australian Ambassador to the United Nations was to, '... support the US in all substantive and procedural proposals on the matter.'[65]

This about face in Australian policy would have been impossible without favourable public opinion and a media environment to sustain it. The change in public opinion, in turn, could not have been achieved without the biased and controlled reporting coming out of Panama, and the efforts of the American information service to push it in the local media.[66]

There are indications that this strategy of exploiting the media to gain international legitimacy and mould world opinion will be a feature of similar 'closed' and semi-expeditionary limited conflicts in the future.

The Media Unleashed

It is often the case that one of the aims of limited conflict is restoration of the democratic rights, which is put forward as part of the rationale for action. The return to normalcy implies the restoration of a free press and the lifting of any military restrictions on the media. This is exactly what happened in Panama, when President Bush informed the world that 'the situation has been stabilised and democracy has returned ... under President Endara.'[67] Unfortunately, what had begun as a political triumph in the handling of the press began to turn sour as soon as the media was free to do its job.

The first major event to capture media attention was the military's failure to capture its prime target, General Noriega. It was a failure that would descend into farce before the operation was over.

On Christmas Eve, 1989, with the Panamanian resistance in collapse, Noriega appealed to the Papal Nunciature in Panama City for temporary asylum. The Vatican refused to grant political asylum, but nevertheless admitted Noriega to its protection. From that point, the Nunciature declined to hand Noriega over to either the United States or the newly formed Endara government – which the Vatican had not yet recognised – because neither had any formal extradition treaty with the Vatican.[68] The Vatican's reply to a United States request to surrender Noriega was that it could not hand him over to 'an occupying power' and the United States, anxious not to do anything to try to undermine the sovereignty of the new Endara government, took second place in the negotiations once the Vatican had recognised the new regime.[69]

In the meantime, however, US forces surrounded the Nunciature with armoured vehicles, snipers, checkpoints and constant helicopter patrols.

They bombarded the embassy with loud and violent rock music, including songs with messages such as 'Nowhere to run', and 'I fought the law and the law won.' General Thurman, whom the media had christened the 'Maxatollah', directed armoured vehicles to rattle the mission gates. He began driving up to the Nunciature himself two or three times a day to deliver the latest inducement or threat from Washington.[70] Thurman's increasingly eccentric handling of the Nunciature situation was fully reported by the media. This coverage led to widespread criticism, with one commentator describing it as:

> The most atrocious, barbaric and unsophisticated act I've ever seen by a military commander... it's so childish, like one kid standing on a street corner and yelling names at one another.[71]

The United States administration was further embarrassed when the world was treated to media coverage of the arrest of the Cuban ambassador to Panama, Lazaro Mora, by United States military forces who took him away in an armoured vehicle. This was followed by the equally visible searching of vehicles entering and leaving the Cuban, Nicaraguan and Libyan embassies, each of which had been ringed by American troops since the first day of the invasion. There was a forced entry and search of the Nicaraguan Embassy in Panama City, with Ambassador Antensor Ferrey complaining that he and his staff had been ordered out of the Chancery at gunpoint by some sixty United States soldiers.[72] America was further embarrassed by pictures flashed around the world showing the Vatican's ambassador being forced to stand by at gunpoint while his car was searched by US Special Forces.[73] With the media free to report, Noriega's delaying tactics were making a mockery of the invasion and revealing the Endara government as little more than a puppet regime.

But this exposure provided only a taste of what was to come once the shooting war was over.

The Pentagon's initial claim was that, apart from a few minor problems, the operation had been a major success. It had been well executed and pointed the way for future low intensity conflicts. But the media suggested otherwise, with one report stating that '... the invading forces were never expected to lose.' Rather, the victory had raised '... a number of awkward questions that suggest the military's planning is not up to date.'[74]

The criticism began to get more pointed with further investigation. Less than two weeks after the initial assault, one media report had 400 civilians killed and 2,000 wounded. An estimated 13,000 Panamanians were displaced, with 5,000 left homeless by what was described as '... a style of fighting more suitable for a world war rather than a surgical strike designed to decapitate a drug dealing Dictator's army.'[75] The official losses released by the United States military in Panama in mid-January listed 314 Panamanian military and 202 civilians killed for a loss of 23 US servicemen.[76] This was immediately challenged by the CBS *60 Minutes* program, which reported a civilian tally of more than 4,000.[77] In April, after continued complaints, the Endara government authorised the exhumation of a mass grave containing the bodies of 125 Panamanians killed during the invasion. All were wrapped in standard United States military green body bags. Mrs Isabel Corro of the Committee of Relatives from the US Invasion, claimed that there were about another eight such mass graves. The Endara Government then put the civilian death toll at 650, more than double the earlier official estimates.[78]

Over the next few months the story worsened The *Los Angeles Times* claimed that the lasting impressions of December 1989, were little more than '... fiction, now being opened to massive revision.' The original Pentagon tally of enemy losses was downgraded from an original 300 to 50 and the 'cocaine' found in Noriega's quarters, news of which had been taken at face value by the world media, proved to be talcum powder. The Pentagon also admitted, some four months after the action, that there had been sixty cases of misconduct by United States forces during the campaign. Finally, earlier reports of the gallantry of American servicewomen in combat were questioned.[79] The matter was debated in Congress, with Mrs Patricia Schroeder, an influential member of the House Armed Forces Committee stating:

> In the heat of battle, you expect something to be distorted, but this has really gotten to the point where you'd think it was almost a public relations war. They're destroying their own credibility. The whole thing looks more and more like a carnival.[80]

The Pentagon's public affairs spokesman, Pete Williams, said that the military may have circulated some inaccurate accounts but he knew of no cases of deliberate misinformation.[81] There is, however, sufficient doubt to reinforce the belief that restrictions on media access during the initial operation were designed to prevent the press from reporting the true situation or to encourage them to follow stale leads which would excite little interest from a public whose views had already been formed by the immediacy of the military controlled images from the battlefront.[82] General Powell, the then Chairman of the Joint Chief of Staff Committee, reflected the military lessons that had been learned when he later admitted:

We did not plan well enough for reintroducing civil government. Our press arrangements produced recriminations on both sides. We were slow in getting the press pool to Panama and to the action... Consequently, the press ate us alive, with some justification. In the future, I knew, we had to do a far better job'.[83]

Conclusion

There can be little doubt, in the face of compelling evidence, that there was a deliberate decision to first exclude, then contain the media in the Panama intervention. While Powell gives no confirmation in his autobiography and gives only a passing reference to Woodward's account of events,[84] there can be no doubt that the decision to limit the media was taken at the highest political levels and endorsed by the military; and it was taken in spite of the recommendations of the Sidle Report. The fact that there appeared to be no planning for the involvement of the media despite the long work up period, also points to a longer-term policy of exclusion and containment aimed at controlling the all-important national and international public opinion during the initial, vulnerable stages of the operation.

From a political point of view, Panama did produce the initial dazzling public relations success boasted of by General Brady, and there is little doubt that both the military and administration readily appreciated the benefits that flowed from such a tight control. It was only when control was lifted and the media was able to fulfil its proper function that the failures and problems became evident. By then, however, the news value of the event had declined, and the opportunity for various publics to make informed decisions had passed.

When this model is compared to the combat and post-combat media control brought down in the Gulf, which closely resembles Panama as a semi-expeditionary limited conflict in a country with limited indigenous press, it becomes apparent that this was a lesson well learned and quickly adopted as part of policy.

From the small amount of unclassified evidence which is available, it is apparent that the planning and deployment took place in secret, and that the media was deliberately excluded from the initial and politically vulnerable first few days of combat. When the media was eventually admitted into the theatre of operations, it was subject to strict controls that went far beyond any valid needs of operational security. The media was also exploited in an attempt to demonise Noriega as a 'personal enemy', in an effort to enlist national and international support. Finally, there is evidence that both the military and the administration suffered some embarrassment when media restrictions were lifted in the aftermath, allowing journalists to unearth the negative information which had been suppressed by the military while it had control of the means of access and communication.

From these conclusions, and building on the factors which emerged from the Grenadan intervention, we can further expand on the way the media will be handled in future semi-expeditionary limited conflicts. Arrangements would include most, if not all of the following factors, probably implemented in sequence. Each factor will impact directly on the media, either in the lead up to the conflict, during the conflict, or in its aftermath.

There will be a tendency to identify and 'demonise' a selected personal enemy. This will be done for two reasons: first, to identify a focus of enmity when no direct threat is posed to the home nation and, second, to isolate opposition leaders or the 'victimised' population at large, because of their use in restoring stability after the conflict. This will rule out the stereotyping of the past, such as the callous images of bespectacled Japanese of World War II or even the more recent 'Argies' of the Falklands.

While demonisation continues, a process of secret planning will commence behind the scenes. This will go well beyond valid contingency plans and be accompanied by the deployment of preparatory intelligence, special forces and offensive communications assets. Next will come the destabilisation of the target regime through intelligence or political means, underlined by a series of strong diplomatic signals aimed at highlighting the intractability of the target. There will also be a program of sanctions or economic isolation, accompanied by a series of major diplomatic signals. We will then see the sudden deployment or build-up of an overwhelming superiority of forces under strict security classification and covered by probable denials and deceptions.

The exclusion of the general media and some form of delay in the deployment of any form from cooperative media arrangements will follow, aimed at ensuring freedom of media scrutiny in the first few hours or days of the operation. We can then expect the implementation of the tightest exclusion and containment of the media possible, based on the concept of operational security, and depending on the remoteness or isolation of the target and levels of indigenous media. This limitation will be matched by an increased level of pre-edited and censored military coverage, reinforcing an image of success, and made widely available to the national and international media through government agencies.

Finally, we can expect a search for legitimacy through local political organisations, regional groupings, client states and allies who owe some form of indebtedness, and through the United Nations. This will be achieved using a combination of diplomatic lobbying, political inducement or pressure. There will also be the exploitation of international media by the sustained and ongoing provision of pre-digested source material and selected personal briefings in support of the aims of the belligerent nation. Afterwards, there will be the publicised deployment of relief teams and assistance to a 'welcoming' population that expresses its relief at the removal of the personalised target enemy, these sentiments being appropriately expressed on placards written in English. This will probably be followed by effusive praise for allied force participation and subsequent state visits to recognise the contributions of allied or supporting government leaders.

In the case of Panama, there was a defined and declared moment of success, after which the media was allowed to operate normally. While it was a feature of the campaign, the dangers of having an open and unrestricted media on the ground so quickly were readily appreciated, and made it less likely that restrictions would be lifted so quickly in the future. Apart from this modification, the general model set out above, with some variations dependent on geographical and political factors, can be expected to prevail. What will remain constant is the maintenance of a secret agenda by the military and government to ensure maximum exclusion and containment of the media, while paying lip service to the public's right to know and the duty of the media to keep them informed.

9

The Gulf Conflict: The Ascendancy of the Military

The evidence of the case studies to this point shows that the balance of power has swung inexorably in favour of the military and, increasingly, to a politico-military coalition, to control of the media in time of limited conflict.

The Falklands, Grenada and Panama shared the characteristics of expeditionary conflicts, affording an ideal environment for the military to exploit the advantages inherent in a monopoly of transport, access and communications. But these advantages had to be balanced against strong representations made by the media after each event, as well as later complaints from civil libertarian groups in both the United States and the United Kingdom.

In the aftermath of the Falklands and Grenada, media complaints led to the establishment of inquiries at the highest levels of government. The resulting opinions, put forward by both the British parliamentary inquiry and in the Sidle Report, generally favoured the public's right to know. The reports recommended the introduction of new cooperative measures for the management of media-military relations and largely assuaged the fears of the media. Even so, the arrangements reflected the widespread acceptance that such campaigns had been 'one off' deployments, mounted in circumstances that would probably never again be repeated. The hard fact was that similar circumstances would reappear in the Gulf – a theatre of war in which the remote and inhospitable terrain would again confer the advantages of an expeditionary campaign, albeit to a lesser extent than in some more recent conflicts. And the experience and evidence of the Gulf war shows that, despite the promises of greater media freedom and increased cooperation, the military and the politicians had developed a firm appreciation and acceptance of the benefits of an ever tighter media control.

The American-dominated United Nations expedition that expelled Saddam Hussein from Kuwait was a masterpiece of planning, command logistics, and execution. The conflict remains a classic example of our earlier definition of a limited conflict in that it was fought within strict geographic and weaponry limits. It was also subject to continuing background negotiations between the belligerents – negotiations involving the United Nations, various religious and regional groupings, and initiatives in personal diplomacy. From the media point of view, the conflict can be classified as an expeditionary campaign. It was mounted in inhospitable terrain, in extremes of climate, and in an area with little or no support infrastructure. These advantages were exploited by the military to minimise independent media reporting during each phase of the allied force build-up in the Gulf and throughout the actual conflict.

Another relevant factor in the Gulf war is that it was waged without the use of conscripts, the main American and allied forces using only regular and volunteer National Guard troops and reservists. This limited popular concern over casualties and minimised dissent in the field, of the kind that could be expected from troops conscripted against their will.[1] There is also evidence of manipulation of the media, if not the conscious use of misinformation. In the case of Australia, there was an element of farce in the handling of the media, and yet another example of exclusion and containment for political reasons. The pattern which emerged in the Gulf followed that of the Falklands, Grenada and Panama, as the United States government utilised the media in its attempts to build national and international public support and secure the legitimacy afforded by United Nations backing.

Only now, some five years after the event, is the hard evidence of media manipulation beginning to emerge. There are allegations of major battles that went completely unreported, suggestions that enemy force levels were less than half those given at the time, and claims of inflated success rates for the high technology weaponry that figured so prominently in the media imagery of the war.[2] More importantly, there is now compelling evidence that the media was stage managed and manipulated to an extent never before encountered in Western liberal democracies.

The Gulf conflict also introduced a new factor – that of the media being utilised as both an avenue for diplomatic signals and for information, if not actual intelligence, by both sides. And, for the first time since Harrison Salisbury attempted to report the Vietnam war from Hanoi, audiences witnessed accounts from behind 'enemy' lines, by reporters such as Peter Arnett who held no ideological or political bias. Networks also resorted to the use of 'once removed' expert commentators on a worldwide scale that beggared the Falklands experience; in the case of Australia, this led to unprecedented political attacks on commentators and the national broadcaster, on the alleged grounds of anti-allied bias. The Western world also witnessed the demonisation of Saddam Hussein, matched by the equally impressive media rehabilitation of President Hafez Al-Assad of Syria and the Arab world in general.

Because of the problems of security classification, especially the grey area of 'cyber warfare', it seems likely that much more remains to be revealed. In much the same manner in which it took two years before the truth behind the deliberate exclusion of the media in Panama was made public, so too will it be many years before the truth behind both the conduct of the war and media policy in the Gulf emerges.[3] From a media point of view, there are also the questions of why both Britain and the United States consistently ignored intelligence reports that Saddam Hussein planned to invade Kuwait, and misled the world into believing that the next target was Saudi Arabia when this appears to have been untrue.

Above all, the United States military, along with the other participating forces, went into the conflict with the benefit of a well developed media policy designed to contain and minimise press scrutiny to the military's own advantage. The media had no response and meekly went along with the pre-prepared military policies of restriction. Hackworth later expressed his feelings on the effects of media control:

> It blows me out how badly the media covers the defense story… All the flacks (public affairs officers) do is spin, deceive, and promote their service. This takes thousands of people and costs the taxpayer hundreds of millions.[4]

This case study will examine the political and military benefits that accrued from this policy of media containment and the resultant 'bloodless' and sanitised coverage. That coverage revealed, on Australian television screens at least, only one dead American soldier.[5] Once again, as they did after Grenada and Panama, representatives of the press in the United States belatedly took the issue of media policy to the government. The fear now, however, is that having achieved what many within the military see as a vindication of the media debacle in Vietnam, other Western military forces will follow what is rapidly becoming a set pattern for media-military relations in time of limited conflict.

The handling of the media in the Gulf conflict typifies this emerging pattern. The military first ensured secrecy in planning. Both sides then employed exclusion, deception and misinformation to manipulate the media in pursuit of their war aims. The Western contributors to the allied effort also exploited the media in the demonisation of Saddam Hussein, using negative images to enlist public support and to legitimate their actions internationally. During the campaign itself, tight restrictions were placed on the media. These restrictions were the subject of formal complaints after the event, and were met with the same expressions of concern and intentions to implement more suitable cooperative arrangements as in the past. Finally, the military and government later engaged in considerable revision of aspects of the campaign, revealing inconsistencies which point directly to the earlier use of deception and misinformation.

Background to the Campaign

Kuwait is sited at the northern end of the Persian Gulf, south of Iraq and the western mouth of the Shatt al-Arab waterway. Its people have always lived under the threat of their larger more powerful neighbours. Iraq in particular has entertained long-time claims over Kuwait and threatened invasion in 1937 and again in 1961. On each occasion, the menace was rebuffed by the deployment of British forces. Nevertheless, annexation remained on the Iraqi agenda and another attempt was made on Kuwait in 1973. This time the Iraqis were deterred by a combination of international opinion and a strong Saudi military reaction. But Iraq's claims have provided an ideal external issue for a troubled leadership, and further demands were lodged in 1978 for the offshore island of Bubiyan in the approaches to the Shatt al-Arab. These claims were overtaken by more pressing issues and left in abeyance, however, while the newly installed president, Saddam Hussein, engaged himself in the 1980–88 war with Iran.[6]

Early in 1990, Iraqi attention turned once again to Kuwait. Saddam Hussein began to push for an increase in the OPEC price of oil and for reparations from Kuwait of some US$2.4 billion for oil which he claimed had been illegally pumped from the Iraqi section of the disputed Rumaila oilfield.[7]

Apart from the logic of the economic argument, Saddam spoke from a position of strength. His million-strong armed forces were the largest, most battle hardened and experienced conventional military force in the Middle East; 95 per cent of Iraq's high technology weaponry had been supplied by France, the United States, West Germany, Egypt, Brazil and Chile.[8] Further, Iraq possessed a formidable chemical and, it was claimed, biological arsenal. In addition, and perhaps most importantly, it had embarked on a nuclear weapons program which, according to Bulloch and Morris, '... would eventually give it nuclear parity with Israel.'[9]

Saddam also spoke from the self-assumed position of the inheritor of the mantle of Saladin and Nasser, as the leader of the Arab world. The Iraqi president saw himself, and was largely recognised, as the protector of the moderate Arab states against the threat of Iranian Islamic fundamentalism. It was a protection that he felt the wealthy Gulf states should recognise through financial assistance to fund his post-war reconstruction. This was despite the fact that they had already almost totally funded his war with Iran. On another level, the Saddam Hussein saw himself as a regional counterweight to the vacuum posed by the collapse of superpower rivalry between the United States and the Soviet Union following *glasnost*. Most importantly, though, after the bitter years of war with Iran, the Iraqi people needed a national rallying point or external diversion. That diversion was to be the annexation of Kuwait.[10]

Iraqi preparations for war began in late June and early July 1990 with the deployment of forces to the Iraqi-Kuwaiti border. These deployments were spearheaded by the Hammurabi Division of the elite Republican Guard, and the movements were dutifully picked up by American satellite reconnaissance. By mid-July more than 35,000 men from three first line armoured divisions were within sixteen to fifty kilometres (ten to thirty miles) of the border. There was, however, no matching communications traffic, ammunition dumping or logistical preparations, nor the sort of careful Soviet-style rehearsal pattern established by the Iraqis in their recent war with Iran.[11] Consequently, the American intelligence community did not see invasion as an imminent danger. CIA Chief, William Webster, dismissed the prospect as '... just sabre-rattling to push the price of oil up and achieve other demands put forward by the Iraqis.'[12]

At a media breakfast on 19 July 1990, US Secretary of Defense, Richard (Dick) Cheney, stated that the United States would take seriously '... any threat to US interests or US friends in the region.'[13] Beyond that observation, the Americans appeared to accept the Iraqi assurances, delivered through their Ambassador to Iraq, April Glaspie, that Saddam Hussein had no intentions on Kuwait – or, at least, not the whole of Kuwait.[14] Even so, Washington took guard and reinforced Cheney's warning by deploying a token naval force in the Gulf for joint exercises. The Americans also met a request from the United Arab Emirates for tanker aircraft to enable full-time air patrols. These decisions were taken as a diplomatic signal of support. By the end of July, however, the Iraqi force had increased to more than 100,000, with reports of helicopter assault forces also being deployed. To some within the Pentagon, this overkill in numbers without the normal accompanying signals traffic and command and logistics support still looked like a bluff. On 24 July, the Chairman of the US Joint Chiefs of Staff, General Colin Powell, ordered the Commander of the Florida-based Central Command, General Norman Schwarzkopf, to review the then current Operational Plan 90–1002 for the deployment of a reaction force. This called for the marshalling of a 100,000 man force spearheaded by F–15 fighters and airborne troops on 30 days notice.[15] General Powell also called for a new two-tiered response; tier one was to include a range of retaliatory plans while the second was designed to halt Saddam and protect the region.[16]

The actual conduct of the campaign, the allied participation, and the tactics used, lies well beyond the scope of this chapter. However, in the early hours of 2 August 1990, Saddam Hussein's forces rolled across the border and within five hours had taken Kuwait in the face of little more than token resistance. The invasion was immediately condemned by the United States which, after gaining a reluctant invitation from the Fahd ruling house of Saudi Arabia, began to build an allied, but predominantly American, force of over 400,000 under the command of General Schwarzkopf. Iraq took Western hostages and concluded its remaining differences with Iran, a move which freed troops for the threatened battle in the south. It then prepared confidently to wait out the United Nations-imposed economic sanctions.

The United States-led coalition, however, was intent on action. On 29 November, United Nations Security Council Resolution 678 (1990) set a deadline of 15 January 1991 for the withdrawal of the Iraqi force. Subsequently, after initial problems of readiness, on 17 January, the United States build-up, codenamed 'Desert Shield', became 'Desert Storm' and allied air attacks were launched against targets in Iraq. The air battle was won decisively, the victory believed to have been achieved at least partly by an as yet unacknowledged technical intelligence coup which introduced a virus into the Iraqi air defence and command and control system.[17] The resulting computer blackout, along with the normal range of jamming capability, allowed the allied airforces to pound the Iraqis for some thirty-nine days. With absolute air superiority established, the allied ground forces went on to rout the Iraqis, inflicting grievous losses at little cost to themselves. The pursuit was called off once the Iraqi mainforce had withdrawn, and Saddam Hussein was allowed to retain his leadership.[18]

The Harnessing of the Media

There can be little doubt that media was used as part of a deception aimed at cloaking the real war aims of the United States. Immediately following the Iraqi invasion of Kuwait, US President George Bush met with General Powell to discuss the military situation. He was called out of that meeting to talk to a press pool and there, according to Woodward, in answer to a reporter's question on whether he was contemplating sending troops, Bush replied, 'I am not contemplating such action'.[19] Yet immediately before that same meeting, Bush had been briefed by Powell and Schwarzkopf on the implementation of either a 'tier one' limited air strike, or the full 90–1002 intervention deployment plan. In fact, the elements identified for a pre-prepared air-attack plan had already been upgraded to alert status and the President had authorised a CIA covert operation to destabilise the Saddam Hussein regime.[20]

As the United Nations had already condemned the Iraqi invasion, the United States was in a position to claim legitimacy for any independent intervention it might mount against Iraq. This would avoid charges that the United States was only pursuing an oil protection policy. Thus the first step towards legitimising American actions lay in the declaration by Bush that the United States had been invited in to 'defend' Saudi Arabia against what he termed 'naked aggression.'[21] This was widely disseminated through White House and Pentagon information networks, and internationally through the United States Information Service (USIS). Yet, as Woodward observes:

> There never seemed any danger of that. For all the talk of Saddam's plans to attack the Kingdom, it never seemed likely. The Iraqi deployment, once Kuwait was taken, was entirely defensive, and the much cited move towards the Saudi border was merely the pushing out of frontlines and tripwires which any prudent commander would undertake when setting up defensive lines. All the evidence was that suggestions of possible moves into Saudi Arabia by the Iraqis was merely propaganda.[22]

Darwish and Alexander go further, claiming that American officials have since admitted that there was '... no evidence to suggest that Saddam Hussein was going to invade Saudi Arabia. In fact, the American move was designed to prevent him, with his missiles pointing at Saudi oilfields, from dictating Arab oil policy and world prices.'[23] Certainly, CIA photographic evidence gave no indication of a force poised to move into the Saudi oilfields.[24] And according to Woodward, despite all the talk of the defence of Saudi Arabia, the allied build-up was clearly aimed at the overthrow of Saddam Hussein.[25] The wider economic and strategic considerations that guided President Bush beyond the simplistic idea of the defence of Saudi Arabia is confirmed by Powell, who has Webster, the CIA Director claiming that:

> The Iraqis are within eight tenths of a mile of the Saudi border. If Saddam stays where he is, he'll own twenty per cent of the world's oil reserves. And a few miles away, he can seize another twenty percent. He'll have easy access to the sea from Kuwaiti ports. Jordan and Yemen will probably tilt towards him, and he'll be in a position to extort the others. We can expect the Arab states to start cutting deals. Iran will be at Iraq's feet. Israel will be threatened.[26]

The transmogrification of this public aim of the 'defence of Saudi Arabia' into the 'liberation of Kuwait', took place almost concurrently with the build-up of the American force to predetermined levels capable of taking offensive action. According to one source, the decision to force Iraq out of Kuwait had been taken as early as 5 August, two days before the meeting with Defense Secretary Cheney and King Fahd at which the invitation to defend Saudi Arabia had been arranged.[27] This was despite evidence that Washington was in receipt of a secret report, commissioned by General Schwarzkopf, that stated that Iraq had by then already begun to withdraw its crack Republican Guard divisions from Kuwait.[28]

By late January, following Iraq's rejection of the United Nations demand to withdraw and abide by the United Nations Resolutions passed since 2 August, the goal posts had once again been moved. This time President Bush claimed that '... the final aim is only now taking shape: the toppling of the Regime and the capture of Mr Saddam Hussein.'[29] At no time was there any official announcement of this extension of American war aims. The change was gradual and was fed to the public in America – and the twenty-eight other allied nations – through the media. As Woodward has observed, the administration knew that it would take seventeen weeks to prepare to defend Saudi Arabia and eight to twelve months for a full offensive capability '... but no one was even hinting that the nation had started down that road.'[30]

A less subtle exploitation of the media came during the build-up, with high profile preparations for a major amphibious landing by the US Marine Corps later revealed as a deliberate deception. As Morris reports it:

> Schwarzkopf also recognised that the work of the media could be beneficial to his cause. He made sure that the media pools were allowed extensive coverage of the Marines' rehearsal assault. As he expected, media military consultants spoke at length on the various TV networks (at least one of which was accessible to the Iraqis) and speculated on the impending assault of occupied Kuwait by naval forces.[31]

There was also a form of passive deception, in the lack of correction of any speculation that aided the United States and its allies. At a press briefing, when asked about the use of the media in this role, Schwarzkopf responded:

> I guess the one thing I would say to the press that I was delighted with is in the very, very early stages of this operation, when we were over here building up, and we didn't have much on the ground, you all had given us credit for a whole lot more over here. As a result, that gave me quite a feeling of confidence that we might not be attacked as quickly as I thought we were going to be attacked. Other than that I would not like to get into the remainder of your question.[32]

This use of the media to further its war aims was not restricted to the United States. Saddam Hussein used the international media to present his case to the Arab world as a *jihad* aimed primarily at Israel. American sources also claim that Saddam invoked local religious sentiments by highlighting damage to mosques.[33] He also used the media to highlight the realities of the collateral damage inflicted by the allied air forces. In doing so, Saddam Hussein successfully 'humanised' the war through haunting television coverage of the civilian casualties, at the expense of the clinical images presented by the Americans. In addition, he emphasised what he described as the neo-imperialist oil policies of the West as the real reason behind the conflict.

The regional media was used by Iraq to enlist support against what Saddam Hussein warned would be the invasion of '... Jewish, and brazen American women soldiers into the holy lands and shrines of Mecca.' He used similar vivid, but nonetheless telling phrases to describe the profligate record of some of the more self-indulgent ruling families of the Arab states.[34] Saddam also exploited the Western media, in particular television, with his clever handling of the hostage situation, which he managed to keep on Western and world television screens for some weeks. This exposure reached its peak when he appeared with the children of hostages.[35]

So sensitive was Saddam Hussein over his image that Darwish and Alexander claim his decision to release the women and children hostages was in response to a taunt by a British woman on British Television that it was '... not very gallant to hide behind women and children.'[36] But he was also inclined to bravado, threatening the 'mother of all battles', a scorched earth policy in defeat, and taunting the Americans that they would be unable to sustain the appalling casualty levels that Iraq had become inured to in its eight year battle with Iran. This strategy was so successful that, according to Darwish and Alexander, it resulted in:

> ... a number of leading retired military figures as well as top strategists (presenting) an intellectual argument against the war based on the possibility of very high casualties amongst allied troops as well as the devastating effect on the world economy of blazing oil wells.[37]

As Ambassador Jean Kirkpatrick put it from the American side, Saddam Hussein had:

> ... pursued this (media) campaign in the United Nations, in foreign capitals and in TV studios around the world. All were targeted with the peace initiative released in the name of the (Iraqi) Revolutionary Command Council.[38]

But while he used the international media for his own propaganda purposes, Saddam Hussein imposed restrictions on Western reporters in Iraq and strictly censored sensitive information such as military casualties. It has been claimed that reporters who stayed, such as Peter Arnett of CNN, were channelled into filming only civilian casualties from allied bombing. The Americans accused Saddam Hussein of staging events for the media, such as the damage to what the Iraqi's claimed was a baby milk factory, and in the use of 'professional passers by': individuals who appeared suspiciously fluent in English both in their command of the language and in the signs they carried.[39]

Finally, there was the unprecedented action of the political leaders of the United States and Iraq broadcasting to the publics in their opposing nations. President Bush's videotaped address, recorded on 12 September and broadcast on 16 September, was relayed uncensored on Iraqi national television. It was, however, followed by a lengthy commentary which, amongst other charges, denounced Bush as a 'liar' who wanted to be '...

dictator of the whole world.'[40] Saddam Hussein, in turn, invited Ted Koppel of ABC (US) News, and Dan Rather of CBS News for interviews and later gave Peter Arnett of CNN a direct interview for world consumption.[41]

In an oddly one-sided response, the American reaction to Iraqi exploitation of the media was one of fury. President Bush enlisted the aid of a specialist media adviser early on to help with what was seen as a propaganda war.[42] But, for the first time, in any conflict, the peoples of both nations were able to watch media coverage, complete with political and military interpretation, of each other's war effort. In the case of Iraq, Saddam Hussein is reported to have watched CNN and other American programs continuously, with much of the coverage being relayed through the Iraqi networks.

For the American viewer, CNN afforded not only comment from the enemy capital, but such vivid imagery and intelligence information as real-time visual confirmation of the air attacks.

CNN and its high-profile reporter, Peter Arnett, are reported to have enraged American military leaders with their coverage of bombing attacks, particularly when CNN reports suggested that the 'baby milk factory' was just what the Iraqi's claimed to be.[43] Few journalists would dispute Arnett. He was after all, an experienced journalist, on the spot, and, as Taylor reports, his network had had the foresight to set up a 'four wire' direct telephone communications system, which allowed continuous independent contact as opposed to the normal operator connected systems with reliance on local power supplies.[44] The Pentagon, however, stuck by its original claim that the factory was a '... facility for biological weapons.'[45] As a result, Arnett suffered some of the opprobrium afforded earlier 'non partisan' commentators, such as Harrison Salisbury in Vietnam. At one time, Arnett was accused in Congress of being an Iraqi sympathiser, a biased reporter during the Vietnam war, and married to a woman whose brother was '... active in the Viet Cong.' These charges, voiced by Senator Alan Simpson, had no foundation.[46] Fortunately, Arnett's reputation, like Salisbury's, was such that he was able to answer his critics.[47] And, as Ted Turner, the head of CNN put it, the network was '... fortunate to have on site, in the most difficult circumstances, a seasoned combat correspondent.'[48]

Still, Arnett's presence in the Iraqi capital was seen by most Western military officers as at least letting down the side. General Peter De La Billiere, the British Force Commander, stated:

> I also found it difficult to accept that Western media had any legitimate role in Baghdad. The principle of a free Press, as I understand it, is that the media report everything which happens.

Reporters in the heart of enemy territory were completely muzzled and could send out only what Saddam Hussein allowed them to. They were, in effect, mouthpieces for the enemy, whose aim was to destroy and kill our own servicemen.[49]

The fact is that, in addition to restricting and, in the case of Iraq, censoring the coverage of the conflict, both sides exploited all branches of the media, both national and international, in a bid to muster support, propagandise, gain intelligence, and influence world opinion by personal and diplomatic signals.

The Press and the Demonisation of Saddam Hussein

While, as previous cases show, it is usual for the media to be harnessed to the will of the government and military in limited conflict, the media war in the Gulf was unprecedented in its intensity. This use, or abuse, of the press showed up particularly strongly in the demonisation of Saddam Hussein – a figure who, only a few years previously, had been supported by the West in Iraq's war against Iran.

This exploitation of the media to demonise an enemy leader is a strategy often pursued as a precursor to limited conflict. In the absence of any direct threat to the home nation, and to justify the conflict as a moral act of liberation, popular outrage must be focused on the leader of the target nation. This was so in the case of General Manuel Noriega in Panama and was again the case with Saddam Hussein in the Gulf. In contrast, from the Iraqi side, there is little evidence of personal vilification of President George Bush or his cabinet. Rather, the Iraqi attack was ideological, with the United States leadership portrayed as 'evil' neo-imperialists and 'lackeys' of the Israelis.[50] But Saddam Hussein went almost overnight from being a friend of the United States to a 'tyrant and brutal dictator.' In his actions, he was portrayed as having 'devoured' Kuwait. This was an interesting depiction in light of the United States' own suspect rationales for going into Vietnam, Grenada and Panama. Saddam was also accused of perpetrating a 'cruel hoax' on the world in his February 1991 offer to withdraw.[51] He was labelled 'an aggressor' and a 'tyrant' who '... shed the blood of his people on the altar of his own ambitions.'[52]

This near instant transmogrification from friend to fiend is perhaps best summed up by the American evidence given to the United Nations Human Rights Commission. In this it was argued that, in addition to being a 'torturer' guilty of 'atrocities', Saddam Hussein:

Took power by assassination, kept it by murder, left hundreds of thousands of dead in a war of aggression against Iran, gassed and obliterated the Kurds, obliterated Kuwait ... oppressed his people through torture, execution and denial of rights and fundamental freedoms ... and now ... (visited) the terror and tragedy of war on his own people by his unjust invasion and occupation of Kuwait.[53]

This line was adopted by the media around the world, and nowhere more than in the Arab nations committed to the United States coalition. Dr Edward Said summed it up:

Today's Arab media are a disgrace, it is difficult now to speak the plain truth in the Arab World. The Egyptian and Saudi press seem almost without exception committed to the destruction of Iraq; their pages permit few demurrals and little trace of reservation or doubt.[54]

Articles vilifying Saddam Hussein appeared in the American, British and Australian media, many by 'special correspondents' and accompanied by line drawings that physically demonised the Iraqi President.[55] The British tabloid press needed no encouragement. The London *Sun* plastered its front page with the headline 'Bastard of Baghdad', referring to the capture of two British pilots, while the *Daily Star* declared 'The bastard is torturing our boys.'[56] British force commander De La Billiere described Saddam Hussein as a brutal dictator who ruled through fear and treated human beings as expendable pawns.[57] General Powell, more aware of the wider media war that was developing, became concerned, hoping to widen the target beyond Saddam:

The demonising made me uneasy, I preferred to talk about the 'Iraqi regime, or the Hussein Regime'... I thought it unwise to elevate public expectations by making the man out to be the devil incarnate and then leave him in place.[58]

President Bush had different ideas, fearful of the political ramifications of peace:

If he'd (Saddam Hussein) pulled out totally from Kuwait and left his forces along the border, we would have been in a terrible bind... The US and its coalition partners would have had to keep a large force in Kuwait, but American public and congressional support would have evaporated[59]

An enthusiastic media backed Bush, caught up in the game of presenting the alternatives in simplistic terms of good and evil. Alan Pizzey of the American CBS network referred to the alleged deliberate release of oil into the Gulf as '... the first time in history that nature has been a direct target.' It was a blinkered view that completely ignored the American defoliation of nearly five million acres of forest in Vietnam.[60]

The Quest for Public Opinion and Legitimacy

With Saddam Hussein recreated as a monster to be destroyed, the United States followed what is now becoming a set pattern in seeking the international legitimacy it needed for its actions. The United Nations was the prime target. This entailed close lobbying of both the General Assembly and the Security Council. The extent of support, however, depended largely on international public opinion and this, in turn, was shaped largely by the media within the home nations.

There can be little doubt that the voluminous background information and opinion-leading articles, provided by the USIS to all branches of the media throughout the coalition countries, directly influenced the tone of media coverage.[61] The result was that the Security Council passed the critical resolution, calling on Iraq to withdraw from Kuwait by 15 January 1991, on a vote of twelve to two, with China abstaining. Once that deadline had expired, the resolution allowed all member states cooperating with Kuwait to

> ... use all necessary means to uphold and implement Security Council Resolution 666 (1990), and all subsequent relevant resolutions, to restore international peace and security in the area.[62]

The United Nations votes, however, were not obtained without cost. According to Draper, the United States wrote off around US$7 billion from Egypt's debts and a further US$6 billion was retired by the Gulf states. Syria gained almost US$3 billion, the Soviet Union received US$1 billion in aid from Saudi Arabia and credit guarantees from the United States, and Turkey was assured US$500 million a year in military aid. Yemen had US$70 million annual aid from the United States cut off for voting the wrong way. It can be assumed that these examples were followed in other cases.[63]

The media took little note of the fact that, once the United States had obtained the legitimacy it needed, the United Nations was relegated to the back seat. Indeed, once the United Nations mandate had been achieved, and once the coalition was established, all of the United States official media information concentrated on the United States leadership of the war.[64] As previously noted, however, the information effort was not all one-sided and Saddam Hussein's Ministry of Information was not new to media manipulation.[65]

The Saudis also sought to influence media coverage of the conflict and hired the prestigious firm of Hill Knowlton for a total of nearly US$12 million to sell their side of the story. The hiring was done by an American-based group called Citizens for a Free Kuwait. As a senior executive of Hill Knowlton later put it, the campaign had the simple objective of making sure that there was adequate public support for Desert Shield and the subsequent operation Desert Storm. Publicity techniques included press conferences showing torture and other abuses by Iraqis, distribution of tens of thousands of 'Free Kuwait' T-shirts and bumper stickers, the organisation of university rallies, and the saying of special prayers in churches. Hill Knowlton developed programs for government officials, businessmen and – after Saddam Hussein released oil into the Gulf – environmentalists. According to the company, President Bush was 'kept informed' of what was being done.[66]

One of the publicity stories emerging from this process resulted in worldwide media coverage of claims that Iraqi soldiers had thrown babies out of incubators in the brutal takeover of a Kuwaiti hospital. The story was taken as fact by Amnesty International and Congress. There were further reports that photographs of the 'atrocities' had been displayed in Congress and journalists could only cringe when the stories were later revealed as complete fabrications.[67] The reports however, were eagerly taken up by the media at the time. Only when the star witness was found to be the daughter of the Kuwaiti Ambassador to the United States, and no hard evidence was forthcoming, was the story dropped.[68] It was later revealed that out of the US$12 million paid to Hill Knowlton, only US$17,861 was coughed up by the 'Citizens', the remaining US$11,852,329 being paid by the Kuwaiti government.[69]

Radio also played an important role in forming opinion, since it knows no physical or geographical boundaries. In the Gulf it was used especially for 'black' propaganda and psychological warfare. Taylor reports that in the Gulf war the 'black' broadcasts

> ... appeared to be emanating from disaffected groups inside Iraq and Kuwait, when in fact they were coming from transmitters within coalition-controlled areas.'[70]

Such stations, and others operating under names such as 'Voice of Free Iraq', 'Radio Free Iraq', and the Kuwaiti-based 'Voice of the Gulf', are believed to have been sponsored by the CIA. They played a major part in the demonisation of Saddam Hussein and his government, as well as in calls for uprisings and rebellion by religious and ethnic minority groups. They also broadcast calls for surrender to individual units.

During the American deployment, the Voice of America (VOA) broadcast news reports to the Arab world fifteen hours a day in Arabic and eighteen hours a day around the world in English. VOA also broadcast continuously in Arabic on the same frequency as Radio Baghdad. Because of their proximity in Dhahran and the strength of transmission, these VOA programs could be heard by any Iraqi who had a transistor radio. The Iraqis retaliated by jamming American broadcasts on 3 August 1991. According to Shulman, however, by September it had given up the unequal task. Radio Baghdad attempted a similar offensive campaign, with the 'black' Holy Mecca Radio and the overt Iraqi 'Voice of Peace' station.

The Iraqis also attempted to flood the Arab world with short wave signals and transmitted two hours a day on shortwave to North America. But almost all of these stations went off the air within a very short time. Overall, the limited Iraqi effort was swamped by the American and other allied outputs, notably the French and British overseas services.[71]

The importance of the media in forging the image of an enemy in the absence of any real national threat, and the exploitation of the media in fostering and maintaining national and international support, cannot be overstated in limited conflict. As Virginia Trioli summed up the situation in the Gulf for *The Age* (Melbourne):

> At a time when nations are involved in a war of such appalling consequence and terror that their need to know the truth is of dire importance, the media doesn't believe the military and some members of the public do not trust the media.[72]

In the Gulf, millions of dollars were spent by both sides on propaganda aimed at achieving popular support and international legitimacy, with most of the effort directed towards the media. Such action emerges as a continuing thread in our case studies and seems likely to be a feature of future limited conflicts.

The Media on the Battlefield

Immediately the Gulf conflict erupted, the Pentagon Pool system (Department of Defense National Media Pool) for managing media on the battlefield was swamped by reporters who wanted to cover the conflict.

The Pool was a small but practised organisation. It had been deployed during the naval response to an earlier Gulf crisis in July 1987 and its availability had been honed in a number of practice callout drills.[73] It was evident from the outset, however, that the Iraqi invasion of Kuwait had the potential to be a major news story, and the Pool system quickly came under legal challenge on the grounds that the exclusion of non-pool media was unconstitutional unless the military could show a bona fide security justification for their action.

The challenge was mounted in the United States District Court in New York by a group of nine news organisations and four journalists who argued that the 'security' provisions were no more than a cover designed to allow the military to manipulate the media.[74] The journalists involved were banned by the military for their pains, but it hardly mattered because, within hours of launching the largest military attack since World War II, the official system for supporting reporters who were covering the operation had collapsed.[75]

When President Bush first ordered the troops into the Gulf on 8 August 1990, Secretary of Defense Cheney refused to allow reporters to accompany them. In the face of intense media criticism, however, he relented and, on 13 August, a pool of seventeen reporters accompanied by six media escorts was authorised.

Despite this apparent change in policy, the United States military followed the pattern that had emerged from the previous involvements in Grenada and Panama, and imposed a blackout on the first thirty six hours of the war. There is little doubt that this was a conscious media-management decision. Andreacchio, who served under Schwarzkopf, claims that Vietnam was the catalyst. Andreacchio noted that there had always been friction between the media and the military:

> ... but during Vietnam, it had turned ugly. Virtually every officer in military service blames the media for the American defeat in Vietnam. While we were fighting the Viet Cong, the media was fighting us. We won the battles with the VC, but lost them with the media.[76]

Schwarzkopf, Andreacchio claims, was a typical military officer who would have shared those views: 'Although he'd probably never admit it publicly, he takes a sceptical view of the media. Sure he'll smile from the platform but his real feelings surface the instant a reporter gets a little pushy.'[77] His British subordinate, General De La Billiere, took a more open approach, drawing on his experiences in the Falklands. He felt that, while the media presented difficulties, the drawbacks were outweighed by their role in mustering political and public support on the domestic front.[78]

But the Vietnam experience dominated and, from a military perspective, the media was seen to present a danger. Based on the lessons of Vietnam, it was assumed that a prolonged war on television would quickly become insupportable. According to Woodward, General Powell believed that such a televised war would:

> ... instantly bringing home the action, death, consequences and emotions even more graphically than during Vietnam. The reporters and the cameras would be there to record each step, vastly complicating all military tasks.[79]

Instead, it was decided that the world's publics would see a very limited and antiseptic version of the war. The media would be kept away. Even videos from the gun cameras showing attacks were going to be distortions when they were made public, so that '... the terror of combat would not be heard by the public.'[80]

On their arrival in the theatre of operations, the United States media team set up the Joint Information Bureau (JIB), to handle the media from a base in Dhahran.[81] Journalists were formed into 'pools' or Media Reporting Teams (MRTs). This initial system broke down as the action in the Gulf increased in scope and intensity, and with the arrival of increasing numbers of journalists. By the thirty day mark, the media contingent had grown to more than 800, rising to over 1,600 by the eve of the ground war. Because of the increasing numbers, new pools were instituted, but only 131 reporters were allotted to them. The remainder had to rely on what the pools produced and what the military fed them.[82] The coordination of the pools was later handed over to the journalists themselves, resulting, says Fialka, in '... an internal fighting that never stopped.'[83] Schwarzkopf also imposed strong security and travel restrictions on the non-pool media. According to Morris:

> Those not assigned to pools would have access to several military briefings held in Riyadh, one by CENTCOM and two others by British and Saudi commands. In addition, unaired background briefings were provided to the media. Otherwise, *travel within the theatre of operations by media reps was prohibited.* (Emphasis added)[84]

Colonel David Hackworth, a much decorated veteran and probably the most successful of all media representatives who covered the Gulf, said that units were instructed to treat unescorted media as hostile. As a non-pool member, Hackworth complained that he had '... more guns pointed at (him) in two months by the military who were into controlling the press than (he) had in all (his) years of actual combat, all of them American.'[85]

Guidelines for the media were initially instituted on 7 January 1991, concurrent with the arrival of the first pool. The guidelines reflected the voluntary arrangements recommended in the Sidle report and spelled out twelve categories of information that should not be reported. These included troop numbers and weapon systems, details of future operations, rules of engagement details, all intelligence matters, troop deployments and locations, and the effectiveness or otherwise of the enemy. They also banned information on air activities and the activities of special forces, tactics, search and rescue systems, information on friendly capabilities, tactics, and possible losses.[86]

A week later, the instructions were superseded by supplementary guidelines which spelled out how information could be gathered. These said that all interviews had to be conducted in the presence of a military escort and all copy, videotape and photographs had to be cleared by a security review system prior to transmission. Appeals could be taken first to the JIB and then directly to the Pentagon. In the case of continued dispute, the choice whether to publish or not lay with the media outlet. In reality, such a decision would involve news that would by then be stale. Perhaps the most important provision in the supplementary guidelines, however, was that they explicitly forbade any non-pool reporters access to forward areas.[87]

The rationale behind these restrictions relied on the familiar claims of 'operational security' and 'the safety of the media.' In a survey conducted by the New York based *Freedom Foundation*, the majority of correspondents said they had at some point violated the guidelines, with 68 per cent saying they knew colleagues who had done so. One respondent went so far as to say that anyone who said they did not was a liar.[88]

According to Powell, each of the two principal spokesmen, Lieutenant General Tom Kelly in the Pentagon, and the Deputy Director of Operations at Schwarzkopf's HQ, Brigadier Richard Neal, were carefully selected after exhaustive 'auditions'. Kelly, because he came across as Norm in the sitcom *Cheers*, and 'Butch' Neal, because he projected a sense of 'unflinching honesty'.[89] Morris says it was Neal's experiences with the body count system in Vietnam that caused him to disallow any questions on casualties.[90] But the military also complained about the quality of the media, a charge echoed by Hackworth who described some of them colourfully as not knowing 'a tank from a turd.'[91]

Under the military pool system however, even the uninformed-informed and unsuitable could claim their place in a pool when their turn came around. Fialka, who spent almost five months in the Gulf, claims that this practice was exemplified by the presence of a reporter from a women's magazine who spent her time writing about the sex lives of the female soldiers and the drugs used by medical units.[92] Fialka also points to at least three instances of 'out of pool' status and communications priority being extended to favoured reporters.[93]

It is doubtful that the military was greatly concerned over the lack of hard reporting from the Gulf, as neither Washington nor Riyadh welcomed the media coverage of the war in the first place. In fact, as Powell revealed later:

> Early in the buildup the Saudis made a simple announcement. They were not going to allow any reporters into their country. That we knew, could not stand. You do not send nearly half a million Americans, plus thousands of other nationals, halfway around the world to prepare for a major war and then impose a news blackout.[94]

Yet this, of course, subject to the allowance of favourable, or self provided coverage, was exactly what the military wanted. Schwarzkopf originally echoed these feelings, he was instrumental in rebuffing a second, later call by the Saudis for the withdrawal of all reporters. It was crucial, he said, '... not to repeat the mistake we'd made in Grenada, where the military had stonewalled.' This time, it would be different, and he laid out rules for his own dealings with the media, including one that said 'Don't ever lie to the American people'.[95] In practice however, these ideals did not last long in the face of what were seen as more pressing military and political imperatives. Schwarzkopf in particular was worried about the security issue, echoing the Duke of Wellington, when he complained at the time that '... I was also convinced that our own newspaper and TV reports had become Iraq's best source of military intelligence.'[96]

But because of the scale and duration of the operation in the Gulf, the military was unable to implement the outright initial exclusion of the media that had been used with such success in Grenada and Panama. But, based on the general thinking that media coverage should be limited, they did the next best thing and imposed a policy of containment, exploiting to the full the difficult nature of the terrain and the resulting media reliance on the military for mobility and communications. This is reflected in the comments of journalists surveyed on the level of censorship, with the majority of them stating that limited access was the biggest barrier to timely and accurate reporting.[97] And there is little doubt that this attitude reflected the Bush administration's views on the way the conflict should be reported. According to a study done by *The New York Times* after the conflict:

> President Bush and his inner circle had vowed from the start of the deployment to the Persian Gulf in mid-August to manage the information flow in a way that supported their political goals, quoting Secretary Cheney as saying that, I look on it as a model of how the Department ought to function ... The system provided better coverage than any other war in history.[98]

Indeed, it was a public relations triumph from the official point of view. As Peter Robinson, a noted Australian defence correspondent, summed it up at the beginning of the campaign:

> We are in essence being asked to believe that nothing has gone wrong, that a perfect military operation has proceeded without pain to the personnel involved, that there are no tensions between a variety of tenuously linked allies and that there are no problems of supply or command structures which might seriously inhibit the effectiveness of the UN supported force.[99]

Most of the media agreed with this interpretation of the coverage of the war, and journalists began to complain, in both Washington and the field. They complained that the pool system had tilted the balance of power in favour of the military. The use of the pool system and limitations on access had made the military *de facto* assignment editors. It allowed the military to choose what reporters would be able to see and when and where they would be able to see it.[100]

In theory, the bigger pools were to have been rotated among the bigger units, while a 'rapid reaction' group would be whisked from place to place as the battle developed.[101] But, in practice, the system opened the door to a form of indirect censorship never before seen on the battlefield. As Judd Rose of ABC news complained, instead of covering the B–52 bombing effort, journalists were shunted off to cover the 'unsung heroes' of the motor pool.

Another problem was the regular briefings by the military that took on a life of their own. The briefings proved immensely popular with home audiences, giving the impression that the public was getting the news straight from the horse's mouth. In reality, the sessions were so stage managed that they gave the media little chance to probe or analyse. They also had the effect of undermining the credibility of the media. As MacArthur points out, the public was not slow in contrasting the purposeful and self assured military briefers with the bumbling and un-informed media.[102] The situation became so bad that the American television program *Saturday Night Live* aired a skit satirising the performance of the press corps and lauding the military.[103] To General Powell, there was '... a touch of truth behind the hilarity', and the skit was '... proof that we had won the battle for public opinion'.[104]

Events like the coverage of the motor pool were staged because of the absolute blackout on coverage of sensitive issues such as the B–52 bombing missions.[105] There was also manipulation and implied censorship in the selective release of the official television footage from combat aircraft, which formed a major part of the television coverage. As *Newsweek*, put it:

> They selected highlights from the most successful missions. Reporters were not shown tapes of bombs or missiles that went astray. And no one, except the Iraqi victims, witnessed the old fashioned onslaught of the giant B–52 bombers dumping loads of bombs on troops cowering in their bunkers. The B–52s attacked targets that were outside the range of television's prying eye.[106]

This 'sanitised' approach to coverage was encouraged, in complete contrast to the blanket ban on the bloody effect that the weapons had on those at the receiving end. Military spokesmen referred to 'targets' which, although they contained living people, were presented to audiences like images in a video game. The sanitisation was even more pronounced when it came to friendly casualties. Reporters were not allowed to photograph any allied wounded soldier without the consent of the patient, the doctor and the soldier's commanding officer. The fact that this permission would not be given was evidenced by the charge that one divisional commander would not allow photographs of any of his troops unless they had their helmets on and their chinstraps buckled.[107] Further, reporters were not allowed to record any visual or audio footage of any personnel '... in agony or severe shock.'[108] At home, in the United States, there was a matching ban on recording the arrival of coffins at Dover Air Force Base. When the ban was challenged on constitutional grounds by the American Civil Liberties Union, the court decided that access should be denied on the basis that the arrival of dead soldiers presented a risk to national security.[109]

The security guidelines issued by the military were also challenged by journalists. Although the Pentagon responded with their usual promises to review the rules, they remained substantially unchanged. In some cases, according to Hackworth, the restrictions were actually increased.[110] In addition, the rules were enforced by a local memorandum that threatened reporters with deportation, or even death, if they went within 99 kilometres (62 miles) of the Saudi/Kuwaiti border without a military escort.[111] The biggest complaint, however, was that once they had submitted their copy for review, the journalists lost control of it. The military had absolute control over the movement of copy and had the ability to delay transmission for unspecified periods of time. Gettler quotes the *Washington Post*'s veteran foreign correspondent as saying '... they don't know how to transmit copy like I don't know how to drive a tank.'[112]

The military further banned reporters from driving their own vehicles and outlawed cellular phones or other independent means of transmission. These rules were strictly enforced by the escorts. When reporters asked to use the Saudi phone system, this was declared 'off limits' because of a 'terrorist threat.'[113]

The individual complaints by journalists are too numerous to list and there is little doubt that they represent only the tip of the iceberg. They include roadblocks being ordered to turn media back at all times despite the presence of escorts and prior permission being given, the detention of reporters by individual units, delays in transmission of copy, staged interviews and events, and inexperienced and even hostile escorts. Particular reporters were banned from press conferences for asking questions that were deemed to be 'out of bounds' by the escorts or briefing officers. According to one report '... the antics of the escorts and public affairs officers would have made a Marx Brothers movie.'[114] But the most frequent complaint was the denial of access to allied casualties and religious services, and the limitations on pool access. Few complained about the security reviews. Rather, journalists viewed the reviews as unnecessary, since they themselves had used common sense in protecting operational security. Instead, the issue for reporters was the prior restraint of limiting access to specific areas. Other journalists complained of an excessive, and sometimes 'silly' use of security classification for routine information. A more serious charge was a loosening of the guidelines in order to achieve 'positive' coverage or the tendency of escorts to silence individual soldiers when it was perceived there might be a problem. Delay was the overriding problem, coupled with a multi-tiered review system.[115] Another more insidious form of censorship was achieved by allowing the Saudi government to control the issue of visas to the media. Initially the Saudi policy was to issue only one to each organisation, but this was later reversed after strong representations to Washington.[116] Fialka relates incident after incident in which reporters were hampered or frustrated. These range from outright inefficiency and malice on the part of the military, to actual physical violence.[117] As Draper interprets it, '... so many reporters went though the same ordeals that they take on a systematic character.'[118]

Hackworth took issue with the kitting out of journalists with all the paraphernalia of the military, claiming that some, as a result, '... fell in love with the Army.' The escorts, or 'thought police', as Hackworth termed them, approved of this as encouraging 'positive bonding.'[119]

In complaining about the fact that Defense Public Relations was more interested in propaganda than fact, Robert Manof, the Director of the United States-based Centre for War, Peace and News Media, argued that operations in Saudi Arabia were managed like an American political campaign with imagery as the dominant concern.[120] Hackworth was more direct:

> I was very unhappy with the military's paranoia and their thought police who control the press. Although I managed to get out on my own, we didn't have the freedom of movement to make an independent assessment of what the military was all about. Everything was spoon fed. We were like animals in a zoo and the press officers were the zookeepers who threw us a piece of meat occasionally.[121]

Despite these limitations, Hackworth managed not only to accurately predict the outcome of the war as a non-pool correspondent, but to do it within the first two or three days. On the other hand, the military had been harsh in the controls they placed on themselves. So important did they see the media as a weapon to be exploited in the transmission of diplomatic signals, that the newly installed Chief of the United States Air Force, General Michael Dugan, was sacked by Defense Secretary Cheney for talking to the press out of turn. Dugan's crime was his admission that the military had targeted Saddam Hussein and his family. Among the reasons listed for Dugan's dismissal by Cheney were '... the potential revelation of classified information, the acceptance of assassination as a weapon and the discussion of operational plans.'[122] Dugan's response was that he was ambushed by a media he was trying to court, his words were taken out of context, and a background brief was relayed as firm policy.[123] The hard facts are that Dugan was sacked because he interfered with the delicate diplomatic signalling going on at that time. There is evidence, however, that Dugan's hard line, combined with his sacking, led the Iraqis to revise their belief that the United States would not go to war.[124]

The way that the media was stage managed, controlled and manipulated in the Gulf war had no precedent in any previous conflict. Hackworth has described the situation as a media triumph for the military and the administration, '... a lovely bloodless, corpseless war, just the sort the politicians love.'[125] Nothing was said of the enormous casualties suffered by the Iraqi forces. Indeed, casualty numbers were suppressed by *both* sides in their political interests.

Despite the growing technological superiority, reach and immediacy of the global media – advantages which should have allowed the press to break free of the military – the media was kept largely in the dark through the exercise of these policies. Censorship as such was not even necessary. In fact, only 0.035 per cent of the reports filed during and after the war had to be sent to Washington for review. Of these, according to the Pentagon, only one was changed. There was no need. The media simply did not have access to the battlefield. An executive of the American Broadcasting Corporation, Walter Porges, who reviewed the pooled television coverage of the war, is quoted by Fialka as saying, 'I guess you could call it censorship by lack of access... There were a couple of big battles that nobody's seen any pictures of yet'.[126]

No one except the military was allowed to film or witness the awesome destruction wreaked by the B–52s on static positions, or what some saw as the unnecessary pounding afforded the retreating Iraqi forces as they withdrew from Kuwait.[127] No one saw the major tank battles.[128] No one witnessed the casualties from friendly fire that were ten times higher than those recorded in any other war fought by American forces.[129] No one was allowed to witness or report the death and destruction.

'There were no dead Iraqi soldiers', said Donald Mell, a photo editor for Associated Press. According to Fialka, Mell, reviewed thousands of photographs taken by over forty photographers on the battlefield. He observed, 'It was what we didn't get that bothers me... We had these massive tank battles, but I did not see a picture of an American tank being fired during the whole thing.'[130] Even the officially released, carefully sanitised and selected footage, such as the images shot through aircraft gun-cameras, was a distortion. In media terms, the war was reduced to little more than a high technology video game which never showed the bloody end results or failures. It might have been great television and grand theatre, and it might have delighted the government and the military, but it was not journalism. It was a new, passive form of censorship and manipulation, more dangerous and more threatening to the public's right to know and the media's duty to inform than has ever been seen before. In the words of the US News and World Report team, if anyone lost the war besides the Iraqi army, it was the press:

> Disorganised, anarchic by nature and chronically competitive among themselves, the news reporters were no match for the machine of the US Central Command and the Pentagon ... As a result, the news that came from the Persian Gulf was the news the

military wanted presented ... Many reporters seethed with the knowledge that their coverage was inadequate. But they simply could not get to the story to cover it.[131]

The problem was that defence and defence reporting had simply gone out of fashion. As Peter Braestrup put it:

With the end of the draft in 1972 and the influx of women into journalism, the culture gap between journalists and the U.S. military had widened greatly since Vietnam. Increasingly, tactics, logistics, weaponry, and military language had become as foreign to most American reporters – and their lower echelon bosses – as the basics of American football were to, say, Kuwaitis.[132]

As Macarthur put it, 'Few did not count Desert Storm as a devastating and immoral victory for military censorship and a crushing defeat for the press'. But as he went on to say, few American journalists complained at the time and fewer still were capable of meeting the military on their own terms.[133] According to Fialka, most were mentally prepared to cover another Vietnam where reporters could shift, unescorted from unit to unit as the action dictated. Most of us he said,

... were not prepared for a war of total rapid movement over dynamic trackless, extremely dangerous battlefield, where someone without tactical vehicles, navigation equipment, military radios and protection could easily get lost or killed.[134]

The Unfolding of the Truth

It is only now that evidence presented by the American media is beginning to show the extent to which the press *was* kept blindfolded and gagged. As happened during the Falklands, Grenada and Panama, the earlier sweeping claims of complete military success are now being revised.

According to a report by the Congressional House Armed Services Committee, Iraq's total order of battle of 43 Divisions was actually around 34 per cent under-strength. Instead of the Pentagon's estimate of an enemy force level of 540,000, or the 623,000 claimed by General Schwarzkopf, there were probably less than 300,000 Iraqis, and only 50,000 front line troops.[135] According to Representative Les Aspin, the Chairman of the House Armed Services Committee, the total enemy facing the 700,000 coalition troops could have been as low as 180,000.[136]

These revised estimates are in sharp contrast to the picture – disseminated by the Pentagon throughout the build-up phase in Saudi Arabia – of more than half a million Iraqi troops facing the allies over a well prepared defensive line. It also undermines the pre-emptive warnings issued to the press that allied troops would face heavy losses in a head-on campaign.

The earlier estimates of the Pentagon and Central Command, that 100,000 Iraqi soldiers died during the war, are also open to doubt. US News staff, using credible calculations based on accepted kill/casualty ratios, estimated that, given force levels of a quarter of a million, the Iraqis would have suffered only 12,500 to 25,000 casualties and from 3000 to 8000 killed during the hostilities.[137] While the numbers are not small, they are well below the earlier official claims.

Another area where figures were drastically revised was in the performance of some of the precision guided munitions, in particular the Patriot anti-missile system that starred in the television imagery of the war. At the time of the conflict, the Pentagon claimed that 45 out of the 47 Patriot engagements had been successful, a kill rate of around 96 per cent. By April 1993, the estimate had been revised to a probable 52 per cent success rate, with the Pentagon highly confident of that assessment in only 27 per cent of engagements. Using more rigorous criteria than the United States military radar data that accepted proximity as a 'kill', the American General Accounting Office (GAO) reduced the success rate to 9 per cent.[138] In later evidence to Congress, the Congressional Research Service stated that, even when using the Army's own criteria, they could only confirm that no Scud warhead had been destroyed by a Patriot missile.[139] Later, in the subsequent unclassified report to Congress in April 1992, entitled *Conduct of the Persian Gulf War*, Defence Secretary Cheney admitted only to the fact that the Patriot system 'helped' counter the Scud missile threat.[140]

Other claims of success were made which, in retrospect, could hardly have been supported by military intelligence at the time. In January 1992, General Schwarzkopf announced on the American television program *Meet the Press*, that all thirty of the Iraqi Scud missile fixed launching sites had been destroyed by bombing and that '... as many as 16 mobile launchers – out of an estimated 20 – had been destroyed.' In fact, out of the total fifty fixed and mobile Scud launchers the Iraqis had on their order of battle, a total of eighty-one were reportedly wiped out by the time the war ended – at least according to the official military press briefings.[141]

In addition, the claim by the US Air Force, based on actual combat footage, that they had destroyed four mobile Scud launchers in one sortie

– footage which was widely run on American and world television – was later found to have been an attack on Jordanian fuel tankers. The military was soon alert to the falseness of this claim, as the original video tape evidence was refuted within days by Pentagon analysts using computer enhancement. Yet at no time was there any retreat from the official line. As Powell states:

> The next day our photo reconnaissance experts came to me with pictures that were hard to deny, four burned-out hulls of tanker trucks, certainly not Scuds. I let the story stand, without correcting it. Norm's (Schwarzkopf) burdens were so heavy and preserving his equanimity so important that I did not want to undercut him.

It was left to a CNN camera crew to provide the proof when they filmed the destroyed vehicles from ground level.[142]

Post-operational reports by the United Nations Special Commission charged with the destruction of Iraq's weaponry indicate that only twelve Scud missile fixed launching sites were actually destroyed and that no missiles were destroyed by allied bombing during the war.[143]

As with the campaigns in the Falklands, Grenada and Panama, where tight media control had been exercised, it was only well after the event, when the public interest had waned, that claims of success were revised downward. This often occurred in the light of new and compelling evidence, the result of fine investigative reporting. But, as in those earlier conflicts, the later revisions counted for little when compared to the political benefits of the first, official images. And unpleasant as it may be to accept, the polls show that Americans, buoyed by the jingoism that has become a feature of limited conflict, initially supported the concept of restrictions on the media at the time of the Gulf war, as they had during Grenada and Panama. According to Fialka, polls taken by the Gallup Organisation and Princeton Survey Research in January 1991 showed that a substantial majority of Americans felt the media coverage made it harder for the United States to prosecute the war. Americans also felt that the press was not overly controlled by the military and an astounding 79 per cent supported military censorship.[144] Only when the full story became known did the figures change and people begin to question the wider issues of the public's right to know.

The fact that the public is still amenable to the patriotic jingoism of the past, and that this patriotism overcomes wider considerations, has not been lost on the politicians. It was certainly not lost on President Bush, whose popularity soared dramatically as a war leader, just as Prime Minister Margaret Thatcher's had in the Falklands campaign.[145]

The Media Response

The American media kept a close watch on the development of the Pentagon Pool and made major representations to the government over what they saw as deficiencies in the deployment of the pool during the earlier Gulf naval crisis.[146] There was also a continued and increasing level of complaint from the mainly American media throughout the Gulf war, both in the field and in Washington. The battle continues. Major submissions have been made to the United States government by the Ad Hoc Media Group and the American Society of Newspaper Editors. The Inter American Press Association has also issued a major statement condemning the Gulf war censorship on constitutional grounds. The general line of complaint has been in the delay and control over information, and concern that these practices should not be perpetuated. Thus, in a letter to Defence Secretary Cheney on 25 June 1991, the Ad Hoc Media Group stated:

> We believe that the Pentagon Pool arrangements during Operation Desert Storm made it impossible for reporters and photographers to tell the public the full story of the war in a timely fashion. We believe it is imperative that the Gulf war not serve as a model for future coverage.[147]

The letter was accompanied by a comprehensive factual account of obstacles encountered by members of the media in the Gulf. The Ad Hoc Media Group also forwarded a set of ten principles which they believed should govern future arrangements for news coverage of the United States military in combat. These stated:

1   Independent reporting will be the principal means of coverage of US military operations.
2   The use of pools should be limited to the kind envisioned by the Sidle Commission. Pools are meant to bring a representative group of journalists along with the first elements of any major US military operation. These pools should last no longer than the very first stages of a deployment, the initial 24–36 hours, and should be disbanded in favour of independent coverage. Pools are not to serve as the standard means of covering US forces.
3   Some pools may be appropriate for events or in places where open coverage is physically impossible. But the existence of such special purpose pools will not cancel the principle of independent coverage. If news organisations are able to cover pooled events independently, they may do so.

4 Journalists in combat zones will be credentialled by the US military and will be required to abide by a clear set of military security guidelines that protect US forces and their operations. Violations of the guidelines can result in suspension of credentials or revocation of credentials and expulsion from the combat zone.

5 Journalists will be provided access to all major military units.

6 Military public affairs officers should act as liaison but should not interfere with the reporting process.

7 News material, words and pictures, will not be subject to prior military security review.

8 The military will be responsible for the transportation of pools. Field commanders should be instructed to permit journalists to ride on military vehicles and aircraft wherever feasible.

9 The military will provide PAOs (Public Affairs Officers) with timely, secure, compatible transmission facilities for pool material and will make these facilities available whenever possible for filing independent coverage. In cases when government facilities are unavailable, journalists will, as always, file by any other means available and will not be prevented from doing so. The military will not ban communications systems operated by news organisations.

10 These principles will apply as well to operations of the standing DOD National Media Pool System.[148]

The principles were in turn adopted by the American Society of Newspaper Editors, which sent a letter to Defense Secretary Cheney endorsing the principles and reiterating fears that '... the press experiences of the Gulf War must never be repeated.' The Society went on to say that, in the Gulf, the media simply did not have the freedom of movement and access needed to provide the independent observation and accountability which was its responsibility.[149]

The American Society of Newspaper Editors also advised of moves for a meeting of major media groups later in that year to formalise further representations. At their annual meeting held in May 1991, the President of the Society, Burl Osborne, had put the position that the press had been 'clobbered' during the Gulf, but warned that the American people generally supported the sort of strict controls that had led to this situation. The problem, Osborn said, was that '... we, the press failed to persuade people that timely first hand reporting will in the long run best serve the public interest and that we do understand the need for military security.'[150]

Michael Gettler of the *Washington Post* summed up the overall view of the media, observing that the flow of information to the public was generally '... blocked, impeded or diminished by the practices of the Defence Department.' The press, according to Gettler was never allowed to tell the full story.[151]

The response was as expected. No official comment from the Defense Department or the Pentagon, other than Cheney's statement that 'If we had to do it tomorrow, I would start with what we've just done.'[152] Although Cheney suggested that the government might be willing to listen to recommendations, the military conceded nothing. Brigadier Neal, the military's official spokesman in Riyadh, had already spelled it out: 'I can tell you, the pool system is here to stay.'[153]

The hardline attitude prevailed in the new guidelines, produced in May 1992, after eight months of negotiations between the Defence Department and senior staff of some twenty news organisations. In the end it was agreed that 'open and independent reporting' would be the principal means of coverage during future conflicts involving United States forces. The media, for its part, undertook to field better prepared correspondents in the future. Yet despite these and other recommendations reminiscent of the Sidle Report, it was accepted that '... even under conditions of open coverage, pools may be appropriate for specific events, such as when at extremely remote locations or where space is limited.' It was agreed that pools should be as large as possible and should be disbanded as quickly as possible. But the old concepts of operational security and the safety of news teams still prevailed.[154]

The painless, bloodless, sanitised success in the Gulf had its political benefits, a fact not lost on politicians. A poll taken in Australia the day after Prime Minister Hawke's statement releasing Royal Australian Navy ships for offensive action with the allied task force, revealed that 80 per cent of respondents supported his actions; 70 per cent were still in favour a month later, in February.[155] Polls in Great Britain showed 56 per cent support for the war, with only 13 per cent against the use of British forces.[156]

In August 1990, 60 per cent of American voters approved the way in which President Bush was handling his job. The onset of the Gulf crisis added twelve percentage points to this tally, with three Americans out of four expressing their approval for the President.[157] Interestingly, public support for the President's stance had fallen to under 50 per cent by November 1990,[158] but it soared once the battle was underway; 79 per cent of Americans approved the decision to attack and 70 per cent believed the war should have been prosecuted into Iraq.[159]

The American public also generally approved of the way in which the administration and the military were handling the media. A survey on public attitudes to the general concept of censorship indicated that opinion had been evenly divided on the issue since the mid-1980s. During the Gulf conflict, that opinion changed, however, with a two-to-one majority approving the statement that '... military censorship is more important than the media's ability to report important news.'[160] Against this background of support it is difficult to see why any government would wish to change what to them is a winning formula.

Given the apparent political gains to be made from assertive military action, many would argue that a bid to boost presidential popularity lay behind the July 1993 US missile attacks on selected intelligence targets in Baghdad.[161] The twenty-four Tomahawk cruise missile attack was ordered by President Bill Clinton – on the basis of 'compelling evidence' – in retaliation for an alleged Iraqi-sponsored threat on the life of former President George Bush during his April visit to Kuwait.[162] Despite the highly publicised reports from Iraq of civilian damage and even the death of a leading Iraqi artist, public opinion polls by CNN showed overwhelming support for the President's action. Two thirds of those polled voiced their support, with only 23 per cent disapproving.[163] President Clinton gained the added bonus of defusing concern over his attitude to the military who remember his anti-Vietnam stance and who are still smarting over his support for homosexuals within the forces.

Conclusion

The immediate conclusion is that, in the Gulf conflict, the military followed the familiar pattern of deliberately denying media access to the earliest phase of operations, followed by a policy of media containment and limitation. As before, the carefully thought out voluntary programs for media military cooperation were overridden by the political imperatives for a controlled media. Again, the military exploited to the full the advantages inherent in an expeditionary campaign in remote and inhospitable terrain with little local infrastructure. This, along with the distances involved and the speed of the operation, forced the media to rely on the military for transport, maintenance, communications and access. And it allowed the military to dictate terms. When combined with the restrictions imposed by the guidelines – which allowed the military to limit coverage of negative issues and gave them the right of review – the military was able to control what the media was allowed to see, and where and when they could see it. This power was enhanced by the military's ability to delay transmission of copy because of their near monopoly of communications.

The subjugation of the media was matched by the proactive involvement of the military in the provision of selected pre-edited and positive news to all branches of the media. As a result, the military was able to control the media image of the conflict. More importantly, it was able to control the vital first image. The end result was that, despite thousands of feet of television footage and the deployment of the latest technology, major battles went unreported. The realities of war and any real analysis was foregone in favour of a politically acceptable, sanitised war which showed nothing but success.

It was evident too that the military used the media not only to present its own policies in the best possible light, but to deceive and misinform the Iraqis. The main weapon of censorship, that of limitation of access, was widespread enough to point to a secret agenda at all levels of command, to minimise the impact of the media. The media was well prepared with the latest high technology equipment, but the potential of that equipment was negated by delays in security reviews and access. In addition, the military held the reserve power of electronic jamming should it have been necessary.

The media itself was unprepared for war. It was divided by competition and could not deploy the expertise in defence that it routinely maintained in other specialist areas. While there were some instances of excellent analysis, all too often the media fell into the trap of reflecting the administration's chosen policy line. This was demonstrated particularly in the demonisation of Saddam Hussein. Finally, and perhaps most disturbingly, the public once again was quick to lend its initial approval to military and government restrictions imposed on the media, in the face of outdated perceptions of the duties of the citizen in time of conflict.

Both the administration and the military clearly benefited from this control. As a result we can expect that future limited conflicts will see a more sophisticated and expanded application of the military initiatives for media control identified following analysis of the Panama campaign. This will confirm the ascendancy of the military over the media. The pattern of media-management adopted is also likely to exhibit identifiable characteristics.

As a preliminary step, there will not just be the selection of a popular cause but, in the absence of any defined enemy that poses a threat to the home nation, exploitation of the media in singling out an acceptable personality or group for 'demonisation'.

While planning is underway, a closely controlled pool system backed up by strict access and escort provisions, and requirements for tight review of copy, will be developed. There will be a formalised policy of containment for independent media.

To fill the news vacuum created by these measures, there will be an increase in the release of selected and pre-edited military-shot media footage and the development of controlled press conferences once operations commence. Governments and the military will make direct approaches to the public through the immediacy of television, at the expense of the traditional role of the journalist as a watchdog and interpreter. There will also be a policy of no corrections to media handouts until well after the event, with any revisions to the original claims released slowly when public interest has subsided.

All of this can be expected to be played out against the background of a well planned, rapid and successful operation, after which the public relations emphasis will be on the professionalism of those involved, with excessive praise for allied forces.

The overall success of these factors, or variants of them, primarily in the shielding of the military from scrutiny but also in the voter benefits afforded the politicians, points to a future which will further reduce the public's right to be informed through the media. The only caveat is that, in line with previous case studies, this form of media containment or partial exclusion can only work for a limited period. If, as in Vietnam; and as may well have happened in the Gulf, such a limited conflict becomes protracted and involves high levels of casualties, then the ascendancy of the military may be challenged and broken as the global media brings to bear the full weight of its capacity for independent news gathering and communications.[164]

10

The Media and United Nations Peace-keeping

Peace-keeping is an important aspect of the changed nature of war at the end of the twentieth century. In the forty year period from 1948 to 1988, the United Nations was involved in thirteen separate peace-keeping operations. In the eight years since, it has undertaken twenty-three such deployments, almost twice as many as in the previous four decades, and the demand for peace-keeping shows no signs of diminishing.[1]

This sudden enthusiasm for peace-keeping is closely linked to the subsidence of Cold War tensions and the decline of superpower interest in a number of situations which were previously the subject of East-West rivalry.[2] In the renewed spirit of global cooperation which has emerged since the end of the Cold War, many states are looking to the United Nations in the expectation that the good offices of the Secretary General will be used to address a wider range of conflicts and matters of international concern than was possible in the past.[3]

The result has been an expansion of the peace process and the creation of new and qualitatively different tasks for military personnel involved in peace-keeping operations. While United Nations troops still patrol the truce lines, their new assignments include duties as diverse as the provision of electoral assistance, protection of humanitarian relief efforts, training local police, and the disarmament, cantonment and demobilisation of armed forces.[4]

The media has adapted quickly to these changes, turning the spotlight from the East-West dimension of conflict to the suffering produced by violence and repression. Press reports have aroused public concern and added to calls for international action. But the media has been slower to appreciate that a commitment to peace-keeping is not the same as involvement in traditional forms of conflict. The distinction is important because, although decisions about peace-keeping also involve choice, those choices take the citizen into a decision making arena entirely different to that of limited conflict.

For citizens of the Western world, the decision whether or not to support peace-keeping rarely raises questions of national survival or personal safety. But it does raise the question of the individual's moral obligation, as an international citizen, to uphold the principles of the Charter of the United Nations. Among other things, those principles commit the world body

> ... to take effective collective measures for the prevention and removal of threats to the peace, and for the suppression of acts of aggression or other breaches of the peace, and to bring about by peaceful means, and in conformity with the principles of justice and international law, adjustment or settlement of international disputes or situations which might lead to a breach of the peace.[5]

More importantly, with the expansion of the peace process, international commitment raises the question of how far the citizen's obligation to the United Nations should extend beyond the more traditional forms of peace-keeping to intervention in communal conflict and implementation of activities which might properly be described as 'nation-building'. Recent initiatives in these areas embrace purposes and principles laid down in the Charter which seek to '... [solve] international problems of an economic, social or humanitarian character and ... [promote and encourage] respect for human rights and for fundamental freedoms ...'[6]

Ultimately, the citizen must ask the question of whose values are to be imposed on decision making in these important domains of international concern. This becomes a key issue when the major powers, and the United States as the unquestioned military superpower, dominate the politics of peace processes.

This chapter considers the place of peace-keeping and the newer concept of peace-making in international conflict management, the management of United Nations peace-keeping, the influence the media is able to exert on peace processes, and the concept of state and individual obligation to the United Nations.

The recent peace-keeping and peace-making initiatives in Somalia, Cambodia and Haiti, each of which displays elements of nation-building activity, will be discussed in following chapters to demonstrate how the expansion of the peace-process has affected the task of the peace-keeper, and how particular attitudes and values are projected by the media when covering peace-keeping situations.

The Media, Peace-keeping and Limited Conflict

The diplomatic and military requirements of United Nations peace-keeping are quite different to the demands imposed by limited conflict. There has been some tendency, even in defence circles, to think of a continuum of political and military confrontation descending from conventional war down through limited war to peace-keeping operations.[7] Whether in conventional or limited war, however, confrontation proceeds from an attitude of belligerence towards another party.

This is completely at odds with peace-keeping philosophy.

Peace-keeping calls for an unbiased stance and the maintenance of goodwill on the part of the United Nations and its forces. Where the object is to legitimise collective international action aimed at preventing or containing conflict, those forces must be, and must be seen to be, impartial.[8] Further, in discharging the qualitatively different tasks which identify the new-style peace-keeping, peace-keepers must be able to work to alleviate suffering and create conditions in which a situation can be negotiated to settlement, or otherwise resolved, without themselves becoming embroiled in conflict.[9] Because of this, while some violence may occur during peace-keeping operations, it is usually contrary to the interests of the peace-keeping initiative to dwell on the loss of life at the expense of efforts to reduce tension. The goals of the United Nations may be compromised if the focus of attention shifts away from the peace process.

The media environment for United Nations peace-keeping also differs from the environments for conventional or limited war. The time frames for conventional war make development of media management systems both expedient and desirable, and the assumption of an overriding obligation to the state justifies media control if voluntary restraint is not observed. In limited war there is usually a more tenuous hold on public support and, as the case studies demonstrate, the emerging doctrine has been to get in, get the job done, and get out – hopefully before the media has a chance to become fully engaged and, in any case, under conditions in which the media is tightly controlled.

Peace-keeping offers no similar prospects for media control.

The media impacts upon United Nations peace-keeping through its role as a chronicler of crises and commentator on the international actions designed to address them. But while the United Nations has an interest in the way its activities are reported and may exercise some control over the flow of information, it can generally claim no right to restrict media scrutiny of peace-keeping operations. Indeed, any attempt to do so would run counter to the openness and trust on which peace-keeping is built.[10] Nor can the United Nations rely on swift resolution of disputes to deflect media attention from its activities. From the United Nations' perspective, there are some situations in which the longevity of the peace initiative is considered a measure of its success in preventing a recurrence of hostilities, rather than an indication of failure.[11]

In spite of these differences between peace-keeping and limited conflict, one of the consequences of comparison with swiftly concluded limited wars is a tendency to assume that successful peace-keeping will be of short duration also. But international disturbances rarely attract the attention of the United Nations if they are likely to be resolved easily; and in the situations of communal conflict which are increasingly the focus of international attention, swift conclusions appear remote possibilities at best.[12] The record speaks for itself.

The reality is that no peace-keeper who has intervened in a communal conflict has yet been able to withdraw after successfully restoring peace between the combatants.[13] After thirty years, United Nations troops still patrol the corridor between Greek and Turkish Cypriots, having achieved some reduction in tension but gaining little in trust.[14] In Lebanon, the United Nations force is, by the United Nations' own admission, prevented from implementing its mandate.[15] In Rwanda and Bosnia in the 1990s, similar situations of unresolved, and perhaps unresolvable, conflict exist.[16] Elsewhere, when the peace-keepers have departed or the intervention finalised, as with the Indian Army from Sri Lanka, or simply withdrawn, as with the United Nations from Somalia, the conflict has continued.

The practical effect of this is that, with the best of intentions and broad agreement on objectives, there is considerable scope for media coverage to conflict with peace-keeping aims. As the complexity of the issues involved in United Nations' interventions increases, so does the potential for conflict between the media and any peace-keeping force. The situation arises because the media has no responsibility for risk assessment or for the success of operations. The attention-grabbing potential of a particular incident may be at odds with the need for sensitivity in handling the problems confronting a peace-keeping force, and the immediacy of a story may override the need to present a peace-keeping initiative in perspective.[17] At the end of the day, media optimism can turn quickly to disenchantment if the results of peace-keeping do not live up to expectations.[18]

The Management of United Nations Peace-keeping

In part, such problems arise because choices in peace-keeping have never been totally under the control of the United Nations as a world body. The traditional doctrine, pre-dating both the United Nations and the League of Nations, is that peace-keeping is a job for great powers.[19] Although the doctrine may not be consciously expressed today, the most powerful states in the United Nations are still able to bring political and economic leverage to bear on matters affecting their interests. Consequently, although United Nations Secretary-General Dr Boutros Boutros-Ghali has argued that 'Peace-keeping is a United Nations invention',[20] the claim is true only to the extent that United Nations peace-keeping requires the parties to a dispute to abide by the principles for peaceful resolution of conflict laid down in the United Nations Charter.

United Nations peace-keeping in practice combines notional commitment to these principles with pragmatic decision making and implementation, under a structure and process which are systemically biased towards the interests of the most powerful members of the organisation. This situation arises because the United Nations has no military force of its own to deploy, and no structures capable of assembling such a force quickly.[21]

Military systems plan and organise operations at three levels of war – strategic, operational and tactical – which have equivalent application in peace-keeping. Within the United Nations, the Security Council provides political direction at the strategic level to initiate peace-keeping, while peace-keepers in the field implement resolutions at the tactical level. However, the operational level of control – the link between the strategic and tactical levels of activity – is virtually absent from the United Nations structure.[22]

The lack of an operational level in United Nations peace-keeping increases the reliance of the organisation on member states for structural support. This, in turn, gives the states providing that support a disproportionate degree of influence over peace-keeping processes. The effects are seen particularly in the dependence of the United Nations on member state contributions to meet the costs of peace-keeping and its reliance on those with highly developed military infrastructures and technological capabilities for the provision of logistic support.

With the current high level of peace-keeping activity, the United Nations is more than ever dependent on the wealthier states to sustain its operations.[23] As a result, although the United Nations 'invention' of internationally sanctioned peace-keeping relies for its legitimacy on the idea that moral responsibility is shared widely among member states, ultimately the process of choice in dealing with threats to world peace is heavily influenced by the dominance and capability of powerful states (including permanent members of the Security Council) whose decisions may be based on political self-interest.[24]

The distortions created as these powers shape United Nations responses to their own ends are particularly evident in the United States relations with the world body. As the predominant superpower and the only state with the combination of financial and logistic resources needed to respond quickly in support of United Nations initiatives, the United States is in a strong position to influence the organisation's strategic decision making.[25] In the crisis in Somalia, for example, it was accepted that the United States was the only power capable of reacting in the time frame envisaged.[26]

But it is not simply a matter of the major contributors asserting themselves in operational control of the peace-keeping process. In the absence of an effective United Nations command structure there is a further dissipation of authority among all participating national forces at the tactical level of peace-keeping. This is demonstrated by the historical tendency for peace-keepers to refer to their own governments for advice on matters of policy.[27] Nor is this the only effect of weaknesses in strategic decision making and operational control observed in the field. Peace-keeping at the tactical level may be hampered by other factors such as inadequate channels of communication with United Nations headquarters, lack of field intelligence, lack of mobility, and inadequate training and preparation of peace-keeping forces .[28]

To dwell on issues that have their origins in the politics of peace-keeping, however, is to fail to do justice to the peace-keepers on the ground. Theirs is the most difficult job of all.[29] At the tactical level, structurally-induced deficiencies are compounded whenever the problems facing peace-keepers escalate. Escalation may lead to a revision of United Nations expectations and changes to the peace-keepers mandate. It also tends to attract media scrutiny. Depending on media perspectives, escalating problems can change public perceptions and support for a peace-keeping mission, and change the priorities of individual states.

Media Influence and Commitment to Peace-keeping

With peace-keeping, as with conflict generally, the penalties increase as time passes without resolution of an issue. For the media, escalating problems, heightened tension or simply failure to achieve the objectives of a deployment, signal the creation of 'news'. They sound a warning that the original intervention was poorly conceived, the objectives are unrealistic, or the forces on the ground are not suited to the demands of the task.

The newsworthiness of any particular event aside, the potential for media coverage to conflict with peace-keeping aims stems primarily from the presentation of peace-keeping issues in contexts which reflect the world view of the media's audience. Where there is congruence between the views of an audience and those of their government, the media becomes an effective vehicle for the interpretation of national interest. However, there is a degree of fluidity in this interpretation, and nowhere is this more clearly demonstrated than in the relationship which develops between national interest and international concern in areas such as commitment to peace-keeping.

It has always been the case that those human tragedies which are publicised, are determined by media access to areas in crisis and subject to media priorities. To some extent, they become media constructs.[30] This remains true in the post-Cold War era. Media presence and the images broadcast to the outside world create pressure for peace-keeping by raising levels of awareness and translating that awareness into international concern.

The United Nations' intervention in Somalia came as a response to just such media coverage.[31] With Somalia racked by a succession of famines and refugee problems, the United Nations, along with other agencies, was providing humanitarian assistance to the country for some time prior to the 1992 peace-keeping deployment. But similar problems were being experienced in other parts of the world and peace-keeping interventions could have been considered for Liberia, Mozambique or the Sudan at the same time. An earlier commitment to Rwanda might have forestalled the later human tragedy in that part of the world. Why, then, was Somalia chosen for peace-keeping? One answer appears to be that Somalia was the choice of the Western and, in particular, the United States media.

For months prior to the United Nations peace-keeping initiative, the media had been at work, beaming pictures of starving Somali children into the six o'clock news and recounting tales of disaster for the Sunday papers. But the imagery was not just that of disaster in a far off land with an exotic culture. As Pilger has pointed out, the 'warlords' and 'gangs' of 'gunmen' in Somalia gave journalists the ideal enemy to report on.[32] And just as the images of human suffering evoked public sympathy, so the media calls for international intervention to curb the activities of the 'gunmen' provided a rationale for reporting the issue.

The media's continuous quest for the sensational can also be used effectively by the parties to a conflict. Vietnam used the media to focus attention on the excesses of the Khmer Rouge after Vietnamese forces had overrun Cambodia in 1979. While there was international criticism of Vietnam on one level, the images of horror which were broadcast from Cambodia enabled Vietnam to claim the moral high ground in rescuing the Cambodian people.[33] Journalists covering the conflict in Bosnia have observed that the warring parties in that conflict are adept at manipulating the media to exert influence in the United Nations. This is confirmed by United Nations reports that the Bosnian government forces, for example, shelled Bosnian-held Sarajevo immediately before a Bosnian envoy was to visit the United Nations in New York – the object being to blame the Bosnian Serbs and get the desired images into the media at the right political moment.[34]

Press reports which place a matter on a national or international agenda, however, do not necessarily translate into government acceptance of the issue as one worthy of national commitment. Even with the considerable coverage given to Somalia during 1991–92, both the *Washington Post* and the London *Times* devoted more space to events in the former Yugoslav republics of Croatia and Bosnia-Hercegovina than to events on the Horn of Africa. It was not until Secretary-General Boutros-Ghali charged members of the Security Council with the double standard of being more concerned with events in the former Yugoslavia (because of its European associations) than with Somalia, that the United Nations' membership – and the United States in particular – was mobilised.[35]

The subsequent decision by the United States to opt for a concerted peace-making and peace-keeping effort in Somalia – in the face of calls from its European allies for stronger action in a disintegrating Yugoslavia – underlines the link between national interest and commitment to peace-keeping.

In a peace-keeping environment in which resources are always at a premium, one of the attractions of intervention in Somalia – from an American government perspective – was that the objectives were deemed to be both affordable and achievable.[36] This still left the United States with the problem of rationalising the decision to support intervention in Somalia against equally strong calls for United Nations action on Bosnia-

Hercegovina. It could be validly argued that the apparent Serb territorial ambitions in Bosnia presented a much greater threat to international security than did the problems in Somalia. But the American media fell in behind their government as soon as the intervention in Somalia was announced. The message was that Somalia was the intervention that the United States could afford. It was not lost on the American public.

This brings out a contrasting aspect of the role of the media in the interpretation of national interest: the tendency for press coverage to conform to an officially sanctioned view of the world amenable to government officials. Indeed, for some media outlets – such as *USA Today* and *Time* – the stated goal is to present a national perspective which legitimates the government position, as opposed to striving for a full reporting of the facts or an unbiased account of events.[37]

It is indicative of the different priorities adopted by the United States and its European allies, that the American press fell into line with its government's decision to support intervention in Somalia, while the British press continued to echo their government's position calling for more decisive action in the former Yugoslav republics.[38] European questioning of the desirability of intervention in Somalia continued until the commencement of the peace-keeping deployment itself, when the immediacy of reporting events – the sensational story – took over from discussion of the issues.

The media therefore is able to influence commitment to peace-keeping in two ways: by bringing an incident to an audience's attention and placing it on the national agenda, and then by presenting the government view on the situation and reflecting audience reaction. Thus the relationship between national interest and international concern is established.

As a result of this relationship, the individual's moral obligation, as an international citizen, to support intervention in the interests of peace, tends to be expressed as a reaction to incidents rather than a response to issues. Thus, in the summer of 1993, when President Clinton advised his NATO colleagues that, in Bosnia, '... the last thing that was needed was more tough talk and no action', there continued to be no action until a bomb exploded in a Sarajevo marketplace. It was then that the 'CNN-induced outrage' of the American population obliged the administration to act.[39]

Nevertheless, perceived national interest is the final arbiter of commitment to peace-keeping and, to that extent, the lessons of Vietnam have not been forgotten. An adverse sequence of incidents can still produce a media-led reinterpretation of national interest and governments can generally be relied upon to react accordingly. When the ongoing cost of a deployment is called into question, the objectives of United Nations peace-keeping are likely to be questioned – and perhaps rejected – by the public in countries providing operational support.

The Concept of Obligation to the United Nations

The United Nations is not a world government. As Secretary-General Boutros-Ghali has pointed out, 'The United Nations is a gathering of sovereign States and what it can do depends on the common ground that they create between them.'[40] This observation in itself provides some insight into the special problems facing United Nations peace-keeping in its interaction with the media.

The arguments of Hobbes, Locke and Rousseau provide a justification for the existence of the state and the operation of the social contract, at least in the face of threats to national and personal survival.[41] Kant, however, took the ideas of these theorists further to use the social contract as a test of the justice of laws. From this he postulated that all subjects should be equal before the law and should have equal freedom to pursue their own ends. It is significant, in view of the focus of this chapter, that Kant extended his argument to apply those same conclusions to international relations.[42]

Kant argues that the existing relation between states is lawlessness. In accordance with the idea of the social contract, therefore, it is necessary to establish an alliance for mutual protection in which states will protect one another against external aggression while, at the same time, refraining from interference in one another's internal affairs.[43] By implication, the individual, who is obliged by the social contract to uphold the moral codes and laws prevailing within his or her own society, cannot reasonably seek to extend the application of those values to the peoples of some other state. The social contract assumes that individual populations are responsible for the type of contract struck with their states. It is this kind of philosophy which found expression in the League of Nations and, following World War II, the United Nations.

In defining the obligations of states, this philosophy that individual populations have international obligations flows through to the operation of international law. However, the jurists' view is that individual states cannot fulfil collectively the role which a world state could be expected to play. States have their own political, historical and other reasons for ensuring their existence, and must exercise their own judgement as to the desirability of supporting international initiatives as the dimensions of their international relations change.[44] In international law, then, the obligations of individual states to the United Nations are heavily circumscribed, with the 'looseness' of wording in many international agreements allowing wide latitude in interpretation and implementation.

Conclusion

The United Nations' absolute dependence on its wealthier member states to meet the costs of peace-keeping and for logistic support is not likely to change while the demand for peace-keeping remains at a high level.[45] As a result, although the United Nations relies for its legitimacy on the idea that moral obligation to support its purposes and principles is shared widely among member states, ultimately the process of choice in dealing with threats to world peace is heavily influenced by the dominance and capability of powerful states, including permanent members of the Security Council, whose decisions may be based on national interest.[46] It is here that the sense of obligation becomes distorted.

When world politics were dominated by East-West rivalries, the actions of the powerful states in pursuit of their own interests limited the functioning of the United Nations severely.[47] These limitations affected not just decisions to initiate action, but the continuation of operations in progress, and were evident from the first hesitant steps towards United Nations peace-keeping. Referring to the rejection of an early initiative to deploy a small force in Palestine in 1948, Boyd observes that:

> For the first time, a Secretary-General ... found that the great powers responsible for saddling the UN with a decision that required strong executive action were ratting on it – and on him – once things got really nasty.[48]

This situation has not changed simply because Cold War tensions have subsided. Rather, the United Nations is more than ever dependent on the developed nations of the West to fund and support its proliferating peace-keeping and peace-making activities. And it is now more than ever dependent on a single superpower – the United States – for much of that support, particularly when an initiative must be implemented swiftly.

The United States, while quick to deny any role for itself as the 'world's policeman', also acknowledges that it has a defining role in reacting to some international crises.[49] On the one hand, in the post-Cold War environment, this situation fuels debate as to whether the United States or the United Nations should control major international operations.[50] On the other, it begs the question of the extent to which the choices made ostensibly by the United Nations or its Security Council reflect the values of the United States. During a week in which United States President Clinton asserted the world's right to intervene in Haiti to restore democracy, his Commerce Secretary was warming to the task of promoting the commercial interests of the United States in China – and making no mention of human rights.[51]

Because of the dominance of the United States as a world power, it is useful to consider the impact of the United States on United Nations peace-keeping in the post-Cold War era. It is useful, also, to consider how that involvement is presented by an international media dominated by United States-based organisations. Despite all concepts of international obligation, as an individual or as a nation state, the relationship between the media and United Nations peace-keeping cannot be considered in isolation from national interest and the relationship between the media and the state.

The three cases of United Nations peace-keeping and peace-making which follow – Somalia, Cambodia, and Haiti – consider the impact of direct and indirect United States involvement, and the way that involvement has been rationalised by the media.

11

Somalia: The Uninvited Intervention

In theory, participation in the processes of the United Nations gives all states an equal voice in peace-keeping. In practice, economic and political realities mean that the degree of influence exercised by a state tends to increase with its power and interest in any particular problem. Unlike other states, however, the United States has an overriding interest in all peace-keeping decisions and, because of this, American interests intrude heavily on the peace-keeping environment.

This intrusion does not stem just from the exercise of control over American economic and military contributions to United Nations peace-keeping. Rather, the United States is motivated to protect its position as the predominant superpower, and this causes it to assess any proposal for international intervention against its own priorities.

But there are also inherent contradictions in the American approach to diplomacy. As Henry Kissinger has observed:

> In the twentieth century, no country has influenced international relations as decisively and at the same time as ambivalently as the United States. No society has more firmly insisted on the inadmissibility of international intervention in the domestic affairs of other states, or more passionately asserted that its own values were universally applicable. No nation has been more pragmatic in the day-to-day conduct of its diplomacy, or more ideological in the

pursuit of its historic moral convictions. No country has been more reluctant to engage itself abroad even while undertaking alliances and commitments of unprecedented reach and scope.[1]

Nowhere in recent years has the effect of these contradictions been more evident than in the American contribution to the United Nations intervention in Somalia.

From a moral viewpoint, Somalia appeared to offer an opportunity to showcase the determination of the international community in asserting the dignity and worth of the people of one of its poorest states. With the United States still buoyed by belief in its ideological supremacy following the end of the Cold War and its military success in the Gulf, American support for the intervention was never in doubt.

Somalia was no longer of strategic significance to the great powers. Nor did regional states have any particular stake in domestic Somali politics. The situation invited the type of peace-making initiative which would demonstrate to the world the great powers' commitment to order and the achievement of humanitarian goals, their determination to relieve suffering and protect the weak.

From a pragmatic, United States government perspective it was significant that the objectives in Somalia seemed more achievable, while being less costly and certainly less problematic, than any alternative action which might have been contemplated in response to calls for intervention in Bosnia-Hercegovina. Indeed, support for the intervention in Somalia could be used to deflect demands for more forthright action in the former Yugoslav republics, while at the same time bolstering support for United Nations Secretary-General Dr Boutros Boutros-Ghali.

These factors combined to bring the United States to the fore in the Somalia intervention, an operation which proved far more difficult in practice than it appeared on paper. In the end, the intervention absorbed some 28,000 troops and 2,800 other United Nations personnel[2] in a fruitless attempt to construct a system of order within which the international community could recognise a rebuilt Somali state. The extent of United States influence posed questions about the ongoing relationship between the United States and the United Nations – something which went well beyond the rationale for the intervention itself.[3]

Such questions were barely considered by an international media which had invested considerable resources in covering Somalia at the expense of other crisis areas. This media was more concerned with taking credit for influencing the decision to intervene than it was with analysing the situation in which the United Nations force would be deployed. As a result, it fell in behind the deployment with an enthusiasm which echoed the kind of patriotic support encountered so often in the lead-up to more nationalistic military adventures. At the same time, the media moved to consolidate its capacity to cover events in Somalia independent of the military. The lessons of the Gulf were not to be quickly forgotten.

This case study looks at the role the media played in the lead up to intervention in Somalia, the coverage of attempts to capture the 'fugitive' warlord Mohamed Aidid, and the slide into disillusionment as the objectives of the Somalia deployment slipped from the grasp of America and the United Nations. These events have been selected for their chronological sequence which traces the pattern of declining media and public support for a peace-making operation which effectively descended into war.

Background to the Crisis

Somalia covers an area of some 638,000 square kilometres (about 250,000 square miles) of generally arid country on the Horn of Africa. Its population is estimated to be about 9 million.

A land of limited natural resources, Somalia has been plagued throughout its history by internal disputes over access to waterholes and grazing lands. Although the people share a common language and claim descent from a common ancestor, Somalis are divided internally into clans which are inwardly focused and fiercely protective of their territorial interests. Traditionally the clans have banded together only when the equilibrium among them has been disturbed, returning afterwards to their exclusionary ways.[4] This tendency to internal conflict has always kept stability at a distance. It did not bode well for Somalia's future after the former United Nations trusteeship gained its independence in 1960, and it should have added a cautionary note to calls for intervention in the 1990s.

Given the nature of traditional Somali society, it is perhaps not surprising that the post-independence Somali government was marked by nepotism and abuse of privilege. However, the country struggled on as a relative democracy until 1969 when the president was assassinated and Major General Mohamed Siad Barre seized power in a military coup.

To secure his political base, Siad Barre used harsh measures to suppress the clans and centralise power in Mogadishu. His strategy was to replace the ingrained clan loyalty with a nationalist Somali consciousness which included reference to Somalis living beyond the country's borders in Kenya, Djibouti and Ethiopia. At the same time, he showed a growing inclination towards Marxist rhetoric – a move which coincided with increased economic and military aid from the Soviet Union.[5] In return, the Soviets gained port facilities to sustain their Indian Ocean activities and established a foothold on the Horn of Africa.

In 1977, emboldened by Soviet support and revolutionary upheaval in neighbouring Ethiopia, Siad Barre seized the opportunity to invade and incorporate the Ogaden region of that country into a Greater Somalia. This attempt to stir Somali nationalism beyond the country's borders led to the ill-fated Ogaden War in which the Soviet Union at first supported both sides before switching its economic and military backing to Ethiopia – a larger country which could provide it with a firmer base for its activities in the region.[6] As a result, Somalia not only lost the war but was swamped with two million refugees from the Ogaden. Coming on top of existing problems caused by drought and political repression at home, the military disaster only served to underline the declining position of the Somali government.[7] Siad Barre lost any hope of establishing broad-based legitimacy, but more than ever needed a benefactor to supply the military and economic resources to maintain his power.

In 1980, relief came in the form of aid from the United States, in exchange for American access to port facilities and permission to install infrastructure to support the Rapid Deployment Force it was positioning in the region.[8] Significantly, the United States made no serious attempt to encourage reform in Somalia and, to that extent, it can be argued that the American aid provided to prop up Siad Barre contributed to the further regression of Somali society.[9]

But Siad Barre's repressive measures – his massacres of rival clans and politicians – could not go unanswered forever. The clans turned to armed resistance, at first individually and then cooperatively. Finally, in 1989, a credible counter-force emerged in the form of the United Somali Congress (USC).

The USC was funded by a wealthy Somali hotel owner, Ali Mahdi Mohamed. Its military wing was led by 'General' Mohamed Aidid, a former army officer with both Italian and Soviet military training. Although there was a subsequent split between Ali Mahdi and Aidid, increasing military and political coordination between the rebel factions soon gave the clan-based militias the upper hand against the badly weakened government.

As the tide of battle turned the Somali army mutinied and, in January 1991, Siad Barre was forced to flee, eventually finding political asylum in Nigeria. Ali Mahdi seized his chance and declared himself president with the support of only his immediate followers.[10] Aidid, who had led the military action against Siad Barre, was deprived of the recognition for victory which he felt he deserved.

The new shake-out of alliances left Aidid and Ali Mahdi vying for power in the Somali capital, Mogadishu. Elsewhere the clans returned to their old ways and their own interests. But ill-disciplined militias held sway throughout much of the country and, as a two-year drought worsened, gangs armed with the weaponry that the two superpowers had provided began to plunder the people for food and possessions.[11] While an estimated 300,000 Somalis died from the effects of the drought and a million fled to neighbouring countries, the gangs looted everything of value including all electrical wire in Mogadishu, which was sold as scrap copper.[12] For all practical purposes, the Somali state had ceased to exist.

The Road to Intervention

With the overthrow of the Somali government, media interest in the country waned. Throughout 1991, events in the former Yugoslav Republics of Croatia and Bosnia-Hercegovina attracted more attention than did Somalia, and calls for United Nations intervention focused primarily on addressing the troubles in Europe. Interest in Somalia stirred again in December 1991 when United Nations Secretary-General Perez de Cuellar informed the Security Council that he intended taking an initiative to restore peace to the country, but the renewed coverage provided at best a superficial overview of Somalia's problems.[13]

Chief among those problems, according to press reports, was the effect of famine. Certainly, famine was a factor which prompted the Secretary-General's review of the situation, and famine was a factor that international audiences could relate to. The wretched, skin-and-bone images of starving Somalis moved Western audiences and aid agencies to ask how such suffering could be permitted in the post-Cold War climate of global cooperation. However, the suggestion that peace might be restored to Somalia in the process of ameliorating the effects of famine masked the real problem. In Somalia there were no recognised government structures with which dialogue might be opened[14] and never before had the United Nations contemplated entering a country uninvited. It was not the provision of humanitarian aid, but the problem of dealing with an anarchic society from which all semblance of legitimate government had disappeared, which posed greater difficulties.

However, the same anarchy which created difficulties for the United Nations allowed the media a great deal of freedom. For the cost of purchasing protection from the militias, journalists in Somalia could go where they liked, when they liked.[15] Within the anarchy, the media also found the ideal enemy to report on. As Pilger observed:

Like the British in pith helmets, they (the media) are facing amorphous 'gangs' of natives led by 'warlords'. On the TV screen, Somalis are dehumanised. There are no good Somalis, no wise Somalis, no professional and organised Somalis. There are only those 'warlords' and their 'gunmen' and, of course, their pathetic victims.[16]

The ease with which access could be bought from those same 'gunmen', and the imagery of social disintegration which journalists were able to record, ensured Somalia's place as a priority media event. It meant that Somalia attracted a degree of attention that was not accorded to similar disasters elsewhere and it increased the pressure on the United Nations to respond.[17] Reports, however, concentrated on the problems facing aid organisations and the violence in a society where government had collapsed, without making the logical connection that aid was simply another resource to be controlled – as far as possible – by those who possessed the arms.

The situation confronting the United Nations was exacerbated by this media coverage because it created an expectation that the crisis in Somalia could be addressed as an aid problem. However, the organisation was poorly placed to intervene in any case. It had removed its staff from the country with the overthrow of Siad Barre and – lacking established channels of communication – committed a series of diplomatic blunders in its efforts to broker a cease-fire. Assistant Secretary-General James Jonah's first bid for peace only aggravated tensions between Ali Mahdi and Aidid, and undermined the position of neutral clans and that of the United Nations. A tenuous cease-fire was eventually secured and the United Nations Operation in Somalia (UNOSOM) established in March 1992.[18]

With the decline in fighting, media interest in Somalia subsided.[19] Then, by mid-1992, as outbreaks of violence brought the flow of aid to a halt, the realisation dawned that UNOSOM had not actually been implemented. The failure of the United Nations to act on its intentions raised the media profile of Somalia again.

In the United Nations, the situation necessitated a series of difficult choices to devote substantial resources to UNOSOM. This led the international organisation into an argument over priorities, which culminated in new Secretary-General Boutros Boutros-Ghali criticising the Security Council for being more ethnocentrically concerned with the 'rich man's war' in the former Yugoslavia.[20] Such criticism applied to the Western media as much as to the United Nations member states against which it was levelled. But the media, which had directed far more attention to the Bosnian situation, barely noticed. It was too busy criticising the United Nations for not following up on its resolutions.

This was somewhat unfair, as the office of the Secretary-General could do little more than open the door to intervention.[21] The organisation possessed neither the resources nor the means to deploy a peace-keeping force, and the reluctance of the great powers to respond was unmistakable. In the first half of 1992, tiny Cape Verde offered the Security Council a more ambitious agenda for intervention than did the United States.[22]

The American view, expressed in Congress, was that the West should simply 'flood [Somalia] with food' so that it ceased to be a high-stakes item stolen by those with arms. This simplistic approach to confronting the crisis dealt with the question of intervention by noting that the United States and the United Nations were caught between a desire to provide humanitarian relief and the prospect of exacerbating the violence by deploying peace-keepers.[23] The view demonstrated an inadequate appreciation of the problem in Somalia, but it nevertheless ensured that, in the final analysis, the United States would support the position of the Secretary-General.

Such support was necessary while the European media were questioning the priority which Boutros-Ghali accorded Somalia. *The Times* went further to attack the credibility of the Secretary-General, referring to a 'whispering campaign' against him and suggesting that he might not be able to hold his position. It even quoted an unnamed Western diplomat as saying that Boutros-Ghali was keen to get action in Somalia because he had a 'bad conscience' about his failure to get a settlement when it was part of his responsibilities as Egyptian Foreign Minister.[24] Nevertheless the Secretary-General's bitter rebuke galvanised the membership into action and, within a month, the first five hundred Pakistani peace-keepers had been flown into the Somali capital, Mogadishu.

Still the problem was far from solved. The use of force was deeply ingrained in the Somali culture and United Nations 'stop-start' approach to intervention could only be interpreted as a sign of weakness which the major players in Somalia would seek to exploit. This was compounded by the apparent disjuncture between appreciation of the situation on the ground and comprehension of the problem at senior levels within both the United Nations and the United States.

In Somalia, the Secretary-General's special representative, Algerian diplomat Mohammed Sahnoun, had already criticised the United Nations for its ineffectiveness in comparison with other aid agencies and for its failure to come to terms with realities.[25] There was a media outcry when it was found that United Nations agencies were paying for the protection of relief convoys in the same way as private aid donors but, as a United Nations military official was quoted later as saying, any action to end the protection payments would have been 'like opening up a second front.'[26]

In spite of these difficulties, Sahnoun worked hard to have the initial deployment of 500 peace-keepers accepted, particularly by Aidid who possessed the strongest force in Mogadishu and who resented the United Nations intrusion. The deployment lifted the flow of aid briefly but, within weeks, it was halted again when the wing of an American cargo plane was allegedly hit by a bullet. Pilger argues that such occurrences were a relatively minor occupational hazard which did not deter private aid donors,[27] but the incident brought the United States food airlift to a stop while an increase in the peace-keeping force was discussed. Sahnoun felt he was close to having Aidid accept a larger deployment when Boutros-Ghali unilaterally announced a decision to strengthen UNOSOM with a further 3000 peace-keepers, upsetting Sahnoun's delicate negotiations.[28] Aidid threatened to send the new troops home in body bags and, shortly after, in October 1992, Sahnoun resigned, his best efforts at diplomacy thwarted by the United Nations itself.

Throughout October and November 1992, the situation in Somalia continued to deteriorate, but the media invested more in highlighting the apparent failure of the United Nations relief efforts than it did in examining the reasons for Sahnoun's resignation. In Britain, where the call had always been for stronger United Nations action in the former Yugoslav republics, *The Times* described Sahnoun as having resigned in frustration with the United Nations bureaucracy.[29] It was another way of expressing displeasure with the directions taken by the Secretary-General. In contrast, in the United States, where the administration continued to support Boutros Ghali and was moving towards sponsoring a major intervention in Somalia, the *New York Times* reported that Sahnoun had been forced to resign because of his critical outbursts.[30] The different media perspectives generally reflected conformity with their respective government's views.

The stakes were raised towards the end of November when, in a letter to the Security Council, the Secretary-General reported on the continuing decline in Somalia and outlined a number of response options. Now, one month after Iraqi diplomat Mr Ismat Kittani had been appointed to replace Sahnoun, *The Times* expressed regret at the loss of Sahnoun's 'diplomatic finesse and understanding of Somalia's extremely complex tribal allegiances.' Belatedly, *The Times* called upon the Secretary-General to restore Sahnoun's expertise to the Somalia mission.[31] But this was little more than a British attempt to shore up opposition to the developing American push for a real show of force.

The Secretary-General's recommendations for action were couched in terms of the need for a response which would restore the conditions for effective peace-keeping. In making his recommendations, Boutros-Ghali also noted that the United Nations lacked the command and control capability to mount such an operation itself, and that this would necessitate resorting to collective member state action under Chapter VII of the United Nations Charter. On 3 December 1992, the Security Council adopted, unanimously, Resolution 794 (1992), authorising the use of 'all necessary means to establish as soon as possible a secure environment for humanitarian relief operations in Somalia.'[32]

No one – least of all the American media – was surprised when the United States offered to lead the new Unified Task Force (UNITAF) to restore order. The *Washington Post* supported the use of force to protect the flow of relief supplies and accepted as a *fait accompli* American leadership of the intervention.[33] Official briefings in preceding months had paved the way for concerted United Nations action, and it was tacitly recognised that the United States was the only state capable of rapid implementation of the recommendations. This gave America considerable latitude in specifying the form that the response should take, as well as in stipulating the terms and conditions under which its forces would participate.[34]

In announcing the American commitment, President George Bush observed that the United States could not act alone, but '... some crises in the world cannot be resolved without America's involvement.'[35] The extent of that involvement was soon evident. Retired American Admiral Jonathan Howe quickly replaced Ismat Kittani as the Secretary-General's special representative in charge of UNOSOM. There was some Third World resistance to the appointment of an American force commander, but the Turkish Lieutenant-General Cevik Bir, being from a NATO country, was an acceptable compromise – and his deputy was an American. UNITAF was implemented within days of its announcement, with Marine General Joseph Hoare describing the Pentagon's contingency plans for the protection and delivery of aid as 'militarily not too complex.'[36]

In retrospect, it seems likely that press coverage over previous months reflected briefings provided by American officials who had knowledge of the plans in hand for intervention but made no disclosures. If the media was thereby encouraged to present a particular view of the Somali situation to bolster public opinion, to the detriment of more accurate reporting, the media paid little heed once the course of events became clear. The 'story' in Somalia had always been more significant for its entertainment value than for the issues involved.

'Shoot to feed' was the line that the London *Times* used to sum up the UNITAF peace-making mission[37] and the wider media quickly warmed to the theme. Although it was reported that Pentagon officials were less optimistic than the American government on the time frame for the operation,[38] this was not allowed to dampen the expectation that the forces of good, particularly those of the United States, would triumph over evil in Somalia as surely as they had in the Gulf a year or so previously.

On the road to intervention, the media never really stopped to examine the issues. But it was there in force. On 9 December 1992, just five days after the announcement of UNITAF, Operation Restore Hope commenced with 1600 American Marines storming ashore in Mogadishu, their night vision goggles rendered useless by the television lights and photo-flashes of some 250 waiting reporters. The journalist-combatant ratio of 1:6 compared with a ratio of about 1:300 at the height of the Gulf War; and, on this occasion, at least, there were legitimate concerns about the potential hazards of uncontrolled media access.[39] It was an indication of things to come.[40] Coverage exploded as journalists swarmed across the country, free of the restraints of the pool system which had plagued them in the Gulf and reviving, for the military, all the horror of the Vietnam experience.

The 'Fugitive' Warlord

Although Aidid had resisted the deployment of UNOSOM peace-keepers, both he and Ali Mahdi initially cooperated with the Americans and the UNITAF deployment. In some ways, this was not surprising. The success of Operation Restore Hope was predicated on suppressing resistance by an overwhelming show of force and, in the world of realpolitik, the clan leaders were obliged to adopt lower profiles while the formidable allied forces – spearheaded by the Americans – spread out from Mogadishu to clear the way for aid distribution.[41] Aidid and Ali Mahdi also had an eye to the future. A claim to legitimacy could be established by demonstrating commitment to, and support for, the peace-making effort. As a result, the operation commenced in a climate of polite cooperation, with clan leaders even willing to collude in the allied public relations campaign. Stephen Smith, writing for *New Statesman and Society*, observed of an early incident:

There was no criticism from them [Aidid and Ali Mahdi] over the deaths of two Somalis after French troops opened fire at a roadblock on the day they first trod Somali soil. Clan leaders tacitly endorsed an allied snow job, which made out that the truck carrying the victims had rammed the barrier, and that the legionnaires only discharged their weapons after coming under attack. Reporters at the scene, however, said the lorry had been unable to brake promptly on the wet road, and disputed the French claim of firing second.[42]

And it was not just the Somali leaders who bowed to UNITAF in explaining away this incident. Smith adds that, 'Curiously, some news organisations that had had people on the spot went along with the official remake the morning after.'[43] Only the desire to patriotically identify with the UNITAF 'team' could explain why some elements of the media would suppress their knowledge of the true situation.

But if it appeared that Operation Restore Hope commenced with the task force troops, clan leaders, and media standing shoulder to shoulder in support of UNITAF, each had a different view of the hope that was to be restored.

For the United States administration, the UNITAF objective was narrowly focused on securing the situation for the distribution of humanitarian aid. United Nations Secretary-General Boutros Boutros-Ghali, however, was keen to develop the humanitarian mission into a more substantive operation to rebuild the Somali nation.[44] Disarming the populace was seen to be essential to this higher aim and was quickly adopted by the media as part of the objective. The *Washington Post*, for example, argued that:

> ... many Somalis hope that the American soldiers, by taking away the unchallenged authority of Somalia's warlords and gunmen, also will break the political logjam that has stalled all previous attempts to reconcile Somalia's myriad warring clan factions.[45]

In the circumstances, the American administration was wary about such action. United States Special Envoy Robert Oakley correctly pointed out that weapons were an important part of the Somali culture and reasoned that if American soldiers began confiscating weapons, they could quickly become the enemy. But this view was presented in conjunction with an alternative assessment that total disarmament could actually be completed in a just few months. The report concluded with the judgement that 'If the U.S. proves unwilling to undertake this part of its mission, then the result will be like the end of the Gulf War – a job half done.'[46]

For Western audiences, such journalism, coupled with images of the overwhelming strength of UNITAF, created the impression that restoring order to Somalia was simply a matter of will. However, lessons from similar situations elsewhere supported Oakley's view and suggested that any attempt to disarm the Somali populace would more likely result in costly failure. The Americans would have been aware, also, that columns of the militia forces' 'technicals', light utility trucks with heavy machine guns mounted, had been crossing the desert to safe havens in Ethiopia ahead of the UNITAF deployment. There, presumably, the technicals would be mothballed until the United Nations forces withdrew.[47] Such actions sent clearer diplomatic signals about the hopes of the clan leaders than the polite cooperation of Aidid and Ali Mahdi as the United Nations operation commenced.

It was because of this perhaps that UNITAF troops initially accepted surrendered arms or took guns from individual Somalis, but refrained from any attempt to seize the arsenals of clan leaders.[48] However, this policy could continue only as long as there was progress towards some kind of peace settlement. It was in setting the agenda for peace that the positions of clan leaders, and the position of Aidid in particular, became clear.

Early in January 1993, United States President George Bush visited Somalia and toured areas where American troops were in action. While Bush was in Mogadishu, inter-clan fighting erupted in parts of the city and there were violent demonstrations against Secretary-General Boutros-Ghali outside the United Nations compound. The demonstrations were believed to have been organised by Aidid, who had indicated that he wanted the United States, and not the United Nations, to mediate at any peace talks.[49]

Bush left Somalia claiming success for Operation Restore Hope. But he also noted the need for a firmer approach on security and promised that some American troops would remain while security was in doubt.[50]

Within days, United States Marines stormed part of Mogadishu controlled by Aidid, destroying buildings and seizing weapons and ammunition. Next, they shut down the arms market in Mogadishu. On 14 January 1993, the first Marine was shot and killed in a running battle near Mogadishu airport.[51]

The more aggressive stance taken by UNITAF could only bring the Americans into direct confrontation with Aidid. Aidid's powerful forces held sway in much of Mogadishu and, arguably, he commanded the support of a substantial part of the population. Predictably, the American actions were met with demonstrations of opposition from Aidid supporters, and clashes with UNITAF troops intent on quelling the disturbances led to the deaths of Somali civilians. Aidid's reaction was to denounce the United States for firing on his supporters, who rampaged through Mogadishu defying calls to lay down their arms.[52]

On 3 March 1993, the Secretary-General made recommendations to the Security Council for the transition of UNITAF to UNOSOM II. Due to continuing concerns with security, however, he suggested that UNOSOM II be endowed with similar enforcement powers to UNITAF, to enable it to continue with the task of restoring 'peace, stability, law and order.'[53] This decision to combine the peace-keeping and peace-making roles carried significant risk, not just because the tasks were potentially incompatible, but because failure could place in jeopardy the standing of the United Nations in international peace processes. Nevertheless, the Security Council gave the necessary mandate for the expanded UNOSOM II for an initial period through to 31 October 1993.

Meanwhile, in Somalia the level of violence grew, exploding to new levels on 5 June when more than twenty Pakistani peace-keepers were killed while attempting to inspect weapons storage sites in Mogadishu. The United Nations Security Council immediately condemned the action and called for the arrest and punishment of those responsible. The blame for the incident was placed on Aidid, and the United States offered to head the operation to bring the killers to justice.[54]

The new campaign saw the violence escalate further. The United States brought in sophisticated airborne firebases, AC–130H Spectres, to attack Aidid's strongholds. It also conducted large scale operations on the ground. But while the United Nations gradually destroyed Aidid's ability to wage war, it also increased his popularity at a cost to itself. The peace-keepers found themselves effectively at war with Somalia. The result was inevitable. Amid general rioting, United Nations troops opened fire on a crowd of Somalis, killing fifty, mainly women and children. It was, observed *The Times*, the first civilian massacre by United Nations troops. The Somalis hit back in anger against all foreigners. Several foreigners, including journalists, were killed in retaliation. Aid workers retreated to their sandbagged compounds while a Somali radio station called for the United Nations to leave the country.[55]

On 18 June 1993, the United Nations ordered the arrest of Aidid for 'war crimes'. It was embarrassed a few days later when the 'fugitive' warlord was interviewed in hiding by two American media organisations. Aidid proclaimed his determination to defy the arrest warrant and maintained his innocence in relation to the killing of the Pakistani troops. The United Nations response was to issue a reward poster for his capture. The poster, which was to be dropped by helicopter over Mogadishu, was immediately dubbed a 'Wild West' tactic by journalists, and its advice

that recipients could bring in Aidid 'in person' was interpreted as a tacit invitation to produce a corpse.[56]
For the media, such developments only added to the entertainment value of the Somalia 'story'. But images of suffering still overshadowed any analysis of what was occurring. *Time* summed up the situation:

> Gone are the tragic images of vacant-eyed skeletal children dying by the thousands in Somali villages. In their place are equally troubling images of shell-shattered civilians and Mogadishu mobs, fists raised in anger against the mounting violence that has marked the two months since the U.S.'s handover to the U.N. peacekeeping mission in Somalia.[57]

Time also drew attention to the continuing role of the United States in Somalia, the extent to which the campaign to capture Aidid had come to dominate the United Nations mission, the anger of the Somali people, and the divisions appearing in the ranks of UNOSOM II:

> Anger is focused squarely on the U.S. The helicopters and missiles responsible for the civilian carnage are almost entirely American. While U.N. military forces are ostensibly led by Turkish General Cevik Bir, his second in command is American, his staff is predominantly American, and the real boss in Somalia is American, U.N. special representative Jonathan Howe, a retired Navy Admiral. The determination to decapitate Aidid's faction is considered an American interpretation of the U.N. resolution calling for the capture of the Somalis responsible for the ambush of the Pakistanis. A total of 35 peacekeepers have died since May, none of them American. 'The U.S. is quick to stir up trouble with air strikes,' said a Pakistani peacekeeper, 'but it is my men and other Third World soldiers who always draw the tough assignments on the ground.'[58]

And it was on the ground that cracks began to appear in the UNOSOM II facade.

In July 1993, the United Nations demanded that Rome recall the commander of the Italian contingent in Somalia, General Bruno Loi, for insubordination. Loi, it was alleged, had refused to carry out orders before checking with his government. Italy rejected the call and sent an envoy for urgent discussions with the UNOSOM II leadership.[59] While this event and the associated decision to redeploy the Italian forces outside Mogadishu were well reported, most media paid less attention to the background to the incident than they did to the issue of Loi's consultations with Rome.

In this instance, the *Sunday Times*, was one newspaper which did canvass the issues. According to the paper, the controversy arose because of Loi's refusal to attack Checkpoint Pasta – a key Mogadishu street corner controlled by Aidid's forces. Loi calculated that he could have lost up to seventy men in a battle to take the Checkpoint and, after consultation with Rome, decided to persuade Aidid to back down by force of words instead of arms. Loi succeeded, and reoccupied Checkpoint Pasta a day ahead of the United Nations deadline.[60] That the Italians had communicated directly with Aidid's forces offended the Americans, who did not share the Italian view that there was still room for diplomacy. The real issue, as *Time* magazine indicated, was not Loi's consultations with Rome, but the American-led aggression in Somalia which was turning the UNOSOM II peace mission into a war operation.[61]

However, while media coverage canvassed the incompatibility of peace-keeping and peace-making, there was little serious discussion of the desirability of dealing with Aidid other than as a 'fugitive warlord' for whom a reward had been offered, or of the implications of United States command of operations. The action against Loi may have been presented as a reminder that all forces were under United Nations control, but in reality the offence was that the Italians had challenged United States leadership and doctrine on how matters should be handled.[62]

On 26 August the United Nations released a report of its investigations concluding that Aidid had '... personally authorised the 5 June attack on Pakistani forces serving under the United Nations flag.' At the same time, four hundred members of the United States Army Rangers – including the elite Delta Force counter-terrorism unit – were deploying in Mogadishu. 'Whatever (the) units within the task force are there for, you'll have to draw your own conclusion,' was the quoted response to a media question on the Special Forces' mission.[63]

Their task was soon evident. On 30 August, fifty Rangers using twelve helicopters conducted a raid on two buildings outside the 'approved sector' in Mogadishu. One building was empty, but the occupants of the other were detained – until they were found to be employees of the United Nations Development Program. The raid had apparently been part of an attempt to capture Aidid and the Rangers had mistakenly believed the buildings to be Aidid's command centre.[64]

Ten days later, there was another debacle. The *New York Times* reported a major battle in which two American Cobra attack helicopters and Pakistani tanks and armoured personnel carriers lent support to American and Pakistani peace-keepers who had come under fire while attempting to clear a roadblock. As many as one hundred Somalis were believed to have been killed in the fighting, including women and children. A Pakistani soldier was also killed, while four peacekeepers were wounded, including two Americans. Major David Stockwell, the chief United Nations spokesman in Mogadishu, justified the shooting of women and children as a ...

> last-ditch, last resort effort to protect the United Nations troops... We saw all the people swarming on the vehicles as combatants... We've seen this before. If they reach our soldiers they tear them limb from limb.[65]

As unpalatable as the images may have been to Western audiences, the statement reflected the basic reality of combat in Somalia. According to United Nations special representative Jonathan Howe, the tactic of Somali militiamen mingling with women and children to deter United Nations forces from firing back, was one favoured by Aidid;[66] and this reference to Aidid linked the battle to the focus of the United States and United Nations mission in Somalia. There could be no doubt, however, that audiences were having difficulty reconciling the trend of events with the original humanitarian goals of the operation. The *New York Times* expected the incident to heighten debate over the United States role in Somalia; Congress noted that there had been eleven American combat deaths and called for the withdrawal of the remaining 4,700 United States troops.[67]

Then, in one disastrous week, the American resolve to capture Aidid was destroyed.

Early in October 1993, some fourteen American Army Rangers were killed and seventy-seven wounded in a major battle with Aidid's militia. Two American Blackhawk helicopters were also shot down, and the pilot of one was captured by the Somalis. Relief troops took ten hours to fight their way through to the embattled Rangers. In the newspapers of the West there were pictures of the dead bodies of American servicemen being dragged through the streets of Mogadishu, and television footage of the helicopter pilot being questioned by his Somali captors. United States President Bill Clinton ordered a further 2,000 troops to Somalia, but gave an undertaking that all American forces would be withdrawn within six months. If the deteriorating situation had not sapped the will of the American people, the sight of the bodies of their soldiers being beaten and spat upon in the streets of Mogadishu was the last straw.[68] A *Time* survey revealed that 89 per cent of Americans now wanted their forces withdrawn and, for 96 per cent of those surveyed, the highest priority was securing the release of the captured helicopter pilot.[69] There were fears that Somalia would become 'another Vietnam'.

In October 1993, a British adviser with the United Nations in Somalia, John Drysdale, resigned his position blaming the United States for provoking war in Somalia by 'irrationally' turning against Aidid.[70] His view reflected that of Sahnoun and Loi, who had also departed the scene questioning the policy towards Aidid. At the same time, a unilateral cease-fire declared by Aidid held, causing Pakistani Commander Brigadier-General Ikram Hasan to comment that Aidid had demonstrated that he had 'considerable control' over the militia. Hasan further observed that Aidid was probably only doing what he needed to do to survive.[71] But the media never stopped to consider whether it had taken the wrong tack in falling into line with the view that Aidid was of no significance in the bigger picture within Somalia.

Aidid's cease-fire gave the United States the breathing space it needed to negotiate the release of the captured American pilot. But it also fostered a division between the United States and the United Nations, as the United States abandoned the hunt for Aidid and opened the door to a political settlement. Howe was made a scapegoat by both the United States and the United Nations for 'personalising' the hunt for Aidid.[72] Howe's defence was that he was only trying to carry out the wishes of the Security Council. A few days later, the *New York Times* put the view that it was Boutros-Ghali's fault – that he was autocratic, obstructionist and bent on personal revenge against Aidid.[73] It was not until the end of October, some two weeks later, that the United Nations officially abandoned the hunt for Aidid. The parallels between the independent exercise of United States national policy in relation to the United Nations mission, and the similar episode with Italy a few months before, failed to attract media comment.

Aidid, who had effectively seen off both the United States and the United Nations, did not receive even belated recognition that he exercised a degree of control within Somalia and retained some capacity to coordinate Somali responses.[74] At the end of the day, he was not militia leader or even a 'warlord'. In what may have been intended less as a slight on Aidid than on the Americans for encouraging the United Nations intervention in Somalia – contrary to the position preferred by Britain – the London *Times* suggested that the might of the United States had been foiled by a 'crafty local chieftain.'[75]

In December 1993, Aidid, the 'fugitive warlord', was flown to Ethiopia on an American military aircraft to take part in reconciliation talks with other Somali factions. According to reports, Aidid did not speak to Ali Mahdi.[76] The battle lines in Somalia, it seemed, were much as they had been after Siad Barre's flight in 1991. But Somalia was no longer a headline story with the media. The interest disappeared along with the change in United States policy.

Disillusionment and Defeat

Somalia was not a traditional United Nations peace-keeping operation. The peace-making objectives of UNITAF always carried the possibility of descent into limited war and, in the planning and execution of UNITAF in particular, it is difficult to escape the conclusion that the operation was conceived by the United States as a campaign not unlike limited war. The UNITAF objectives were to be secured in just six weeks. The object was to get in, get the job done and get out. And within the constraints imposed by action under the flag of the United Nations, the conduct of the operation and relations with the media were typical of the approach to limited conflict.

In the first place, in Somalia as there had been in Grenada and Panama, there was complete secrecy in planning. At about the time that UNITAF was being implemented, the American ambassador to the United Nations, Edward Perkins, claimed that the United States had been examining the possibility of direct intervention in Somalia for some five months. If so, planning must have commenced about the time of the decision to deploy the first 500 peace-keepers in mid-1992. According to Perkins, the Americans had been waiting only for a United Nations invitation to take action.[77] No hint of this was given to the media.

While planning was in progress, however, the media was encouraged to demonise the Somali leadership. Over time, the members of the 'militias' which had overthrown Siad Barre became 'gunmen' and their leaders 'warlords'. The 'gunmen' were the focus of enmity for audiences sympathising with the victimised Somali population, and such sympathy was easily evoked by reference to the many Somalis who allegedly wanted the 'gunmen' disarmed.[78]

Ultimately, demonisation focused on Aidid as the most powerful 'warlord' in Mogadishu, and the campaign against him was intended to erode his power base. This was the closest any strategy could come to destabilisation in a country which was already destabilised – where no recognised institutions of control existed.

The targeting of Aidid began in the latter part of 1992, when Secretary-General Boutros-Ghali made his unilateral decision to increase the peace-keeping force in Somalia and Aidid threatened to send the soldiers home in body bags.[79] The media made much of Aidid's threat while ignoring the fact that at the time he had been negotiating with the

United Nations, apparently in good faith. But the course to direct intervention had already been set and, from that point, Aidid's name was connected with every obstruction to, or setback in, the United Nations operation in Somalia.

Legitimacy was not an issue in Somalia as the United Nations action was seen as an appropriate response to concern over the suffering of the Somali people. For the United States, legitimacy was bestowed by the United Nations invitation to take action – the invitation for which the Americans were waiting. Legitimacy also came from association with other contributor nations in the UNITAF and UNOSOM II deployments.

Finally, UNITAF was based on the concept of deployment of overwhelming superiority of forces to achieve its objectives quickly.[80] This concept had proven its worth in Grenada and Panama. In the Gulf, two years previously, it had virtually been marketed by the media and the military as the key to limiting the number of casualties and its apparent success had captured the popular imagination.

But not everything went according to plan in Somalia.

Because peace-keepers are not parties to the situations they seek to control, they have no mandate to manage the flow of information about operations. The media could not be controlled in Somalia the way they had in the Gulf; nor could they be restricted or simply shut out as they had been in the Falklands, Grenada and Panama. For the military, the free reign enjoyed by journalists raised the spectre of another Vietnam. Initially, however, the media in Somalia were patriotically behind their respective country's contributions to the United Nations effort, in apparent anticipation of another easy victory. It was the only as the cracks began to appear in UNITAF's secure environment that the media began to question the feasibility of the mission. And as the cracks widened and the focus of the mission shifted to the hunt for Aidid, what was left of media optimism turned swiftly to disillusionment.

The change was to be expected. While the peace-keeping environment differs in important ways from other conflict situations, the basic tenet that penalties increase as time passes and the situation remains unresolved still holds. However, in a peace-keeping situation, it is likely that disillusionment will set in and legitimacy will be undermined more rapidly as problems escalate than would be the case in a traditional limited conflict. This is not just because of the absence of media controls or a result of concern over the deaths of troops whose role is supposed to be peace-keeping. It is because perceived national interests over-ride the sense of international commitment and make it easy for both governments and the media to lay the blame for any failure at the feet of the United Nations.

In Somalia, the interests of the United States and the United Nations were directly linked in UNITAF and UNOSOM II. But there was a separation of the ways once the United States administration took the decision to withdraw – and the United Nations bore the brunt of media disaffection.

After giving up pursuit of Aidid, President Clinton was portrayed as acting in the best interests of the United States in 'struggling to extract himself from the Somali quagmire.'[81] In contrast, the United Nations was described as 'putting a diplomatic figleaf over its exoneration of the murderous warlord' for abandoning the hunt in favour of a commission to investigate armed attacks on United Nations personnel.[82]

The media depicted the United States as a victim and the United Nations as a failure. Almost twelve months after the commencement of the intervention, with the situation beyond redemption, a report in *Time* observed that 'while America's attention was focused at home, the goals of the mission [had] shifted dangerously.'[83] The report stated that the United States had had 'misgivings [about the mission] from the start' and attributed the loss of American lives in the hunt for Aidid to the United Nations command and control structure which had been 'unable to rush well-equipped troops to the ... rescue' of American forces.[84]

But it seems unlikely that the United States was utterly devoid of influence over operations in Somalia and there is a certain irony in President Clinton's observation that 'If the American people are saying 'yes' to UN peacekeeping, the United Nations must know when to say 'no'.'[85] It is hard to be gracious in defeat.

Conclusion

There can be no denying that aid, particularly military aid, supplied to Somalia by the Soviet Union and the United States over a twenty year period contributed to the eventual collapse of the Somali state. It is difficult to reconcile this with the view, expressed by the media, that the United States contribution to the United Nations effort was in some way altruistic – that this was a region in which no United States geopolitical interests were at stake.[86] It would have been more accurate to say in which there were *no longer* any United States geopolitical interests at stake. Ignoring this aspect of the crisis led to the uncritical reporting of President Bush's characterisation of the Somalia intervention as 'God's work.'[87] No one asked if it had also been 'God's work' when the superpowers were supplying the arms which laid the basis for the situation.

There can be no denying also that drought and famine brought on the crisis in Somalia and provided the images which triggered the humanitarian effort. Media presentation of these images against a background of social disintegration encouraged the belief that Somalis would respond to the distribution of aid by reverting to a peaceful and orderly way of life. But the suggestion that the problem in Somalia might be solved by flooding the country with food[88] assumed, in effect, that aid in sufficient quantities might lead to a revision of the entire Somali social and political structure. The idea that members of Somali society would automatically choose to emulate the ideals of the West if only they were given enough to eat, ignored the fact that famine caused by drought was only part of the problem and affected only part of the country.

The arms sent to the Horn of Africa by the major powers exacerbated the problems of prolonged drought by increasing the destruction and cost of competition between the clans, but the internal struggle for supremacy was only an extension of the age-long and traditional Somali war of survival. This is something that the media, the United States and the United Nations all alluded to at various times, but never took fully into account. Failure to consider this aspect of the situation led the United Nations to ignore the political dimension of the arms problem and view it primarily in humanitarian terms.[89]

The leadership of the movement which had overthrown Siad Barre had legitimate expectations of external recognition and this, too, was withheld while the United Nations and the United States adopted the position that there were no suitable political structures within Somalia with which dialogue could be opened. The clan-based militias and their leadership offered the only realistic hope of reconstructing Somali society, but they were dismissed as irrelevant to the re-establishment of the Somali state.

This action led directly to the violence which followed the deployment of UNITAF and UNOSOM II. The United Nations forces on the ground tried to avoid dwelling on the violence. However, predictably enough, the media eagerly ran with it, to the detriment of presenting a more balanced picture of the problems in Somalia and the objectives sought by the peace-keepers. From beginning to end in Somalia, entertainment took priority over informed analysis. The initial media optimism, based on the media's own narrow view of the situation and fed by unrealistic American predictions of a quick resolution, soon turned to a disenchanted attribution of blame to the United Nations when expectations were not met.

In retrospect, it may be argued that much of what happened on the ground in Somalia could and perhaps should have been anticipated. But whether the debacle in Somalia could have been avoided if intervention had taken more account of the political situation is a moot point. What Somalia demonstrated above all is that, while the United Nations is seen as the voice of its membership and to some extent can act as the representative of collective world opinion, in reality the peace-keeping agenda is set by the major powers. This situation is exacerbated by structural weaknesses in the United Nations peace-keeping mechanism which necessitate reliance on major powers in the implementation of peace-keeping and creates difficulties for the world body in controlling the agenda once operations have commenced. There could be no clearer demonstration of this than in the role played by the United States in the Somalia peace-keeping deployment.

Early in 1995, the last of the of the United Nations forces withdrew from Somalia and the country dissolved once again into civil war. The media accorded the event just a few brief paragraphs. The 'story' had largely gone from Somalia when the bulk of the Western nations' troop contributions were withdrawn some twelve months earlier. In September 1995, the plight of Western aid workers caught in the continuing struggle between Aidid and Ali Mahdi brought Somalia to the headlines once again,[90] but the story lay in the Western interest, not in the Somali suffering.

In June 1996, the United States indicated that it would not be supporting Dr Boutros-Ghali's bid for a second term as United Nations Secretary-General. The media told the story:

> The US has been unhappy for several years with Dr Boutros-Ghali's leadership which it believes contributed to the failure of UN missions in Somalia and Bosnia.[91]

Then, in August 1996, Aidid was reported to have died of a heart attack following a gunshot wound. *Time* magazine observed:

> Should (Aidid's) removal turn out to be the key to peace, the irony will be that it was his removal that the U.N. and the U.S. were seeking to accomplish three years ago.[92]

It was as if a chapter of history had closed. If the military learned anything about relations with the media from the United Nations initiative in Somalia, it was that media loyalty is still – first and foremost – a national loyalty. While the political penalties for failure in limited war might be severe, when things go wrong in peace-keeping there is always the United Nations to blame.

12

Cambodia: The War
the Media Forgot

In the early 1990s, more than two decades of political instability in Cambodia were brought to an uncertain conclusion as a result of a United Nations peace-keeping initiative.

The United Nations operation in Cambodia took place at the same time as its intervention in Somalia. There were similarities in the two situations in that both Somalia and Cambodia were dysfunctional states. However, there were vast differences in the way the interventions were conceived and implemented. Whereas Somalia was media driven and, to an extent was finalised because of media pressure, Cambodia was the war the media forgot.

Like Somalia, Cambodia was an exercise in the re-establishment of order, although it had less to do with the end of the Cold War than with the international response to the new strategic balance.[1] Cambodia was, in many ways, a casualty of the Vietnam war. Because of its geographic location, it was first drawn into the war and then, in the aftermath, became the battleground on which competing regional interests played for strategic positions against a victorious Vietnam.

Throughout the 1980s, as the full horror of what had taken place in Cambodia became evident, there were international calls for an end to the war in Cambodia. But with a Vietnam-backed puppet government installed in the Cambodian capital, Phnom Penh, and Vietnamese 'expansionism' opposed by China, the United States and the regional Association of Southeast Asian Nations (ASEAN), there was little hope of gaining international support for any peace initiative.

It was not until the end of the Cold War that the possibility of a solution emerged. The continuation of confrontation by proxy in Cambodia made little sense with Vietnam's main benefactor – the Soviet Union – consumed by its own domestic and economic problems. As a result, Vietnam became increasingly susceptible to pressure to withdraw from its neighbouring state. Convincing the Cambodian parties to the conflict to cooperate was another matter. But, at the end of 1990, as the international community was becoming increasingly preoccupied with the Gulf war, the powers then engaged in trying to get Cambodian peace talks to work delivered a warning: unless the warring parties in Cambodia came to an agreement soon, the world would be too involved elsewhere to continue an interest in the situation.[2]

The result was the most ambitious peace-keeping exercise the United Nations had ever undertaken. But where the peace-making exercise in Somalia carried many of the hallmarks of limited conflict in its attempt to establish order, Cambodia remained predominantly an exercise in diplomacy, with the United Nations intervening on behalf of the parties.

Because of the different circumstances, and because the situation did not dissolve into conflict as it did in Somalia, the part played by the media in Cambodia differed significantly from the critical role it assumed in Somalia. Indeed, the Cambodian experience is best addressed in the historical context of more than twenty years of war during which international perceptions of the conflict were shaped. It is a history which casts doubt on the claim of triumph for the eventual United Nations intervention.

Background to the Conflict

Cambodia, along with Vietnam and Laos, is one of three former French possessions in Indochina. It occupies an area of about 181,000 square kilometres (about 70,000 square miles) bordered by Vietnam in the east, Laos in the north, and Thailand in the west and north west. Its southern coast fronts the Gulf of Siam. The country has a population around 6 million, 96 per cent of whom are Khmers, the rest mainly Chinese and Vietnamese.

Most of Cambodia is a large, low-lying basin draining into the Tonle Sap (Great Lake) in the centre. The Tonle Sap, in turn, drains into the Mekong River, the lifeblood of states of the region. At flood time, the river reverses its flow and the lake fills from the Mekong.

Cambodia has a history of ancient civilisation influenced by Indian culture. In contrast, Laos and Vietnam have been influenced more by China. From the ninth to the fifteenth centuries, the Khmer people had a great kingdom in the area that is now Cambodia. This was followed by a protracted period of instability in which Siam (now Thailand) and Vietnam alternately struggled for control of the region. Always, the cohesion of the Khmer people defeated them.[3] Vietnam finally withdrew shortly before France established a protectorate over the area in 1863, with the great Vietnamese mandarin Phan Thanh Gian observing:

> Our intention, in principle, is not at all to take over this country; we wish following heaven's example to leave these men to live and exist ...[4]

Ironically, more than a century later, Vietnam would find itself again withdrawing from Cambodia, uttering similar sentiments.

The French protectorate quelled regional antagonism. It reversed Cambodia's decline and established the state borders that are still disputed today. But the French invested little in Cambodia's development. They set in place a civil service (staffed mainly by Vietnamese) and followed the pattern established by Thailand and Vietnam of selecting Cambodian kings who would cooperate in legitimising their control. In 1941, they enthroned Prince Norodom Sihanouk, an eighteen year old whose youth and accommodating nature seemed to equip him well as a protector of colonial interests.[5]

During World War II, Japan occupied most of southeast Asia. The Vichy French administration in Cambodia, however, was left largely undisturbed until the beginning of 1945. It was then, as the war turned against them, that the Japanese ousted the French, persuaded King Sihanouk to declare independence, and installed a new government headed by the Cambodian nationalist Son Ngoc Thanh.

When the French returned at the end of 1945, they found a different Cambodia. Sihanouk capitulated to the French and Thanh was arrested and exiled.[6] But his short-lived regime had given Cambodians a sense of nationalism; bands of armed guerrillas, with no particular unifying ideology except a desire for independence, made the countryside largely ungovernable. In the circumstances, some concessions were unavoidable and, the following year, France granted Cambodia autonomy within the French Union. While France still retained control of the police and the military, the important change was in the abolition of the absolute monarchy and the establishment of a constituent 'consultative' National Assembly. Young King Sihanouk, who had entered party politics, joined the ranks of the opposition.

The new Cambodian government charted a turbulent course. The Democratic Party, which sought full independence and European-style democracy, held a majority. But it faltered in the face of the conservative opposition and, in 1953, Sihanouk's chance came. He dissolved the squabbling National Assembly and began campaigning for Cambodian independence. France, fighting a losing battle in Vietnam and unwilling to face the same in Cambodia, transferred state power to Sihanouk's Royal Government of Cambodia in November of that year. Sihanouk became a hero to his people and would continue to rule over his country in various capacities, as Chief of State, Prince, and Prime Minister, for the next eighteen years.[7]

While there had long been a communist movement in Cambodia, it was significant that independence was achieved without their participation.

The Khmer communists had joined with the Vietnamese to follow the Viet Minh strategy of winning the war in Vietnam first. It was to be a costly mistake. When the French conceded in Vietnam, the Khmer communists found themselves with no standing in their own country and were unable to obtain the international recognition and support secured by the Viet Minh. Unlike the Vietnamese and Lao communists, they were not seated at the table for the peace talks in Geneva and came away feeling isolated and frustrated. As Becker put it:

> Like their earlier experiences with the French, the Thai, and the Japanese, Geneva was to the Cambodians an example of why they could not trust foreigners. [8]

After Sihanouk's deal with the French and the Geneva talks, the Khmer communists were left with little to fight for – neither independence nor democracy. They then had to rebuild from the grassroots while Sihanouk actively sought to destroy what little organisation they possessed. Their efforts were a slow process assisted only by Sihanouk's contradictory policies and increasingly eccentric personal behaviour.[9] While in other circumstances this might have led to instability, Sihanouk managed to maintain his position for a time by playing off different groups internally and pursuing a policy of neutrality with the superpowers and China.[10]

With a United States-backed war raging in South Vietnam during the 1960s, however, the situation was bound to become increasingly difficult. Sihanouk predicted an eventual communist victory in his neighbouring state and, ever pragmatic when weighing up political affairs, was concerned to keep the United States out of Cambodia. America's involvement in the November 1963 assassination of South Vietnam's President Ngo Dinh Diem only served to heighten his fears for his own position. Sihanouk reacted by renouncing all American aid and, in 1965, severed diplomatic relations with the United States.[11]

With the Americans already distrustful of Sihanouk, the CIA lent support to Son Ngoc Thanh and the Khmer Serei (Free Khmers) who were assisting in the war against the communists in South Vietnam. The Khmer Serei made occasional forays against the Khmer communists, but the real value of Son Ngoc Thanh to the Americans was that he had shown genuine political leadership in the 1940s and, with his deep hatred of Sihanouk, had the potential to step into the vacuum if Sihanouk should ever be toppled.[12] As the war in South Vietnam dragged on, this appeared increasingly likely.

Sihanouk's political manoeuvres in the mid-1960s were followed by a rapid succession of governments of both the Right and the moderate Left. With the loss of substantial amounts in aid, the economy became increasingly unstable and Sihanouk began to accumulate enemies across the full spectrum of Cambodian politics. Even the former King's immense popularity with ordinary Cambodians was eroded. Peasant revolts erupted in some areas but were quelled with ruthless efficiency.[13] Meanwhile, the Khmer communist movement was growing in strength and Sihanouk was claiming that they wanted to drag Cambodia into the Vietnam war.[14]

Then, in 1969, a 'Government of National Salvation' was returned under General Lon Nol, the man who had been Sihanouk's police chief and military leader for years. The Lon Nol government immediately set about dismantling Cambodia's failed economic programs and began to vie with Sihanouk for control of the country's foreign policy.

In January 1970, Sihanouk went to France for a holiday. While he was gone, members of the government organised mass demonstrations against the use of Cambodia's northeast border region by North Vietnamese and Viet Cong fighting in South Vietnam. Sihanouk reacted by threatening to remove Lon Nol and his associates for trying to destroy Cambodia's peaceful relations with the communist powers. But his absence from the country placed him at a disadvantage. On 18 March, Lon Nol and his supporters staged a coup d'etat with the support of the Cambodian Army, promising to create a Khmer Republic that would be modern, democratic and truly neutral.[15]

There was immediate speculation about external involvement in Sihanouk's overthrow. This was not surprising given that the CIA-connected Son Ngoc Thanh had been heavily involved in its planning[16] and that the United States had already commenced bombing suspected North Vietnamese bases in Cambodia.[17] But there were also compelling domestic reasons for the action, given Cambodia's state of decline. The challenge facing the Lon Nol government was that, as the war in South Vietnam began to encroach on Cambodia's borders, the country had become increasingly embroiled in a civil war between communist and non-communist forces. However, if the coup leaders believed they could redress the problems, their steps to distance themselves from the communists ensured that their actions would bring war and not peace. The Lon Nol government declined to cooperate with China and North Vietnam and, within days of the coup, the new regime was involved in border disputes with the communists. In May 1970, the United States invaded Cambodia to chase down communist forces. If it did so as an ally, it failed to inform Lon Nol until the invasion had begun.[18]

In the meantime, Sihanouk, who was prohibited from returning to Cambodia, had retreated to Beijing. There he joined forces with the still small Khmer Rouge, led by Pol Pot. From Beijing, Sihanouk announced the formation of the National United Front of Kampuchea (NUFK) and a government-in-exile, the Royal Government of National Union of Kampuchea. China and Vietnam immediately saw that their best interests would be served by backing the NUFK. This was to be a major turning point in Cambodian history.[19]

The Path to Tragedy

In the early months of the new regime, Phnom Penh engaged in fiercely anti-Vietnamese propaganda which resulted in the deaths of many ethnic Vietnamese living in Cambodia and the flight of more than 200,000 as refugees. There was also a disastrous military campaign to drive out the Vietnamese communist forces, leading to the loss of major portions of Cambodian territory.[20]

It was American concern to save the endangered Lon Nol government which led to the invasion of Cambodia in May 1970. But, if the introduction of 31,000 American and 43,000 South Vietnamese troops shattered any illusion that the Lon Nol regime might remain neutral, a more important consideration was the alienating effect it had on the Khmer people. By the United States own admission, the ill-disciplined conduct of invading South Vietnamese forces antagonised the local population and compared poorly with the 'exemplary' behaviour of North Vietnamese troops in the country.[21] American ground forces withdrew some two months after the invasion began, but the United States continued the battle with a massive bombing campaign. According to Hood and Ablin:

> The destruction was unimaginable ... The bombers hit wedding parties and funerals, rice fields and water buffaloes, villages, hospitals and monasteries... the bombing did as much to alienate the population from the Khmer Republic as to kill the Khmer Rouge.[22]

In all, the Americans dropped more explosives on Cambodia than were dropped on Japan during the whole of World War II.[23] By the end of 1970, most of the roads and railways were impassable, and half the country's schools had closed. Refugees swelled the population of Phnom Penh from 600,000 to over 2 million in less than twelve months.[24] Food was scarce and, in the end, inflation was rampant. The United States provided humanitarian aid, but its massive and fruitless injection of funds into the Cambodian military destroyed what was left of the economy.[25] North and South Vietnamese forces remained in Cambodia for a further two years, turning the country into a major battleground for the Vietnam war.

These circumstances probably only served to drive the Khmer peasants towards the communists and the opportunity was not wasted. The Khmer Rouge, using taped exhortations from Sihanouk, recruited from the Khmer peasantry in the name of the NUFK. From an estimated 800 men under arms in early 1970, the Khmer Rouge grew to 12,000 by the end of the year and to 40,000 by 1973.

The bombing of Cambodia also fuelled the anti-Vietnam war movement in the United States. In the end, the campaign was halted by The United States Congress on 15 August 1973.[26] The Khmer Republic was expected to fall soon after, but held on for another twenty months while the communists strengthened their hold on the countryside. Already the harsh and unpopular programs of the Khmer Rouge were driving more refugees towards Phnom Penh. However, they found little solace there, with the failing Lon Nol regime barely propped up by the United States.[27]

Before Phnom Penh fell on 17 April 1975,[28] the hardship was being felt by all Cambodians. The area under cultivation for rice had dropped from 2.4 million hectares (6 million acres) at the start of the war to just over 400,000 hectares (1 million acres) at the end of the bombing campaign. In addition, as Hood and Ablin point out:

> Between 500,000 and 1 million people were killed. Approximately 3,400,000 had become refugees. The population of the capital had

grown from 600,000 to 3 million. Of fourteen hundred rice mills, eleven hundred were destroyed. Seventy-five percent of the draft animals were killed. And so on. By any measure, the result was horrifying.[29]

And the horror was not to stop. The Khmer Rouge began removing Sihanoukist elements from its structure and denouncing 'non-Khmer' city dwellers. It also identified Vietnam as the 'long-term acute enemy' and began to purge its ranks of Cambodian communists thought to be sympathetic to Vietnam.[30]

Once in power, the Khmer Rouge proclaimed a new state – Democratic Kampuchea – and instituted a program which, years later, would be described as genocide against its own people. They closed the country's borders and isolated it from the outside world. Urban dwellers were evacuated to the countryside and almost the total population was eventually relocated to collective farms. Pol Pot and the Khmer Rouge had determined to rebuild Cambodia literally from nothing and all vestiges of the past, of the industrialised and 'intellectual' world, were to be erased. Pilger, one of the few journalists to follow events in Cambodia closely, described a small part of what had happened on his return to Phnom Penh years later:

> At the edge of the forest there appeared a pyramid of rusting cars like objects in a mirage. The pile included ambulances, a fire engine, police cars, refrigerators, washing-machines, generators, television sets, telephones and typewriters. 'Here lies the modern age,' a headstone might have read, 'abandoned April 17, 1975, Year Zero.' From that date, anybody who had owned such 'luxuries', anybody who had lived in a city or a town, anybody with more than a basic education or who had acquired a modern skill, anybody who knew or worked for foreigners, was in danger. Many would die.[31]

In spite of the new tragedy that overtook the Cambodian people with the declaration of Democratic Kampuchea, the Khmer Rouge implemented its programs behind a veil of secrecy which shielded the rest of the world from the full horror for some years. Essentially, the strategy of the Khmer Rouge was to destroy the social structures of the old society and this involved reducing former members of the middle and upper classes, and the former intelligentsia, to the hardest physical labour in the manner of the poorest peasants. Thus, members of these classes were not just persecuted because of their formal education, but suffered in the name of creating a 'classless' society. At the same time, soldiers, village leaders and the cadres of the communist party were recruited from among the poorest of the peasantry. Typically, they were young teenage boys, and their fanaticism and intolerance were exploited in building the Khmer Rouge's new society. The absolute power placed in the hands of these individuals could lead to random executions for the merest show of insubordination.[32]

Internally, many of the strategies adopted by the Khmer Rouge reflect the fact that Pol Pot saw enemies everywhere, within his own party as well as among the professional and educated elites, religious and ethnic minorities.[33] Externally, the same paranoia led to two features of the country's foreign policy which would be significant in terms of later developments. These were Democratic Kampuchea's close cooperation with the People's Republic of China (PRC) and its hostility towards Vietnam.

Democratic Kampuchea's aggressiveness and belligerence towards Vietnam are difficult to comprehend as a rational action. As Hood and Ablin have argued,

> ... it seems ridiculous and implausible that the leaders of a weary country with 6 million people would confront a neighbouring country with 50 million people and one of the largest armies in the world.[34]

But Pol Pot's internal policies were no more rational and the conflict with Vietnam (and to a lesser extent Thailand) could be seen as deriving to some extent from Kampuchea's alignment with the PRC.

The conflict – ostensibly a border dispute – continued until February 1978, when Vietnam made its last serious attempt to resolve the situation. The Vietnamese proposed an end to hostilities, troop withdrawals from both sides of the border, and international supervision of an agreed settlement. When Kampuchea rejected the offer, Vietnam took steps to consolidate its international position in advance of stronger military action. It moved firmly into the Soviet camp, increasing tensions with the PRC, as well as between Vietnamese and ethnic Chinese living in Vietnam. At the same time, it dropped its demand for reconstruction aid as a precondition to diplomatic normalisation with the United States; America declined the invitation. Then, in May 1978 there was a massive rebellion in Cambodia's eastern provinces and, the following month, thousands of 'boat people', refugees from both Vietnam and Cambodia, took to the open seas, while many more made the trek from Cambodia into Thailand. At the same time, many ethnic Chinese from Vietnam fled into China and open conflict broke out between Vietnam and the PRC. The United Nations High Commission for Refugees stated that one million people had fled Vietnam and Cambodia, but primarily Vietnam.[35]

The international community began to grasp the enormity of the tragedy that was overwhelming Indochina, but the flight of refugees from Cambodia had only just begun.

On 25 December 1978, Vietnam invaded Cambodia in force and, within three weeks, had taken Phnom Penh and secured all but the region bordering Thailand. The invasion was purportedly undertaken at the 'invitation' of a group of Cambodian communists, comprising former Khmer-Viet Minh and defectors from the Pol Pot regime, led by Heng Samrin . Three days after the fall of Phnom Penh, Heng Samrin declared the People's Republic of Kampuchea (PRK).

Heng Samrin inherited a country in disarray. Difficulties during the first phase of reconstruction, during 1979–80, were increased by the lack of educated Cambodians – testimony to the destructiveness of the Khmer Rouge policies. Because of this, much administration, from the local level up, relied initially on the resources of the Vietnamese.

Vietnam was able to deflect some of the international criticism that its actions drew by immediately allowing the international media into Cambodia and placing the full horror of the Pol Pot regime on display.[36] However, the overthrow of the Khmer Rouge also saw a large part of the population become refugees, whether as a result of the conflict or simply because they saw the chance to escape to a better life elsewhere. And it was the refugee problem that would attract most attention from the international media.

It is estimated that there were about 850,000 refugees from Cambodia between 1975 and 1981, the bulk of them in the years 1979-81. Most ended up in UNHCR camps on the Thai-Cambodian border. In the early years, however, many were forcibly repatriated by the Thais, with heavy loss of life.[37] In addition, there were the refugees from Vietnam itself, which ensured that the Western media would focus more on Vietnam as the source of the problem. Becker makes the telling point:

> [The] mysterious flight of the boat people is a major key to understanding the Vietnamese-Cambodian War and the dreadful consequences of that triangle of disputes between Cambodia, Vietnam and China which ignited the Third Indochina War...
>
> The boat people composed a deadly flotilla of complaints against Hanoi; the South China Sea was a graveyard for the Vietnamese forced out by the new regime. More than that, their small craft were the equivalent of thousands of red warning flags proclaiming that the ills of postwar Vietnam had exploded and that explosion was pushing Hanoi to extremes. Vietnam was angry and frightened, afraid of China and Cambodia, afraid that nothing

would succeed ... particularly not the dream of one, cohesive Indochinese communist bloc headed by Hanoi.[38]

The Western media usually failed to relate the Vietnamese perspective and presented Vietnam simply as an expansionist power. And even though by 1983 Vietnamese participation in the control of Cambodia had been reduced to less than half the 1979 level,[39] the continuing role of Vietnamese advisers and the presence in the country of some 150,000 Vietnamese soldiers was enough to ensure that the Heng Samrin regime was regarded as a puppet government.

Against this, there was an increasing tendency, in the early 1980s, to compare what had occurred in Cambodia under the Khmer Rouge with Nazi Germany, and to refer to it as a 'new holocaust'. But competing views on what had happened meant that the calls for action remained muted.

Throughout the 1970s, there had been little mainstream media attention to events in Cambodia or the precursors to the situation. Those analyses which were undertaken tended to reflect a strong ideological bias. Early in the history of the Pol Pot regime, Ponchaud wondered that '... so few voices [should be] ... raised in protest against the assassination of a people,'[40] but both Gomes and Vickery queried claims made about the degree of human destruction.[41] Gomes described the part played by the United States in creating the situation in which the Khmer Rouge rose to power and implemented its programs - a role evident from the history of Cambodia in relation to the Vietnam war. Gaddis, in contrast, sought to attribute the lay the blame on North Vietnam.[42]

With competing retrospective interpretations of history, it was comparatively easy for a media serving Western audiences generally ideologically opposed to communism, to portray Vietnam as the villain, particularly when confronted with the immediacy of the refugee problem. The Western view of Cambodia in 1981, summed up in a *New York Times* survey of changes in southeast Asia since the end of the Vietnam war, concluded that the standard of living and state of peace in regional countries rejecting communism had continued to rise, while Vietnam and Cambodia were mired in war and social upheaval.[43]

Throughout 1981 the United States exploited the media by raising allegations of Vietnamese use of chemical weapons against the Khmer Rouge. The United States put forward 'evidence' to support its stance but a United Nations investigation was unable to either confirm nor deny the use of chemicals.[44]

It was against this background of a demonised Vietnam that the West, and specifically the United States and the United Kingdom, continued to provide aid and training to the Khmer Rouge during the 1980s, thus adding to the problems of the region, even while the extent of the earlier destruction was becoming evident.[45] Indeed, in 1981, United Nations discussions on a possible peace settlement included conditions which would have allowed for the return of Pol Pot after elections had been held.[46] This concession reflected the pursuit of Western interests through backing for the Khmer Rouge. At the same time, Vietnam's abandonment of support for communist forces elsewhere in southeast Asia was rejected as a cynical attempt to gain favour with the United States and ASEAN.[47] But, clearly, it was not only the Vietnamese who were pursuing their perceived national interests.

As Shawcross point out, what took place in Cambodia '... hardly demonstrates real improvement in international conduct.'[48] Indeed, the Cambodian tragedy was, to some extent, a by-product of regional and global rivalries and the real deficiency in media coverage lies in the failure to report in context. The fact is that when Vietnam lifted the veil of secrecy on Cambodia - when it revealed the atrocities, the instruments of torture, the piles of skulls - it provided the media with a story.[49] The images of horror were newsworthy but, at the same time, they deflected what might otherwise have been more in-depth analysis of the motives of the international players involved, including Vietnam itself. Cambodia was seen as a buffer against Vietnamese 'expansionism' but, as Chanda argues, the 'bloodletting' which occurred in the 1970s and early 1980s left Cambodia too weak to be a real buffer.[50] As a result, Vietnam incurred the suspicion and hostility of China, the United States and ASEAN, and the Western media reflected the official line. It did so even while the worst excesses of the Khmer Rouge were becoming evident.

Sadly, as Shawcross points out, the story of Cambodia is not atypical today.[51] In the 1990s, the examples of Rwanda and Bosnia confirm the observation and raise serious questions about the reasons for which political groups resort to, and populations participate in, what would otherwise be considered 'inhuman' behaviour. It took more than another decade of appeals to the international conscience to address the tragedy in Cambodia. Even then, the solution appears to have owed more to international compromise than any moral decision to redress the injustices of the past.

The Ambitious Mission

While Sihanouk appears always to have been prepared to hedge to retain his position, there seems little doubt that he was able to read the Cambodian political situation well. In the early 1960s, he predicted that the Vietnam war would end in a communist victory, and it was probably for this reason that he preferred to tolerate the incursions of his communist neighbours, rather than welcoming American attempts to expel them. But Sihanouk's apparent acceptance that the communists would prevail did not mean that he shared their commitment. In 1973, Sihanouk visited areas of Cambodia held by the communists and asked Premier Zhou En Lai of the PRC to warn United States Secretary of State Henry Kissinger that the longer the war continued the more radical its outcome would be.[52] The advice, however, went unheeded. Indeed, there was probably little that could have been done to change the course of events at that point.[53]

In the early 1980s, the position in southeast Asia consolidated into firm opposition to Vietnam and its perceived 'expansionism' in Cambodia.[54] By 1982, Vietnam controlled most of the country, opposed by a fragile coalition of the Khmer Rouge and non-communist groups based along the Thai-Cambodian border. Sihanouk nominally led the government-in-exile represented by the new political grouping but, numerically, the coalition was dominated by the Khmer Rouge.[55] In Cambodia, the situation developed into what was effectively a civil war between the coalition forces, supported by ASEAN, and the Vietnam-backed forces of the PRK. Internationally, the conflict was complicated by Soviet support for the PRK, Chinese support for the Khmer Rouge, and United States support for the non-communist forces. The ASEAN nations – affected to differing degrees by the refugee crisis[56] – were now seen as the first line of defence and enjoyed fairly solid support from the West. They were even prepared to put aside their longstanding distrust of the PRC while they sensed a greater threat from the Soviet Union's links with Vietnam. The PRC was particularly supportive of Thailand which bore the brunt of the refugee problem.[57]

In 1983 there was a change of government in Australia, and the Labor Party came to power under Prime Minister Bob Hawke. The Hawke government held strong views on Australia's role in the Vietnam war and was determined to play an active role in settling the Cambodian crisis. It also sought to re-establish relations with Vietnam. The positions taken by ASEAN and the United States, however, made it clear that independent action – particularly any initiative to establish bilateral relations with Vietnam – would not be welcomed. Because of this, the Hawke government concentrated on exploring options for a settlement in Cambodia.[58]

Soon after the Vietnamese invasion of the country, ASEAN had put forward a regionally-sponsored resolution in the United Nations, expressing concern for the situation in Cambodia. In 1983, Australia withdrew from co-sponsorship of this resolution on the grounds that it was too one-sidedly critical of Vietnam and did not take sufficient account of the human rights abuses which had occurred under the Khmer Rouge. Other Australian proposals, including a call for a war crimes tribunal in Cambodia, were welcomed by the Vietnamese, but not by ASEAN who saw such moves as undermining the regional position. It took some years for a consensus to begin to emerge on a possible solution. When it did, the consensus was that Vietnamese forces should withdraw from Cambodia under arrangements which ensured that Pol Pot and the Khmer Rouge could not return to power, while conditions were created for free and fair elections and the return of refugees, with the guarantee of a future Cambodia that would be neutral, independent and non-aligned.[59]

In 1988, hope emerged for a break in the deadlocked confrontation, when the United States began to pressure the PRC on its continuing support for the Khmer Rouge. This was allegedly done by planting unsubstantiated stories in the media, suggesting that China was prepared to give asylum to top Khmer Rouge leaders.[60] The strategy finds parallels in the steps taken to shape the media context of a situation before engaging in military action. At the same time, Indonesia moved to host informal talks between the warring Cambodian parties, resulting in the two Jakarta Informal Meetings in July 1988 and February 1989. Although the meetings did not produce substantive outcomes, they clarified some of the issues and were assisted by Vietnam's announcement, in January 1989, that it was prepared to withdraw all its forces from Cambodia by September of that year. Vietnam's decision was probably influenced by the end of the Cold War and the likely decline in Soviet economic aid. By mid-1989, however, France sensed that the climate was right for a full international conference on Cambodia. The result was the Paris International Conference on Cambodia (PICC), convened under joint Indonesian leadership, in July and August 1989. The PICC failed, although it came close to achieving its aims.[61]

Vietnam proceeded to withdraw its forces more or less on schedule. However, instead of adding to the momentum of the peace process, the withdrawal led to a resurgence of fighting and a hardening of diplomatic positions. Although international opinion remained strongly in favour of a comprehensive peace settlement, no agreement could be reached on the composition of the proposed transitional administration. In particular, there were difficulties over the role suggested for the Khmer Rouge, despite the fact that it would be only one of four factions involved and its former leadership would take no part.[62]

In November 1989, a new peace proposal was put forward by Australian Foreign Minister Gareth Evans. To avoid the power-sharing issue which had been the central point of contention, and to constrain the role of the Khmer Rouge, it was proposed that the United Nations be directly involved in the civil administration of Cambodia during the transitional period while elections were held and the Cambodian state re-established. The idea was not entirely new. As early as 1981, Sihanouk had proposed a United Nations trusteeship and, in 1989, United States Congressman Stephen Solarz had also put forward the specific idea of a neutral United Nations interim administration. According to Evans and Grant, discussions Evans had with Solarz in October 1989 were crucial in shaping Australia's thinking on the proposal.[63]

The final peace proposal was prepared by Australia following the Informal Meeting on Cambodia which took place in Jakarta on 26–28 February 1990. *Cambodia: an Australian Peace Proposal* (known more commonly as the 'Red Book' for the colour of its cover) outlined a comprehensive settlement, an enhanced role for the United Nations in an interim administration in Cambodia, the organisation of elections, reconstruction, and the guarantee of a sovereign and neutral Cambodia.[64]

There were still diplomatic hurdles to be overcome but, by 1991, Pol Pot's patrons had grown tired of him in a confrontation that no longer made strategic sense.[65] In October of that year, Agreements on a Comprehensive Political Settlement of the Cambodian Conflict were signed in Paris (the Paris Agreements) and the United Nations was invited to establish the United Nations Transitional Authority in Cambodia (UNTAC). The move was fully supported by the Security Council in Resolution 718 (1991) of 31 October 1991.[66]

The 22,000-man UNTAC mission was heralded as the most ambitious peace-keeping operation ever undertaken by the United Nations. With expenses approaching US$2 billion, it was also one of the most expensive.[67] The media generally accepted the peace settlement and heralded it as marking a great step forward in international cooperation. For this reason, the legitimacy of the exercise was never in doubt.[68] However, major power interests had not been replaced by altruism, and there were those who questioned what had been conceded to arrive at a settlement. Pilger described the peace plan as 'vague and sinister'. He noted the 'new, cleansing jargon' employed to reclassify the Khmer Rouge as a 'faction' and the failure to mention genocide. But the mention of genocide would have served little purpose. The peace plan specifically prohibited the retroactive application of criminal law; the Khmer Rouge were granted immunity from prosecution[69] and as long as the governments of Western liberal democracies were looking the other way, so to was the mainstream media.

Media Attitudes to the Khmer Rouge

There can be no doubt that the Cambodian people suffered more than a decade of death and destruction from the time of the United States and South Vietnamese invasion of their country in 1970, through the American bombing campaign, the years of the Khmer Rouge and Pol Pot, to the vicious civil war which followed the Vietnamese takeover in 1979–80. But histories recorded by outside observers tend to reflect the political biases and perspectives of those observers. For Pilger and others, there was no doubt about what the Khmer Rouge had done and the continuing threat that they presented. It was the rehabilitation of the Khmer Rouge that led Pilger to argue that the peace process was compromised from the beginning. In November 1992, he wrote:

> One year ago, the *Observer* reported: 'If Cambodia's peace process remains on course ... it will be because of Khmer Rouge restraint.' Since the United Nations arrived here, Khmer Rouge 'restraint' has included a full-scale military offensive in the north, where it has nearly doubled its area of control. Indeed, Pol Pot's men in black are now virtually everywhere in Cambodia, thanks to a 'peace process' that has provided them with both a Trojan horse and a veto.[70]

Certainly, the part played by the Khmer Rouge in recent Cambodian history is contentious, but the 'truth' about the Khmer Rouge and Pol Pot is far from settled. Scott described the problem within Cambodia:

> To speak to Cambodians is to hear painful accounts of what happened to them in the years between 1975 and 1979 when the Khmer Rouge ran the country and about 1 million Cambodians, or one in eight, died from starvation, disease or execution. The tales are brutal and sad, but what is equally tragic is that so often no one seems clear about who is to blame. Pol Pot is the only answer most can come up with; the Khmer Rouge period has become 'Pol Pot time,' as if every brutal act can be laid at his feet alone.
> This transformation of the Khmer Rouge period into 'Pol Pot time,' into an official version, is one of the central themes of Cambodia... Cambodia's leaders have been content to turn the Khmer Rouge period into an emblem of modern barbarity – an

Asian genocide – empty of content about what really happened and why.[71]

However, while the media reported the horrors, they showed little interest in investigating the real story. The United States had opposed the Khmer Rouge and supported Lon Nol in the early 1970s. But, by 1977, when Ponchaud was drawing attention to the 'assassination of a people' in Cambodia,[72] United States was already shifting towards support for the Khmer Rouge as America's strategic interests in opposing Vietnam assumed priority. Pilger has detailed the observations he made after the Vietnamese takeover. He has also detailed the attacks he suffered for reporting what he saw and heard of both the brutality of the Khmer Rouge and the assistance they received from the West.[73] But Pilger is in no doubt about what took place, and he criticises writers such as Shawcross who blur the distinctions between the Pol Pot period and what occurred later. According to Pilger, Shawcross attempts to shift most of the blame to the Vietnamese, whom the West had demonised as marauding invaders. In accordance with American policy, Cambodia was cut off from all economic assistance – and even trade with American companies – after the Vietnamese intervention.[74]

Other writers, such as Gomes,[75] are equally adamant that the Khmer Rouge have been misrepresented. Gomes' views are not those of the mainstream, but his explanation of events shows why contrasting perspectives must at least be entertained. According to Gomes, the forced evacuation of Phnom Penh was not an act of oppression but a necessary step to get the starving population out into the countryside where they could be fed. Nor, according to Gomes, did the Khmer Rouge pursue a policy of persecuting the educated 'elite'. Rather, educated Cambodians were more likely to have resisted the rebuilding strategies of the Khmer Rouge and to have sought to escape as refugees. Gomes is equally critical of refugee reports of atrocities, on the grounds that the refugees were unlikely to be a representative sample of the population.

However, despite the perspectives that may be adopted to serve a particular point of view, there can be little doubt that the basic strategy of the Khmer Rouge was to isolate Cambodia from the rest of the world while they built a new society based on fundamental communist principles. It is also clear that many people were executed or died during the three years of Khmer Rouge rule. At the same time, the Khmer Rouge received both direct and indirect support from the West because it suited the West's political purposes.[76]

This situation made it difficult for Western governments to encourage the media to demonise the Khmer Rouge. On the one hand there were the reports of those such as Pilger and Silber[77] who had covered the situation following the Vietnamese takeover, and whose stories lent credence to the claims of severe political oppression, torture, and genocide of the Khmer Rouge. On the other, there was the evidence of previous Western support for the Khmer Rouge. The answer is provided by Scott: the Khmer Rouge period became 'Pol Pot time' and all the brutality of the Khmer Rouge was identified with the movement's leadership.[78] As long as the Khmer Rouge leadership was removed, then the bulk of the Khmer Rouge could be distanced from its more 'misguided' elements and policies. This was similar to the strategy of distancing a people from its leadership, encountered in limited conflict.

The media readily accepted this position and needed little encouragement to compare Cambodia under Pol Pot with Hitler's Germany rather than Stalin's Soviet Union.[79] The comparison with Hitler left the role of communism out of the equation,[80] perhaps to gain PRC and Russian support for a peace settlement. More importantly, this attitude demonised Pol Pot personally and enabled Vietnam to be rehabilitated as the saviour of Cambodia. Vietnam was able to withdraw with honour while the Khmer Rouge were allowed to participate as another 'faction' represented in the peace process. References to 'genocide' were euphemistically replaced with statements of '... the need to ensure in Cambodia a non-return to policies and practices of the recent past.'[81]

In 1990, as progress towards a peace settlement was being made, Sihanouk stated he would agree to anything the Khmer Rouge wanted. He was quoted as saying 'The Khmer Rouge are not criminals. they are true patriots.'[82]

In these attitudes to the Khmer Rouge, the full picture of the compromise on Cambodia is revealed. As Evans and Grant argue:

> If it were simply a matter of adopting a strategy that would effectively isolate and marginalise the Khmer Rouge, not very many voices would be heard in strenuous opposition. But the critical point was that the Khmer Rouge could not be effectively isolated and marginalised, and its military influence nullified, so long as it continued to be supplied, especially by China, with arms, money and diplomatic support.[83]

So it was that the continuing role of the Khmer Rouge was determined outside Cambodia, by international actors. In the end, it was not the alleged new commitment of the United Nations to lift up and protect those who were too weak to care for themselves that mattered. It was not basic human rights or a new world order that weighed 'Pol Pot time' in the balance. Old fashioned politics, rather than the findings of an independent media, determined the way the Khmer Rouge would be presented to global audiences.

Cambodia in Transition

United Nations Security Council Resolution 718 (1991) established a Supreme National Council of Cambodia (the SNC) recognised as 'the unique legitimate body and source of authority in which, throughout the transitional period, the sovereignty, independence and unity of Cambodia [were] enshrined.' The SNC was chaired by Prince Norodom Sihanouk and comprised the four Cambodian parties to the peace agreement – the Front uni national pour un Cambodge indépendent, neutre, pácifique et coopératif (FUNCINPEC), the Khmer People's National Liberation Front (KPNLF), the Party of Democratic Kampuchea (PDK), and the State of Cambodia (SOC).[84] FUNCINPEC was the pro-royalist party (led by Sihanouk's son, Prince Norodom Ranariddh), while the KPNLF was the other non-communist faction. The PDK represented the Khmer Rouge, its forces now renamed the National Army of Democratic Kampuchea (NADK). The SOC was the Cambodian government installed by Vietnam. It was now headed by Hun Sen, who had replaced Heng Samrin in 1985. At the United Nations-sponsored elections, Hun Sen's faction campaigned as the Cambodian People's Party (CPP).

UNTAC was established by United Nations Security Council Resolution 745 (1992) of 19 February 1992, for a period not to exceed eighteen months. It became operational on 15 March 1992.

Difficulties arose almost as soon as UNTAC commenced its operations. Phase I of the cease-fire, which had been in effect since the signing of the Paris Agreements, was to be followed on 13 June by the cantonment, disarming and demobilisation of the various forces. Well before that date, however, it was apparent that the PDK/NADK was not cooperating.[85] The PDK introduced its own interpretation of the Agreements as they related to verification of the withdrawal of foreign forces and the role of the SNC. The PDK also refused to allow UNTAC forces to be deployed in areas under NADK control, and did not provide the required information on force strengths and matériel.[86]

Part of the problem may have been that, by June 1992, only part of the UNTAC force was in place, and the inability of the United Nations to quickly deploy its full force reduced the level of trust it could command.[87] Any advantage to be gained by the swift deployment of overwhelming force, an established tactic in limited conflict, was lost. Relations with the PDK were to remain a problem and not all difficulties could be attributed to failure on the part of the United Nations. UNTAC forces came under attack in areas where the NADK were known to be present. By the end of the year, the United Nations had formally condemned the PDK for its failure to observe the Paris Agreements and called for sanctions against the PDK/NADK. The media, which had never quite accepted that the Khmer Rouge should be integrally involved in the peace process and avoided use of the term NADK, strayed from the official line and began demonise Pol Pot's forces.[88] Pilger criticised the United Nations for its continuing 'appeasement' of the Khmer Rouge.[89] There were also charges that UNTAC was insufficiently aggressive in pursuing human rights objectives.[90] These developments find parallels in limited conflict where the media typically questions the course of any operation which is protracted or which the media believes is deviating from its objectives.

The United Nations determined that the peace process and preparation for elections should continue[91] but, by the end of 1992, UNTAC was under strain as the international media became increasingly critical of the United Nations' apparent impotence.[92] Typical media-management strategies were implemented to control the situation. UNTAC personnel were forbidden to talk to the media without permission and 'media control officers' were deployed within the publishing offices of political parties and factions in an effort to prevent the dissemination of inflammatory propaganda. It was alleged that UNTAC officials had also banned certain correspondents from covering United Nations operations because they had written 'unfriendly articles' about UNTAC.[93]

In February 1993, the Secretary-General reported to the Security Council that UNTAC was proceeding on schedule with electoral preparations, the SNC having set the election dates for the end of May. But he also reported that neither the PDK nor its recently formed National Unity of Cambodia Party had filed official registration to participate in the elections. Shortly before the elections, the PDK advised that it could no longer attend SNC meetings because there was insufficient security and that it was withdrawing 'temporarily' from Phnom Penh.[94]

There were some difficulties in the lead up to the ballot, with the NADK using terror in an attempt to abort the process, and the SOC employing the remnants of its state apparatus to coerce Cambodians into voting for the CPP; the CPP suggested that votes would not be secret.[95] UNTAC banned opinion polls in an attempt to limit intimidation.[96] However, apart from a few minor incidents, the elections were peaceful and went ahead as planned. This, apparently, was a disappointment to those in the media who were expecting more violence.[97] But, as the vote count began, tensions began to rise. There were early complaints of electoral irregularities from the CPP, which trailed FUNCINPEC by less than 1 per cent in the early tallies. The strength of these complaints prompted the SNC to request that UNTAC cease announcements about the results of the elections until the issues could be addressed.[98] When the result was declared, FUNCINPEC won with more than 45 per cent of the vote, compared to 38 per cent for the CPP. Eighteen other political parties shared the remainder of the votes. The turnout of just over 4 million voters represented approximately 90 per cent of registered voters.[99]

The Khmer Rouge capitalised on the defeat of its old enemies from the Hun Sen regime by calling for FUNCINPEC and Prince Ranariddh to be given full rights as winners of the election. The CPP responded with Hun Sen warning of a 'bloodbath' and declaring secession in six provinces in the east of the country.[100] The eventual solution saw a deal which allowed Prince Ranariddh and Hun Sen to share power as co-prime ministers.

On 27 August 1993, the United Nations Security Council welcomed the Secretary-General's reports on Cambodia and approved the UNTAC withdrawal plan. On 24 September, Prince Norodom Sihanouk, as Head of State, formally promulgated the Constitution adopted by the new Constituent Assembly; Cambodia became a constitutional monarchy which was 'independent, sovereign, peaceful, neutral and non-aligned.'[101] President Bush of the United States was to call Cambodia the 'international community's greatest triumph' heralding a golden age for human rights in that country and giving it 'a new lease of life.'[102]

In a style reminiscent of limited conflict outcomes, the claims were all for resounding success. But the Khmer Rouge were still active and some United Nations-sponsored programs – such as mine clearing – were making slow progress. Osborne noted that the political compromises already made did not augur well for the functioning of a democratic system and that, away from Phnom Penh, little had changed. He conceded that Sihanouk's description of Cambodia as 'the most corrupt country in the world' was probably correct.[103]

The Aftermath - the Failure of the Media

Three years after the election, assessments of the outcome in Cambodia vary. But, with the exception of incidents such as Khmer Rouge kidnapping and murder of foreigners, Cambodia attracts little attention from the media. Serious analysis does not bring headlines.

Shawcross and Pilger were critical of each other's assessments of cause and effect in pre-UNTAC Cambodia. In the aftermath, however, they agreed that the prospects for continuing stability were not good.

In May 1994, Shawcross acknowledged that there had been important achievements. He noted that in pre-UNTAC Cambodia, political terror and murder were institutionalised, but that UNTAC had compelled Cambodia to sign the United Nations covenants on human rights and freedom of the press. 'Those,' stated Shawcross, 'are now standards to which the Government can be held. Cambodia now has one of the most free presses in South-East Asia – although the Government is considering a tough new press law.'[104] In the end, the standards were to no avail. Shawcross acknowledged that human rights were abused by the CPP 'apparat' which still dominated the country.[105] And, in late 1994, the government clamped down on the domestic media, which had been highly, and colourfully, critical of the government's performance. The official explanation was that the government was simply trying to ensure responsible journalism.[106]

Shawcross further reported that, in the twelve months since the election, the Khmer Rouge had driven further into Cambodia than at any time since the Vietnamese overthrew them in 1979. The Cambodian army was as ineffective as ever. Real soldiers often were not paid, while there were many 'phantom' soldiers on the military payroll whose salaries were pocketed by corrupt officers. The small army was alleged to have some 2,000 generals, many of whom were not even soldiers. They had simply bought their rank in order to be able to intimidate and extort more effectively. 'As in the Lon Nol years,' Shawcross observed, 'money and factionalism still define political life.'[107]

In July 1995, Pilger's assessment of the future for Cambodia was even more bleak. The Khmer Rouge were apparently still operating with impunity from large bases inside Thailand and moving with relative ease in up to 50 per cent of the country, more than they controlled before the arrival of the United Nations advance force in 1991.[108] Mainstream media reports were divided between warnings that the Khmer Rouge could return to power, and claims that an amnesty was depleting their ranks.[109] The peace settlement was supposed to create a Cambodia which was 'independent, sovereign, peaceful, neutral and non-aligned.' But, according to Pilger,

> The UN has produced report after report showing that the Thais hold the key to peace in Cambodia... without the support of the Thai military, the Khmer Rouge would wither on the vine. But neither the UN secretary-general nor any western or regional

leader has condemned the Bangkok government and demanded that it close the border and the Khmer Rouge bases on its soil.[110]

Conclusion

Many of the world's major powers contributed to the tragic political history of Cambodia: French colonialism, Japanese occupation, American support for the military government of Lon Nol during the Vietnam war, Chinese backing for the genocidal Khmer Rouge and, finally, Soviet assistance to the Vietnam-backed Hun Sen puppet government.[111]

It is easy to believe, taking the official Western line, that the United Nations intervention in Cambodia was, in the end, an act of conscience, a realisation by the international community that the Cambodian people had suffered enough. But the underlying objective of a neutral Cambodia shows that the interests of the great powers had not been forgotten, and the continuing toleration of the Khmer Rouge suggests that humanitarian goals continue to be compromised in favour of strategic objectives.[112] Indeed, the management of the media throughout the Cambodian peace process indicates little that is different from limited conflict, except that the time frames were longer and, due to the internationalisation of the effort, manipulation and restriction more difficult to achieve.

There may not have been secrecy in the planning of UNTAC. It was, after all, the outcome of years of stop-start negotiations. But there was at least some secrecy regarding its objectives. Pilger quotes United Nations spokesman, Eric Falt, as saying, 'You must understand that the peace process was aimed at allowing [the Khmer Rouge] to gain respectability.'[113] Only such an objective could explain the continued tolerance of the Khmer Rouge despite widespread acknowledgment of its record of atrocities and continuing human rights abuses. Few citizens of the West would accept that the Khmer Rouge were entitled to any respectability, yet their governments conceded it respectability for political purposes.

The approval granted the Khmer Rouge is further demonstrated by the fact that peace moves were not seriously mooted until after the Vietnamese invasion of Cambodia. And then it was the Vietnamese who were demonised, not the Khmer Rouge whose atrocities the Vietnamese drew attention to. It was also the Vietnamese-backed State of Cambodia government that was de-stabilised by economic sanctions, particularly the unilateral sanctions of the United States, as well as by Western support for the Khmer Rouge. Even so, as long as it had Soviet backing, Vietnam could probably have held out in Cambodia. It was the end of the Cold

War that brought the change in circumstances. By unanimously backing a regional initiative, the great powers brought legitimacy to the peace efforts. Vietnam could offer withdrawal as a concession once the outcome appeared inevitable. There was little to conceal in the buildup of UNTAC. It was a vast force in terms of United Nations deployments. Each of the contingents brought with it elements of its national press. The tasks were also diverse, demanding and open to risk of media exposure. But the United Nations lost the advantage because it was slow to deploy its full force. UNTAC was anxious that the media should not emphasise any problems this might cause in the peace process and has been accused of attempting to 'muzzle' journalists who reported deficiencies. Where necessary, the United Nations also restricted the media to ensure the success of its operations, such as when it withheld election results.

Finally, although many of the outcomes of the peace plan had not been achieved and other tasks, including mine clearance, were proceeding only slowly, the United Nations show-cased Cambodia's election results as evidence of its 'triumph' and withdrew to leave a factionalised government facing a recalcitrant Khmer Rouge, still indirectly supported by the West through Thailand. Yet there was little media controversy over the conduct of UNTAC, because the military side of the operation had been well managed. The elections were a media story. The continuing Cambodian struggle was not – except when Westerners were kidnapped and murdered.

According to Pilger:

> Six years ago, when the United States and its friends were constructing the 'peace process' and Margaret Thatcher was demanding the inclusion of Khmer Rouge in the Phnom Penh government, a British diplomat told Eva Mysliwiec of Oxfam: 'Cambodia is of no strategic value ... it's expendable.'[114]

And what of the 'expendable' Cambodians and their feelings towards the Khmer Rouge? In 1996, a split in the Khmer Rouge brought the possibility of a deal that would restore some of the former Khmer Rouge leadership to positions of power in Cambodia. The *Economist* observed that:

> Foreigners ... may feel squeamish about the return of the Khmer Rouge, in any form, to Cambodian politics. But foreigners do not have to live there, nor pay the price of peace, if that is what it turns out to be.[115]

In summary, the lack of media coverage and media analysis was one of the major reasons why Western audiences failed to understand the real motives of their governments and the United Nations in a peace process which was nowhere near as altruistic or successful as was claimed. Despite the work of one or two dedicated journalists, in the main the media preferred to forget Cambodia, first because the situation was too complex and, second, because they chose to avoid the complexities and accept instead the simplicities of the official line.

13

Haiti: A Domestically-Driven Intervention

The collapse of international communism following the end of the Cold War was held out by the West as evidence that the market had triumphed. The market system, it was argued, would now spread unfettered around the globe, carrying the Western liberal democratic ideology with it. But if that was the rhetoric of the champions of the West, there were many in the Third World who were less optimistic about the benefits of market-led development, and who could point to situations where Western business interests had taken precedence over a commitment to democracy. The West has always been, and remains, selective in its support of the drive for democracy.

Haiti is a typical case. The 1991 military overthrow of President Jean-Bertrand Aristide – the charismatic priest who had come to power in the country's first fully free democratic elections in almost three decades – was met with a poorly enforced embargo by the Organization of American States (OAS) and a token multinational monitoring system.

The United States, which wields enormous influence in the OAS, was largely to blame for the ineffectiveness of the response. President George Bush, pressured by American investors in Haiti, failed to invoke the full range of available measures and then proceeded to dilute the meagre sanctions that were put in place.[1] Aristide's brand of left-leaning populism did not endear him to the United States and the American administration's commitment to Haitian democracy was reflected in its response.

Central America and the Caribbean Islands are not critical to a stable international system, but the United States interventions in Grenada and Panama, and its intrusion into the politics of other countries in the region, are testimony to America's willingness to impose its values when it is in its interest to do so. However, it was not the overthrow of a struggling democracy or the human rights abuses in the Haitian countryside which pricked America's conscience. It was the influx of Haitian refugees escaping to Florida in a flotilla of crude wooden boats which galvanised America to act.[2]

The United States responded to exiled President Aristide's call for restitution of constitutional order in Haiti when it was confronted by a refugee problem that was not just a matter of international concern, but that was domestically unacceptable. That response followed the now well developed formula for limited conflict intervention.

The operation was planned in secret, with media excluded. Legitimacy was secured through the backing of the OAS and the United Nations, and preparation was made for the deployment of overwhelming force against a low risk target, to secure objectives quickly. As in Somalia, the media were on the ground well ahead of the troops once the intervention was announced, aided this time by Haiti's proximity to the United States. But this time the military campaign was so closely connected to domestic political issues that the media was able to exercise a degree of independence and authority at odds with the control that had become a feature of so many recent campaigns. The result was a depth of coverage that, for a time at least, held the promise of limited conflict coverage that gave audiences a relatively balanced picture of the situation in its proper context.

Background to the Campaign

Haiti is one of the poorest countries in the world. It is the second largest of the chain of islands that stretch in an arc from south of the tip of Florida to Trinidad, just north of Venezuela. Situated on the western end of the island which it shares with the Dominican Republic, Haiti occupies just under 28,000 square kilometres (about 11,000 square miles), or roughly one third of the land mass.

The population of Haiti numbers just over 6.6 million people, 95 per cent of whom are black. The remaining 5 per cent are of mixed race but it is this minority group which has traditionally exercised economic and political power. The language is a French-based Creole and the major religion is Roman Catholicism blended with voodoo.[3] The country's gross national product has never risen above $US3 billion. At the time of the intervention, Haiti's armed forces consisted of some 7,500 personnel operating in a gendarmerie/police role, with responsibility also for immigration and fire fighting. The forces were equipped with six armoured personnel carriers, nine light artillery pieces, some light mortars, four patrol craft, two combat aircraft and ten other transport liaison aircraft, all of them propeller driven.[4]

Haiti was only the second country in the Western hemisphere to gain independence from its colonial masters. The original French possession, known as Saint-Domingue, was a model slave-based economy ruled over by a small white land-owning class. In 1791, the black slaves (80 per cent of the population) rose in revolt under the leadership of Dominique Toussaint and Jean-Jacques Dessalines.[5] After nearly a decade of bloody conflict, Toussaint emerged victorious. Napoleon Bonaparte despatched a force of 40,000 men to retake the colony in 1802 but, within two years, the French had withdrawn for good, defeated by a combination of climate, disease and a desperate resistance determined not to accept a return to slavery.[6]

Haiti declared its independence on 1 January 1804. The nation was in ruins, but it had forged a fierce brand of anti-authoritarianism and nationalism. This is evidenced by Dessaline's statement at the declaration of independence:

> We will write this Act of Independence using a white man's skull as an inkwell, his skin for parchment and a bayonet as a pen.[7]

Lack of political skills and economic infrastructure, however, condemned Haiti to poverty, and the fear that Haiti's example might encourage other slave populations to revolt led to its ostracism by the United States and other members of the international community. Haiti's independence was eventually recognised by France in 1825. Despite this, without cheap slave labour there was little export income and, as the years went by, the country sank further into poverty.

In 1898, the United States defeated Spain in the Spanish-American War, acquiring Puerto Rico and virtual control of Cuba. As a newly arrived force in the international community, Washington saw the Caribbean as an American sphere of influence. There were few resources at stake, but the United States had to be seen to dominate its own 'backyard' and, in the first three decades of the century, America launched over thirty military interventions in the region.[8] Haiti received its share of attention.

Between 1908 and 1915, the inherent political instability in Haiti worsened. Seven successive leaderships bankrupted the nation by buying arms from the United States to maintain short lived regimes.[9] Following its by now standard response to such instability in the region, Washington invaded in July 1915. The ostensible reason was to protect the lives and property of American citizens, but the real reasons were strategic and economic.

The United States was in the process of taking control of strategic areas around the Panama Canal and had earlier attempted to purchase the Haiti peninsula because of its command of the Windward Passage. Haiti had also recently defaulted on a US$21 million debt to American banks.[10] The stated aims of the invasion were to maintain order, to provide an environment conducive to American investment, and to build public works.[11] Once the Marines were ashore, however, Washington installed a puppet president and had him ratify a treaty legalising the invasion. The Marines were to stay for a further nineteen years, during which they faced constant and increasing public resentment. It was not until 1934, after a depression ravaged America had turned inwards and President Roosevelt had denounced unilateral action at the 1933 Inter-American Conference, that they withdrew.[12]

The longest American overseas occupation in history did little for the Haitian people. Economic improvements only matched population increases, and no attempt was made to provide the education or other reforms on which a lasting democracy might be built. Consequently, when the Marines withdrew, Haiti returned to its previous pattern of corruption and instability. The best efforts to promote change had little impact on the country's desperate situation. Then a deterioration in the economy in the 1950s led to a political crisis in 1957. Four provisional governments rose and fell in that year until Francoise Duvalier, or Papa Doc, was elected president. Duvalier proclaimed Haiti the world's first black republic and encouraged the awakening of a black consciousness in the Haitian people.

Duvalier rapidly increased his grip on power, installed himself as dictator for life and eliminated any free political expression or opposition. The key to this power were the Tonton Macoutes, his private army, who were used to terrorise the populace into submission.[13] The severity of his rule was reflected in the fact that by 1970, an estimated one million Haitians had left the island.

Little changed with Duvalier's death in 1971, when leadership passed to his son, Jean-Claude – or Baby Doc. By 1985, Haiti was the poorest nation in Latin America with static economic growth and a declining per capita income.[14] Economic collapse was not far behind. Food riots escalated into widespread unrest and, in February 1986, Baby Doc was forced to leave the country.

His departure left a power vacuum which was filled by a military interim government pending elections in 1987. These elections, and those a year later, were marred by violence. The winner of the 1988 election was overthrown by the army within a month. The following year, the military-installed President was overthrown by the rank and file of the army led by General Avril. Then Avril himself was forced to step down in the face of unrest and was replaced by the Supreme Court Justice, Ertha Pascal-Trouillot.

Free presidential elections held under the watchful eyes of more than a thousand foreign observers were conducted in December 1990. Victory went to the populist candidate, Father Jean-Bertrand Aristide. Before he could take office, however, the former head of the Tonton Macoutes, Dr Roger Lafontant staged a coup and declared himself president. In sharp contrast to previous coups, the people and the army revolted and the interim president, Pascal-Trouillot was restored to power.[15] Aristide himself was inaugurated on 7 February 1991, with every hope that democracy might be an attainable objective.

United States Involvement

The United States intervention in Haiti had its origins in the Haitian Army's second ousting of Aristide on 30 September 1991. The leaders of the coup were the head of the defence force, Lieutenant-General Raoul Cedras, Port-au-Prince police chief, Colonel Michel Joseph, and Army Chief of Staff, General Philippe Biamby. The catalyst for the confrontation lay in Aristide's plans to dismantle the army and replace it with foreign trained security forces loyal to him.[16] Aristide fled to exile in Venezuela, and then the United States, amid international condemnation of the coup. The United States and the United Nations, however, took no immediate action against the military junta which seized control.

Over the next eighteen months, various diplomatic overtures failed to persuade the Haitian military to return power to the democratically elected president. However, international opinion continued to harden in the face of widespread human rights abuses and a steadily increasing flow of refugees to the United States. It was the refugee situation which finally spurred America into action, although a hard line was taken against fleeing Haitians, many of whom rightly feared political persecution at home.[17]

Finally, in June 1993, the United Nations imposed economic sanctions against the regime preventing sales of military goods and petroleum to Haiti.[18] With a matching trade embargo imposed by the OAS and the cessation of American and other international aid, it was obvious the effects would soon be felt by the fragile Haitian economy.[19] It is perhaps not surprising, then, that at the same time that the United Nations was imposing its sanctions, Haiti's military rulers were persuaded to engage in talks to restore the elected government. The result was the signing of the Governors Island agreement between Aristide and the military high command on 3 July 1993. The agreement provided for the immediate appointment of Robert Malval as interim Prime Minister and the restoration of democracy, with Aristide's return to the presidency, by 30 October 1993.[20]

However, if the Haitian military expected the United Nations to remove its sanctions following the Governors Island agreement, they were wrong. The Security Council waited until the end of August, as Malval prepared to be sworn in, before voting to lift the oil embargo. The sanctions would only be removed in line with progress towards the return to legitimacy and, in the event, Malval found himself little more than a figurehead as the military stubbornly clung to power.

Then, on 12 October, the United States was humiliated when the *USS Harlan County* carrying a United Nations-sponsored contingent of 200 United States marines and 25 Canadian engineers to prepare for the return of the president, was prevented from landing at Port-au-Prince by a mob of anti-Aristide demonstrators, apparently organised by members of the security forces.[21] A further blow came when the safety of the United Nations/OAS International Civilian Mission (ICM), fielded in Haiti to monitor human rights, could no longer be guaranteed and had to be withdrawn.[22] These humiliations came on top of losses and continued failure in Somalia, at a time when a CNN/*USA Today* survey showed United States President Clinton down to a 52 per cent disapproval rating in his handling of foreign affairs. Ominously, 67 per cent of Americans surveyed disapproved of the dispatch of American troops to Haiti.[23]

On 14 October, the United Nations reimposed all sanctions and, two days later, the United States despatched six warships with orders to stop and search any vessels suspected of violating the embargoes.[24]

Haiti's economy deteriorated rapidly, but the worsening conditions had little effect on the military, who continued to refute the Governors Island agreement and cracked down against internal opposition. By early 1994, killings by the security forces were estimated to be running at about fifty a month and United Nations observers were unable to move safely in the Haitian countryside.[25] American resolve hardened in May when the military installed 80 year-old Supreme Court Justice Emil Jonassaint as president.[26] The United States and United Nations responded with further economic sanctions and the neighbouring Dominican Republic was persuaded to put a stop to petrol smuggling over the border.[27]

At the same time, the flow of refugees increased to a flood as increasing numbers of Haitians took the risky thousand mile sea voyage to Florida. The situation reached a crisis point in July with 5000 refugees being picked up by the United States Coastguard in the first week of the month. America dealt with the difficult and politically untimely crisis by diverting many of the refugees to Panama and other Caribbean countries.[28] But it had to do something more.

The United States had already ordered the suspension of air services and financial transactions with Haiti,[29] effectively isolating the country and sending its regime the clear warning that they were a target for intervention. By late July the United States was seeking explicit United Nations approval to invade.[30]

The Search for Legitimacy

The Clinton administration had been openly canvassing the possibility of a military solution in Haiti since October 1993.[31] The *Harlan County* incident could not be ignored but, while 'gunboat diplomacy' still had its place in United States foreign policy, the response in Haiti had to be more than that of a superpower reasserting its authority. There had to be substantial reason to intervene and − if possible − a rationale which tied the situation more closely to the interests of the American public. With the resurgence of the refugee crisis some months later that rationale was established. In May 1993, President Clinton spelled out the situation. First, Clinton said:

> ... it is in our own backyard. Second, we've got a million Haitian Americans. Third, we've got several thousand Americans in Haiti. Fourth, we believe that drugs are coming through Haiti to the United States. Fifth, we face the possibility, the continuous possibility, of a massive outflow of Haitian migrants to the United States.[32]

Nevertheless, caution prevailed. The lessons of Somalia and the reservations expressed by Congress and the American public were enough to forestall immediate action. As a result, even while the path to direct intervention was being prepared in secret during June and July

1994, President Clinton was making conciliatory offers to 'buy off' the Haitian military leaders.[33]

As these attempts were rebuffed, exercise of the military option became increasingly likely. Unlike Panama in 1989, however, the less than enthusiastic public response to a military solution highlighted the need for the legitimacy of any such action to be established. The need was both regional and global.

The United States had already begun to lobby members of the OAS. At the meeting of the OAS in Brazil in June, the United States had gained the organisation's endorsement for the by then near-total trade embargo imposed by the United Nations.[34] The United States also achieved early success in its attempts to line up 'flag' nations within the region, enabling Washington to claim some thirty countries in the Western hemisphere as willing to support, or prepared to join, a multinational military intervention.[35]

But the wider legitimacy was provided by the United Nations. The initiative came from the American Ambassador to the United Nations, Mrs Madeleine Albright. In July 1994, Albright presented a plan for a possible American led, multinational, United Nations-monitored invasion of Haiti aimed at restoring democracy. The request was made on behalf of a group termed 'the friends of Haiti', made up of the United States, Argentina, Venezuela, Canada and France.

While discussions on this proposal took place behind closed doors,[36] the Security Council took into account the most recent report of the Secretary-General which presented three options for solving the crisis. The first option was to expand the existing United Nations mission in Haiti with military forces from member states, under the direct command of the United Nations vested in the Secretary-General. The second was to allow a multinational force – with no limit on the proportion of the force provided by any one state – to restore order and to rebuild the country. The third option was to allow a multinational force to restore order, and then replace that force with a United Nations peace-keeping force for the reconstruction of the country.[37]

Not surprisingly, the Security Council took the third option, since it would be impossible to obtain the necessary troops for option one, and no member nation was likely to volunteer for the messy and expensive clean-up job foreshadowed by option two. The third option also matched the level of involvement anticipated by the United States.

Under this option, the operation would take place in two phases similar to the intervention which had been planned for Somalia. The first phase would see the deployment of a multi-national force to establish and maintain a 'secure and stable environment'. The second would transform the intervention into a standard peace keeping mission with up to 6000 troops financed by the United Nations and directed by the United States. The wording of the draft resolution – sponsored by Argentina, France, Canada and the United States – sought approval for a multi-national force to use 'all necessary means' to intervene to restore constitutional rule in Haiti and to restore security and stability.[38] On 1 August 1994, the United Nations Security Council accepted the recommendation and passed Resolution 940 (1994), authorising a multi-national intervention in Haiti to end the crisis.

The resolution passed the Security Council on a vote of 12–0. Brazil and China abstained, and Rwanda was absent. Strong opposition, however, was voiced by leading Latin American nations. Brazil criticised the resolution for attempting to solve the problem of violence with more violence, while Cuba, with some justification, charged the United States with having spent decades 'arming and supporting' those whom it now wished to expel. Mexico opposed the resolution because of the dangerous precedent it set for future interventions. [39]

Mexico clearly had a point, since Article 2 of the United Nations Charter forbids foreign intervention in the domestic affairs of member states. Chapter VII of the Charter, however, allows intervention when there is a threat to international peace. This provision had provided the rationale for the essentially humanitarian intervention to relieve the plight of the Kurds in Iraq, following the Gulf war. Security Council Resolution 688 (1991) determined that Iraq's repression of the Kurds threatened international peace and security in the region. This, in turn, set the precedent for the intervention in Somalia, which was authorised under Security Council Resolution 794 (1992). Intercession to protect the Kurds could be justified as a necessary action to maintain stability in the aftermath of the Gulf war, but Somalia was the first specific instance of the sovereign rights of a nation being over-ridden by an externally based, and possibly biased, decision that the crisis threatened international peace.[40]

The precedent afforded by Somalia, in which the United Nations moved to restore order in the face of what was seen through predominantly Western eyes as a dangerous anarchy, signalled a move away from the rights of national sovereignty to a more global perspective in which humanitarian issues rise above state borders. However, it was convenient, in the case of Somalia, to point also to the collapse of the state apparatus as a circumstance overriding the provisions of Article 2 of the Charter. Haiti took this trend a step further. There was clearly no threat to international peace and none was mentioned in the resolution. There may have been humanitarian concerns, but these alone did not justify intervention. Nor had the Haitian state ceased to exist. Security Council Resolution 940 (1994) instead referred to the 'unique character' of the situation in Haiti, and stated that the Security Council was '... gravely concerned by the significant further deterioration of the humanitarian situation in Haiti ...', continuing systematic violations of civil liberties, the desperate plight of Haitian refugees, and the recent expulsion of the ICM. It determined that the circumstances called for an exceptional response.[41] In effect, the Article 2 principle of non-interference in the domestic affairs of sovereign states, which has long been accepted as a cornerstone of the United Nations relations with individual members, was brushed aside in favour of the interpretation of a one-off situation that justified the intervention.

In retrospect, there appears to have been no legal basis for breaching Haitian sovereignty, nor any reason to believe that the situation leading to Security Council Resolution 940 would not arise again in the future. This, along with reports that Soviet compliance at the Security Council was only given as part of a trade off for a free hand in Georgia, lends credence to the view that the United Nations was once again manipulated by a major power intent on pursuing its national interests.[42] Certainly, the United States-inspired resolution stands in stark contrast to the initial United Nations reaction to the coup in 1991. At that time, the Security Council declined to vote on a resolution condemning the Haitian junta, on the grounds that any such action would violate the long-held principle of non-interference.

Under the circumstances, Mexico had valid concerns over the setting of a precedent that allowed major powers on the Security Council to legitimise their actions in the belief that their particular set of moral values, or simply their national interests, had priority over the sovereign rights of others.[43] But Mexico was not the only state to be concerned.

Having gained regional and international approval for the intervention, President Clinton still needed to establish the legitimacy of the action at home. Both the Senate and House expressed misgivings, with the Senate voting 100 to 0 that United Nations approval did not constitute Congressional approval for direct intervention. Opinion polls showed the nation split over whether to invade, with 75 per cent of those surveyed opposing the United States going it alone. This latter prospect was particularly galling to Clinton who, despite the earlier optimism, was having difficulties in drumming up 'flag' contingents.[44]

Faced with this situation, Clinton despatched naval forces to Haiti but put any implementation of the United Nations authority to invade on hold. While the use of force was an option, the President's judgement was that it was premature to act at that point.[45]

By mid-September, American public approval of Clinton's handling of the Haitian crisis stood at 31 per cent, with 47 per cent disapproving. With support for any military action remaining low, the focus remained on diplomatic measures. But a spearhead force of eighteen warships with 6000 US Marines and special forces were deployed off the coast of Haiti as a demonstration of intent.[46] The force was reported to be backed by some 1500 troops from seventeen other nations, to be sent in once the situation had been secured.[47]

It was later revealed that special forces units were already active and that a psychological warfare program was put into place ahead of the invasion. This consisted of leaflet drops and parachute delivery of thousands of transistor radios locked into the broadcast frequency of a new offshore shipborne radio station called Radio Democracy. At the same time, daily speeches by Aristide were broadcast from American planes circling over Port-au-Prince.[48] For the benefit of the Haitian junta, the United States administration talked up the intervention, stating that the full invasion force of more than 20,000 would be going 'in any event' and would establish civic order in 'a couple of months.'[49] The final warning came in a televised Presidential address that warned the Haitian leadership that their time was up. President Clinton delivered a blunt warning: 'The hour has come for Haiti's dictators to go ... they should leave now or we will force (them) from power.'[50]

The Occupation

Two days after the Security Council Resolution 940 was passed, President Jonassaint declared his country to be in a 'state of siege.' This was accompanied by stern and belligerent warnings from the Haitian military leader, General Paul Cedras, promising a 'tough, implacable' fight in defence of the island. Speaking on American television after rejecting the American offer of a comfortable exile, Cedras warned that the people would resist and that the United States would face '... a massacre starting with a civil war.'[51]

With the battle lines drawn and thousands of American troops poised to invade, President Clinton made a televised address to inform Americans that he had exhausted all attempts at diplomacy. Clinton made the address in an attempt to convince Americans that their 'overwhelming aversion' to the planned military operation was misplaced. At the same time, he despatched former President Jimmy Carter, retired General Colin Powell, and Georgia Senator Sam Nunn in a final bid to persuade Haiti's military leaders to relinquish power.[52]

The deadline for an agreement passed with Cedras still refusing to step down. Finally, according to the *Washington Post,*

> ... Biamby walked into the room where they were negotiating and told Cedras the planes were on the way... How Biamby knew American planes were enroute to Haiti is officially unexplained. Senior administration officials hint that the television networks, which knew planes roaring off with paratroopers from Polk Airfield in North Carolina would be a sure sign of invasion, had leaked that news and it found its way to the Haitian military.[53]

It was enough. After some sixteen hours of negotiations, the junta was persuaded to step down voluntarily, just in time for the recall of airborne and special forces some seventy-three minutes into their flight to invade.[54] The deal, as one commentator put it '... avoided what would have been a bloody and, for Mr Clinton, a politically unpopular offensive military operation that would have been undertaken at night under dangerous conditions.' It also allowed a clearly relieved and exultant Mr Clinton to claim that his policies had achieved their goal of restoring democracy in Haiti. The agreement, he said, had come '... only because of the credible and imminent threat of a multinational force.'[55]

On 20 September, 3000 United States troops landed in Haiti. Cedras and his senior officers were pensioned off at a cost to the American taxpayers of US$12.5 million and a promise of amnesty which, as part of the deal, allowed the military leaders to remain in Haiti. Aristide, although reported to be bitter at the American concession which left his major opposition still in the country, and 'outraged' at official statements indicating that he supported the deal, announced that he would return 'without vengeance.'[56]

The actual 'invasion' or occupation, was described by one correspondent on the scene, as '... more like a slightly out-of-control open air rock concert than a potential war zone.' But apart from some minor problems, it was an efficient and peaceful operation, with the capital securely held by midday on 20 September. General Hugh Shelton, commanding the American forces, confirmed that he had received full co-operation from the military leaders, who were due to relinquish power by 15 October.[57]

What violence there was, came from a clampdown on pro-Aristide demonstrations followed by United States tolerated looting of government military posts and police stations. There was also mob violence against suspected 'attaches', the name given to police informers or enforcers.[58]

There was only one major incident, when a young Marine platoon leader exchanged fire with Haitian police leaving eight Haitians dead and two more who later died of wounds. While the circumstances leading to the exchange were not clear, the deaths were denounced by the Haitian military as atrocities.[59]

The return of Aristide was delayed, possibly because he was negotiating secretly with Washington for higher levels of support while he still had the leverage of placing the final seal of legitimacy on the American intervention. However, apart from some early rumours that an attempt was being made to form a Haitian resistance group, Aristide's eventual return was uneventful. Within six weeks the bulk of the American forces had begun to withdraw, leaving to Aristide the far more difficult task of rebuilding the nation, and to the United Nations the problem of security.

The Role of the Media

In line with what has by now become the standard procedure in organising such interventions, the media was excluded from the planning phase of the Haiti operation and given only that information which the government needed as part of its diplomatic signalling campaign. As an example, as late as July, only two months before the actual intervention, the Clinton administration was busy using the media to deny any such intentions while laying the groundwork for intervention and running airborne and maritime exercises.[60]

As in previous campaigns also, the media was enlisted to galvanise the world's information elite, the opinion makers who could put Haiti on the agenda for their respective audiences. The aim was to present the Haitian military leaders and the situation in Haiti in the worst possible light, while highlighting the humanitarian role of the United States.[61] This had the dual effect of alerting and preparing the world for a possible invasion while applying subtle pressure on world governments to support the United States through positive statements which would be reported in their respective media.

In this case, however, the media played an important role beyond the control of either the military or the government. Since domestic politics was a major factor, and since the problem was a longstanding one, familiar to both the media and the American public, the media was afforded an opportunity to play out their traditional role of dispassionate observer.

The Clinton administration initially proposed a news blackout during the first six or eight hours of the invasion, but relented after discussions with major television networks. The final agreement involved a voluntary embargo on '... all broadcast video depicting or describing troop landing locations during the first hour of the intervention.'[62] In practical terms, there was probably no other option. The media had a large contingent on the ground in Haiti. Its presence increased as the confrontation escalated, and was ready and waiting when the American troops arrived. The hotels, it was said, bristled with television camera equipment and satellite dishes.[63] The response made by General Cedras to every American initiative, threat or pleading, was faithfully reported. There were also background or 'colour' pieces, which provided an insight into the victim nation's thinking at levels never before encountered in limited conflicts.

But nowhere did the media play out its role better than in its editorials, both print and electronic. It was here that the issue was debated at an informed level and it was here that the overriding issue of domestic politics was considered. Indeed, in the United States, the central issues were discussed in depth, with considerable objectivity. However, it must be recognised that the higher profile accorded Haiti, and the greater impact of reporting on the situation, were due solely to the domestic and presidential issues involved. Even within the United States, the thoroughness with which Haiti was treated lessened the further the news outlet was from the imperatives of American internal politics.[64]

In the wider global media, it was business as usual for the United States government information agencies and military as they prepared a flow of pre-digested articles designed to provide the background ambience needed to secure public and international support for their actions. As a result, the general run of media comment on Haiti in the Western media was negative. There was routine use of such descriptions as 'repressive', 'corrupt' and an almost mandatory use of the term 'illegal' in American official documents and statements. This was reflected in the media which adopted such terms as 'the pariah nation'. When headlining news from Haiti, State Department briefings constantly gave the impression that United States Embassy staff and American citizens were in danger from what were described as '... escalating human rights violations.' Critics were answered with the statement that the invasion was inevitable and necessary because of the '... deplorable conditions and the suffering of the people who have been denied democracy ... and the persistent pattern of human-rights abuses.'[65]

Father Aristide presented something of a problem, but generally the earlier American condemnations of the priest as a Marxist psychopath and anti-American populist were turned around to depict him as some form of latter day Martin Luther King.

An earlier CIA profile which had portrayed Aristide as 'mentally ill', a 'psychopath' and 'a killer', was fortuitously revealed to have been based on '... false evidence supplied by the Haitian military.'[66] The media was also replete with messages that supported the United States position and Aristide: reports from conveniently anonymous respondents in 'colour' pieces. 'Ronald', a social worker, was quoted as saying of Aristide that '... everyone wants him back. That is the only way we can breath again.'[67] There was a matching spate of 'placed' articles and news reports which highlighted the undoubtedly poor human rights record of the military junta. In a re-run of the way in which Saddam Hussein was vilified while President Assad of Syria was rehabilitated, so too was there no reference to the fact that there was little difference in human rights abuse between Haiti and the Dominican Republic – the United States newly enlisted ally next door.

At the same time, the Haitian leadership was systematically demonised. In May 1994, as the new wave of refugees headed for the United States, President Clinton had accused the regime of extending its slaughter of civilians and of bringing a '... reign of terror and poverty on their people.' For the past several weeks, Clinton said, the administration had been receiving reports of 'civilians' as well as Aristide backers '... being not only murdered but mutilated.'[68] The Haitian leadership was later branded by the State Department as an MRE – a 'morally repugnant elite'. Such labels have considerable media appeal. In an attack echoing the condemnation of Manuel Noriega in Panama some five years earlier, Cedras himself was targeted by the United States Justice Department which identified the General as '... one of many officials who profited from drug shipments through the island.'[69]

Almost every reference to the Haitian military referred to them as 'thugs' – or worse. They were also ridiculed. The Haitian navy had '... immaculate uniforms but only one ship with working engines', helicopters were 'in pieces', and the main armament of the 7000 soldiers was described as '... a bottomless supply of 150-proof rum, and a force of voodoo priests ...' The Haitian military were '... not afraid of women and children, they will shoot a man who is bound up like a pig, but they will not stand and fight.' According to yet another anonymous source '... they dance and sing ... and talk big, but when they hear 'boom boom' ... here the report described its anonymous alleged informant as wiggling two fingers to simulate a man running away.[70] 'Jean', an anonymous Haitian soldier, was quoted making comments typical of those run in several Australian newspapers on 19 September 1994, as invasion was imminent.

In the Brisbane (Australia) *Courier Mail*, the report stated: 'It's over ... the Haitian army will not resist ... we'll look out for ourselves first ... we are not going to protect these people, he [Jean] added, referring contemptuously to Gen Cedras, Brigadier General Philippe Biamby, the chief-of-staff, and Michel Francois, the capital police chief.'[71]

At the same time, in a manner reminiscent of bogus reports of the buildup of Iraqi force levels as insurance against possible military setbacks in the Gulf war, reports were leaked of Haiti's secret acquisition of heat seeking missiles that could threaten the helicopter mobility of the planned invasion force.[72]

During the deployment, American forces were officially depicted as being welcomed as liberators. A half page, unattributed story reprinted in an Australian newspaper, the Brisbane *Courier Mail*, painted the official picture: 'Thousands of cheering and waving Haitians scrambled atop advertising signs, market stalls and walls in the capital to welcome the soldiers.'[73] Print reports and electronic images – many of them supplied by the military in the early days – routinely depicted Haitians raising their arms in welcome to helicopters and waving small American flags. It would not be too cynical to suggest that the flags had been brought in with the invasion force, since they would not have been in great demand in pre-American-controlled Haiti.

To the extent that it was necessary to justify allowing Cedras to remain in Haiti, the military leader was rehabilitated from a drug runner and a thug who had created a 'reign of terror', to a respectable leader. Far from leading the coup against Aristide, Cedras, it was now claimed, had saved his life.[74] In much the same manner as Aidid had gone from warlord to statesman in Somalia, President Clinton stood by as former President Carter told Congress that Cedras was not a dictator and to call him that was 'plain wrong.' Further, to force such a man into exile, also would be 'wrong.' General Cedras and the Haitian psyche, it seemed, had been misunderstood all along. Cedras' main concern, said a senior Clinton administration official, was not himself but that he could not leave his country and see it fall into a civil war.[75]

But once the intervention was under way, the Haitian leadership was dealt with in a more stereotypical manner. General Cedras was reported to be haggling over his payout and was portrayed as a spent force. When Cedras appeared at a funeral for those killed in the exchange of fire with the Marines, the ceremony was denigrated as being poorly attended and Cedras and his 'tattered command' isolated and exhausted.[76] The ceremony in which he stood down was stage-managed for the media, with a hostile crowd 'jeering and hooting', and the slightly built Cedras overshadowed by the large physical presence of an obviously disapproving General Shelton.[77] There was to be no doubt as to the unpopularity of the departing Cedras. As yet another unsourced report put it:

> ... the once-omnipotent Cedras seemed small ... as he announced he was resigning ... The sound of 5000 joyful people buried the tubas and trombones of Cedras's military band playing the national anthem with an impromptu version of Auld Lang Syne. Then Cedras's voice ... faded amid an underamplified sound system and the crowd's shouts of 'hoodlum' and 'thief.'[78]

As a final indignity, the report continued, American troops had to protect Cedras, firing warning shots as his departing vehicle was stoned.

Even FRAPH, the pro-Cedras right wing Revolutionary Front for Advancement and Progress, was rehabilitated at the time Cedras agreed to stand down. FRAPH was reported to have pledged its support for Aristide and democracy. On 1 October, however, a bomb blast at a pro-democracy rally – which killed five and injured many more – was sheeted home to FRAPH. They were once again relegated to 'thugs' and 'gunmen' despite any evidence beyond the by now mandatory drugs said to have been found in the FRAPH headquarters.[79] FRAPH had to be blamed; for anyone else to have committed the act would have negated the official line that the population was overwhelmingly pro-Aristide. According to force commander Shelton, four of the 'primary thugs' were detained: 'They were known dealers in arms, they were known attaches, they were known ninjas.'[80]

In the same way, the looting which followed the collapse of the military regime was portrayed as a just response by an oppressed people. The invading force stood by as Haitian mobs destroyed not only police stations, but the homes of suspected informers and international relief agency stores.[81] There was some suggestion that the Haitian police shot by the Marines in the only major exchange of fire during the invasion, were attempting to prevent looting when the Marines interceded. But United States military spokesman, Colonel Barry Wiley, stated that it was '... clear that our Marines acted in self defence.'[82]

With the arrival of Aristide, optimism ruled. Unattributed colour pieces once again showed 'happy Haitians' cleaning the 'filthy' city streets in preparation for his return. The actual reception and greeting showed the smiling face of the United States military, this time with a deferential General Shelton greeting Aristide. But once Aristide was home, the world media went silent, almost as if a switch had been turned off. There was hardly a mention of the handover to the United Nations force, or of the detailed aid and nation rebuilding program which followed.

The United States military and government had learned the lessons of Panama well, especially when dealing with a situation in which there was the potential for the media to be both independent and politically-oriented. Once the handover was complete and the first of the troops had been successfully withdrawn, the media had played its allotted part. It was no longer needed, in case it reported on anything that could cast doubts on the value or long-term success of the operation. The media, too, had other interests to turn to.

Conclusion

Haiti was a limited conflict, conducted under the aegis of the United Nations, and it followed the pattern that has now become the norm in such conflicts.

There was secrecy in planning. It is not yet clear, but it appears that planning for the invasion of Haiti went well beyond normal contingency plans and was conducted by a separate, politically aware planning team. On the other hand, there is clear evidence that, while planning was underway, the Haitian leadership was demonised, with the three leading members of the junta singled out for special attention. In addition, the Haitian military as a whole was denigrated. It was difficult to smear the clean living General Cedras with the sexual excesses attributed to Noriega in Panama, but it was relatively easy to use the emotive link with drugs. The same tactic was used against FRAPH. As usual, care was taken not to implicate the Haitian people as a whole, since they were needed to act out their welcome to the 'liberating' invading forces.

While firm evidence is yet to emerge, there is reason to believe that the United States Embassy directed a major espionage and de-stabilisation effort against the regime in the lead-up to the actual invasion. There is also reason to believe that intelligence operatives and special forces had been deployed in some strength over a long period. Attempts had been made to isolate the target nation by initiatives such as economic and political sanctions, and by international means such as the United States trade, finance and travel embargo, as well as the wider United Nations sanctions.

The United States search for legitimacy has been well documented and demonstrates the now set pattern of exploiting regional and international groupings to share responsibility for the actions of the major initiating power. Even limited content analysis of the media coverage of the Haiti intervention reveals the exploitation of local and international news media in support of these objectives.

During the buildup and deployment, the media was used in the same way that it had been in previous campaigns, both to signal intentions and, as an insurance policy, to emphasise the possible difficulties. The media was also used to highlight the awesome power and inevitability of the threat that was posed to the Haitian regime. This served to improve the American bargaining position. While the pool system appeared to have been implemented without the usual delay, this may have been due to the fact that the media was already present in force. The military could do little to control that media which was already in place, but needed a trained pool of reporters which could concentrate on the military issues as a counter to the overwhelming political debate developing in the United States.

In summary, Haiti was a classic case of the United States following the strategy of using force to impose its will on a selected 'no risk' target. This is underlined by the fact that Haiti was a small backward nation, subject to the whole economic, diplomatic and military power of the United States government. At the same time, that same government studiously ignored the greater and far more demanding humanitarian issue of Bosnia. This is especially relevant given the fact that it is the United States which has distorted United Nations policy, most clearly in the case of Haiti, by widening the ambit of intervention to superpower-decided 'humanitarian' issues.

On the other hand, while the United States government deployed the full weight of its news and information agencies to enlist and maintain international support, because the campaign was so closely linked to domestic political issues the media was still able to exercise a degree of independence. To that extent, the situation was at odds with the dependency and control that has been a feature of many recent limited conflict campaigns. The politicisation of the campaign, along with the ease of media access and long lead time for the intervention, not only afforded media independence but enabled it to provide a more wide-ranging critique of the entire effort. To some extent, this relegated the pool system to little more than a sideshow.

The impact of domestic political needs and the power and authority this afforded the media is perhaps the most interesting factor to emerge in the study of the Haiti intervention. It appears to have forced the United States administration to greater efforts to sway public opinion through the manipulation of the media. But these efforts, although successful on the international scene, were largely blunted in the far more important domestic arena. The evidence of the case therefore suggests that a military campaign could be aborted at a late stage if public support was not forthcoming.

It is here that a glimmer of optimism emerges in what has been an increasingly pessimistic pattern of media control in limited conflict over recent years: a media doing its job of educating the people still has the power to decide the issues, and perhaps to influence the political decision to engage in limited conflict or a peace keeping-deployments. But the media must seize the opportunity. This perhaps is the real message of the Haitian campaign.

14

Conclusion:
An Uncertain Future

There should be no doubt that the global reach and immediacy of the new media and communications technologies, and the ability of those technologies to shape both national and international public opinion, has made the media a major player in limited conflict and peacekeeping deployments. Given the rapid progress and far reaching advances in communications over recent years, the media can be expected to become increasingly influential in the future, especially when the ability to inform is matched with better educated world audiences. These audiences, and Western audiences in particular, now expect both sides of every argument to be presented to them through the media.

In the normal course of events, such developments could be expected to have a significant impact on the way conflict is reported and debated within the international community. Already the new global media is beginning to blur the lines of sovereignty, and even culture, as it fulfils its primary task of entertainment.[1] As our examination of post-World War II conflict has shown, however, where national military ambitions are concerned, governments have increasingly held the media in check through the imposition of deliberate policies of exclusion, containment and manipulation.

The arguments put forward in this book have been based upon two major premises which help to define the problem this creates in media-

271

military relations. The first is that, because of the mutually assured destruction inherent in nuclear, biological and chemical warfare, the future international ambitions of the major powers will be achieved through limited conflict, in contrast to the total commitment required for the great wars of national survival which engulfed our world in the early years of the twentieth century. The second is that the limited conflicts stemming from this change in the character of confrontation will afford the citizen discretionary choices, in contrast to the assumed duties and obligations of the citizen which applied in wars of national survival.

These changes in the approach to war have placed a new priority on public opinion in time of conflict and created a new challenge for the media. The challenge arises because the newly liberated citizen, no longer bound by the patriotic imperative of unquestioning duty to the state, has to be persuaded to support the government and the military in limited wars which are often fought in remote areas and generally pose no threat to the survival of either the citizen's or the nation. On the other hand, it is the military's appreciation of the importance of public opinion which has resulted in the development of sophisticated media management systems designed to marginalise the media in time of war and minimise its impact.[2] If the flow of information is effectively controlled, governments and the military are better able to present their own sanitised versions of successfully prosecuted wars.

Because it has been fragmented and unprepared, the media has been trapped into cooperative arrangements set up by the military on the ostensibly sensible pretexts of ensuring operational security and the safety of the reporters. But both these concepts remain ill-defined and their interpretation rests entirely with the military.[3] Nowhere in any Western liberal democracy has there yet emerged an independent media forum able to hold its own with the military. The media is also limited by the need to compete, the cost of coverage, lack of specialist expertise and audience expectations. As a result, the media has few defences against the sort of manipulation that was seen in Grenada, Panama and the Gulf campaigns.[4] The only saving grace for the media, and for the public's right to know, is the lesson of Vietnam and Panama. That is, that if the military should meet with any major setback, or if the conflict should become protracted, then carefully controlled containment and channelling of the media will be to no avail. Given enough time in any war, the media should be able to install its own support and communications systems, enabling reporters to make more independent judgements and disseminate information through global networks. The installation of such systems would not be without problems in many conflict situations, but protracted conflict, high casualty levels and lack of success can only sharpen a cynical public's appetite for news.

It is the fear of public disaffection and withdrawal of support for the military that has encouraged Western liberal democratic governments and their armed forces to develop systems for media management and control.[5] This fear was expressed by Generals Colin Powell and Norman Schwarzkopf during the Gulf campaign. It was a constraint on the Clinton administration when planning the invasion of Haiti. But, outside government and military circles, the implications of the new media management systems which have been developed in response, and the limitations these systems place on the media in its duty to inform, are not yet fully appreciated.[6] In the majority of our case studies, the evidence points the home audiences of nations engaged in limited conflict tending to accept military claims that some restriction of the freedom of the press, and hence of the public's right to know, is necessary in time of war.

The development of the theoretical argument suggests that these circumstances arise because little thought has been given to changes in the citizen's obligations to the state as the nature of war has changed. This can be explained by the observation that theory usually lags behind technical development. But there has also been relatively little theoretical discussion of the changed nature of war within the wider context of the social contract. Indeed, a close examination of recent social contract literature indicates that there is still an almost automatic acceptance of the age old concept that everything becomes subordinate to the state in time of war.[7] Beyond Rawls, few, if any, have examined the changes that have freed the citizen of obligations predicated on the threat of personal or national survival, leaving the citizen free to take a position based on the merits of the situation.[8] But even though Rawls has made a significant contribution, his central thesis focuses on the issue of conscientious objection. Only the military appear to have comprehended that the obligations of the citizen to support government policy have changed and to have recognised the consequent importance of winning the media battle for public opinion.

A Slow Awakening

While a relationship between the media and public opinion has existed for as long as there has been a mass media and audience to be reached, relations between the media and the military were shaped over three distinctly separate periods. These began with the imperialist period, when the media largely took on the role of retailing the exploits of their respective military forces to the jingoistic and nationalistic populations that made up mass circulation audiences. With little questioning of national policy and the reporting of war generally far removed in time and place from the home nation, the media posed little immediate threat to military objectives in the imperialist campaigns.

It was a different matter in the second period – what has been referred to as the golden age of war reporting – which covered the period from the Crimea and the American Civil war in the mid-nineteenth century, to the Franco-Prussian War of 1870 and the Russo-Japanese war of 1904. During this period, the correspondents' new weapon of cable communications raised the spectre of more immediate reporting, with the prospect of coverage affecting the conduct of war. The military responded by limiting access to the means of communication and instituting formal systems of censorship. At the same time, new problems emerged to confront the media. Modern wars were now being fought on numerous fronts over great distances.

The third period, from World War I to World War II, drew the media in as full partners to governments in what were perceived to be wars of national survival. Patriotism reigned supreme. The willing acceptance of the war aims of governments were also reflected in the between-war conflicts. In the Spanish civil war, for example, patriotism and nationalism were replaced by an ideological commitment that brooked no opposition.[9] But, if it seemed to governments and the military that the true role of the media in war had been defined by subordinating the ability to report to government objectives, it was only because little thought had been given to the political and social contexts in which that situation had arisen.

As the case studies demonstrate, the military's appreciation that the perceived rights and obligations of the citizen in time of limited conflict might be changing was slow to emerge and accepted only as a result of the media impact of the Vietnam war. Despite the alarm bell conflicts of Korea, Indochina and Algeria, the importance of public opinion, the capabilities of the emerging communications technologies, and the power of the increasingly internationalised media, were largely ignored. They were ignored despite the fact that the theoretical questions of how to handle a media that saw itself free of the imperatives applying in a war of survival had already begun to emerge in the Korean conflict.[10]

These warnings were ignored when the French government was faced with a loss of popular will to carry the fight in Indochina as the French public made their decision on the merits of the case as it was presented to them, largely through the media.[11] The warnings were again ignored by the French during the Algerian conflict, where the result was open dissent and revolt as major segments of the home community weighed up the merits of the conflict and 'found' for the opposing forces.[12]

In Northern Ireland, the problem came into even sharper focus as the British were faced with attempting to control a free media exercising its right to report what was happening in a working democracy. To the surprise and chagrin of both the military and government, the British and Irish press largely rejected the outdated notion of patriotic support for the official line on events and afforded government policy and military action a high level of scrutiny. When the issue was finally recognised and addressed in Northern Ireland, the response was a policy of deceit and denial, backed up, as a last resort, by legal sanction. It is a policy that continues to this day.[13]

In each of the post-World War II conflicts, the media felt itself able, for the first time, to report what it saw, free of national or patriotic constraints, in limited conflicts which had little direct impact on the public in the home nation. The media was also speaking to audiences who were no longer constrained by the imperatives of personal survival or the duties and obligations of national survival. At the same time, the reach and immediacy of news coverage was being extended by technical advances, above all by the penetration of television.

Limitation of access, direct and indirect censorship, and resentment of adverse although accurate reports, can be traced back to the earliest days of the war correspondent in which the military first attempted to negate the media challenge to the monopoly they held on the reporting of war.[14] But it was a situation that could not last in the face of the changing media environment and a newly enfranchised public.

Vietnam: The Catalyst

As we saw in Chapter 5, the Vietnam experience was the catalyst for change. For the first time, both government and the military came face to face with the reality of dealing with a free media able to influence public opinion, especially through the immediacy and credibility of the visual images provided by television.[15]

In terms of the case analyses presented in this study, Vietnam is classified as an 'open' conflict. The United States administration had almost no way of controlling media coverage when government commitment to the war was ideologically based on the restoration of democratic liberties in the theatre of operations and there was a constitutionally guaranteed freedom of speech in the home nation. The situation was made worse for the military as the deployment coincided with near-saturation penetration of television in the United States. The result was the first ever 'television war', in which the realities of war were brought dramatically and graphically into the living rooms of the home nation.

In spite of this situation, the American military went to war on the outdated assumption that they could still demand the traditional patriotic support of both press and public they had enjoyed in previous wars. This support was received in the early days when the conflict was largely covert. But as the American presence grew and the stakes became higher, the United States administration was unable to maintain its deliberate policy of tactical, strategic and national deception in the face of an increasingly critical media able to disprove many of the government's claims. Media exposure began in the field as reporters lost confidence in official military statements. The cynicism and critical reporting that this produced was then brought to bear upon the wider deceptions played on the American public by successive administrations.[16]

Importantly, however, as Hallin and Thayer, and now even the American military have argued, although the media informed the public, they did not shape the popular disillusionment and disapproval that followed.[17] That disillusionment resulted largely from a conscious choice by an intellectual elite who did not feel themselves bound by any obligations to the state, but saw themselves free to make up their own minds on the merits of the situation. Their protests permeated through to the mass audience who, faced with a continuing lack of success in the conflict, turned against their government and its unflagging optimism. There is no doubt, however, that without a critical media able to reveal the true situation and reinforce public opinion, the eventual swing against the war would have taken much longer.

In summary, the United States went into the Vietnam war with outdated expectations of public and media support. It quickly found that both the media and a significant part of the nation's intellectual leadership had developed a sense of independence and were willing to exercise their freedom of choice. The American military had neither the right nor the ability to limit or censor the media, and their response of deception at all levels foundered on the realities of protracted war. Such circumstances inevitably point to a no-win situation. Public dissent was sure to follow.

One lesson was clear. The only solution for the military in open conflicts, where there is no rationale for the control or censorship of the media, lies in winning – and winning within a relatively short time.

The Falklands: The Beginnings of a Response

The problems of an uncontrolled media revealed by Vietnam were not lost on the British. But when the time came to address a similar media challenge in the Falklands, Britain was to enjoy the full benefits of a classic 'expeditionary' campaign. This conferred advantages which were exploited to the full by both government and military. As the British Chief of Defence Force later admitted to Parliament, everything, including the public's right to know, was subordinated to the prime aim of winning.[18] In the case of the media, this included the use of disinformation, misinformation, and deception, as well as direct and indirect censorship. There is clear evidence of political support for these measures, as well as of the political priority given to retailing information aimed at enlisting and maintaining national and international support.[19]

That the authorities largely succeeded in this was due to two factors. The first was a generally uncritical media which responded to the renewed sense of nationalism induced by government exhortation. The second was that the carefully controlled flow of information over a relatively short campaign always pointed to an ever increasing success, culminating in a decisive victory. The relatively short time frame and remoteness of the area of operations did not allow the media to deploy their own means of communication which would have facilitated independent global reporting.

But once the initial public euphoria over victory in the Falklands had worn off, there were widespread calls for an inquiry into the restrictions on the public's right to know. This resulted in a parliamentary inquiry which generally condemned the constraints which had been imposed on the media.[20] The military, however, remained unrepentant and the end result was not a relaxation, but a refinement of the existing systems of media management.[21]

The main conclusion that can be drawn from the Falklands campaign is that it became, by default, the testing ground for a pattern of media control which would become the reference point in planning future limited conflicts where the military held the advantage of a 'closed' or 'expeditionary' deployment. Such a 'closed' conflict enables maximum exploitation of the dependence of the media on the military for communications and support. On the home front it can be similarly matched by political exploitation of the resulting media vacuum, evidenced by the presentation of a carefully sanitised government version of events. This media strategy, in combination with the military strategy of concluding any limited conflict as quickly as possible, gives rise to an expectation that the public's right to know will be overridden at every opportunity in favour of the political imperative of maintaining national and international support.

Grenada and Panama: A Pattern of Media Management

Still smarting from what was perceived as the media's betrayal of the military in the Vietnam war, the Pentagon was quick to appreciate the benefits of the controls available to the British in the Falklands.[22] The lessons of the Falklands were quickly incorporated into the American media strategy in Grenada, where circumstances afforded advantages similar to those offering in an expeditionary campaign. The measures taken included exclusion of the media from the planning phase of the operation and the initial assault, and the imposition of constraints when exclusion could no longer be justified. On the ground, there was censorship by delay and restriction of access. For the first time, there was electronic jamming of alternative channels of communication.[23]

It can only be concluded that these policies were deliberately designed to avoid any possible military or political embarrassment during the vulnerable first few days of the operation. Once the situation had stabilised, the media was allowed to cover the operation in order to publicise its success.[24] In the meantime, pre-edited and favourable coverage generated by the military was released to news networks in an attempt justify what later transpired to be a far less successful operation than was at first reported.

The measures adopted by the military were mainly those of exclusion to preserve operational security and a professed inability to guarantee the safety of journalists. But while the media was excluded from the battlefield, it was exploited to the full in the demonisation of the Grenadan government and in publicising a generally spurious threat to the welfare of American students on the island.[25] The media was also used to foster claims of legitimacy for the operation and to harness regional and international support.[26]

Once again, this policy of limiting media scrutiny paid off politically, with the majority of Americans acknowledging the patriotic call to protect the forces involved. The operation was also of short duration and, at the time, it was accepted that the demand for restrictions prevailed over the wider needs of a free media and the public's right to know. But the later outcry from the journalistic profession was such that it led to a formal investigation by the Pentagon into the handling of the media, the *Sidle Report*.[27] The terms of reference precluded an examination of military aspects of the invasion of Grenada but called instead for a determination of ways in which the competing needs of the media for access, and the military for operational security, could be accommodated. The overall recommendation, in both intent and spirit, was that the media should accompany any future United States troop deployments, to serve the American public's right to know, subject only to the valid requirements of operational security.

But this recommendation, and the voluntary Pentagon Pool system for media coverage that it resulted in, was totally ignored in favour of the political and military benefits of exclusion when American forces were deployed in Panama.

As the case study of Panama shows, the military were ready with an official explanation for the exclusion of the media – the plans for deployment of the pool had been mislaid. However, as Woodward revealed in 1991, a deliberate decision had been taken to exclude the carefully selected and practised members of the media pool from both the planning of the operation and the actual deployment.[28] Not only was an announcement of the deployment delayed in order to avoid news comment on the first day of the operation, but no journalists were allowed in until the fighting had been concluded. The Defence Department provided official footage taken by military camera crews which gave the impression that the campaign was over on the first day and only mopping up operations remained.[29]

Once again the media was harnessed to demonise a symbolic enemy, in the absence of any real threat to the American public or state.[30] This time it was America's former agent of influence, General Manuel Noriega. And, once again, public support remained high for the duration of the operation, because of the military's ability to manipulate the flow of information. The subsequent delay in capturing Noriega imbued the campaign with the characteristics a protracted conflict and allowed the media to assume its rightful role. Once the objectives of the operation had been achieved with the installation of a new government in Panama, there could be no further justification for media restrictions.

This time, seizing its freedom, the media was quick to highlight inadequacies in the search for Noriega and also began to exploit opportunities to glean what it could on the conduct of the operation. The findings revealed an operation that was seriously flawed, both politically and militarily.[31] But Washington's aims had been achieved and the positive images provided by the military at the time of the conflict carried the day for the government. This developing pattern suggests that the United States military, along with other ABCA (America, Britain, Canada, Australia) states, were now following a policy of deliberate and increasingly refined media management, designed specifically to deal with the conditions of limited conflict.

The Gulf War: The Primacy of Politics

Control of the media during the Gulf war followed the pattern that was established in the Falklands and refined in Grenada and Panama. The pattern included secrecy in planning, demonisation of the enemy, exploitation of the media to enlist national and international support, and the exclusion of the media during the initial phases of the operation. The resultant news vacuum was filled by official coverage favourable to the military. Later criticisms were stonewalled.

In the Gulf, the media were excluded from the planning stages of the initial deployment and the deliberations leading to the change of war aims from that of the defence of Saudi Arabia to offensive action in Kuwait.[32] The demonisation of Saddam Hussein was used to rally national as well as international support, and the media was immediately co-opted for these tasks.[33] The Gulf also demonstrated the familiar pattern of exclusion of the media from the early action, when both the military and the administration were most vulnerable.

Beyond these measures, however, the Gulf campaign lent itself to complete media management through absolute control over the means of communication, transport and access. So powerful were these weapons that there was no need for actual censorship. Censorship was achieved primarily through denial of access and delay in transmission,[34] backed by a blanket decision not to allow media access to any event that was not strictly controlled.[35] This was offset by a flow of favourable military sourced information to fill the vacuum created by media restrictions. Material ranged from information provided at carefully controlled briefings which bypassed journalists on the spot, all the way to carefully sanitised television coverage of high technology weaponry in action.[36] The combination of credibility afforded by the briefings and novelty of the new weaponry was enough to satisfy domestic and international audiences. The media on the ground was left humiliated and floundering as they were forced to run with what was available. Only the few who broke loose from the restrictions were able to provide any independent critical analysis, and they had to battle against the credibility afforded official briefers in uniform.[37] At the same time, external commentators were silenced by the lack of hard information, while an official policy of deceit made a mockery of prudent military assessments based on known factors of weaponry, range and order of battle.

Much the same story emerged from the media who accompanied the major allied forces.[38]

The full story of the media coverage of the Gulf campaign is yet to be told, but formal complaints from the industry point to a depressingly similar trail of limitation, denial, delay, harassment, inefficiency and deliberate deceit.[39] Another problem that has not yet been fully explored is the political influence of political and ethnic lobbies. The activities of the Jewish lobbies in the United States and Australia during the Gulf campaign point to what could emerge as a major factor in the conduct of limited conflicts in the future. The only redeeming feature emerging from the Gulf has been the subsequent investigative reporting and Congressional and other inquiries that have forced the military to sharply revise their earlier optimistic assessments of success. Nevertheless, the United States military and administration appear quite satisfied with the end results of their media management and the United States Defense Department does not anticipate changes in any future operations of a similar nature.[40]

For the media, the overwhelming evidence of the Gulf experience points to the harsh reality that the campaign to liberate Kuwait was perhaps the most under-reported and media-managed conflict in history. The media's epitaph was written in Draper's description of 'the humiliation and degradation to which American and allied journalists were subjected by the US Army in the field.'[41]

The Peace-keeping Experience

As we have seen, it is apparent that peace-keeping adds a new dimension to relations between the media and the military and takes the role of the media into unfamiliar territory.

For the media, balancing national and international interests poses a singular challenge when support for United Nations objectives demands a high level of national commitment. High costs can be incurred maintaining forces in areas which are remote from the contributing country. The circumstances which lead to peace-keeping also are rarely conducive to rapid restoration of order and withdrawal of the peace-keeping force.[42] As we saw with limited conflict, a population will withdraw its support for national political and military objectives when a conflict which does not impact upon that population directly becomes protracted or when casualty lists are increasing. For the same reasons, any tendency for peace-keeping to deviate from its expected course will quickly bring a deployment under public scrutiny. The course of the United Nations intervention in Somalia demonstrates the point.

The American public and media were generally optimistic about the prospects for the success of the United States-backed peace-making and peace-keeping operations in Somalia. But if victory in the Gulf had generated an expectation that much smaller conflicts could be resolved by display of sheer strength, the reality was quite different. The media image of Somalia as a humanitarian disaster created by failures in aid distribution quickly faded as the international effort to restore order descended into limited conflict. Where Western audiences had anticipated a grateful Somali people, they encountered images of hate and violent demonstrations against the United Nations. Faced with unanticipated loss of life and the probability of lengthy conflict, the American public's support for the United Nations intervention quickly dissipated. Images of the bodies of American servicemen being paraded through the streets of Mogadishu resulted in calls for the immediate withdrawal of American forces.

The bitter experience on the Horn of Africa resulted in far greater caution when the prospect of United States intervention in Haiti arose. Government caution was fed by the American media which, assisted by the Haitian refugee problem, placed Haiti firmly on the domestic political agenda. As a result, Haiti demonstrated that there were still circumstances in which the public could claim its right to debate the issues and influence government decisions to engage in limited conflict or peace-keeping deployments. In this respect, Haiti was not a Grenada or a Panama. Even if the Haitian junta only capitulated when the invasion force was more than an hour into its flight, public opinion obliged the United States administration to leave the door open to diplomacy until the last minute.

The lessons from one may have been applied by the media in its approach to the other, but the American experiences with Somalia and Haiti underline the fact that media loyalty is first and foremost a national loyalty and a reflection of the fact that audience loyalty is also national rather than international.

From a military perspective, however, there may be little difference between preparing for peace-keeping operations and preparing for limited conflict. This is almost certainly the case when a major power has its own agenda in relation to a peace-making or peace-keeping initiative and commences planning in anticipation of a United Nations intervention. The United States positions on Somalia and Haiti illustrate the point.

In Somalia as with Grenada and Panama, there was complete secrecy in planning, with the United States waiting only for a United Nations invitation to take action.[43] No hint of this was given to the media. In the same way, the media was excluded from the planning phase of the Haiti operation and given only that information which the government wanted to publicise as part of its diplomatic signalling campaign. While there may be considerable media speculation on the possibility of intervention, based on observation of preparatory military exercises and troop movements, a government may still engage in denial, as the Clinton administration did with Haiti, until the Security Council passed a resolution approving its intentions.[44]

Just as in limited conflict, when planning for a United Nations intervention is in progress, the media may be employed to demonise identifiable leadership figures. As soon as international attention was focused on Somalia, the members of the 'militias' which had overthrown Siad Barre became 'gunmen' who were the focus of enmity for audiences sympathising with the 'victimised' Somali population.[45] 'General' Mohamed Aidid, who had coordinated the militias in the overthrow of Siad Barre, was recast as a 'warlord'. Ultimately, demonisation focused on Aidid as the most powerful warlord in Mogadishu and his name was connected with every obstruction or setback to the United Nations intervention.[46] The Haitian leadership was also systematically demonised once the possibility of armed intervention came under consideration. President Clinton accused the Haitian regime of bringing a '... reign of terror and poverty on their people'[47] and the State Department branded the junta a 'Morally Repugnant Elite.' The Haitian military were routinely referred to as 'thugs' and the leader of the junta, General Cedras, was alleged to be profiting from the drug trade.

The situation in Cambodia differed from that in Somalia and Haiti as the international forces were an invited presence. The major Western powers also had a position to protect. During the time that serious peace negotiations were under way, there was a desire to deflect attention from the reality that the United States and others had supported the brutal and genocidal Khmer Rouge both tacitly and materially for many years because of their ideological opposition to the Vietnamese presence in Cambodia.[48] Instead, the Vietnamese, whom many would argue had rescued the Cambodian people from the Khmer Rouge, were demonised. The position was similar to that in other United Nations interventions where major powers took part without acknowledging their sometimes less-than-honourable connections with the situation in the recent past. The relative absence of conflict (despite the non-cooperation of the Khmer Rouge in the final implementation of the Paris Agreements) made Cambodia less of a media event during the UNTAC deployment. The massive deployment of force was emphasised, although there was little attention to the way the troops were able to be deployed. This, in part, may have been due to the difficulties the media encountered in moving about within Cambodia. There were still media restrictions, principally in relation to the coverage of the elections, but these were applied for the protection of voters rather than to protect the operations of the military.[49] There were also restrictions on the announcement of election results as soon as voting irregularities were alleged.[50]

As with some of our examples of limited conflict, the UNTAC deployment may have been less successful than was originally claimed. However, there were no newsworthy major difficulties in the deployment and the media did not subject the situation to in-depth retrospective analysis.

The United Nations has now arrived at a crossroad with its new initiative into peace-making and uninvited interventions in what might otherwise be considered the domestic affairs of member states. Some of these initiatives clearly have taken on characteristics more typically associated with limited conflict, but with the advantage that the action is automatically legitimated by United Nations sponsorship. Relations between the media and the military in these situations can be expected to reflect the emerging pattern of media management in limited conflicts.

While there is less scope to contain the media when operations take place under a United Nations flag, in situations where the media is still reliant on the military for access and communications, the same restrictions still apply.

The problem for the United Nations is that the media tend to cater for national rather than international audiences. This means that if a deployment fails to achieve its objectives, the United Nations is left open to criticism and calls for the withdrawal of individual national troop commitments, even when the states complaining most about the inadequacies of the United Nations are those which drove the deployment in the first place.

The Pattern in Review

This summary of the individual case studies points to the emergence of carefully developed and increasingly refined policies of exclusion and containment of the media in time of limited conflict. These policies can also be expected to apply to some extent in peace-keeping and peace-making deployments. They have been designed to allow an initial period of deployment free of media scrutiny, a strategy which minimises the potential for political embarrassment that would result from any military setbacks. The policies also facilitate ongoing maintenance of the favourable image needed to maintain public support for and acceptance of military operations. Such restrictions have been readily accepted and supported by the liberal democratic governments who implement them under the military rationale of maintaining security and protecting the lives of journalists.

The development of these media management policies is the result of the Western military community's close study of the factors likely to affect the outcome of future operations and its acceptance that the nature of war and the social contract duties and obligations of the citizen have changed. But the changes are not yet fully appreciated by the public in Western liberal democracies, nor by the media that serve them. The results of the polls conducted during the conflicts covered by the case studies suggest that most people believe that the constraints and requirements of patriotic wars of survival still apply. As a result, the public are susceptible to demands for their patriotic support for broad restrictions to safeguard security and are prepared to lend unconditional support to their military forces, but only in short, successful, limited conflicts.[51] The media, which must follow or reflect audience expectations, is also susceptible to these demands. As a result, both the public and the media are open to manipulation for a limited time. It is only when a population is confronted with lack of success or a protracted conflict that public opinion appears to shift.

Against this, the new high technology global media could facilitate a shift in audience thinking if the breadth and depth of reporting were matched to immediacy of coverage. However, other than in the Vietnam war, where media technology was still relatively primitive, the media has not yet had the chance to demonstrate the capabilities of the new communications systems and other media technologies now available. It is precisely the fear of unleashing these technologies and an internationalised media, together with the political penalties of a hostile public opinion that might result, that has led to the emergence of politically-backed military policies designed to muzzle the media and manipulate public attitudes towards limited conflict. *Newsweek* summed up the situation neatly with respect to the Gulf war: 'The globalization of news (a new idea) ran smack into national allegiance in wartime (an old idea).'[52] By the time the media realised this, however, the pattern of government and military media management strategies was firmly in place.

The strategies and the rationales for these policies are readily identifiable. First, because of the need to carefully manage media coverage of conflict situations, the political direction and military planning for such operations has increasingly been predicated on the need for short, sharp, successful campaigns shielded by increasingly sophisticated policies designed to exclude or contain the media. In every case study, this policy of exclusion was designed to allow governments to fill the resulting news vacuum with their own versions of events, in an effort to enlist and maintain public support for as long as possible.

Second, in every case study when this pattern emerged, the rationale has rested on the twin pretexts of the safety of reporters and operational security. This last appeal is unquestionably a valid factor in the planning and conduct of military operations. But it has also allowed the military to exploit the public's outdated and uninformed perceptions of themselves as bound by the duties and obligations which pertained in wars of survival.

Third, in conjunction with the policy of excluding the media from the military planning phase, there has been a separate effort to harness and exploit the media in the demonisation of a selected figurehead enemy. This did not happen in Northern Ireland, where the enemy was portrayed as faceless terrorism. Nor did it happen in Vietnam, where Asian communism fitted the popular idea of an acceptable enemy in the anti-communist crusade of the time. It was also absent in the Falklands conflict, where the Argentinians were presented as the enemy and the rationale for war rested on liberating the British citizens of the occupied islands.[53] But, in the limited conflicts that followed, in the Americas and the Gulf, and to a lesser extent with Aidid in Somalia, Pol Pot in Cambodia and Cedras in Haiti, a figurehead was necessary. It was necessary, first to make up for the lack of any real threat to the home nation, and second because the target population had to be distanced from the guilt of the figurehead in order to be liberated and rehabilitated as allies.[54]

Finally, the one factor that is constant in all the case studies is the exploitation of the media to enlist national and international support, to gain the 'legitimacy' needed to engage in the action.[55] But to an increasing degree, as the cases show, media cooperation to this end has been rewarded with attempts to then exclude the media from the actual area of operations. Where denial of access is difficult or cannot be maintained for a sufficient period, it has been replaced by restrictions which limit the movement of reporters until the political situation no longer makes exclusion acceptable. The policy preference is for the resulting news vacuum to be filled by the military, to ensure positive first images which will be effective in harnessing and maintaining public support.[56] Once the conflict is over, any subsequent investigation of the handling of the media – usually brought on by complaints from the media themselves – can be dealt with by revised estimates of success rates and admissions that have long lost their newsworthiness.

This pattern can be confidently expected to form the basis of the military's handling of the media in future conflicts.

A Far Reaching Problem

The implications for the media, the military, and the public's right to know arising from these changed media-military relations are far reaching. They are also a matter for concern, as governments and the military are inclined to defend their media policies as having minimal social impact.

From a government point of view, restrictions based on the pretexts of operational security and the safety of reporters are entirely justified. They can rightly argue that if a force is deployed by a democratically elected government, then the troops involved are entitled to security of operations, no matter what level of disagreement or protest might exist within the community. They can also make the valid point that the best source of advice on the level of danger facing reporters covering a conflict, is the military itself.

The military has a sound case when it argues that media support must take second place to operational demands, especially in the initial stages of a deployment, particularly if the deployment is opposed, and during resupply and medical evacuation. However, as was demonstrated in the Grenada and Panama deployments, voluntary arrangements between the media and the military outside the areas of immediate necessity can also be overridden in the interests of 'maintaining security'.[57]

As a result, no matter what commitment may be made to the concept of the public's right to know, governments and their military advisers have recourse to a formidable arsenal of acceptable arguments which may be used to advance a hidden agenda of media limitation and containment. The powers of indirect censorship, measures such as denial of access or delay in the transmission of copy, that are available to the military to preserve security, can make direct censorship unnecessary.[58]

The evidence of the case studies is that governments are aware of the considerable military and political advantages that stem from current media management policies. As a result, it is likely that the hidden agenda of media control will form the basis for the future handling of the media in similar situations, while authorities continue to pay lip service to the public's right to know. At the same time, they will place the onus of cooperation and responsibility on the media, noting risks that could accrue from breaches of security and the problems of protecting reporters in dangerous locations..

The implications for the media are grave. The problem is that while the military has recognised the problem and has set in place unified and considered policies, the media emerges from the case studies as fragmented, unprepared and bedevilled by the concerns of competition and cost. Even specialist organisations such as CNN tend to respond to situations rather than prepare for them. Few news organisations maintain the levels of expertise or organic defence knowledge which would allow them to compete with the military on near equal terms. Despite the media industry response to the restrictions imposed during Grenada and Panama, and the work done by organisations such as the Freedom Foundation in its critique of the handling of the media during the Gulf conflict, there is no organised, central, specialist defence media lobby within the working media in any of the major democracies.[59]

Apart from the newly formed Australia-based International Defence Media Association, there is no organised specialist international lobby group able to present a unified and independent point of view to counter the dominance of the military.[60] But an independent council representing defence media interests could facilitate discussion of issues such as access, censorship, and the broader problem of freedom of expression in wartime, prior to conflicts. Left until a crisis situation arises, these issues are unlikely to be the subject of balanced discussion in an environment already being shaped by media manipulation and government appeals to patriotism. As it is, the lack of cohesive opposition to the military's policies and guidelines has weakened the position of the media in their ability to challenge future restrictions or to widen debate on the public's right to know and the duty to inform them.

The answer for the media lies in a far greater awareness of these changed circumstances and in developing the ability to organise as a separate entity from the military in order to provide a significant lobby. Such an entity may be represented on officially constituted cooperative bodies, but would retain a reserve position with the aim of safeguarding the rights of the media. From such a position, the media might regain a measure of independence in covering conflict situations.

The biggest challenge, however, lies in the implications of current media management policies for the public's right to know. The challenge arises because the public is largely unaware of the degree to which coverage of limited conflict is restricted and distorted, and because they have not been educated to exercise their increasing democratic freedoms of choice. The evidence from polls reported in the case studies indicates that attitudes have changed little since World War II.[61] There remains a widespread perception of a duty to support the nation's armed forces wherever or whenever they are deployed. It is an attitude reinforced by governments in their attempts to enlist and maintain support through demonisation of the enemy and calls to patriotism. The community also is very susceptible to what they can appreciate as commonsense appeals to operational security and the safety of the media. As a result, intellectual protest based on the citizen's freedom to choose whether to support their government's position on a conflict, in the absence of any threat to personal or national survival, is invariably denigrated as being unpatriotic and ideologically based.

Government exploitation of the lack of community awareness of the right, and the need, to judge a conflict on its merits, is aided to a large extent by the media which is shaped by conformity and which tends to reflect prevailing opinion. Even if the media was moved to adopt a more objective line, the early polls in any limited conflict campaign tend to overwhelmingly favour the government and military in the imposition of censorship. Indeed, experience has shown that any attempt by more serious media outlets to critically analyse a situation attracts penalties in the form of loss of audience.[62]

When these arguments are drawn together, the future outlook for the public's right to know and the freedom of the media to inform them, looks increasingly poor. Beyond one or two notable exceptions, there is no body of literature on this topic. Apart from Rawls, every social contract theoretician has accepted the concept that all rights and duties become subordinate to the good of the state in time of war. No one has explored the issues in the light of the changed nature of war and the emergence of limited conflict, peace-keeping and peace-making. Understandably, it is in the interests of democratic governments to keep silent over this changed situation, while sheltering behind the rationale of their media management policies. This allows them to pursue sometimes questionable ends in diplomacy while claiming the support of a public still wedded to an outdated concept of automatic support for government and military objectives. The media itself is unprepared – if not uninterested – and, lacking public support, is largely ignored by governments when the issues of freedom of the press and the public's right to know are raised. It is only now, after the media disaster of the Gulf and the military debacle of Somalia, that the subject is being taken up as a major area of study in the universities.

In summary, the situation is that governments hold both the high moral ground and the whip hand, the media is unprepared and weak, and there is a lack of public awareness of the rights of democratic communities whose complacency leaves them open to government manipulation by outdated calls for patriotic support.

Nevertheless, the three day missile attack by the United States in the Gulf in September 1996, codenamed 'Desert Strike', provided heartening evidence of a new sophistication and independence by the global media in its handling of the issue. The lessons of the Gulf war, it would seem, had been more accepted than many realised at the time. A content analysis of British, Australian and European media coverage showed a marked degree of cynicism, with leader writers and specialist defence and foreign affairs commentators immediately rejecting the United States official line and concentrating on the relevance of the action to American domestic policy.[63]

Greg Sheridan, the foreign affairs editor of *The Australian*, immediately labelled it '... the authentic Gulf Lite, with all the trimmings ...', stating that it was almost impossible to see any military purpose in the strikes beyond the re-election of President Clinton.[64] In London, Simon Jenkins went further, condemning the strike as hypocritical. As Jenkins stated:

> U.S. foreign policy is now content free. Gone is the grand strategy, gone with the Cold War. In its place are what are called 'boutique' issues, taken off the National Security Council's shelf when required for domestic consumption ... opened at the bidding of a lobbyist, but if it fails to show a quick profit, the shutters come down quickly.[65]

This critical line was reflected around the world, backed up by the cutting edge role of the cartoonists, some of whom showed Iraqi-bound missiles labelled 'Help re-elect President Clinton'.

It is true, that the crisis did not develop to the point where it attracted the sort of determined political involvement that saw the setting up of government propaganda campaigns such as we saw in the Gulf. Nor yet did we see any threat to Israel which might have necessitated the unleashing of the coordinated attacks in the media against anyone who questioned the war, such as we saw during Desert Storm.

Despite this we saw for the first time, perhaps, the beginnings of a coming-of-age by the global media: a new sophistication and sense of purpose that promises much for the public's right to know. The downside, revealed by the first American polls, was that 79 per cent of United States voters nevertheless approved of the missile attacks and 73 per cent backed their president's overall handling of the Iraqi situation.[66]

The Media and the Military: The Way Ahead

The experience of the post-war years suggests that the nature of war has changed. The potential for mutually assured destruction has made the major national confrontations of the past too costly for the industrialised world. In the future, the liberal democracies of the West will pursue their international ambitions through limited conflicts.[67]

These limited conflicts, almost by definition, will be so constrained in order to avoid uncontrollable escalation, that they will pose no threat to the survival of the citizen or the state. As we have seen, in this changed environment the citizen's conditions of obligation have diminished from near total abrogation of rights and automatic support for the state in the common interest in time of war, to a state of discretionary choice. In the absence of any direct threat to national survival, then, the citizen will have the luxury of making up his or her own mind on the merits of any conflict.

No longer assured of the automatic support that prevailed in time of common threat to personal and national survival, the state will have to work to enlist and maintain the support of the citizen in order to prosecute war. As a result, public opinion has become a major factor – if not the major factor – in the successful prosecution of limited conflicts.

In this changed environment, the media, in turn, assumes a greater importance than in the past, for the media too have been liberated from the supporting role allocated to them in previous wars of survival. Yet the media have been slow to rise to the challenge. Analysis of media coverage of the Falklands, Grenada, Panama and the Gulf shows that some elements of the media were only too willing to be swept along with the tide of enthusiasm and to act as cheerleaders for their own forces. This is understandable to some extent, especially when patriotic support is the prevailing mood of the home nation audience whose views they must respect. To its credit, however, the media has made some attempts to exercise the new independence arising from the changed nature of war, even if it has done so through retrospective analysis of events and without fully appreciating the implications of the changed obligations of the citizen in the post nuclear age.

The capacity for independent assessment and reporting has been reinforced by an increasing independence in communications and dissemination of information through the global media. The capacity for independence increases the potential for the media to break free from military constraint, while globalisation has conferred on the media formidable power to influence national and international public opinion. Another factor is the liberating influence of the digital phone and Internet to ordinary citizens around the globe. While limited to the individual, the impact of that informal individual information could have major international repercussions when broadcast through formal media organisations. That the military has long recognised these changes is evident from their approach to public affairs. As a result, the military has moved into a closer alliance with government in the development of new and increasingly sophisticated media management systems designed to control the press in time of limited war.

The end product of analysis of individual case studies points to a predictable pattern in the conduct of operations and the accompanying control of the media. This pattern applies equally to limited conflict and peace-keeping and peace-making deployments, with the caveat that there may be limits in restricting media coverage of United Nations-sponsored operations. Otherwise the pattern varies only in minor detail, depending on such factors as terrain and the remoteness of the conflict. In general, the approach can be codified in chronological order of its application:

1 *Secrecy in Planning*: This constitutes long-term secret planning that goes well beyond normal contingency plans. Such planning will be undertaken by a special political and military group which, while having full access to contingency plans and normal staff resources, will generally comprise a discrete organisation with high level political input. Knowledge of the options in military action that this group sets in place will be restricted to the most senior political levels with the mainstream military relegated to an implementation role.

2 *Demonisation of the Opposing Leadership*: If political factors determine that the deployment should be presented as being for the benefit of an oppressed population, the political strategy will normally revolve around the demonisation of a selected leader. The primary aim is to identify a focus of enmity for the home nation of the deploying force. A secondary aim is to distance opposition leaders or the 'victimised' population in the country of deployment from the source of the conflict. This allows those opposition groups and the wider community to be given a role in the eventual restoration of stability.

Demonisation is achieved by playing on the excesses, both real and imagined, of the selected leader. It will normally centre on around the issue of human rights and the leader's private habits. Truth will be a secondary issue and no consideration will be given to local custom or circumstances in meeting the overriding need to discredit the leader or, in some cases, the leadership group.

It is at this level that the media will first become involved, through background briefings to favoured journalists and arranged interviews with government leaders, refugees or exiled groups hostile to the regime. This will be accompanied by a flow of carefully slanted briefing notes or 'factory' written articles and photographs, which will be made available to the media. The target media will be both national and international. The overall aim will be to galvanise local media leaders and the international information elite into accepting that a problem does exist, and to condition them to explain to their constituents that the blame rests with the demonised leader.

3   *De-stabilisation of the Target Regime*:   De-stabilisation may be engineered using economic, political or diplomatic means. Common strategies include economic sanctions and economic isolation, or the freezing of assets held within the home or allied nations. A target regime may be further embarrassed by the sponsorship and acceptance of any available exiled claimants to power, and the fomenting of pubic unrest and support for any local opposition. Embargoes are likely to be imposed on all but essential and humanitarian supplies. Diplomatic measures may be employed to highlight the intractability and irrationality of the regime. Such measures may be accompanied by a carefully graduated military response, blockades and, possibly, clandestine insertion of preparatory intelligence personnel, special forces and offensive communications assets.

4   *The Search for Legitimacy*:   Unless an issue is a matter of extreme and direct concern to a population, the quest for public approval is likely to be accompanied by efforts to secure declarations of support from regional political groupings or from the United Nations. Where intervention is anticipated attempts may also be made to enlist 'flag' nations to demonstrate support for the action. These ends will be achieved using a combination of diplomatic lobbying or economic inducement, such as relief from existing loan repayments or the promise of additional loans, and the application of political pressure where necessary.

Again, the media will be expected to play a major role in explaining the 'rightness' of the cause. The international media will be especially targeted in order to apply pressure on particular governments. The source of most of the material for this purpose will be specialist government media organisations of the belligerent nation. These organisations will provide ready-made articles and selected facts and interviews to suit local requirements.

5 *The Buildup and Deployment*: Once the target state has been economically and politically isolated, and its demonised leadership has been sufficiently discredited internationally, the next step calls for the deployment of vastly superior forces. This will normally take place under tight security.

Based on the pattern of the past, there will if possible be some fabricated reason for excluding the media, aimed at ensuring freedom from media scrutiny in the first few hours or days of the operation when the deployment is at its most vulnerable. In all probability, this will be followed by as tight a containment as possible of what limited media is subsequently allowed in. These measures will be justified on the grounds of operational security and their success or otherwise will depend on the level of isolation of the target state. It may be expected that any pool system will be exploited to restrict coverage even further. The ability of the military to select and deploy the pool could also be used to positively ensure lack of coverage.

These restrictions will be matched by a corresponding increase in the level of pre-edited favourable coverage compiled by the military, all of it designed to ensure the projection of a favourable first image and to reinforce the picture of success and cooperation. The full weight of censorship will also be applied with probable exploitation of the military's absolute control of media traffic to delay or deny the dissemination of alternative information completely. Any media complaints at this treatment will be held over by the government until the conflict is concluded.

The military may further neutralise the media by presenting daily briefings themselves direct to the public.

The only time that the media would be unleashed is when the news must, by its nature, be favourable to the operation. This will include media being flown in to witness the deployment of relief teams or assistance programs, pro-intervention demonstrations, or the installation of a new regime. The media would also be assisted to cover subsequent victory celebrations or visits by allied political leaders.

6 *The Aftermath*: A feature of any successful limited conflict or peace-keeping deployment will be the rapid evacuation of the force, with the longer-term task of nation-building handed over to the sponsoring entity which provided the initial legitimacy – in

most cases, a regional grouping or the United Nations. The media will be neither encouraged nor assisted at this point, because it is in this phase that they will be in a position to examine the performance of the deployment and, perhaps, to uncover the artifices used to misrepresent the situation in the lead up to and implementation of the operation.

At this point, the military will move to distance themselves from any further comment on the operation. Any claims of mismanagement, unlawful acts, or other pejorative issues, along with any proven exaggerations, will be disclaimed. With the situation no longer a news event, and the public in all probability still caught up in a carefully orchestrated sense of nationalistic pride, it will be easy to argue that the media should be emphasising the national success rather than looking for ways to criticise the effort. Matters of concern will be dissected and analysed in intellectual circles, but they are not likely to be an issue for the popular media or to grab the attention of the voting public.

The evidence of past behaviour suggests that this pattern of close political and military liaison will continue to apply in future limited conflicts and peace-keeping deployments. The only variables will be the level of domestic political concern or international objection and the only saving grace for a generally unprepared media, lacking the central control or organisation to counter this form of pre-planned manipulation, is if the military should receive a setback or the conflict becomes protracted. Such a situation makes it difficult for the military to maintain popular enthusiasm. It also affords the media the opportunity to break free of its political and military constraints and use independent means to present a critical analysis.

Once free of the moral and physical limitations, and depending on the remoteness of a conflict, the artificial barriers imposed by the military would soon be breached by the full weight of an internationalised media. Beyond controlling access to field units or communications systems, the military would be powerless and appeals to patriotism based on operational security would mean little to third party national media crews.[68] No matter what the nationality of the reporter, short of recourse to rifle and bayonet censorship, the news would be relayed into international networks within minutes.

Once information is in the global media network, news would be available on a worldwide basis. The information simply cannot be contained, short of jamming airwaves and restricting private satellite dish receivers. Such draconian measures would not be politically sustainable in time of limited conflict. But even if such censorship was put in place, the news would still spread through the normal peacetime traffic of newspapers, journals, international travellers, word of mouth and, more importantly, the Internet. In the end, time would become the enemy of the operation.

In conclusion, the nature of war has changed, as have the obligations of the citizen in time of limited conflict. This change has placed a new priority on securing public opinion in the type of military operation that the nations of the West have engaged in during the post-war years. The situation is appreciated by both democratic governments and their military forces and has been met by the development of policies to harness the media in the quest to enlist and maintain public opinion. Those policies of containment and control are now firmly in place and will form the pattern of the future unless the public can be educated to claim its freedom to decide in time of limited conflict and the media can press its own case for the right to inform them.

If these reforms cannot be achieved and governments do not respond to the needs of the media in time of limited conflict, then the outlook for the public's right to know under a democratic system of government remains grim. The only certainty is that increased control and improved media management systems await us in the future.

NOTES AND REFERENCES

Chapter 1

1. American Society of Newspaper Editors Annual Conference, Boston, May 1991.
2. von Clausewitz, K.M., *Vom Kriege*, Berlin, 1832, p. 1.
3. Rapaport, A., *Three Principles of War*. Introduction to *Clausewitz On War*, Pelican, London, 1968, p. 13.
4. Hammond, G., 'Low Intensity Conflict: War by Another Name', in *Small Wars and Insurgencies*, Frank Cass, London, vol. 1, no. 3, December 1990, p. 226–38.
5. As examples of current military thinking that follows the predominance of the military victory, see the US Army *FM–100 Operations Series*, especially *FM100–5 and FM100–10* Low Intensity Conflict, HQ Department of the Army, Washington, 1976.
6. Rapaport, op. cit., p. 47.
7. For a detailed examination of the competing theories of war and the dilemma posed by the development of the nuclear threat, see Aaron R., *Peace and War: A Theory of International Relations*, (Trans) Doubleday, New York, 1966, and *On War*, Anchor Books, New York, 1963, by the same author; Waller, W., *War in the 20th Century*, Dryden Press, New York, 1940; Earle, E. (ed.), *Makers of Modern Strategy: Military Thought from Machiavelli to Hitler*, Princeton University Press, Princeton, 1943; Singer, J., *Deterrence, Arms Control and Disarmament*, Ohio State University Press, Ohio, 1962; Vagts, A., *A History of Militarism*, Meridian Books, New York, 1959; Khan, H., *On Escalation, Metaphors and Scenarios*, Praeger, New York, 1959; Khan, H., *On Thermonuclear War*, Princeton University Press, Princeton, NJ, 1963; Gavin, K., *War and Peace in the Space Age*, Harvard University Press, New York, 1958; and Hayes, C., *Nationalism, A Religion*, Macmillan, New York, 1960.
8. For a detailed examination of the round of post World War II conflicts see Chapter 3, 'The Alarm Bell Conflicts', covering Korea, Indochina and Algeria. For Vietnam, see Chapter 5, 'Vietnam: Deception on a National Scale'.
9. Kissinger, H., *Nuclear Weapons and Foreign Policy*, Harper, New York, 1957, p. 147–9.

10. Woodman, S., 'Defining Limited Conflict: A case of mistaken identity', paper delivered to the International Conference on Defence and the Media in Time of Limited Conflict, Brisbane, April 1991. See also Godfrey, S., *Low Intensity Conflict Contingencies and Australian Defence Policy*, Canberra Papers on Strategy and Defence, No. 34, SDSC, ANU, Canberra, February 1985.

11. *CLIC Papers Series, JCS Publication 1–02*, Army Air Force Centre for Low Intensity Conflict, Langley, Virginia, May 1988. See also *Joint Low Intensity Conflict Project: Final Report*, US Army Training and Doctrine Command, Fort Monroe, Virginia, August 1986.

12. Hammond, op. cit., p. 268–72.

13. *RAAF Air Power Manual 1990*, p. 6–7. Quoted by the Governor-General, Mr Bill Hayden, in his address to the International Conference on Defence and the Media in Time of Limited Conflict, Brisbane, April 1991.

14. *Threats to Australia's Security, Their Nature and Probability*, Joint Committee on Foreign Affairs and Defence, AGPS, Canberra, 1981.

15. Hammond, op. cit., p. 234.

16. O'Brien, W., *The Conduct of Just and Limited War*, Praeger, New York, 1981. For a detailed examination of the concept of limited or low intensity conflict, see Knorr, R. & Read, T., *Limited Strategic War*, Pall Mall Press, London, 1962; Osgood, R., *Strategic Thought in the Nuclear Age*, Heinemann, London, 1979, and *Limited War*, University of Chicago Press, Chicago, 1957 by the same author. See also Halperin, M., *Limited War in the Nuclear Age*, Wiley, New York, 1966 and *Strategy in the Nuclear Age*, Wiley, New York, 1983 by the same author; Khan, H., *Escalation, Metaphors and Scenarios*, Pall Mall Press, London, 1965; Olsen, W., 'The Concept of Small Wars', in *Small Wars and Insurgencies*, Frank Cass, London, vol. 1, no. 1, April 1990; Thompson, L., *Low Intensity Conflict, An Overview*, Lexington Books, Lexington, Massachusetts, 1989; and Michael, H., *Restraints on War*, Oxford University Press, Oxford, 1978.

17. For a detailed examination of the emergence and development of Social Contract Theory, see Barker, E., *Social Contract*, World Classics, OUP, London, 1959 and *Social Contract*, Dover Publications, New York, 1950 by the same author; Lively, J., & Reev, A., *Modern Political Theory from Hobbes to Marx*, Routledge, New York, 1989; Gough, J., *The Social Contract: A Critical Study of its Development*, Clarendon Press, Oxford, 1957;

and Plamenatz, J., *Man and Society*, vol. 2, McGraw Hill, New York, 1963.

18. Locke, J., *First Treatise*, Section 92; *Second Treatise*, Sections 3,11,57,134 and 139, paras. 160–1. See also Laslett, P., *Locke's Two Treatises of Government*, Clarendon Press, London, 1960.

19. Hobbes, T., *Leviathan, or the Matter, Forme and Power of a Commonwealth, Ecclesiastical and Civil*, C. McPherson (ed.), Penguin, London, 1975. See also, Oakeshott, M., *Hobbes on Civil Association*, University of California Press, Los Angeles, 1975; and Hampton, J., *Hobbes and the Social Contract Tradition*, Cambridge University Press, 1985.

20. Rousseau, J., *The Social Contract or Principles of Political Right*, chaps. v, vii. See also Cranston, M., *The Social Contract: By Jean Jacques Rousseau*, Penguin, London, 1968; Vaught, E., *The Political Writings of Jean Jacques Rousseau*, Cambridge University Press, Cambridge, 1915; and Vaughan, C., *Jean Jacques Rousseau, Political Writings*. Blackwell, Oxford, 1962.

21. Bentham, J., *Constitutional Code*, p. 127. For an overview of Bentham and his School, see also Lively & Reev, op. cit.

22. Thomas, H., *An Unfinished History of the World*, Hamish Hamilton, London, 1981; see especially the chapters on 'Population's Great Leap' and 'Urban Man'. For examples of this period of European nationalism and imperialism, see Hobson, J., *Imperialism: A Study*, London, 1902; and Kipling, R., *From Sea to Sea*, London, 1900.

23. Marwick, A., *War and Social Change in the Twentieth Century*, Bodley Head, London, 1974.

24. For a detailed examination of the restrictions imposed on the differing nations, see Luddendorf, F., *My War Memoirs 1914–18*, (trans.), London, 1919; Ferro, M., *The Great War*, Macmillan, London, 1973; Steiner, Z., *Britain and the Origins of the First World War*, Macmillan, London, 1977.

25. Marwick, op. cit.; see also Towle, P., 'The Debate on Wartime Censorship in Britain 1902–1914', *War and Society*, 1975; and McKenzie, J., *Propaganda Boom*, John Giffard, London, 1938.

26. Meyer, A., *Marxism, the Unity of Theory and Practice*, Michigan University Press, Michigan, 1963, p. 4–5.

27. Marwick, A., *Britain in the Century of Total War*, Macmillan, London, 1968.

28. Rawls, J., *A Theory of Justice*, Clarendon Press, Oxford, 1972. For additional material on Rawls' views, see McMurrin, S., *John Rawls: Liberty, Equality and Law*, Tanner Lectures on Moral Philosophy, Cambridge University Press, Cambridge, 1987; and Brennan, G., &

Buchanan, J., *The Reason of Rules: Constitutional Political Economy*, Cambridge University Press, Cambridge, 1985.

29. Parekh, B., *Contemporary Political Thinkers*, Martin Robertson, Oxford, 1982, p. 172–4. See also the Essay by Rawls in Laslett, P., & Fishkin, J. (eds), *Philosophy, Politics and Society*, Blackwell, Oxford, 1979.

30. Parekh, op. cit., p. 199–200.

31. For an examination of the growth of modern media and its acceptances, see *The Australian Broadcasting Tribunal Annual Report 1990* and Denton, R., & Woodward, C., *Political Communications in America*, Praeger, New York, 1985.

32. Barendt, E., *Freedom of Speech*, Clarendon Press, Oxford, 1987, p. 68. See also Akehurst, M., *A Modern Introduction to International Law*, Allen & Unwin, London, 1970; and the Constitutions of Australia, The United States, and West Germany for examples of guaranteed freedom of speech.

33. See the Australian Freedom of Information Act (1981), and similar legislation in the United States, West Germany and Canada. See also the report by the (Australian) Senate Standing Committee on Constitutional and Legal Affairs on the Freedom of Information Bill 1979 and Aspects of the Archives Bill 1978. See also Spigelman, J., *Secrecy and Political Censorship in Australia*, Angus & Robertson, Sydney, 1972; Mathams, R., *Sub Rosa*, Allen & Unwin, Sydney, 1982; Wolfson, S., *The Untapped Power of the Press*, Praeger, New York, 1985.

34. Schumpeter, J., *Capitalism, Socialism and Democracy*, Harper & Row, New York, 1982, p. 289. See also Buchanan, J., *The Limits of Liberty: Between Anarchy and Leviathan*, University of Chicago Press, Chicago, 1975.

35. For a detailed analysis of these two competing theories see Rosen, B., *Holding Government Bureaucracies Accountable*, Praeger, New York, 1982; Lebedoff, B., *The New Elite*, Franklin Watts, New York, 1981; Frank, M., & Weisband, E., *Secrecy and Foreign Policy*, Oxford University Press, London, 1974; and Struve, W., *Elites Against Democracy*, Princeton University Press, Princeton, 1973.

36. Gration, P., address to the International Conference on Defence and the Media in Time of Limited Conflict, Brisbane, April 1991. See also public attitude polls on the Falklands, Grenada, Panama and the Gulf war in chapters in this work.

37. See Barendt, op. cit., especially chap. iv 'Prior Restraint', and chap. v, 'Political Speech'.

38. For examples of the weight of opinion supporting the Government's right to secrecy, see Millar, T., *Australia in Peace and War*, ANU Press, Canberra, 1978, and 'A Special Case for Secrecy', *Quadrant*, June 1981. *Commonwealth of Australia v John Fairfax and Sons Ltd and Others: Commonwealth of Australia v Walsh and Another*, and *Commonwealth of Australia v IPEC Holdings Ltd and Another*, heard before Mr Justice Mason, Canberra November/December 1981. *Australian Law Review Journal*, no. 55, 1981, p. 45–53; also *Attorney-General v Heinemann*, 62 ALJR 1988, p. 345. The Crimes Act 1914, the secrecy provisions, in particular provisions such as Section 16 of the Income Tax Act 1963, and the Copyright Act 1968.

39. *United Nations Convention on Human Rights*, 1954; *United Nations Yearbook 1955*.

40. *United Nations Yearbook 1966–1967*; see also *The Statute of the Council of Europe* (Revised), the *Universal Declaration of Human Rights* (1948), the *UN Convention on Human Rights* (1954), and the *American Convention on Human Rights* (1969). See also Plowman, E., *International Law Governing Communications and Information*, Francis Pinter, London, 1982.

41. *Protective Security Handbook*, 1978, p. 1. See also Gration, op. cit.

42. Hayden, op. cit.

43. Woodward, B., *The Commanders*, Simon & Schuster, New York, 1991, p. 278, p. 26–7.

44. Pilger, John, *New Statesman*, vol. 125, no. 4295, 2 August 1996, p. 26.

45. *The Australian*, 16 December 1991, 23 December 1991 and 29 June 1992. See also *Beyond 2000* TV Programme, 10 December 1991, on the replacement of the existing Intelsat MCS–D and Marisat F1 by the new geosynchronous Inmarsat 2–F3 serving the Pacific Region from January 1991.

46. Interview, Engineering Department. Network Nine, Sydney, May 1990. See also Williams, R., 'Journocam and Beyond – A Look into the Future of ENG', paper delivered to the Society of Motion Picture and Television Engineers, Sydney, September 1992; and Knapp, G., 'Journocam' The One Person News Crew', *Encore!*, 4–17 June 1992, p. 1–2.

47. *Sydney Morning Herald*, 19 August 1991. See also Cribb, T., 'Greenpeace scores Muraroa Media Victory', AFP, 12 May 1992; and *The Australian*, 8 June 1992.

48. *Washington Post*, 17 March 1991; Arnett, P., *Live from the Battlefield*, Bloomsbury, London, 1994, p. 417–9. Arnett's

experience is instructive. On the one hand, he was restricted by the Iraqis in what he could transmit. On the other, he was able to broadcast to the Western world aspects of the war which Western governments might have preferred to suppress.

49. *The Australian*, 6 January 1991. See also *The Australian*, 22 June, 1992.

50. *Sunday Times* (London), 24 August 1990.

51. *The Australian*, 25 May 1992.

52. For an introduction to the growth of the high technology media communications see Oliver, R., 'Tomorrow the World', *Sydney Morning Herald*, 8 May 1991; and 'China Versus the World in Skywaves War', Knight Ridder Newspapers, reprinted *Sydney Morning Herald*, 19 March 1991; Mercer, D., 'Can the Media be Controlled in World War III', *UK Press Gazette*, Souvenir Issue, 1990; *The Australian*, 26 August 1987 and 14 October 1991; *Weekend Australian*, 17–18 August 1991.

53. Leebert, D. (ed.) *The Future of Computing and Communications*, MIT Press, New York, 1991; and Davidson, B., & Davis, S., *Vision: Winning in the Information Economy*, Simon & Schuster, New York, 1991. See also *The Australian*, 8 June 1992.

54. Merill, J., *Global Journalism*, Longman, New York, 1983, p. 325; see especially Merrill's section on Asia and the Pacific. For current Australian statistics, see the *Annual Report of the Australian Broadcasting Tribunal* 1989–1996. For a detailed examination of the new global media audience see Curran, J., Gurevitch, M., & Woollacott, J. (eds), *Mass Communication and Society*, Edward Arnold, London, 1987; Bonney, B., & Wilson, H., *Australia's Commercial Media*, Macmillan, Sydney, 1983; Browne, D., *International Radio Broadcasting*, Praeger, New York, 1982; and Dizard, W., *The Coming Information Age*, Longman, New York, 1982.

55. For Australian statistics on levels of education, see, *Annual Reports, Department of Education*, 1985–96, and *Annual Reports Department of Employment Education and Training*, 1989–96. See also Bing, P., *Contemporary Democracies*, Harvard University Press, Harvard, 1982; Lerner, A., *The Passing of Traditional Society*, Free Press, Glencoe, 1958; and Fowler, R., & Orenstein, J., *Contemporary Issues in Political Theory*, Praeger, New York, 1940.

56. McAllister, I., & Makkai, T., *Changing Australian Opinions on Defence: Trends, Patterns and Explanations*, International Conference on Defence and the Media in Time of Limited Conflict, Brisbane, April 1991.

Chapter 2

1. Burns, T., 'The Organisation of Public Opinion'. In *Mass Communication and Society*, Curran, J., Gurevitch, M., & Woollacott, J., (eds), Edward Arnold Press, London, 1977.
2. *Printing Act 1695*.
3. Aspinall, A., *Politics and the Press 1750–1810*, Home & Van, London, 1949.
4. Hancock, A., & MacCullum, H., *Mass Communications: Australia and the World*, Longman, Sydney, 1971.
5. Ibid.
6. Thomas, H., *An Unfinished History of the World*, Hamish Hamilton, London, 1979, p. 610–2.
7. Ibid., p. 399–402.
8. Letter from Sir Arthur Wellesley, Duke of Wellington, Army Commander in Spain to the Secretary for War, British War Museum.
9. Royle, T., *War Report*, Grafton Books, London, 1989, p. 19.
10. Royle, op. cit.
11. Chapman, C., *Russell of the Times*, Bell & Hyman, London, 1984.
12. Ibid., p. 42. See also Bentley, N., Russell's *Despatches from the Crimea 1854–56*, André Deutsch, London, 1966; and Russell's original dispatches, British War Museum.
13. Royle, op. cit., p. 27.
14. Young, P., & Lawford, J., *History of the British Army*, Barker Ltd, London, 1970, p. 173; see also Fletcher, R., *Revisionism and Empire*, Allen & Unwin, Sydney, 1984.
15. For an example of this style of colonial reporting, see Churchill, W., *My Early Life*, Butterworth, London, 1930.
16. Knightley, op. cit.
17. Ibid., p. 57–8.
18. Cooke, E., *Delane of the Times*, Constable, London 1915, p. 84.
19. Russell, W., *My Diary. North and South*, Bradbury & Evan, London, 1863.
20. Chapman, op. cit., p. 130.
21. Ibid., p. 115.
22. Knightley, P., *The First Casualty*, Quartet, London, 1975, p. 27; see also Sims, R., *The Pentagon Reporters*, National Defence University Press, Washington DC, 1983, p. 3–5.
23. Ibid.
24. Ibid.
25. Adams, E., *Great Britain and the Civil War*, Longmans Green, London, 1925. See also, Andrews, J., *The North Reports the Civil*

War, Pittsburgh University Press, 1955 and *The South Reports the Civil War*, Princeton University Press, 1970 by the same author.

26. Russell, W., *My Diary during the Last Great War*, Routledge, London, 1874, p. 138.
27. Chapman, op. cit., p. 155.
28. Royle, op. cit., p. 45. See also, Steevens, G., *With Kitchener to Khartoum*, Blackwood, London, 1898.
29. Royle, op. cit., p. 85.
30. Ibid.
31. Wallace, E., *Unofficial Dispatches*, Hutchinson, London, 1901, p. 89.
32. Royle, op. cit., p. 88. See also, Churchill, W., *London to Ladysmith Via Pretoria*, Longman, London, 1900.
33. Thayer, C., 'Vietnam: A critical analysis', International Conference on Defence and the Media in Time of Limited Conflict, Brisbane, April 1991. See also Young, P.R. (ed.), *Defence and the Media in Time of Limited War*, Frank Cass, London, 1992.
34. Royle, op. cit., p. 105.
35. *The Spectator*, 24 September 1904 (Library: RMA Sandhurst, UK). See also Knightley, op. cit., p. 61.
36. Furneaux, R., *The First War Correspondent*, Cassell, London, 1944, p. 197. See also *News of War*, London, 1964 by the same author.
37. a'Court Repington, C., *Vestigia*, Constable, London, 1919, p. 253.
38. Ibid.
39. Ibid.
40. Knightley, op. cit., p. 65.
41. Bray, M., *The Relationship between the Government and the Media in Time of War*, Unpublished Thesis, Downing College, Cambridge, 1984, p. 10.
42. Royle, op. cit., p. 115. See also Bray, op. cit., p. 11.
43. Royle, op. cit., p. 119.
44. *The Times: Past Present and Future*, (The History of *The Times*), *The Times* (London), 1952.
45. For background on this period see Swinton, E., *'Eyewitness'*, Hodder & Stoughton, London, 1923; see also Knightley, op. cit., p. 70.
46. See, for example, *The Illustrated War News*, Part 32, 17 March 1915. Articles refer to the Canadian 'boys' under fire for the first time, who '... found time to laugh and joke while the shells were bursting overhead'. In contrast, a mid-Atlantic fire aboard a French liner is attributed to '... an infernal machine secreted in the cargo by German criminals'. Reference is also made to the Germans' 'inhumane' use of inflammable liquid against French trenches.

47. Royle, op. cit., p. 131. See also a'Court Repington, C., *The First World War*, Constable, London, 1921.
48. Gibbs, P., *Realities of War*, Heinemann, London, 1920, p. 27.
49. Background of the development of these organisations and the intense rivalry between them, see Ferris, P., *The House of Northcliffe*, Weidenfeld Nicolson, London, 1972.
50. Gibbs, op. cit., p. 179.
51. Gibbs, P., *Adventures in Journalism*, Heinemann, London, 1923, p. 179.
52. Serle, G., *John Monash, A Biography*, Melbourne University Press, Melbourne, 1982, p. 247. See also Bean, C., *The Story of ANZAC*, vol. 11, Angus & Robertson, Sydney, 1935, p. 781–4; and Rhodes-James, R., *Gallipoli*, Pan Books, London, 1984, p. 312–5.
53. Royle, op. cit., p. 138.
54. *The Times: Past Present and Future*, (The History of The Times), *The Times* (London), 1952, vol. 2, p. 345.
55. Personal correspondence in possession of the authors.
56. Personal interview, Mr G.W.Young. MM..MC. March 1970. WW1 Veteran.
57. For background to the Abyssinian media coverage see Mathews, H., *Eyewitness in Abyssinia*, Secker and Warburg, London, 1937; and Waugh, E., *Waugh in Abyssinia*, Longmans Green, London, 1937.
58. Orwell, G., *Looking Back on the Spanish Civil War*, Collected Essays, Mercury Books, London, 1961, p. 211.
59. Royle, op. cit., p. 15.
60. Minutes of the CID 14 October 1935, cited in Bray, op. cit.
61. *Hansard* (UK), 28 July 1939. See also Thompson, G., *Blue Pencil Admiral*, Sampson Low, London, 1947; and, particularly, Bray, op. cit., p. 21–2.
62. Knightley, op. cit., p. 202.
63. Memo from the Prime Minister to Minister for Information, 22 March 1942.
64. Thompson, op. cit., p. 39; see also Knightley, op. cit., p. 202–13.
65. Interview, Kapitan Baron Von Lederberger, Defence Attache, German Embassy, Canberra, 1987. See also, Winkler, A., *The Politics of Propaganda*, Yale University Press, New Haven, Conn., 1978; Kris, E., & Spier, H., *German Radio Propaganda and the Media*, Oxford University Press, London, 1944; and Glanz & Elan, *Der Propagandatruppen*, Die Welt, Berlin, 2 May 1970.
66. Brzezinksi, Z., & Huntington, S., *Political Power: USA/USSR*, Chatto & Windus, London, 1963.

67. See Divine, D., *Dunkirk*, Faber and Faber, London, 1954; and Collier, R., *The Sands of Dunkirk*, Collins, London, 1961.
68. Hart, L., *Liddell Hart's History of the Second World War*, Pan Books, London, 1970, p. 92–114.
69. Jullian, M., *The Battle of Britain*, Jonathon Cape, London, 1967; see also Murrow, E., *This is London*, Cassell, London, 1941; and Hart, op. cit., chap. 24, 'The Battle of the Atlantic'.
70. Collier, R., *The WARCOS: War Correspondents of World War II*, Weidenfeld & Nicolson, London, 1989, p. 118.
71. Ibid., p. 123.
72. McConnagh, J., 'The Army and the Press in War', *Journal of the Royal United Services Institute*, vol. 98, 1953.
73. Hawkins, D. (ed.), *War Report: D Day to VE Day*, Aeriel Books, BBC, London, 1985, p. 10.
74. McConnagh, J., *The Army and the Press in War*, op. cit.; see also Sixsmith, E., *Eisenhower as Military Commander*, Batsford, London, 1973.
75. Royle, op. cit., p. 195.
76. Ibid., p. 198.
77. Semmler, C. (ed.), *The War Diaries of Kenneth Slessor*, University of Queensland Press, Brisbane, 1971.
78. Lawrenson, J., & Barber, L., *The Price of Truth. The Story of Reuters Millions*, Sphere Books, London, 1985, p. 79–84.
79. Hawkins, op. cit.; see also Royle, op. cit. p. 202.
80. Yass, M., *This is Your War, Home Front Propaganda in the Second World War*, HMSO, London, 1973, p. 58.
81. Hilvert, J., *Blue Pencil Warriors*, University of Queensland Press, Brisbane, 1984; see chap. 9 and, especially, the joint press statement on censorship, April 1944, at Appendix C.
82. Knightley, op. cit., p. 317.

Chapter 3

1. Department of State, *Selected Documents on American Foreign Policy 1941–1945*, Government Printing Office, Washington, 1946.
2. Magdoff, H., *Imperialism: From the Colonial Age to the Present*, Monthly Review Press, New York, 1978, p. 68.
3. For an overview of Imperialism, peaceful self determination and the aftermath of colonialism see Reynolds. C., *Modes of Imperialism*, Oxford University Press, London, 1981; Porter, A., & Holland, R., *Money, Finance and Empire 1790–1960*, Frank Cass, London, 1985;

Hoepli, N., *Aftermath of Colonialism*, H. Wilson Publishing, New York, 1973.

4. For background information on these campaigns and public reactions, see Osanka, F., *Modern Guerrilla Warfare: Fighting Communist Guerrilla Movements*, Free Press, Glencoe, 1962; Kamin, G., *Nationalism and Revolution in Indonesia*, Ithaca, New York, 1952; Hatta, M., *Portrait of a Patriot*, Mouton Press, The Hague, 1972; O'Ballance, E., *Malaya: The Communist Insurgent War*, Faber & Faber, London, 1966; Young, P., & Lawford, P. (eds.), *History of the British Army*, Arthur Barker, London, 1970; and Darwin, J., *Britain and De-Colonisation: The Retreat of Empire in the Post War World*, Macmillan, London, 1965.

5. For a detailed history of Korea and of the Korean War, see Bong-young Choy, *Korea: A History*, Charles Tuttle & Co, Rutland, 1971; Ridgeway, M., *The Korean War*, Doubleday, New York, 1965; and Kim Chun Kon, *The Korean War*, Kwangmyong Publishing, Seoul, South Korea, 1973. For an opposing view, see *History of the Righteous War of Korean People for the Liberation of the Fatherland*, History Research Centre, Pyongyang, North Korea, 1971.

6. Vaizey, J., *The Squandered Peace*, Hodder & Stoughton, London, 1983, p. 158–160. See also Churchill, W., *The Second World War*, vols. v and vi, Penguin, London, 1985; Dulles, F., *American Policy Towards Communist China 1949–1969*, Thomas Crowell Co., New York, 1972; and Alexander, B., *Korea, the Lost War*, Arrow Books, London, 1986.

7. UN Document *S1511*, Resolution adopted by the Security Council, 27 June 1950. See also White House Press Release, 30 June 1950.

8. *United Nations Yearbook, 1950*, New York, 1950. See also Kim Chun Kon, op. cit., p. 345–7; and Smith, B., 'The Whitehouse Story: Why We Went to War in Korea', *Saturday Evening Post*, November 1951.

9. Royle, op. cit., p. 223.

10. Ibid., p. 226.

11. Burgess, P., *WARCO*, Heinneman, Sydney, 1986, p. 112.

12. Royle, op. cit., p. 228.

13. Knightley, op. cit., p. 321.

14. Burgess, op. cit., p. 113.

15. Thompson, R., *Cry Korea*, MacDonald, London, 1951, p. 33–8.

16. Personal Interview, Dennis Warner, October 1991. See also George, A., *The Chinese Communist Army in Action: The Korean War and its Aftermath*, Columbia University Press, New York, 1967.

17. Knightley, op. cit., p. 328–9. See also, Higgins, M., *The Report of a Woman Combat Correspondent*, Doubleday, New York, 1951.
18. Higgins, op. cit., p. 132; see also Knightley, op. cit., p. 330.
19. Royle, op. cit., p. 236–45.
20. Knightley, op. cit., p. 331.
21. Ibid., p. 332.
22. For a more detailed coverage of this disagreement, see, Truman, H., *Memoirs*, Doubleday, New York, 1955 (2 Vols); Whitney, C., *MacArthur: His Rendezvous with History*, Knopf, New York, 1956; and Alexander, op. cit,. chap. 54, 'The MacArthur Hearings'.
23. Hermes, G., *Truce Tent and Fighting Front*, Government Printing Office, Washington, 1966.
24. Personal interview, Dennis Warner, October 1991, and private correspondence with Burchett, 1977. See also Knightley, op. cit., p. 339. For a detailed treatment of the Armistice negotiations, see also Vatcher, W., *Panmunjon*, Praeger, New York, 1958.
25. Personal interview, Dennis Warner, October, 1989.
26. Coverage by co-author, Peter Young, of the student riots in May 1985. The incident resulted in Young's arrest, assault and confiscation of his equipment, and the arrest and long-term imprisonment of his Korean national cameraman.
27. Alexander, op. cit., p. 483.
28. Stoessinger, J., *Why Nations Go To War*, Macmillan, London, 1985, p. 79.
29. Merill, op. cit., p. 323–6, and chap. 1 'The Reach and Immediacy of the New Global Media'.
30. MacDonald, J., *Television and the Red Menace*, Praeger, New York, 1985. See especially chap. 3, 'The Cold War as Entertainment', and Table 4, 'The Military in TV Series in the 1950s', p. 111.
31. Ibid., p. 33–4.
32. For background to the then current military thinking, see Schnabel, J., *Policy and Direction: The First Year*, Office of the Chief of Military History, Washington, 1962; Schnabel, J., & Watson, R., *The History of the Joint Chiefs of Staff and National Policy*, vol. 3, *The Korean War*, Joint Secretariat, Joint Chiefs of Staff, Washington, 1978–79; MacArthur, D., *Reminiscences*, McGraw Hill, New York, 1964; and Miller, J., & Carroll, J., *Korea 1951–53*, Office of the Chief of Military History, Washington, 1956. See also MacDonald, op. cit.
33. For a detailed coverage of the French takeover of Indochina and its eventual fall to the Japanese, see Buttinger, J., *The Smaller Dragon, a Political History of Vietnam*, Praeger, New York, 1958; Legrand,

J., *L'Indochine à l'heure Japonaise*, Legrand, Paris, 1963; and Devilliers, P., *Histoire de Vietnam du 1940–52*, Seuil, Paris, 1952.

34. Osanka, op. cit., p. 254.
35. For a detailed examination of the rise of nationalism and the Viet Minh, see Buttinger, J., *A Dragon Embattled*, vol. 1, *From Colonialism to the Vietminh*, Praeger, New York, 1967. See also Hammer, E., *The Emergence of Vietnam*, Institute of Pacific Relations, New York, 1947.
36. Osanka, op. cit., p. 258.
37. State Department Bulletin, 30 June 1952.
38. For a detailed description of the military campaign, see Fall, B., *Street without Joy*, Stackpole Publishing, Pasadena, 1958; Hammer, E., *The Struggle for Indochina*, Stanford University, New York, 1947; A. Cole (ed.), *Conflict in Indochina*, Cornell University Press, New York, 1956; Trager, F., *Why Vietnam*, Praeger, New York, 1966; Giap, Vo Nguyen, *Unforgettable Days*, Foreign Languages Publishing House, Hanoi, 1978; Honey, P. (ed.), *North Vietnam Today, A Profile of a Communist State*, Praeger, New York, 1962; and Bonnet, G., *Les Guerres Insurrectionelles et Revolutionnaires*, Payot, Paris, 1958.
39. Trager, op. cit., p. 49.
40. Personal interview, M. Lucien Boz, Directorate of Information (1948–51), Paris, 11 March 1977.
41. *Journal Officiel Assemblee de L'Union Francaise*, 19 January 1950.
42. Hammer, op. cit., p. 269.
43. Interview, M. Lucien Boz, op. cit.; see also Hammer, op. cit., p. 298.
44. Merill, op. cit., p. 45.
45. Ibid., p. 75.
46. Hammer, op. cit., p. 297.
47. Servan-Schrieber, J., Editor of *L'Expresse*, in *Le Monde*, Editorial, 30 April 1953 (Courtesy Interview, M. Lucien Boz, op. cit.)
48. Nguyen, Vo Giap. *People's War People's Army*, Foreign Publishing House, Hanoi, 1961, p. 61.
49. Special Operations Research Office, *Casebook on Insurgency and Revolutionary Warfare*, The American University, Washington, 1962, p. 241. For a more detailed background to the economic and political scene in Colonial Algeria, see Julien, C., *L'Afrique Du Nord en Marcle*, Juillard, Paris, 1952; and Barbour, N., *A Survey of North West Africa (The Maghrib)*, Oxford University Press, London, 1959.
50. Special Operations Research Office, op. cit., p. 256.
51. *United Nations Yearbook 1955*.

52. Personal interview, Colonel Adrian de la Foucould, former member of the Centre d'Instruction a la Guerre Psychologique (1957), Paris, May 1977. See also Vaizey, op. cit., p. 236.
53. Special Operations Research Office, op. cit., p. 253.
54. Interview, de la Foucould, op. cit.; see also Special Operations Research Office, op. cit., p. 258.
55. Vaizey, op. cit., p. 236.
56. For a detailed examination of the military and political conflict from 1957 to 1962, see Crawley, A., *De Gaulle*, Collins, London, 1969; Horne, A., *A Savage War of Peace: Algeria 1945–62*, Macmillan, London, 1969; O'Ballance, E., *The Algerian Insurrection, 1954–62*, Faber & Faber, London, 1967; Gillespie, J., *Algerian Rebellion and Revolution*, Praeger, New York, 1967; Brace, R., & Brace, J., *Ordeal in Algeria*, Princeton University Press, Princeton NJ, 1960; Roy, J., *The War in Algeria*, Knopf, New York, 1957; Kraft, J., *The Struggle for Algeria*, Doubleday, New York, 1961; and Mezerick, A., (ed.), *Algeria Development 1959: De Gaulle, FLN, UN*, International Review, New York, 1960.
57. Merill, op. cit., p. 45.
58. Special Operations Research Office, op. cit., p. 256.
59. Ibid., p. 257.
60. Ibid., p. 245.
61. Fanon, F., *The Wretched of the Earth*, Penguin, London, 1967, p. 39.
62. Sartre, J P, Preface to Fanon, op. cit., p. 23–4.

Chapter 4

1. *Northern Ireland Constitution Act.* See also *Northern Ireland. A Brief Survey*, Foreign and Commonwealth Office and Northern Ireland Office, HMSO, London, 1983.
2. Interviews: Chief of Staff, Northern Ireland Command, and Adjutant, 11 Ulster Defence Regiment (UDR), Portadown, 17 March 1988; and CO Royal Scots Guards, Belfast, 18 March 1988.
3. For background on the ban, see North, D. *Silencing the Airwaves*, Macleans, (UK), vol. 98, 19 August 1985; and Merck, M., 'This is not about Ireland', *New Statesman*, vol. 110, no. 2839, 16 August 1985, p. 14.
4. For background to the legislative provisions, see Baker, G., *Review of the Operations of the Northern Ireland (Emergency Provisions) Act 1978*, HMSO, London, 1984.

5. Boyle, K., Hadden, T., & Hillyard, P., *Law and State*, Martin Robertson, London, 1975, p. 40–1.
6. Boyle et al., op. cit., p. 88–9. See also Wilson, T., *Ulster: Conflict and Consent*, Blackwell, London, 1989; and Boyle, K., *Ten Years on: Northern Ireland: The Legal Control of Political Violence*, Martin Robertson, London, 1980.
7. De Paor, L., *Unfinished Business: Ireland Today and Tomorrow*, Hutchinson Radius, London, 1990, p. 137–8.
8. For a detailed examination to the problem of Northern Ireland, see Lyons, F., *Culture and Anarchy in Ireland 1819–1939*, New York, 1979; Privileges, J., *The Making of Modern Ireland*, Faber & Faber, London, 1968; and Miller, D., *Queens Rebels, A Historical Study of Ulster Loyalism*, Praeger, New York, 1978. For a more recent assessment of the progress of the conflict see Jones, D. & Platt, S. (eds.), 'The Long War', *New Statesman and Society* with Channel 4 Television, special supplement, 8 July 1994.
9. Home Secretary Statement, *Hansard*, 15 August 1969. See also *Disturbances in Northern Ireland : The Cameron Commission*, CMD 532, Belfast, 1969, para 160.
10. See *Violence and Civil Disturbances in Ireland in 1969*, CMD 566, Belfast 1972, chaps. 3 and 8.
11. Boyle et al., op. cit., p. 30. See also the Boyle et al. reference to the Sunday Times Insight Team report, *The Rebirth of the IRA*, 1972.
12. Bowyer-Bell, J., *The Secret Army: The IRA 1916–1969*, Cambridge University Press, Cambridge, Massachusetts ,1980.
13. *Report into the Enquiry into Allegations against the Security Forces of Physical Brutality in Northern Ireland*, CMD 4823, London, 1971.
14. Intelligence Briefing, 11 Ulster Defence Regiment, (UDR), Portadown, 17 March 1988.
15. Background briefing, HQ Northern Ireland Command, 18 March 1988.
16. *The Australian*, 2 September 1994.
17. Adams, J., *The Financing of Terror*, New English Library, London, 1986, p. 129–44; and background briefing, HQ Northern Ireland Command, op. cit. In the early 1980s, it was estimated that it cost the IRA approximately half a million pounds Sterling a year to operate (See Janke, P., 'Northern Ireland'. In Thompson, R. (ed.), *War in Peace*, Orbis, London, 1981, p. 281–85.) In the 1990s, its annual revenue is several million pounds. On the other side, an annual revenue three million pounds Sterling is attributed to the Protestant

paramilitaries (See Wichert, S., *Northern Ireland since 1945*, Longman, London, 1991, p. 190).

18. *The Times* (London), 22 January 1992; *The Weekend Australian*, 3–4 September 1994. To put the cost of limited conflict in perspective, the daily cost of British operations in Northern Ireland approximates the annual operating costs for the IRA.

19. Reference Service of the Central Office of Information, London, December 1990.

20. Co-author Peter Young spent two weeks in Northern Ireland as a guest of the British Ministry of Defence. This included attachments to the Royal Scots Guards and the UDR, 13–25 March, 1988. The evidence of a single four-hour night patrol with the UDR gave a very clear indication of a sectarian subjectivity and personal animosity. See also McKittrick, D., 'Cracks in the Pieces of Ireland's Mosaic', *The Independent*, October, 1989.

21. Bowyer-Bell, J., 'An Irish War: The IRA's Armed Struggle, 1969–90', in *Small Wars and Insurgencies*, Frank Cass, London, vol. 1, no. 3, December 1990. See also *The Australian*, 5 July 1989.

22. Eveleigh, R., *Peace Keeping in a Democratic Society*, C. Hurt & Company, London, 1978. See also Bowyer-Bell 1990, op. cit.

23. *The British Press and Northern Ireland*, Socialist Research Centre, London, 1971. See also Rolston, B., (ed.) *The Media and Northern Ireland: Covering the Troubles*, Macmillan, London, 1991. *The Times* (London), 22 January 1992, reported 61 per cent of British survey respondents favouring withdrawal from Northern Ireland.

24. Boyle et al., op. cit., p. 33.

25. The cease-fire was widely reported in the United Kingdom and internationally. See, for example *The Times* (London), *The Guardian*, and the *Washington Post*, 31 August 1994 and through the first week of September 1994, and *The Australian* and *The Weekend Australian*, 1–4 September 1994. See also O'Doherty, M., 'New myths for old', *New Statesman and Society*, 9 September 1994, p. 12–3. The push for peace may be, in part, an attempt by Sinn Fein to broaden its base in the wake of declining electoral support over the past two years. See O'Doherty, M. 'The people who love the Provos', *New Statesman and Society*, vol. 5, no. 205, 5 June 1992, p. 22–4; and *The Australian*, 8 November 1994. For a media assessment of the cease-fire, see Morgan, J. ' Ceasefire brings wary optimism', *UK Press Gazette*, no. 1474, 5 September 1994, p. 2.

26. Continuing negotiations were reported in subsequent months although a level of violence in the form of 'punishment beatings' was maintained by both Republicans and Unionists; see *The Australian*,

31 October 1994. For reports of the Unionist cease-fire, see *The Times* (London), *The Guardian* and international press reports from 13–14 October 1994 onwards, and reports on negotiations in November and December 1994. By mid-1996, there were signs that the negotiations were in difficulty; see Reuters, AFP, AP, *The Weekend Australian*, 20-21 July 1996; Llyod, John, 'The hatred within will always win', *New Statesman*, vol. 125, no. 4297, 16 August 1996, p. 18-9; Fedarko, Kevin, 'A summer of hatred', *Time*, no. 30, 22 July 1996, p. 22-3.

27. O Connor, F., 'A slogan is no substitute for a strategy', *New Statesman*, vol. 111, no. 2859, 10 January 1986, p. 10–1. See also Northern Ireland Press Office Press Notice 423/88, 'Northern Ireland: The Present and Future', dated 10 March 1988.

28. Foot, P., *Why Britain Must Get Out*, Chatto and Windus, London, 1989.

29. *Belfast Telegraph*, 7 April 1970.

30. Rose, R., *Governing Without Consensus: An Irish Perspective*, Faber & Faber, London, 1971, p. 111.

31. Winchester, S., *In Holy Terror*, Faber & Faber, London, 1974, p. 71; Hamill, D., *Pig in the Middle: The Army in Northern Ireland 1969–85*, Methuen, London, 1986.

32. Greaves, C., *The Irish Crisis*, Lawrence & Wishart, London, 1972, p. 194.

33. Winchester, op. cit., p. 71; also *The Silent Voices*, Videorecording Television Co-operative Production Channel 4, London, 1983.

34. Boyle et al., op. cit., p. 35.

35. Curtis, L., *The British Media and the Battle for Hearts and Minds*, Pluto Press, London, 1984.

36. De Paor, op. cit., p. 130.

37. Winchester, op. cit, p. 67. See also Kelly, K., *The Longest War: Northern Ireland and the IRA*, Zed Books, London, 1982.

38. Bowyer-Bell 1990, op. cit., p. 247.

39. *Hansard* (UK), February 1972.

40. For a critical examination of the evidence, see Dash, S., *A Challenge to Lord Widgery's Report on Bloody Sunday*, Defence and Education Fund of the International League of the Rights of Man, in association with the Council of Civil Liberties, August 1972.

41. Boyle et al., op. cit., p. 127; De Paor, op. cit., p. 130.

42. Winchester, op. cit., p. 210.

43. Ibid., p. 212.

44. McKinley, M., 'Northern Ireland : A Case Study', International Conference on Defence and the Media in Time of Limited Conflict, Brisbane, April 1991.
45. Herman, S., & Chomsky, N., *Manufacturing Consent: The Political Economy of the Mass Media*, Pantheon, New York, 1988, p. 12.
46. McKinley, op.cit.
47. *R v the Justices of the Peace for the County of the City of Londonderry (Ex Parte Hume and Others)*, unreported, judgement delivered 23 February, 1972 (see *Northern Ireland Legal Quarterly*, vol. 23, no. 2, Summer 1972, p. 206–7). Lowry L.C.J observed that the regulation was also ultra vires on the grounds that it was not conducive to peace, order and good government, and was excessively far reaching and oppressive. Perhaps it is not surprising that the case was unreported.
48. See *The Northern Ireland Act* 1972.
49. Corbett, J., *Press Bias in Northern Ireland*, unpublished thesis, Ohio State University, Ohio, 1981.
50. *The Guardian*, 10 March 1988; *The Times* (London), 16 March 1988.
51. *The Guardian*, 15 March 1988.
52. *The Times* (London), 17 March 1988.
53. Co-author Peter Young, personal interviews with witnesses, Belfast, March 1988.
54. National Television News, ITN BBC and Visnews coverage, London. 17–28 March 1988.
55. *The Times* (London), 17 March 1988 and 23 March 1988.
56. The tapes were demanded under Section 11 of the Prevention of Terrorism Act and Section 13 of the Northern Ireland Emergency Provisions Act.
57. *The Times* (London), 20 March 1988 and 23 March 1988. Prime Minister Thatcher put the government position squarely: '... the media ... has a bounden duty to everything they can to see that those who perpetrated the terrible crime which we saw on television and which disgusted the whole world are brought to justice'.
58. *The Times* (London), 20 March 1988 and 23 March 1988.
59. *Hansard (UK)*, March 1988.
60. Lord Hill. *Behind the Screen*, Sidgwick and Jackson, London, 1974, p. 209.
61. Ibid.
62. Tugwell, M., *Revolutionary Propaganda and Possible Counter Measures*, Defence Fellowship Thesis, Cambridge, 1977.
63. Hooper, A., *The Military and the Media*, Gower, Aldershot, p. 125.

64. Wright, J., *Terrorist Propaganda: The Red Army Faction and the Provisional IRA*, St Martin, 1991. See also O'Connor, F., *Newsnight Falls for Unionists PR Ploy*, New Statesman, 9 May 1986.

65. *Congressional Record*, May 1985.

66. For examples, see Hooper, op. cit., p. 139 and p. 141–5. See also Greaves, C., op. cit., p. 151; and Boyle et al., op. cit., p. 129.

67. The ban was made by the Home Secretary under the powers inherent in the *1981 Broadcasting Act and the BBC's License and Agreement*. It was lifted as part of confidence-building measures following the September 1994 cease-fire agreement. For a list of the banned organisations see Glover, R., 'Ulster Media Ban like S Africa', *Sydney Morning Herald*, (London Bureau), 21 October 1988.

68. *Hansard (UK)*, October 1988.

69. *Sydney Morning Herald*, 21 October 1988. See also Weaver, R. & Bennett, L., *The Northern Ireland Broadcasting Ban*, Vanderbilt, Transnational Law, No 5/1989; and Wilson, J., 'Cracking Down on Coverage: Britain's Blurred Television Picture', *Columbia Journalism Review*, May/June 1988.

70. *The Economist*, 'Still hoping to say goodbye', 26 March 1988, p. 48.

71. *The Times* (London), 27 February 1976.

72. Eveleigh, op. cit., p. 42.

Chapter 5

1. Yates, L., *Power Pack: US Intervention in the Dominican Republic 1955–66*, Combat Studies Institute, Kansas, July 1988, p. 174.

2. Ward, J., *Military Men*, Michael Joseph, London, 1972, p. 1–14. See also Weigley, R., *History of the United States Army*, Macmillan, New York, 1967; and Ward, J. *The American Way of War*, Macmillan, New York, 1973.

3. *National Security Action Memorandum No. 111*, November 22, 1961. See also Telegram from Nolting to Rusk, 25 November 1961, cited in Porter, G., *Vietnam: A History in Documents*, Meridian Books, New York, 1981.

4. See Chapter 3, 'Post-War Self Determination: The Unheeded Warning'.

5. Merill, op. cit., p. 45–6 and p. 302–53. See also Denton, R., & Woodward, G., *Political Communication in America*, Praeger, New York, 1985, p. 164–70.

6. Hammond, W., *Newsmen and National Defence*, L. Mathew (ed.)., Brasseys (US) Virginia, 1991, p. 23. See also Turner, K., *Lyndon Johnson's Dual War: Vietnam and the Press*, University of Chicago Press, Chicago, 1985.

7. For a detailed examination of the background to the conflict and the course of the war, see Kolko, G., *Vietnam, The Anatomy of a War 1940–75*, Allen & Unwin, London, 1986; Halberstam, D., *The Best and The Brightest*, Random House, New York, 1972; Snepp, F., *Decent Interval*, Vintage Books, New York, 1978; and Karnow, S., *Vietnam. A History*, Penguin, London, 1984. For the earlier years of the war in Indo-China, see Fall, B., *Street Without Joy*, Schocken Books, New York, 1961.

8. Sarkesian, S., 'Soldiers, Scholars and the Media', *Parameters*, September 1987, p. 82–3. Also, Co-author Peter Young interview with H.E. Mr Nguyen Co Thach, DRVN Foreign Minister, Hanoi, 13 May 1983.

9. Graham, S., transcript, International Conference on Defence and the Media in Time of Limited Conflict, Brisbane, April 1991.

10. Co-author Peter Young served with the Combined Studies Division of the CIA in Vietnam and was involved in the forerunner of OPLAN 34A. He served later as Indochina Desk Officer at the Directorate of Military Intelligence in Canberra, 1963–4.

11. Kolko, op. cit., p. 123.

12. Co-author Peter Young interview with Former CIA Station Chief (Danang), Washington, January 1971.

13. *US Congressional Record*, 4 August 1964.

14. Amter, J., *Vietnam Verdict*, Continuum, New York, 1982, p. 63.

15. Kolko, op. cit., p. 125. See also US Senate Committee on Foreign Relations Hearings, *The Gulf of Tonkin: 1964 Incident*, February 1968.

16. Amter, op. cit., p. 63. See also *Congressional Record*, 6 August 1964.

17. *Congressional Record*. 6 August 1964.

18. Ibid.

19. Thompson, R., 'Vietnam'. In Thompson, R. (ed.), *War in Peace*, Orbis Publishing, London 1981, p. 182.

20. Co-author Peter Young's own files when Assistant Military Attache (Intelligence) at the Australian Embassy in Saigon 1965–68.

21. See Venanzi, G., *Democracy and Protracted War: The Impact of Television*, Air Force Review, 1983.

22. Kolko, op. cit., p. 171.

23. Amter, op. cit., p. 124–7.

24. Amter, op. cit., p. 124–7. See also Jacobsen, K., *Television and the War: The Small Picture*, US Naval Institute, Annapolis, 1975.
25. Levering, R., *The Public and American Foreign Policy 1918–1979*, William Morrow & Co, New York, 1978, p. 128.
26. Gallup Polls, December 1967 and 1968 (courtesy U.S. Information Service, Canberra), and Hallin, D., *The Mass Media and the Crisis in American Politics*, University of California Press, Los Angeles 1981. See also Angele, A., *US Armed Forces Public Affairs Roles in Low Intensity Conflict*, Army Air Force Center for Low Intensity Conflict, Langley, Virginia, May 1988.
27. For background to this dichotomy, see Shapiro, M. (ed.), *The Pentagon Papers and the Courts. A Study in Foreign Policy Making and the Freedom of the Press*, Chandler Publishing, 1982.
28. Lunn, H., *Vietnam: A Reporter's War*, University of Queensland Press, Brisbane, 1985, p. 84–95. See also Herr, M., *Dispatches*, Picador, London, 1977.
29. Lunn, op. cit., p. 59. See also Faulkner, F., *'Bao Chi': The American News Media in Vietnam*, University of California Press, Los Angeles, 1981; Elegant, R., *How to Lose a War: Reflections of a Foreign Correspondent*, Encounter, London, 1981, and Bailey, G., & MacDonald, G., *Report or Distort: The Inside Story of the Media's Coverage of the Vietnam War*, Exposition Press, New York, 1973.
30. Carter, F. & Greenberg, C., 'Newspapers or Television: Which do you Believe?', *Journalism Quarterly*, Winter 1965.
31. Clarke, P. & Ruggels, L., 'Preferences Among News Media for Coverage of Public Affairs', *Journalism Quarterly*, Autumn 1970.
32. Hofstetter, R. & Moore, D., 'Watching TV News and Supporting the Military', *Armed Forces and Society*, vol. 5, no. 1, 1979.
33. Hallin, D., *The Uncensored War: The Media and Vietnam*, Oxford University Press, 1986, p. 99.
34. Thayer, C., 'Vietnam: A critical analysis', paper delivered to the International Conference on Defence and the Media in Time of Limited Conflict, Brisbane April 1991. See also Young, P.R. (ed.), op. cit.
35. Westmoreland, W., *A Soldier Reports*, Dell Publishing Company, New York, 1976, p. 82.
36. USMACV/5512/1 5.68.
37. Co-author Peter Young was accredited to the Department of Defence, USMACV, the National Vietnamese Press Centre and the Department of Information in Cambodia, 1971–73.
38. Lunn, op. cit., p. 59.

39. Burgess, P., *WARCO: Australian Reporters at War*, Heinemann, Sydney, 1986, p. 40. See also Herr, op. cit.
40. Westmoreland, *A Soldier Reports*, op. cit., p. 557.
41. Co-author Peter Young, personal notes taken while serving with the Combined Studies Division of the CIA, Danang 1962 and while visiting the Ashau Valley as Assistant Military Attache at the Saigon Embassy 1967.
42. Westmoreland, W., paper delivered to the International Conference on Defence and the Media in Time of Limited Conflict, Brisbane, April 1991. Paper read by General S. Graham, former ATF Commander.
43. Westmoreland, op. cit..
44. Grenville, K., *The Saving of South Vietnam*, Alpha Books, Sydney, 1972, p. 90, 111–5.
45. Hammond, M., 'The Army and Public Affairs: A Glance Back'. In Mathews, L. (ed.) *Newsmen and National Defense*, Brasseys, McLean, Virginia, 1991, p. 1–18. See also Hammond, M., *Public Affairs: The Military and the Media 1962–68*, Centre for Military History, Washington, 1988.
46. Interview, Colonel J. Dermody, former G2, HQ 1ATF Canberra, December 1987. See also Burgess, op. cit., Chapter 17.
47. Stone, G., *War Without Honour*, Jacaranda Press, Sydney, 1972, p. 53.
48. McDougall, D., 'The Australian Press Coverage of the Vietnam War in 1965, *Australian Outlook*, vol. 20, 1966, p. 303–10. See also Jones, K., & Flood, E., *Media Images of ANZAC*, Department of Education, Sydney, 1983.
49. Warner, D., *Not With Guns Alone*, Hutchinson, Sydney, 1977, p. 147,157. Co-author Peter Young was a member of the group involved in this intelligence assessment.
50. Sarkesian, op. cit.
51. Karnow, op. cit., p. 545.
52. Braestrup, P., *The Big Story*, Westview Press, Colorado, 1977.
53. Westmoreland, paper delivered to the International Conference on Defence and the Media in Time of Limited Conflict, op. cit. See also Young, P. (ed.) *Defence and the Media in Time of Limited War*, Frank Cass, London 1992.
54. Kolko, op. cit., p. 319,345. See also Hallin, 1986, op. cit., p. 175–8.
55. Hallin, 1986, op. cit., p. 168. See also Bishop, D., 'The Press and the Tet Offensive: A Flawed Institution Under Stress', *Air University Review*, 1978.
56. Kolko, op. cit., p. 326, 380–1.

57. Maclear, M., *Vietnam: The Ten Thousand Day War*, Methuen, London, 1981, p. 287.
58. Kolko, op. cit., p. 379.
59. Young, P., 'Laos, What's Happening?', *The Bulletin*, vol. 93, no. 4749, 3 April 1971, p. 32–3.
60. Hammond, W., 'The Press in Vietnam as an Agent of Defeat: A Critical Examination', *Reviews in American History*, Washington, 1989.
61. Kolko, op. cit., p. 380.
62. Cubbage, T., 'Westmoreland vs CBS: Was Intelligence Corrupted by Policy Demands?', *Intelligence and Security Review*, United Kingdom, 1985. See also Kolko, op. cit.; Karnow, op. cit.; and Snepp, op. cit. For the Vietnamese position, see Nguyen,T. & Schecter, J. *The Palace File*, Harper & Row, New York, 1986
63. Hammond, 1989, op. cit., p. 312–23.
64. Trainor, B., 'The Military and the Media: A Troubled Embrace'. In L. Mathews (ed.), *Newsmen and National Defense*, Brassey's, McLean, Virginia 1991, p. 121–9.

Chapter 6

1. Personal Interview, General Sir Jeremy Moore, Brisbane, April 1991; see also Sancton, Thomsa, and Gerwin, Larry, 'How the war was won', *Time*, no. 37, 9 September 1996, p. 40-2.
2. Harris, R., *Gotcha! The Media, the Government and the Falklands Crisis*, Faber and Faber, London, 1983, p. 56. For a detailed examination of the military conduct of the conflict see also Bishop, P., & Witherow, J., *The Winter War: The Falklands*, Quartet Books, London, 1982; Dalyell, T., *One Man's Falklands*, Cecil Woolf, London, 1982; Fox, R., *Eyewitness Falklands*, Methuen, London, 1982; Frost, J., *2 Para Falklands*, Buchan & Enright, London, 1983; Hastings, M., & Jenkins, S., *Battle for the Falklands*, Michael Joseph, London, 1983; Sunday Times Insight Team, *The Falklands War*, Sphere Books, London, 1982; Middlebrook, M., *Operation Corporate*, Viking, London, 1985; *The Falklands Campaign: The Lessons*, White Paper, Cmnd 8758, HMSO, London, 1982; and Woodward, S., with Robinson, P., *One Hundred Days*, HarperCollins, London, 1992.
3. U.N. Security Council Resolution 502 (1982), 3 April 1982.
4. Mercer, D., Mungham, G., & Williams, K., *The Fog of War*, Heinemann, London, 1987, p. 18.

5. Foster, K., *The Failure of the Falklands Myth*, Unpublished Doctoral Thesis, Monash University, August 1989. See also Aulich, J. (ed.), *Framing the Falklands War: Nationhood, Culture and Identity*, Open University Press, Philadelphia, 1992.

6. *The Times*, 20 May 1982.

7. Rice, D., & Gavshon, R., *The Sinking of the Belgrano*, Secker & Warburg, London, 1984, p. 53.

8. Sunday Times Insight Team, op. cit., p. 214; Hastings and Jenkins, op. cit., p. 333.

9. Foster, op. cit., p. 59. Some newspapers, such as the *Observer* and the *Financial Times* took a more restrained approach, opposing armed retaliation. *The Guardian* opposed the action throughout. See Hastings and Jenkins, op. cit., p. 135–6.

10. Moore, Major-General Sir Jeremy, 'The Falklands war: A commander's view of the defence-media interface', paper delivered to the International Conference on Defence and the Media in Time of Limited Conflict, Brisbane, April 1991.

11. Evidence before the House of Commons Defence Committee, 9 October 1982.

12. *Report of the Study Group on Censorship*, (The Beach Report), Cmnd 9499, 1985. See also Foster, op. cit.

13. Adams, V., *The Media and the Falklands Campaign*, Macmillan, London, 1986 p. 6. See also Morrison, D., and Tumber, H., *Journalists at War*, Sage Publications, London, 1988, p. 6–7.

14. Harris, op. cit., p. 96. See also Interview, General Sir Jeremy Moore, op. cit., and Mercer, Mungham & Williams, op. cit., p. 42.

15. RN Signal 'Operation Corporate: PR Policy and Guidance on Press Facilities Afloat', referred to during interview, MOD, London, March 1988.

16. Mercer, Mungham & Williams, op. cit., p. 42.

17. Woodward with Robinson, op. cit., p. 109–13.

18. Morrison & Tumber, op. cit., p. 139–43.

19. Hastings & Jenkins, op. cit., p. 332. See also Harris, op. cit., p. 21–3.

20. Morris & Tumber, op. cit., p. 97–8.

21. Memorandum to the House of Commons Defence Committee, dated 20 July 1984. See also *The Handling of the Press and Public Information during the Falklands Conflict*, HMSO, London, 1983.

22. Adams, *The Media and the Falklands Campaign*, op. cit., p. 6.

23. Mercer, Mungham & Williams, op. cit., p. 147.

24. Morrison & Tumber, op. cit., p. 168.

25. Evidence before the House of Commons Defence Committee, vol. 2, p. 440.

26. Harris, op. cit., p. 57; Morrison & Tumber, op. cit., p. 167.
27. Skynet was erratic and its footprint only covered the Falklands some six weeks after the conflict.
28. Interview, technical staff, ITN Television, London, March 1988.
29. Evidence before the House of Commons Defence Committee, *First Report of the Defence Committee*, HMSO, London, 1983.
30. Morrison & Tumber, op. cit., p. 170.
31. Evidence before the House of Commons Defence Committee, vol. 2, 12 July 1982, para 64.
32. Mercer Mungham & Williams, op. cit., p. 149. See also Morrison & Tumber, op. cit., p. 178–83.
33. Harris, op. cit., p. 56.
34. Hastings & Jenkins, op. cit., p. 125.
35. Morrison & Tumber, op. cit., p. 102.
36. Evidence before the House of Commons Defence Committee, vol. 2, 9 November 1982, para 1724.
37. Evidence before the House of Commons Defence Committee, 11 November 1982.
38. Foster, op. cit., p. 1; See also Morrison & Tumber, op. cit., p. 198–200.
39. Pilger, John, *New Statesman*, vol. 125, no. 4295, 2 August 1996, p. 26.
40. Evidence before the House of Commons Defence Committee, 22 July 1982.
41. *Newsnight* went to air on 2 May and *Panorama* on 10 May 1982. See also Morrison & Tumber, op. cit., p. 265–6.
42. *Hansard*, 6 May 1982.
43. See *The Sun, Daily Mail and Daily Express*, 12 May 1982, and Morgan, K., *The Falklands Campaign. A Digest of Debates in the House of Commons*, 2 April to 15 June 1982, HMSO, London, 1982, p. 218.
44. Evidence before the House of Commons Defence Committee, Appendix 1, vol. 2, p. 421.
45. Morrison & Tumber, op. cit., p. 236.
46. Harris, op. cit., p. 84–5.
47. Foster, op. cit.
48. *Sun*, 14 May 1982.
49. Interview, General Sir Jeremy Moore, op. cit.
50. Harris, op. cit., p. 89. See also Mercer, Mungham & Williams, op. cit., p. 131.
51. Harris, op. cit., p. 89. See also Morrison & Tumber, op. cit., tables 12.27, p. 335 and 12.30, p. 341.

52. Foster, op. cit., Appendix A.
53. Evidence before the House of Commons Defence Committee, 27 October 1982.
54. Adams, *The Media and the Falklands Campaign*, op. cit., p. 159.
55. Evidence before the House of Commons Defence Committee, 22 July 1982.
56. Hastings & Jenkins, op. cit., p. 331; Harris, op. cit., p. 137–8.
57. Evidence before the House of Commons Defence Committee, 22 July 1982.
58. Evidence before the House of Commons Defence Committee, 22 July 1982 (Bishop).
59. Evidence before the House of Commons Defence Committee, 22 July 1982 (Snow).
60. Evidence before the House of Commons Defence Committee 27 October 1982 (Appendix B) (Archer).
61. Interview, General Sir Jeremy Moore, op. cit.
62. Times Memorandum, House of Commons Defence Committee, DF 24, 1982, p. 119.
63. Evidence before the House of Commons Defence Committee, 9 November 1982.
64. Haswell, J. *The Intelligence and Deception of the D-Day Landings*, Batsford, London, 1979, p. 37.
65. Evidence before the House of Commons Defence Committee, November 1982.
66. Interview, General Sir Jeremy Moore, op. cit.
67. Evidence before the House of Commons Defence Committee, 27 October 1982.
68. Evidence before the House of Commons Defence Committee, 9 November 1982.
69. Interview, General Sir Jeremy Moore, op. cit.
70. Mercer, Mungham & Williams, op. cit., p. 201.
71. Evidence before the House of Commons Defence Committee, vol. 11, Annex B, p. 416.
72. Interview, General Sir Jeremy Moore, op. cit.
73. *Hansard*, 4 May 1982.
74. For a more detailed analysis and record of the statements see Adams, V., Unpublished Thesis. *The Role of the Commentators during the Falklands*, Department of War Studies, Kings College, University of London, 1986. See also the *Cardiff Study*, Centre for Journalism Studies, University College, Cardiff, 1983; *The Kitson Report*, HMSO, London, 1982; and Wainright, C., 'How the Press Swallowed a Whopper', *The Listener*, 16 December 1982.

75. Appendix to the Memorandum of Evidence to the House of Commons Defence Committee by the *Glasgow Herald*, 22 July 1982.

76. Evidence before the House of Commons Defence Committee, 22 July 1982 (Reuters).

77. Co-author Peter Young, group interview with British defence correspondents, London, March 1988.

78. Woodward with Robinson, op. cit., p. 112. See also Morrison & Tumber, op. cit., p. 205–8.

79. Adams, *The Media and the Falklands Campaign*, op. cit., p.164–72; Adams, *The Role of the Commentators*, op. cit.

80. Evidence before the House of Commons Defence Committee, 27 October 1982.

81. Co-author Peter Young, interviews with ABC and NBC Network News Staff, New York and Washington, July 1988. See also Harris, op. cit., p. 94.

82. Memorandum to the House of Commons Defence Committee, July 1982.

Chapter 7

1. Combelles, P., *Revue du Centre de Documentation et de Recherche sur La Paix et Les Conflicts*, No 48/9, 1991.

2. For a detailed treatment of the history and development of Grenada, see Brizan, G., *Grenada: Island of Conflict, from Amerindians to People's Revolution 1498–1979*, Zed Books, London, 1984. See also *Grenada, The Peaceful Revolution*, Economical Program for Inter-America Community and Action (EPICA), Washington, 1982; Williams, E., *From Columbus to Castro: The History of the Caribbean 1492–1969*, Deutsch, London, 1970; and Thorndike, T., *Grenada: Revolution and Invasion*, Francis Pinter, London, 1985.

3. *Grenada: Whose Freedoms?*, Latin American Bureau, London, 1984.

4. Statement by US Deputy Secretary of State, Kenneth Dams, Louisville, 4 November 1983, US Department of State, *Western Hemisphere Bulletin*, vol. 83, no. 2081, December 1983.

5. OECS Statement, 25 October 1983. See also Valienta, J., & Ellison, H., *Grenada and Soviet Cuban Policy: Internal Crisis and US/OEC Intervention*, Westview Press, Boulder, 1986.

6. OECS Statement, 25 October 1983.

7. US Ambassador Middendorf's Statement, OAS Permanent Council, 6 October 1983.
8. Presidential Letter to Congress, 25 October 1983.
9. Reagan/Charles, Press Conference, 25 October 1983. For the full text, see 'Documents on the Invasion', *Caribbean Monthly Bulletin*, Supplement No 1., October 1983, p. 17.
10. *Grenada: Whose Freedoms?*, op. cit., p. 79.
11. For the full text of the RMC reply to the United States, circulated to the United Nations, see United Nations: S/PV 2487.
12. *Documents on the Invasion*, op. cit. For a detailed and well sourced examination of the CARICOM meeting, see Davidson, S., *A Study in Politics and the Limits of International Law*, Aldershot, 1987. See also Seabury, P., & McDougall, W., *The Grenada Papers*, Institute for Contemporary Studies, Washington, 1991.
13. Statement by the Cuban Communist Party, *Documents on the Invasion.*, op. cit., p. 47. See also, 'An Armed Attack is Imminent', address given over Radio Free Grenada, 23 March 1983 (Reprinted *Free West Indian*).
14. Ambassador Kirkpatrick's statement to the UN Security Council, 27 October 1983. For the full text, see *Western Hemisphere Bulletin.* No. 2081, op. cit., p. 74–6.
15. Ambassador Kirkpatrick's speech to the UN General Assembly, 2 November 1983.
16. Deputy Secretary Dams Loisville, 4 November 1983, in *Western Hemisphere Bulletin*, op. cit., p. 80.
17. For an assessment of the legal argument over Sir Paul Scoon's actions and the full text of the letter, as well as references to Sir Paul's subsequent statements, see Davidson, op. cit., p. 91–100.
18. *Death of a Revolution: An Analysis of the Grenada Tragedy and the US Invasion*, Ecumenical Program for Inter-American Communication and Action (EPICA), Washington 1982, p. 13. See also the statement by the Grenadan representative to the United Nations, United Nations:S/PV 2487, October 1983.
19. For a full text of the five point resolution, see United Nations Document S/16077, October 1983.
20. Tass, 25 October 1983.
21. Davidson, op. cit., p. 138.
22. Ibid., p. 124.
23. See Gilmore, W., *The Grenada Intervention: Analysis and Documentation*, Mansell Publishing, New York, 1984.
24. *Washington Post*, 30 October 1983.
25. Pentagon Press Release, 27 October 1983.

26. Co-author Peter Young, interview, Admiral J. Metcalf III, Brisbane, 15 April 1991.

27. *Washington Post*, 27 October 1983.

28. President Reagan, Press Conference, 3 November 1983.

29. For an overview of the military operation, see Burrows, R., *Revolution and Rescue in Grenada: An Account of the US Caribbean Invasion*, Greenwood Press, New York, 1980; O'Shaugnessy, H., *Grenada: An Eyewitness Account of the US Invasion and the Caribbean History that Provoked It*, Dodd Mead, New York, 1984; and Adkin, M., *Urgent Fury: The Battle for Grenada*, Lexington Books, Massachusetts, 1989.

30. Maurice Bishop Speaks, *The Grenada Revolution 1979–83*, Pathfinder Press, New York, 1983, Appendix II, p. 334–5.

31. Ibid.

32. Metcalf, Admiral J. III, 'The press and Grenada, 1983', paper delivered at the International Conference on Defence and the Media in Time of Limited Conflict, Brisbane April 1991.

33. Evidence before the House Armed Services Committee, Congressional Record, January 1984.

34. *Western Hemisphere Bulletin*, op. cit., p. 69.

35. *Grenada: Whose Freedoms?*, op. cit., p. 33.

36. Metcalf, Defence Media Conference, op. cit.

37. Weinberger, Defence Release, Washington, 27 October 1983.

38. Metcalf, Defence Media Conference, op. cit.

39. *Washington Post*, 27 October 1983.

40. Ibid.

41. Ibid.

42. *Washington Post*, 28 October 1983.

43. *Washington Post*, 30 October 1983.

44. Metcalf, Defence Media Conference, op. cit.

45. Schwarzkopf, H. Norman, *It Doesn't Take a Hero*, Bantam, New York, 1993, p. 296.

46. Metcalf, interview, op. cit.

47. Ibid.

48. Metcalf, interview, op. cit.

49. *Washington Post*, 29 October 1983.

50. Ibid.

51. Ibid.

52. Authors' survey, US major network Newscasts, 23–29 October 1983.

53. *Washington Post*, 29 October 1983.

54. *Washington Post*, 27 October 1983.

55. *New York Times*, 26 October 1983.
56. Ibid.
57. Interview. Union Official (name withheld), CBS, Washington, January 1989.
58. *Washington Post*, 29 October 1983.
59. *Washington Post*, 29 November 1983.
60. Ibid.
61. Caeser, J., 'The Reagan Presidency and American Public Opinion'. In *The Reagan Legacy*, (ed.) Charles Jones, Chattam Publishing, New Jersey, 1988.
62. Metcalf, interview, op. cit.
63. Ibid.
64. Metcalf, Defence Media Conference, op. cit.
65. For the full text of the *Sidle Report*, see Office of the Assistant Secretary of Defence (Public Affairs), News Release No. 450/84, 23 August 1984.
66. *Sidle Report*, op. cit.
67. Ibid.
68. For the full details of the recommendations, see Office of the Assistant Secretary of Defence (Public Affairs), News Release No. 450/84, 23 August 1984.
69. *New York Times*, 10 October 1984; *Washington Post*, 24 August 1984.

Chapter 8

1. Gosnell, P., *Low Intensity Conflict and the US Military*, reviewed in *The National Guard*, October 1989.
2. Woodward, B., *The Commanders*, Simon & Schuster, New York, 1991, p. 278.
3. For a strategic assessment of the Canal Zone, see Sanchez, N., 'US Policy in Central America: A Strategic Perspective', *Defense*, June 1985; Harvey, R., 'Central America: A Potential Vietnam', *World Today*, July/August 1982; Parker, D., 'The Canal is no Longer Crucial to US Security, *Armed Forces International*, Washington, December 1987; Seidenham, P., 'Caribbean, The Urgency Grows', *National Defence*, Washington, December 1982; Seidenham, P., 'Military Aspects of the Canal Issue', *United States Naval Institute Proceedings,* January 1980; and Haskin, F., *The Panama Canal*, William Heinemann, London, 1914.

4. For a background to this period, see Musicant, I., *The Banana Wars*, Macmillan, New York, 1990; Saxon, J., 'Fix Bayonets, Buckle Diplomatic Spurs', *US Marine Corps Gazette*, August 1989; Kenworthy, E., 'Why the United States is in Central America', *Bulletin of the Atomic Scientist*, October 1983; Leogrande, W., 'United States Security and the Caribbean Basin', *NATO's Sixteen Nations*, November/December 1984; Roberts, K., 'Bullying and Bargaining, the United States, Nicaragua and Conflict Resolution in Central America', *International Security*, vol. 15, no. 2, Autumn 1990.
5. For details of this period see *Report on Events in Panama, January 1964*, International Commission of Jurists, Geneva 1964; Montedonico, R., 'Who's Disrupting the Settlement of the Central American Conflict?', *International Review*, Moscow, October 1986; Dinges, J., *Our Man in Panama*, Random House, New York, 1990; and Kempe, F., *Divorcing the Dictator*, G.P. Putnam's Sons, New York, 1990.
6. For background to the formation of Southern Command, see Binder, J., 'On the Ramparts in Central America', *Army*, Washington, May 1987; and Myer, D., 'US Southern Command. Latin America, the US' Strategic Front Yard', *Armed Forces International*, Washington, December 1985.
7. Kempe, op. cit., p. 122–5.
8. Dinges, op. cit., p. 261–5.
9. Powell, Colin, *A Soldier's Way*, Hutchinson, London, 1995, p. 415. See also Kempe, op. cit., p. 156.
10. For background to Noriega's involvement and indictment, see Cockburn, A., 'The General's Secrets', *Nation*, Washington, 29 January 1990; also Baker, J. (interview), *Department of State Bulletin*, No 2153, December 1990; and Schultz, G.P., *Turmoil and Triumph: My Years as Secretary of State*, Charles Scribner's Sons, New York, 1993.
11. Schultz, op. cit., p. 1052.
12. Smolowe, J., 'Sparring (Again) with a Dictator', *Time*, vol. 133, no. 20, 8 May 1988, p. 46.
13. Schultz, op. cit., p. 1053.
14. *Washington Post*, 10 May 1988.
15. UPI, 10 May 1989. Washington is reported to have given US$10 million towards Endara's campaign; see Dorner, W.R., 'Lead-Pipe Politics', *Time*, vol. 133, no. 22, 22 May 1989, p. 40–3.
16. White House Statement, 10 May 1989.

17. Presidential Statement, AP 11 May 1989. See also Thomas, D., 'Crisis in Panama', *Soldiers*, Washington, September 1989.

18. Presidential Statement, President Carlos Andres Perez, AP, 13 May 1989. President Perez's stand was reported in the United States as an attempt to avert unilateral American action by involving the Organization of American States. But Venezuela was, at the same time, facing civil unrest on the domestic front and was desperate for debt relief from the United States.

19. AP Report, reprinted *The Weekend Australian*, 13–14 May 1989.

20. Admiral W. Crowe, Evidence to the Senate Armed Services Committee, May 1988.

21. Press Statement, Council on Hemispheric Affairs, 12 May 1988.

22. *New York Times* and AFP, 12 May 1988.

23. Admiral Zumwalt, AFP, 12 May 1988.

24. *The Independent*, 19 December 1989 (McGreal, C. filing from Mexico City).

25. Woodward, op. cit., p. 83. See also Galvin, J., interview with Woerner, 'Challenge and Response on the Southern Flank', *Military Review*, August 1986.

26. Woodward, op. cit., p. 127. See also 'What's next Noriega?', *Bulletin with Newsweek*, (Australia) 24 October 1989; and Smolowe, J. 'The Yanquis Stayed Home', *Time Magazine*, 16 October 1989.

27. For a detailed examination of the conduct of the campaign, see Ropelewski, R., 'Planning, Precision and Surprise Led to Panama Successes', *Armed Forces Journal*, February 1990; Behar, D., & Godfrey, H., *Invasion, The American Destruction of the Noriega Regime in Panama*, Americas Group, Los Angeles, 1990; Watson, B., & Tsouras, P., *Operation Just Cause: The US Intervention in Panama*, Westview Press, Boulder, 1991; *A Soldier's Eyewitness Account*, Stackpoole Books, Harrisburg, 1990; *Janes Defence Weekly*, December/January 1989/90; Auster, B., 'Military Lessons of the Invasion', *US News and World Report*, 8 January 1990; and Woodward, op. cit. See also Powell, op. cit., p. 414–34. For details of the Panamanian Defence Force (PDF) see the *IISS Military Balance*, 1989/90. See Boswell, B. in *The Australian*, 22 December 1989, for a description of the invasion at the time.

28. Woodward, op. cit., p. 85. See also Galvin, op. cit.

29. Woodward, op. cit., chap. 12.

30. Ibid., p. 139. See also Colucci, F., 'Rehearsal Reaps Rewards', *Defence Helicopter World*, June/July 1990.

31. *Christian Science Monitor*, 5 August 1988.

32. *Washington Post*, 19 March 1990.

33. Brady, P., 'Telling the Army Story', *Army*, 22 September 1990. See also Lowther, W. 'Counting the Hidden Cost: Media Distortions in the Panama Invasion 1989', *McLeans*, 22 January 1990.

34. Boot, W., 'Wading Around in the Panama Pool', *Columbia Journalism Review*, March/April 1990; and Komarow, S., 'Pooling Around in Panama', *Washington Journalism Review*, March 1990.

35. Woodward, op. cit., p. 178.

36. Cheney, R., 'Response to the Hoffman Report', in *Newsmen and National Defense*, ed. L. Matthews, Brassey's, Virginia 1991, p. 107–8. See also Hoffman, F. 'The Panama Pool Deployment: A Critique', *Newsmen and National Defense*, op. cit., p. 91–107, and p. 145.

37. Woodward, op. cit., p. 178.

38. *Sidle Report*. For the full text, see News Release, Office of the Assistant Secretary for Defence (Public Affairs), No. 450/84, 23 August 1984.

39. *US Armed Forces Public Affairs Roles in Low Intensity Conflict*, Army Air Force Centre for Low Intensity Conflict, Langley, Virginia May 1988.

40. *The Australian*, 29 December 1989.

41. Ibid. See also Jaco, C., 'Missing the Action in Panama', *Quill*, November/December 1990; Cloud, S., 'How Reporters Missed the War', *Time Magazine*, January 1990.

42. *Sidle Report*, op. cit.

43. ABC Radio, 29 December 1989. See also 'No Cigars. Military Allowed Insufficient News Coverage of Panama Invasion', *Broadcasting*, 1 January 1990.

44. Hoffman, F., 'Early Bird', *Pentagon News Roundup*, 19 March 1990.

45. Brady, op. cit. See also *US Armed Forces Public Affairs Roles in Limited Conflicts*, op. cit., chap. 1.

46. Survey of coverage – *Time Magazine, Washington Post, Washington Times, New York Times, Christian Science Monitor, New York Daily*, AAP, AFP and Knight Ridder News Service, May 1989 – January 1990.

47. Quoted in Kasper, D., *The Panama Deception*, Empowerment Project (film) 1992.

48. *The Independent*, 2 January 1990.

49. *Sun Herald*, 14 May 1989.

50. *The Times*. (*London*), 22 December 1989.

51. Ibid.

52. *Washington Post*, 22 December 1989.

53. *Congressional Record*, 20 December 1989.
54. UPI, Washington, 21 December 1989.
55. Ibid.
56. Ibid.
57. Terry, J., 'Law in Support of Policy in Panama', *Naval War College Review*, Autumn 1990.
58. US State Department Press Release, 27 December 1989.
59. Justice Department Memo to National Security Council, 3 November 1989. See also Pfaff, W., 'Bush Takes Swing and Misses', *International Herald Tribune*, reprinted in *The Australian*, 27 December 1989; and, Woodward, op. cit., p. 141.
60. Maechling, C., 'Washington's Illegal Invasion', *Foreign Policy*, Summer 1990. See also Church, G., 'Showing Muscle', *Time Magazine*, 1 January 1990; *Canberra Times*, 27 December 1989; and *Sydney Morning Herald*, 3 January 1990.
61. As an example, see United States Information Service releases in Australia, April to December 1989 and January 1990.
62. United Nations Resolution, NAM, 23 December 1989.
63. United Nations Resolution, GA, 27 December 1989.
64. *Sydney Morning Herald*, 17 September 1990.
65. Press Statement: Department of Foreign Affairs, 22 December 1989. For a more detailed critique of Australia's actions at the UN see *Sydney Morning Herald*, 2 January 1990 and 8 January 1990.
66. A limited survey of the *Sydney Morning Herald, Financial Review*, the Melbourne *Age, Canberra Times* and Brisbane *Courier Mail*, over the period 3–19 December 1989, showed an 87 per cent reliance on overseas reporting. See also Editorial, *The Australian* 22 December 1989.
67. Presidential Statement, 5 January 1991.
68. AAP, Reuters, Knight Ridder Services, 28 December 1989.
69. Vatican Statement, 30 December 1989. See also Kneebone, T., statement, US Embassy Spokesman, Panama City 2 January 1990; and *Canberra Times*, 2 January 1990.
70. *The Independent*, 30 December 1989. See also Jaco, S., 'Military to Journalists, Now Hear This', *Washington Journalism Review*, March 1990.
71. Laroque, G., (Director, Centre for Defence Information), statement, Washington, 30 December 1989. See also *The Times*, 27 December 1989; and editorial, *Sydney Morning Herald*, 27 December 1989.
72. *Sunday Times*, 28 December 1989. See also AFP. Reuters, Knight Ridder Services, 27 December 1989; *The Independent*, 23 December 1989; and *The Weekend Australian*, 30–31 December 1989.

73. Associated Press Photo, *Canberra Times*, 29 December 1989.
74. *The Independent*, 2 January 1990.
75. Daniel, L., 'Too Many Innocents Die in Overkill', *Washington Post*, 30 December 1989, reprinted, *The Australian*, 2 January 1990.
76. Woodward, op. cit., p. 195.
77. Ibid.
78. AFP, 'Panama Exhumes US Massacre Victims', reprinted in *The Australian*, 30 April 1990. See also Cockburn, A., 'Beneath a Peak in Darien: The Conquest of Panama', *Nation*, 29 January 1990.
79. Jehl, D., & Broder, J., 'Facts Got in the Way of Panama Victory', *Los Angeles Times*, reprinted in the *Sydney Morning Herald*, 28 April 1990.
80. *Congressional Record*, April 1990. See also Press Conference., former Attorney General, Mr Ramsay Clarke, Panama City, 15 August 1990.
81. 'Facts Got in the Way of Panama Victory', op. cit. See also 'Pentagon Spokesman Speaks', *Editor and Publisher*, 6 April 1991.
82. Cooper, M., 'The Press and the Panama Invasion', *Nation*, 18 June 1990. See also Herstgaard, M., 'How the News Media Let us Down in Panama', *Rolling Stone*, 8 March 1990; Cranberg, G., 'Behind the Invasion: A Flimsy Story and a Compliant Press', *Washington Journalism Review*, March 1990; and O'Sullivan, G., 'The Free Press, Every Military Should Own One', *Humanist*, May/June 1991.
83. Powell, op. cit., p. 413.
84. Ibid., p. 420.

Chapter 9

1. Watson, B., *Military Lessons of the Gulf War*, Greenhill Books, California, 1991. See also Brenner, E., & Harwood, W., *Desert Storm: Weapons of War*, Fontana, London, 1991 (chap. 2, 'Manpower and Materiel'). There were, however, concerns about the casualties and the reasons that they might be incurred; see Buchanan, P.J., 'Declare war or come home'. In *The March to War*, J. Ridgeway (ed.), Four Walls Eight Windows, New York, 1991, p. 127–9 (Reprinted from Mercury News (San Jose), 24 October 1990).
2. See, for example, *New York Times Weekly Review*, 14 July 1996.
3. Woodward, B., *The Commanders*, Simon & Schuster, New York, 1991, p. 178; and Salinger, P., *Secret Dossier: The Hidden Agenda*

Behind the War, Penguin, New York, 1991. See also Chapter 8, 'Panama: A Deliberate Policy of Exclusion'.

4. Quoted by Maitre, H. Joachim, 'Taking Issue', *Defense media Review*, July/August 1996, p. 12.

5. Author's survey of the ABC TV (Australia) and Australian Commercial Networks, 16 January–1 March 1991.

6. For a detailed examination of the historical background to the emergence of Kuwait and Iraq, see Cohen, S., *British Policy in Mesopotamia 1903–1914*, Ithaca Press, London, 1976; Abbas Kelidar, *The Integration of Modern Iraq*, Croom Helm, London, 1979; Mansfield, P., *Kuwait: Vanguard of the Gulf*, Hutchinson, London, 1990; Mechjer, H., *Imperial Quest for Oil: Iraq 1910–1928*, Ithaca Press, London, 1976; Hassan Quaid, *A History of Kuwait*, Dar Asharq Doha Quatar, 1990; Hassan Shabr, *Political Parties in Iraq from 1908–1958*, Dar Al Turath Al Arabi, Beirut, 1989; Trevelyn, H., *The Middle East in Revolution*, Macmillan, London, 1970; Dilip Hiro, *The Longest War*, Grafton Press, London, 1989; Devlin, J., *The Ba'athist Party: A History from its Origins in 1966*, Stanford University Press, Palo Alto, Calif., 1976; and Iskander Amir, *Saddam Hussein: The Fighter, The Thinker and the Man*, Hachette, Paris, 1980.

7. Freedman, L., & Karsh, E., *The Gulf Conflict*, Faber & Faber, London, 1994, p.48; Hilsman, R., *George Bush vs. Saddam Hussein*, Lyford Books, Novato, California, 1992, p. 41; Pimlott, J., 'The Gulf Crisis and World Politics', in Pimlott, J., & Badsey, S. (eds), *The Gulf War Assessed*, Arms & Armour, London, 1992, p. 35–56. The figure of US$2.4 billion is also reported in Darwish, A., & Alexander, G., *Unholy Babylon: The Secret History of Saddam's War*, Gollancz. London, 1991, (see p. 262). But a claim by Saddam Hussein for US$27 billion for the same losses is also reported by Darwish & Alexander (see p. 254).

8. *IISS Military Balance 1989*. See also Darwish & Alexander, op. cit., p. xv; and *Sydney Morning Herald*, 26 January 1991.

9. Bulloch, J., & Morris, H., *Saddam's War: The Origins of the Kuwait Conflict and the International Response*, Faber & Faber, London, 1991, p. 17. See also *Weekend Australian*, 22–23 December 1990; and *Sydney Morning Herald*, 1 October 1990.

10. For a more detailed examination of the current politics of the Arab world at that time and, in particular, Saddam Hussein's assessment of his role, see Bulloch, J., & Morris, H., op. cit. See also Sciolino, E., *The Outlaw State: Saddam Hussein's Quest for Power*, Wiley, New York, 1992; and *Financial Review*, 21 January 1991.

11. Woodward, op. cit., p. 210. See also Friedman, N., *Desert Victory: The War for Kuwait*, Naval Institute Press, Annapolis, 1991.
12. Darwish & Alexander, op. cit., p. 265.
13. Woodward, op. cit., p. 210.
14. Darwish and Alexander, op. cit., p. 268–9; Hilsman, op. cit., p. 43. See also the transcript of the meeting between Ambassador Glaspie and Saddam Hussein of 25 July 1990, in Ridgeway, op. cit., p. 50–3.
15. Woodward, op. cit., p. 217–9.
16. Powell, op. cit, p. 460.
17. US News & World Report Staff, *Triumph Without Victory: The Unreported History of the Persian Gulf War*, Times Books/Random House, New York, 1992, p. 224–5.
18. For a detailed examination of the build-up and conduct of the battle and the new technology which formed such a feature of the operation, see Morris, M., *H. Norman Schwarzkopf: Road to Triumph*, Pan Books, London, 1991; Brennan, E., & Harwood, S., *Desert Storm: The Weapons of War*, Fontana, London, 1991; and Ball, D., *The Intelligence War in the Gulf*, SDSC, Canberra, 1991. See also Rochlin, G., & Demchak, C., 'The Gulf War: Technological and Organisational Implications', *Survival*, vol. xxxiii, May/June 1991; Friedman, op. cit.; Dunnigan, J., & Bay, A., *From Shield to Storm: High-Tech Weapons, Military Strategy and Coalition Warfare in the Persian Gulf*, Morrow, New York, 1991; Mason, R., 'The Air War in the Gulf', *Survival*, May/June 1991; Hiro, D., *Desert Shield to Desert Storm: The Second Gulf War*, Paladin, London, 1992; and Morrison, D., *Television and the Gulf War*, John Libbey, London, 1992.
19. Woodward, op. cit., p. 225.
20. Ibid., p. 227. See also Powell, op.cit., p. 461–8.
21. Presidential Statement, Washington, 16 October 1990.
22. Woodward, op. cit., p. 169–70.
23. Darwish, A., & Alexander, G., op. cit., p. 286.
24. US News & World Report Staff, op. cit., p. 150.
25. Woodward, op. cit., p. 161.
26. Powell, op. cit., p. 463.
27. Smith, J., *George Bush's War*, Holt, 1992, cited in Draper, T., 'The True History of the Gulf War', *New York Review of Books*, 30 January 1992, p. 40.
28. US News & World Report Staff, op. cit., p. ix.
29. *The Australian*, 25 January 1991. See also *The Age* (Melbourne), 28 February 1991. For the full text of the UN Resolutions, see USIS Wireless File, ssF504, February 1991.

30. Woodward, op. cit., p. 280.
31. Morris, op. cit., p. 64.
32. Press Briefing, Riyadh, 27 February 1991.
33. Levental, T., (USIS Director for Counter-disinformation), *Iraq Disinformation Campaign loses Credibility*, USIS 25 February 1991.
34. Bulloch & Morris, op. cit., p. 168–9.
35. Taped interview, CNN/ABC/BBC and others, 23 August 1990.
36. Darwish & Alexander, op. cit., p. 293.
37. Ibid.
38. *Washington Post*, 18 February 1991.
39. Levental, op. cit. See also Arnett, P., 'Debriefings, What we Saw, What we Learned', *Columbia Journalism Review*, May/June 1991.
40. *Sydney Morning Herald* (Reuters), 18 September 1990. For the full text see USIS official text, 19 September 1990.
41. See Arnett, P., *Live from the Battlefield*, Bloomsbury Publishing, London, 1994, p. 397–405, for Arnett's description of his interview with Saddam Hussein. Channel 10 (Australia) which took the CNN feed was quick to boast, 'Channel 10 has exclusive access to CNN and gives you the coverage Dick Cheney watches' (*The Age* (Melbourne), 18 January 1991).
42. McAvoy, K., 'Group Launches Campaign to 'pull plug' on CNN's Arnett', *Broadcasting*, 18 February 1991, see also Cassidy J., 'White House Enlists Expert for TV War', *Sunday Times*, reprinted in *The Australian*, 28 August 1991.
43. Smith, P., *How CNN Fought the War*, Carroll Publishing, New York, 1991, ('The Peter Arnett Controversy').
44. Taylor, P., *War and the Media: Propaganda and Persuasion in the Gulf*, Manchester University Press, Manchester/New York, 1992, p. 91. See also Arnett, op. cit., p. 308–82.
45. Monroe, B., 'Peter Arnett, Anti-Hero of Bagdad', *Washington Journalism Review*, March 1991. See also *Sydney Morning Herald*, 25 January 1991.
46. *Sydney Morning Herald*, January 1991.
47. *Washington Post*, 17 March 1991.
48. *Sydney Morning Herald*, January 1991. See also Smith, P., op. cit.
49. De La Billière, P., *Storm Command. A Personal Account of the Gulf War*, HarperCollins, London, 1992, p. 65.
50. Middle East radio monitoring, Iraqi RCC announcements.
51. Presidential Statement (Address to the American Association for the Advancement of Science), 15 February 1991. Articles in some American papers, particularly in the first few weeks after the invasion, drew attention to America's recent support for

Saddam Hussein at the same time as they described him as a 'tyrant' and compared him with Hitler. See, for example, *Wall Street Journal*, 16 August 1990, and *New York Times*, 18 August 1990.

52. Prime Ministerial Statement, Canberra, 21 January 1991.
53. Blackwell, J., US Evidence to the UN Commission on Human Rights, Geneva, 25 February 1991. See also Starr, P., 'No Vietnam', *New Republic*, 18 February 1991 (Reprinted worldwide by *USIS*). Starr drew a parallel between the stand against Iraq and the World War II battle against fascism.
54. *New York Times*. 11 January 1991.
55. This is evident from any survey of leading American, British and Australian daily newspapers. *The Times* (London), 25 July 1990, branded Saddam Hussein a 'bully'. Later comparisons were made between Saddam Hussein and Adolf Hitler, and the excesses of Saddam Hussein's methods of maintaining power were detailed at length. See for example, *New York Times*, 26 August 1990, 30 September 1990, 6 January 1991 and 2 February 1991; *The Times* (London), 3 March 1991; *The Age* (Melbourne), 13 January 1991, 16 January 1991, 22 January 1991, 23 January 1991 and 24 January 1991; and *Courier Mail* (Brisbane), 26 January 1991.
56. See Barrett, G., 'Tabloids wage gutter (Gulf) war', *The Age* (Melbourne), 25 January 1991. *The Sun* also criticised the French with the question 'Where the ---- were you?' as France refrained from the first air strikes.
57. De La Billière, op. cit., p. 25.
58. Powell, op. cit., p. 491.
59. *The Times* (London), 15 January 1996.
60. Hallin, D., 'TV's Clean Little War', *Bulletin of the Atomic Scientist*, May 1991.
61. As an example of this effort, see Transcript: Richard Solomon, *USIS Worldnet Television hookup*, 31 December 1990.
62. UN Security Council Resolution 678 (1990), 29 November 1990. For a full examination of the UN lobbying campaign, see Darwish & Alexander, op. cit., especially, the appendix, 'Summary of the United Nations Resolutions Covering the Gulf Crisis'. See also Sifry, M., & Cerf, C., *The Gulf War Reader: History, Documents and Opinions*, Times Books, New York, 1991, which reproduces the text of all the resolutions on the Gulf War.
63. Draper, op. cit., p. 42.
64. Bone, J., 'UN Loses Control of Conflict it Started', *London Times* (reprinted in *The Australian*, 16 January 1991). See also USIS Wireless File, Australian issues, December to March 1991.

65. Darwish & Alexander, op. cit., p. 231. Darwish & Alexander make the point that, as far back as 1983, the Iraqis had paid a subsidy of US$2 million to a London-based Arab newspaper with a circulation of less than 3,000 '... just to give certain messages to Arab diplomats, analysts, rivals, friends or neutrals, indicating the direction in which Saddam Hussein wanted events to go'.

66. *Sydney Morning Herald*, 16 April 1991.

67. Dickey, C., *Newsweek* Review of MacArthur, J., *Second Front: Censorship and Propaganda in the Gulf War*, Hill & Wang, New York, 1992.

68. MacArthur, J., *Second Front: Censorship and Propaganda in the Gulf War*, Hill & Wang, New York, 1992, p. 54–6.

69. Ibid., p. 49.

70. Taylor, op. cit., p. 150.

71. Shulman, H., 'One Way Radio', *The Nation* (USA), 13 May 1991. See also Taylor, op. cit., p. 149–53.

72. *The Age* (Melbourne), 24 January 1991.

73. For a background on earlier deployments, see Ahern, T., 'White Smoke in the Persian Gulf', *Washington Journalism Review*, October 1987; and Thompson, M., 'With the Pool Press in the Persian Gulf', *Columbia Journalism Review*, November/December 1987.

74. Danniston, L., 'Suing the Pentagon for Access to War', *Washington Journalism Review*, April 1991; Gersha, D., 'Journalists Protest Desert Storm Pool', *Editor and Publisher*, 11 May 1991; and Robinson, S., 'And TV Will be there', *The Spectator* (UK), (reprinted in *The Weekend Australian* 12–13 January 1991).

75. Fialka, J., *Hotel Warriors: Covering The Gulf War*, Woodrow Wilson Centre Press, Washington, 1991, p. 11.

76. Parrish, R, & Andreacchio, N., *Schwarzkopf: An Insider's View of the Commander and his Victory*, Bantam, New York, 1992, p. 178–80.

77. Ibid.

78. De La Billière, op. cit., p. 63–8. See also *Despatches*, the Journal of the Territorial Army Pool of Public Information Officers, vols. 2 and 3, Autumn 1991 and Autumn 1992.

79. Woodward, op. cit., p. 315.

80. Ibid., p. 375.

81. LaMay, C., Fitzsimon, M., & Sahadi, J. (eds.), *The Media At War: The Press and the Persian Gulf Conflict*, Freedom Forum Media Studies Centre, New York, 1991, p. 16.

82. McMasters, P., 'Cronkite, Williams Trade Pool Views at Senate Hearings: Pentagon and Journalists during the Gulf War', *Quill*, April 1991; *Washington Post*, 17 March 1991; and co-author Peter Young's personal interview with Colonel David Hackworth, Defence Correspondent Newsweek. Brisbane April 1991.

83. Fialka, op. cit., p. 35.

84. Morris, op. cit., p. 61.

85. Hackworth, D., co-author Peter Young's personal interview, Brisbane April 1991.

86. LaMay et al., op. cit., p. 17–8.

87. *Operation Desert Shield: Ground Rules and Supplementary Guidelines*, US Department of Defence, Washington, 14 January 1991.

88. LaMay et al., op. cit., p. 32.

89. Powell, op. cit., p. 529

90. Morris, op. cit. p. 126. See also Schmeisser, P., 'Shooting Pool: How the Press lost the Gulf War', *New Republic*, 18 March 1991.

91. Hackworth, D., International Conference on Defence and the Media in Time of Limited Conflict, Brisbane, April 1991. op. cit. See also Corn, D., 'Flacks, Hacks and Iraq: Military Control of the Media Coverage of Persian Gulf War', *Nation*, 29 April 1991.

92. Fialka, op. cit., p. 40–1.

93. Ibid., p. 9.

94. Powell, op. cit., p. 494.

95. Schwarzkopf, op. cit., p. 398–9.

96. Ibid., p. 443.

97. LaMay et al., op. cit., p. 29–30.

98. *New York Times*, 6 May 1991.

99. *Sun Herald*, 13 January 1991. See also *Sydney Morning Herald*, 7 February 1991.

100. McMasters, op. cit. See also *Washington Post*, 17 March 1991; and Schmeisser, P., 'How the Press Lost the Gulf War: Shooting Pool', *The New Republic*, 18 March 1991.

101. *New York Times*, 12 March 1991.

102. MacArthur, op. cit., p. 151.

103. US News & World Report Staff, op. cit., p. 413.

104. Powell, op. cit., p. 529.

105. Zoglin, R., 'Volleys on the Information Front', *Time*, 4 February 1991. See also Letter to Secretary of Defence Dick Cheney, Ad Hoc Media Group, 25 June 1991 (copy courtesy American Society of Newspaper Editors), signed by seventeen publishers, editors or chief executives of major news outlets.

106. *Newsweek*, Special Gulf Issue, February 1991, p. 41.
107. Draper, op. cit., p. 44.
108. 'Will we see the real war?' *Newsweek*, 1 January 1991.
109. Zoglin, R., 'It was a public relations rout too', *Time*, 11 March 1991. See also LaMay et al., op. cit., p. 22–3.
110. *The Australian*, 7 January 1991.
111. Gersh, D., 'Press Restrictions must GO', *Editor and Publisher*, 6 July 1991. See also *The Times* (London), 25 February 1991.
112. *Washington Post*, 17 February 1991. See also, Rosenberg, J., 'Coping with Copy from the Gulf War', *Editor and Publisher*, 18 May 1991.
113. *Washington Post*, 17 February 1991.
114. Draper, op. cit., p. 44.
115. *Problems of News Coverage in the Persian Gulf War*, compiled by the Ad Hoc Media Group. See also 'War Coverage Debriefings', *Columbia Journalism Review*, May/June 1991; and *New York Times Magazine*, 3 March 1991.
116. Schmeisser, op. cit.
117. Fialka, op. cit.
118. Draper, op. cit., p. 44.
119. *Sydney Morning Herald*, 23 February 1991.
120. Manof, R., quoted in Zoglin, op. cit.
121. Hackworth, International Conference on Defence and the Media in Time of Limited Conflict, op. cit.
122. Woodward, op. cit., p. 294.
123. General Michael Dugan, personal interview, Brisbane April 1991.
124. Bulloch & Morris, op. cit., p. 115.
125. Hackworth, personal interview, op. cit.
126. Fialka, op. cit., p. 6.
127. Garrett, L., 'The Dead: What We Saw, What We Learned', *Columbia Journalism Review*, May/June 1991. See also Nairn, A., 'When Casualties Don't Count', *Progressive*, 4 May 1991; Dority, B., 'Casualties of War', *Humanist*, May/June 1991. For the official view, see also US State Department Fact Sheet, Civilian Casualties at Iraqi Sites', statement by Press Secretary Marlon Fitzwater, 18 February 1991.
128. US News & World Report Staff, op. cit., p. 350–70.
129. Ibid., p. 373.
130. Fialka, op. cit., p. 5.
131. US News & World Report Staff, op. cit., p. 413.
132. Fialka, op. cit., pp. xii–xiii.
133. Macarthur, J., op. cit., p. 8

134. Fialka, op. cit., p. 8
135. US News & World Report Staff, op. cit., p. 404–5.
136. Aspin, L., Congressional Press Conference, Washington 23 May 1992. (USIS Wireless File EPF/508 24 May 1992).
137. US News & World Report Staff, op. cit., p. 406–7.
138. *The Australian*, 13 October 1992 'Missile Company Defends Patriots' (reprinted from *The Economist*).
139. Weekes, J., 'Patriot Games. What did we see on Desert Storm TV?' *Columbia Journalism Review*, July/August 1992, p. 13–4.
140. *Conduct of the Persian Gulf War*, Final Report to Congress, Washington, April 1992, p. xiii.
141. *New York Times*, 24 June 1992; Crispin Miller, M., *Spectacle: Operation Desert Storm and the Triumph of Illusion*, Poseidon Press, Washington, 1992.
142. Powell, op. cit., p. 511.
143. Fialka, op. cit., p. 61–7.
144. Ibid.
145. 'Strong US Support for US Effort in the Gulf Continues', USIS Wireless File EPF515, 15 February 1991. See also Lauterpacht, E., *The Kuwait Crisis: Basic Documents*, Cambridge International Documents Service, Cambridge, 1991.
146. *New York Times*, 23 July 1987. See also *Under Fire, US Military Restrictions on the Media*, Centre for Public Integrity, Washington, 15 January 1991.
147. Letter to Secretary of Defence Dick Cheney, Ad Hoc Media Group, 25 June 1991 (copy courtesy American Society of Newspaper Editors).
148. Letter to Secretary of Defence Dick Cheney, op. cit.
149. Ibid.
150. Osborne, B., address to the Annual Convention of the American Society of Newspaper Editors, Boston, May 1991.
151. Gettler, M., address to the Annual Convention of the American Society of Newspaper Editors, op. cit. See also Editorial, *The Nation*, 27 May 1991.
152. *New York Times*, 6 May 1991.
153. Gettler, address to the Convention, op. cit.
154. *Washington Post*, 21 May 1992.
155. Saulwick Poll, *Sydney Morning Herald*, 24 January 1991, and Morgan Gallup Poll, February 1991.
156. *The Observer, Harris* and *Sunday Times* polls, January 1991.
157. *Washington Post*, 31 March 1991. For a more detailed breakdown of American attitudes towards the Gulf War, see also Lauterpacht, op.

cit.; and 'Strong Support for US Effort in Gulf Continues, USIS Wireless File. Ref EPF515, 15 February 1991.

158. *Australian Financial Review*, 29 November 1990.
159. Roper Centre for Public Opinion, University of Connecticut, July 1991.
160. *Times Mirror* Survey, *The People, the Press and the War in the Gulf*, Part II, 14–18 March 1992.
161. Editorial,. *Sydney Morning Herald*, 28 June 1993.
162. *Time*, 5 July 1993. p. 18.
163. *Sydney Morning Herald*, 29 June 1993.
164. For further reading on the consequences of the conflict, see Bennis, P., & Mousehabeck, M., *Beyond the Storm*, Olive Branch Press, New York, 1991; and Carpenter, T., *America Entangled: The Persian Gulf Crisis and its Consequences*, Cato Institute, Washington, 1991. For a more detailed examination of the media coverage and government deception, see also US News & World Report Staff, op. cit.

Chapter 10

1. *Weekend Australian*, 1–2 July 1995 (report from *The Times*).
2. Berdal, M.R., *Whither UN Peacekeeping*, Adelphi Paper 281, International Institute for Strategic Studies, London, October, 1993 p. 3; Boutros-Ghali, B., *An Agenda for Peace*, United Nations, New York, 1992, p. 1–2.
3. Evans, G., *Cooperating for Peace*, Allen & Unwin, St Leonards, NSW, 1993, p. 100–3; Boutros-Ghali, B., loc cit.; United Nations, *The Blue Helmets: A Review of United Nations Peace-keeping*, 2nd Edition, United Nations, 1990, p. 7–8.
4. Berdal, loc cit.; Michaels, M., 'Blue-Helmet Blues', *Time Australia*, vol. 8, no. 46, 15 November 1993, p. 50–1.
5. *Charter of the United Nations*, Article 1.
6. Ibid.
7. See, for example, *CLIC Papers Series, JCS Publication 1–02*, Army Air Force Centre for Low Intensity Conflict, Langley, Virginia, May 1988; *Joint Low Intensity Conflict Project: Final Report*, US Army Training and Doctrine Command, Fort Monroe, Virginia, August 1986.
8. Holst, J.J., 'Enhancing peace-keeping operations', *Survival*, vol. xxxii, no. 3, May/June 1990, p. 264–75.

9. United Nations, *The Blue Helmets: A Review of United Nations Peace-keeping*, 2nd edition, United Nations, 1990, p. 7–8; Berdal, op. cit., p. 3–4.

10. While reporting on international matters such as peace-keeping may be considered a basic press freedom, the counter argument that the media does not provide sufficient balance in its coverage cannot be dismissed. The problem is that news is not context-free, and national interest influences the context significantly. See Wilkins, L., & Patterson, P., 'Risk analysis and the construction of news', *Journal of Communication*, vol. 37, no. 3, Summer 1987, p. 80–92.

11. *The Blue Helmets*, op. cit., p. 8.

12. Gerlach summed up the task facing the United Nations when discussing the feasibility of a United Nations-controlled army. Such a concept, stated Gerlach, was '... a recipe for fighting endless enemies in intractable situations.' The most difficult tasks are left to the United Nations. (Gerlach, J.R., 'A U.N. army for the new world order?', *Orbis*, vol. 37, no. 2, Spring 1993, p. 223–36.)

13. Rudolph, J.R., Jr., 'Intervention in Communal Conflicts'. *Orbis*, vol. 39, no. 2, Spring 1995, p. 259–73.

14. For recent developments, see *The Times* (London), 16 August 1996; also the *Weekend Australian*, 13–14 January 1996 and 17–18 August 1996;.

15. *The Blue Helmets*, op. cit., p. 152.

16. In November 1995, a peace settlement was reached on the Bosnia conflict. But the agreement, which effectively divides Bosnia along ethnic lines, while maintaining the illusion of a single political entity, did not appear to be conducive to continuing 'peace' in the normal sense of the word. A 60,000-strong NATO force was planned to keep the two sides apart (*The Australian*, 24 November 1995).

17. Putting it another way '... a journalist's definition of a good news story means a catastrophe for someone else.' Wilkins & Patterson, op. cit., p. 80.

18. See Walsh, J., 'The U.N. at 50: Who needs it?', *Time Australia*, no. 42, 23 October 1995, p. 28–35. Walsh describes some of the assessments of United Nations 'failure'.

19. Boyd, A., *United Nations: Piety, Myth, and Truth*, Penguin, Harmondsworth, Middlesex, 1961, p. 29–30.

20. Boutros-Ghali, B., *Report on the Work of the Organization from the Forty-seventh to the Forty-eighth Session of the General Assembly*, United Nations, New York, September 1993, p. 101.

21. Urquhart, Sir Brian, 'A U.N. fire brigade?', *Time Australia*, no. 42, 23 October 1995, p. 44. In Urquhart's words 'A fire brigade that

takes several months to get to the scene of action will inspire no confidence. Only a permanent rapid-deployment force will ensure that the U.N. can fight peace-keeping fires effectively.'

22. Berdal, op. cit., p. 51.
23. Evans, op. cit., p. 117–20; Boutros-Ghali 1992, op. cit., p. 28–9.
24. For example, although Argentina was rebuked by the Security Council for its invasion of the Falklands in 1982, a majority of the Council later backed a resolution calling for Britain not to force military action. The resolution was vetoed by the United States and Britain. As Walsh points out, had the resolution stood, it would have set an interesting precedent for Iraq's invasion of Kuwait in 1990. See, Walsh, op. cit., p. 34.
25. This has become particularly relevant with America's floating of the concept of a 'new world order' following the end of the Cold War. In essence, the issues revolve around America's attempts to develop a post-containment doctrine and are evident, to some extent, in the cases of Somalia, Cambodia and Haiti. For an outline of the debate, see Wallop, M., 'America needs a post-containment doctrine', *Orbis*, vol. 37, no. 2, Spring 1993, p. 187–203; Sicherman, H., 'Winning the peace', *Orbis*, vol. 38, no. 4, Fall 1994, p. 523–44; Thies, W.J., 'Rethinking the new world order', *Orbis*, vol. 38, no. 4, Fall 1994, p. 621–34; and Odom, W.E., 'How to create a true world order', *Orbis*, vol. 39, no. 2, Spring 1995, p. 155–72.
26. Kitfield, J., 'Restoring Hope', *Government Executive*, vol. 25, no. 2, February 1993, p. 20–32.
27. Berdal, op. cit., p. 39.
28. Ibid., p. 39–48.
29. See Prager, K., 'The limits of peacekeeping', *Time Australia*, no. 42, 23 October 1995, p. 40–6, for a brief review of the problems facing peace-keepers on the ground.
30. Benthall, J., *Disasters, Relief and the Media*. I.B. Tauris & Co, London, 1993, p. 26–9. See also Wilkins & Patterson, op. cit.
31. Evans, op. cit., p. 155; Kaufman, L., 'The Media Monster', *Government Executive*, vol. 25, no. 2, February 1993, p. 34–5. McMullen, R.K., & Norton, A.R., 'Somalia and Other Adventures for the 1990s', *Current History*, vol. 92, no. 573, April 1993, p. 169–74.
32. Pilger, J., 'The US fraud in Africa', *New Statesman and Society*, vol. 6, 8 January 1993, p. 10–1.
33. As the case study of Cambodia shows, Vietnam probably did act with some justification and with greater morality than the developed nations. But establishing 'truth' with regard to Cambodia is probably

more difficult than with the history of almost any other conflict – except perhaps Bosnia.

34. ABC TV (Australia), *Lateline* program 'Deadly Images', 15 November 1995.

35. Clark, J., 'Debacle in Somalia', *Foreign Affairs*, ISS. 'America and the World 1992/93', 1993, p. 109–23; *Le Monde* editorial, 9 August 1992.

36. *The Times*, 2 December 1992.

37. For a full discussion of the relationship between government and the media see Chomsky, N., *Necessary Illusions*, CBC Enterprises, Toronto, 1988; and Koch, T., *Journalism in the 21st Century: Online Information, Electronic Databases and the News*, Adamantine Press, Twickenham, UK, 1991, p. 22–7.

38. See, for example, *The Times* (London), 28 July 1992 and 5 August 1992. To support its stand, *The Times* attacked the credibility of the Secretary-General. See Chapter 11, 'Somalia: The Uninvited Intervention'.

39. Sicherman, op. cit., p. 533.

40. Boutros-Ghali, op. cit., p. 1.

41. See Chapter 1, 'The Changed Nature of War and Duties of the Citizen in Time of War'.

42. Lessnoff, M., *Social Contract*, Macmillan, London, 1986, p.92.

43. Ibid. See also Thies, op. cit. Thies questions the argument that, in the 'new world order', war is obsolete for the wealthy democracies. But he acknowledges that there is an increasing gap between rich and poor nations, and suggests that, for the poorer nations of the Third World, modern technology – and modern weapons technology in particular – may be destabilising.

44. Carty, A., *The Decay of International Law?* Manchester University Press, Manchester, 1986, p. 5.

45. Evans, op. cit., p. 117-20; Boutros-Ghali, op. cit., p. 28–9.

46. Indeed, the idea of a new 'concert of great powers' is not far from American thinking on the new world order; see Odom, op. cit, p. 169–70. The admission of Japan and Germany as permanent members of the Security Council would fit with this strategy.

47. Mueller, J., *Retreat from Doomsday*. Basic Books, New York, 1989, p. 99; Boutros-Ghali, op. cit., p. 5–7.

48. Boyd, op. cit., p. 93.

49. Bush, G. 'Conditions in Somalia: Creating a secure environment', *Vital Speeches of the Day*, vol. 59, no. 6, 1 January 1993, p. 162–3.

50. *The Australian*, 2 November, 1993, p. 11.

51. *The Australian*, 16 September 1994; *Courier Mail* (Brisbane), 10 September 1994.

Chapter 11

1. Kissinger, H., *Diplomacy*, Simon & Schuster, New York, 1994, p. 17–18.
2. *United Nations Peace-keeping Operations Information Notes 1993: Update No. 2*, p. 79.
3. For a discussion of the relationship between the United States and the United Nations see Smith, G., 'What Role for America?' *Current History*, vol. 92, no. 573, April 1993, p. 150–4.
4. Stevenson, J., 'Hope restored in Somalia?' *Foreign Policy*, no. 91, Summer 1993, p. 138–54; *The Economist*, 'Somalia: Pause to bury', vol. 322, 1 February 1992, p. 44.
5. McMullen, R.K., & Norton, A.R., 'Somalia and Other Adventures for the 1990s', *Current History*, vol. 92, no. 573, April 1993, p. 169–74.
6. Janke, P., 'The Horn of Africa'. In Sir Robert Keegan (ed.), *War in Peace*, Orbis Publishing, London, 1981, p. 248–53; McMullen & Norton, op. cit., p. 171.
7. Clark, J., 'Debacle in Somalia', *Foreign Affairs*, IISS. 'America and the World 1992/93, 1993, p. 109–23; Gregory, S.S., 'How Somalia Crumbled', *Time*, vol. 140, no. 24, 14 December 1992, p. 30.
8. McMullen & Norton, op. cit., p. 171.
9. *Guardian Weekly*, vol. 147, no. 23, 6 December 1992, p. 7.
10. Clark, op. cit.; McMullen & Norton, op. cit., p. 171.
11. For comment on the arms situation, see Janke, op. cit.; McMullen & Norton, op. cit., p. 171; and Woollacott, M., 'Why Rambo's boot has no place on Somalia's door', *Guardian Weekly*, vol. 147, no. 23, 6 December 1992, p. 7.
12. McMullen & Norton, op. cit., p. 171. A later report in the *New York Times*, 24 January 1993, claimed that streets in Mogadishu had also been torn up to steal the sewer pipes.
13. Based on reviews of coverage in the *Washington Post, New York Times* and *The Times* (London). Between reports of the overthrow of the Somali government and flight of Siad Barre in January 1991, and the rekindling of United Nations interest in the country in December of that year, there was little presented on events in Somalia.
14. Clark, op. cit., p. 116, discusses some of the problems this created. For example, for nine months in 1992, US$68 million earmarked for

Somalia could not be disbursed by United Nations officials 'for lack of a signature from a non-existent Mogadishu government'.

15. Kaufman, L., 'The media monster', *Government Executive*, vol. 25, no. 2, February 1993, p. 34–5.
16. Pilger, J., 'The US fraud in Africa', *New Statesman and Society*, vol. 6, 8 January 1993, p. 10–1.
17. Evans, op. cit., p. 155–6 makes the point that similar disasters in Rwanda, Liberia, the Sudan and Mozambique at the time did not attract the same media coverage as Somalia (although Rwanda was to be catapulted into world headlines in 1994).
18. Clark, op. cit., p. 115.
19. Reviews of coverage in the *Washington Post*, *New York Times* and *The Times* (London).
20. Stevenson, op. cit., p. 138–54; *Washington Post*, 31 July 1992; *Le Monde* editorial 9 August 1992.
21. For a discussion of limitations on the role of the Secretary-General, see Picco, G., 'The U.N. and the use of force', *Foreign Affairs*, vol. 73, no. 5, September/October 1994, p. 14–8.
22. Clark, op. cit., p. 116. See also the *New York Times*, 26 April 1992, for a report that the United Nations dropped an initial plan to deploy 500 peace-keepers in the face of United States objections to the proposal. The *New York Times*, 9 May 1992, carried a subsequent report denying the American objections.
23. *Washington Post*, 27 July 1992 and 29 July 1992.
24. *The Times* (London), 28 July 1992 and 5 August 1992.
25. *Guardian Weekly*, vol. 147, no. 6, 9 August 1992, and vol. 147, no. 7, 16 August 1992.
26. *The Australian*, 11 October 1993.
27. Pilger, op. cit.
28. Stevenson, op. cit., p. 145.
29. *The Times* (London), 30 October 1992.
30. *New York Times*, 1 November 1992.
31. *The Times* (London), 1 December 1992.
32. *United Nations Peace-keeping Operations Information Notes 1993: Update No. 2*, p. 83.
33. *Washington Post*, 1 December 1992.
34. Kitfield, J., 'Restoring Hope', *Government Executive*, vol. 25, no. 2, February 1993, p. 20–32.
35. Bush, G., 'Conditions in Somalia: Creating a secure environment', reprinted in *Vital Speeches of the Day*, vol. 59, no. 6, 1 January 1993, p. 162–3.
36. *The Times* (London), 2 December 1992.

37. *The Times* (London) (editorial), 1 December 1992.
38. *Washington Post*, 1 December 1992; *The Times* (London), 5 December 1992.
39. Kaufman, op. cit.; see also Dobell, G., 'The media's perspective on peacekeeping'; in *Peacekeeping: Challenges for the Future*, ed. Hugh Smith, Australian Defence Studies Centre, Australian Defence Force Academy, Canberra, 1993, p. 41–57. In the words of a Marine participating in the landing, 'The white lights of the cameras just totally destroy night vision. Our forces are practically blind ... Thank God there was no opposition.' But it was also a milestone for the Marine Corps: the first amphibious landing televised live. (*Washington Post*, 9 December 1992).
40. In December 1992, the *New York Times* carried more than 130 reports on Somalia (more than the total for the previous twelve months), while the London *Times* carried 70 reports (Co-authors' review of coverage in the *New York Times* and *The Times* (London)). See also Smith, S. 'Lights on in the shooting gallery', *New Statesman and Society*, 18 December 1992/1 January 1993, p. 18–9, for details of the expenditure on media coverage. Payments for cars, guards and houses exceeded Somalia's gross domestic product. One television channel reportedly paid US$500,000 to airlift sixty pallets of editing gear into Mogadishu and NBC kept six satellite telephones open around the clock.
41. Marlowe, L., 'The gift of hope', *Time*, vol. 7, no. 52, 28 December 1992, p. 22–5; Smith, S., op. cit.
42. Smith, S., op. cit.
43. Ibid.
44. Bonner, R., 'The dilemma of disarmament', *Time*, 28 December 1992, p. 24–5.
45. *Washington Post*, 7 December 1992.
46. Bonner, op. cit. *Time* quoted a former Somali national police chief as saying that only an 'outside authority' could disarm the country because Somalis were 'unable – or unwilling' to disarm themselves. He estimated that it would take four to six months for 'total disarmament.'
47. Smith, S., op. cit.
48. See Smith, S., op. cit., for an assessment of the politics of disarmament See also Marlowe, op. cit., for the Marines' perspective on their task.
49. *New York Times*, 2 January, 3 January and 4 January 1993; *The Times* (London), 1 January 1993. Some 23,000 American troops were deployed in Somalia at the time.

50. *The Times* (London), 5 January 1993.

51. *New York Times*, 7, 9 and 14 January 1993.

52. The type of incident which resulted in the rising tide of violence was covered by all major media. See, for example, the *New York Times*, 25 and 26 February 1993.

53. *United Nations Peace-keeping Operations Information Notes 1993: Update No. 2*, p. 84–5. UNITAF had deployed some 37,000 troops, the bulk of them American. UNOSOM II deployed about 21,000 troops.

54. *New York Times*, 6 June and 7 June 1993; *The Times* (London), 6 June and 7 June 1993. *The Australian*, 9 June 1993. The surviving 80 Pakistanis, surrounded by snipers, were extricated by Italian troops backed by tanks and helicopters.

55. *The Times* (London), 13 June, 14 June, 15 June and 18 June 1993; *The Australian*, 11 June and 18 June 1993. Civilian deaths appear to have been occasioned, in some instances at least, by Somali gunmen using civilians as shields.

56. *The Times* (London) 18 June and 23 June 1993; *The Australian*, 25 June 1993.

57. Michaels, M., 'Peacemaking war', *Time*, vol. 8, no. 30, 26 July 1993, p. 30–1.

58. Ibid.

59. *New York Times*, 15 July 1993; *Washington Post*, 15 July 1993; *The Times* (London), 15 July 1993 and 16 July 1993; *Weekend Australian*, 17–18 July 1993.

60. *Sunday Times*, 18 July 1993.

61. Michaels, op. cit.

62. See *The Economist*, vol. 328, 17 July 1993 and vol. 328, no. 7822, 31 July 1993 for detailed discussion of the role of the United States and its approach in Somalia. The *New York Times*, 16 July 1993, made the point that the Italians were concerned that the United Nations appeared to be taking sides, rather than maintaining an impartial stance.

63. *The Australian*, 27 August 1993. The United States administration had reaffirmed its commitment to Somalia earlier in the month, stating that its forces would remain as long as Aidid remained a disruptive political and military force (*New York Times*, 10 August 1993).

64. *New York Times*, 31 August 1993; *The Australian*, 31 August 1993 and 1 September 1993. This was only the first of the bungled raids that were attributed to poor intelligence.

65. *New York Times*, 10 September 1993; *The Australian*, 11 September 1993. The headlines in *The Australian* were 'Women attack UN tanks' and 'US helicopters fire at children'.
66. *New York Times*, 10 September 1993.
67. *New York Times*, 26 September 1993.
68. See any major newspaper (*Washington Post, New York Times, The Times* (London), *The Australian*) for the week 4 October to 11 October 1993. See also Church, G., 'Anatomy of a disaster', *Time*, vol. 8, no. 42, 18 October 1993, p. 44–55. According to the *Weekend Australian*, 9–10 October 1993, President Clinton justified the fresh deployment of troops by stating that it would be 'open season on Americans' around the world if the United States withdrew because of the killing of its servicemen.
69. Church, op. cit.
70. *The Australian*, 11 October 1993.
71. *Washington Post*, 11 October 1993.
72. *Washington Post*, 11 October 1993.
73. *New York Times*, 16 October 1993.
74. See *The Times* (London), 5 September 1993; *The Australian*, 6 September 1993. There was a message in the fact that the United Nations was paying Aidid US$100,000 a month in protection money at the same time that it had a $25,000 price on his head.
75. *The Times* (London), 11 October 1993.
76. *New York Times*, 3 December 1993; *The Times* (London), 4 December 1993.
77. Ryan, H., 'A New Diplomacy', *Government Executive*, vol. 25, no. 2, February 1993, p. 36–8.
78. Bonner, op. cit.; *Washington Post*, 7 December 1992.
79. Stevenson, op. cit. This was the decision which prompted Sahnoun's resignation.
80. Marlowe, op. cit.; Smith, S., op. cit.
81. *The Australian*, 11 October 1993.
82. *The Australian*, 18 November 1993.
83. See Koch, T., *Journalism in the 21st Century: Online Information, Electronic Databases and the News*, Adamantine Press, Twickenham, UK, 1991, p. 22–7. See also Church, op. cit. The defence by *Time* magazine of the US government position is significant. For some media outlets – such as *USA Today* and *Time* – the stated goal is to present a national perspective which legitimates the government position, as opposed to striving for an unbiased account of events.
84. Ibid.

85. Pick, H., 'Clinton sets limits to UN peace role', *Guardian Weekly*, vol. 149, no. 14, 3 October 1993, p. 1.
86. Ryan, op. cit.; *The Times* (London), 9 December 1992.
87. *The Times* (London), 5 December 1992.
88. See *Washington Post*, 27 July 1992.
89. See, for example, Bonner, op. cit.
90. See, for example, *The Australian*, 20 September 1995.
91. *Weekend Australian*, 22-23 June 1996.
92. Serrill, M., *Time*, no. 33, 12 August 1996, p. 30; see also AP, AFP reports, *Weekend Australian*, 3–4 August 1996.

Chapter 12

1. McMullen & Norton, op. cit., p. 169–74.
2. *The Age* (Melbourne), 9 January 1991.
3. Osborne, M., *Before Kampuchea: Preludes to Tragedy*, George Allen & Unwin, Sydney, 1979, p. 10–1. For a brief history of this period, see also Hood, M., & Ablin, D.A., 'The path to Cambodia's present', in *The Cambodian Agony*, Ablin, D.A., & Hood, M. (eds), M.E. Sharpe, Inc., Armonk, New York, 1987, pp. xv–lix; and Becker, E., *When the War Was Over*, Simon & Schuster, New York, 1986, p. 60–9.
4. Quoted in Osborne, M., *Region of Revolt: Focus on Southeast Asia*, Penguin, Harmondsworth, Middlesex, 1970, p. 22.
5. Hood & Ablin, op. cit., p. xx.
6. See Becker, op. cit. According to Becker, Thanh lobbied the Japanese to invade Cambodia early in the war. He was forced to flee the country, however, and went to Tokyo, where he was trained by the Japanese and became a captain in the Japanese imperial army. With the return of the French, Thanh was imprisoned on Sihanouk's request.
7. Hood & Ablin, op. cit., p. xx–xxi. Sihanouk made it clear that, if he controlled an independent Cambodia, he would fight neither for nor against the Viet Minh. This was an important concession for the French (See Becker, op. cit., p. 92).
8. Becker, op. cit., p. 92–4. The Vietnamese and Laotian communists were seated at the Geneva Conference, but the Khmer communists were not.
9. See Osborne, 1979, op. cit., p. 44–58, for a background on Sihanouk, particularly in the 1960s. Sihanouk's venture into making

feature films in the late 1960s typifies the direction his life had taken.

10. Hood & Ablin, op. cit., p. xxi–xxiii; Becker, op. cit., p. 96–7.
11. Becker, op. cit., p. 28.
12. Osborne, 1979, op. cit., p. 61.
13. Hood & Ablin, op. cit., pp. xxii–xxiii.
14. Becker, op. cit., p. 30.
15. Hood & Ablin, op. cit., pp. xxii–xxiii.
16. Osborne, 1970, op. cit., p. 168.
17. On 18 March, 1969, Nixon ordered a B–52 attack on an area in Cambodia suspected of being a North Vietnamese base. There were further attacks later that year. See Hung, N.T, & Schecter, J.L., *The Palace File*, Harper & Row, New York, 1989, p. 31.
18. Hood & Ablin, op. cit., p. xxiii–xxv; Becker, op. cit., p. 31.
19. Hood & Ablin, op. cit., p. xxiv.
20. Ibid., p. xxv.
21. Ibid. Hood & Ablin quote a U.S. Defence Intelligence Agency report of 8 July 1971 which reported that South Vietnamese troops had indulged in a 'frenzy of raping and looting' in Cambodian villages they overran. By contrast, North Vietnamese troops were known for their discipline and decorum..
22. Ibid., p. xxviii.
23. Hood & Ablin, op. cit., p. xxviii, put the figure at 539,129 tons of bombs – more than three times the amount dropped on Japan. Becker, op. cit., p. 34, puts the figure at 257,465 tons – one and a half times the amount dropped on Japan.
24. Hood & Ablin, op. cit., p. xxv–xxvi. See also Kiljunen, K. (ed.), *Kampuchea: Decade of the Genocide*, Report of a Finnish Inquiry Commission, Zed Books, London, 1984, p. 5–8.
25. Becker, op. cit., p. 34–5.
26. Hung & Schecter, op. cit., p. 220.
27. Hood & Ablin, op. cit., p. xxxi. American aid to the Lon Nol regime in 1974 exceeded the total Cambodian national budget for 1969.
28. South Vietnam fell less than two weeks later, on 30 April 1975.
29. Hood & Ablin, op. cit., p. xxxi.
30. Ibid., p. xxix.
31. Pilger, J., *Distant Voices*, Vintage, London, 1992a, p. 171–2. See also Gomes, C.M., *The Kampuchea Connection*, Grassroots Publisher, London, 1980, p. 147. Gomes claims the 'Year Zero' concept originated in France and he was unable to trace it to Kampuchean documents. Gomes also rejects much of what has been written about the Khmer Rouge.

32. Kiljunen, op. cit., p. 15–7.
33. Hood & Ablin, op. cit., p. xxxvii.
34. Ibid.
35. Ibid., p. xli; Becker, op. cit., p. 402–3; Kiljunen, op. cit., p. 25–6.
36. Pilger, for example, was in Cambodia in the summer of 1979.
37. Kiljunen, op. cit., pp.46-47; Hood & Ablin, op. cit., pp.xliv-xlv. See also Jesser, J., 'The tragedy of the Hmong hill-people of Laos', *Canberra Times*, 11 July 1979, and 'The big fear is of being forced back across the border', *Canberra Times*, 17 July 1979, for descriptions of the problems facing typical refugees at the time.
38. Becker, op. cit., p.356.
39. Kiljunen, op. cit., pp.26-27.
40. Ponchaud, F., *Cambodia: Year Zero*, Holt, Rinehart & Winston, New York, 1977, p193.
41. Gomes, op. cit. Gomes discounts many of the figures quoted by the media - for example, the number of Cambodian doctors who survived - but he provides no alternative assessments of the effects of the Pol Pot regime. See also Vickery, M., *Cambodia 1975-1982*, George Allen & Unwin, North Sydney, NSW, 1984, p.185. Vickery concedes that at least tens of thousands of deaths did occur, but provides statistics which cast doubts on CIA estimates. Nevertheless, the point is made that it was the number of deaths that became the focus of attention in reporting on Democratic Kampuchea.
42. Gomes, op. cit.; Gaddis, J.L., *Strategies of Containment*, Oxford University Press, Oxford, 1992, p.337.Not surprisingly, American analysts blamed North Vietnam for what happened. Gaddis claims that it was North Vietnam, not America, which first violated neutrality. The advent of Pol Pot, he argues, was less a function of the 1970 U.S. military 'incursion' than of Hanoi's final victory over South Vietnam. However, Gaddis appears not to take into account the impact of the American bombing as compared to less intrusive North Vietnamese actions.
43. *New York Times*, 8 November 1981.
44. *The Times* (London), 23 March 1981, 13 June 1981, 26 October 1981, 27 October 1981; *New York Times*, 1, 11, and 24 November 1981.
45. Pilger 1992a, op. cit., pp.171-202.
46. *New York Times*, 18 July 1981.
47. Spragens, J., Jr., 'Why not just say it? National interests still come first.' *Southeast Asia Chronicle*, issue 78, August 1981.
48. Ibid.

49. Pilger 1992a, op. cit., p.206 reports that it was alleged he had been invited in by the Vietnamese, a charge he strongly denies.
50. Chanda, N., *Brother Enemy: The War after the War*, Collier Books, Macmillan Publishing, New York, 1986, pp.409-410.
51. Shawcross, W., *The Quality of Mercy: Cambodia, Holocaust and Modern Conscience*, Simon & Schuster, New York, 1984, p.430.
52. Kiljunen, op. cit., p. 8.
53. See Pilger 1992a, op. cit., p. 176. Pilger asserts that the same conclusion could have been drawn from the CIA's own assessments that the bombing was driving Cambodians towards the communists.
54. See, Sihanouk, Prince Norodom, *War and Hope: The Case for Cambodia*, Pantheon Books, New York, 1980. Sihanouk now identified the war in Cambodia as anti-Cambodian – a position which distanced him from both the Khmer Rouge and the Vietnamese.
55. The coalition formed in Kuala Lumpur on June 1982. It brought together non-communist Sihanoukists and the Khmer Peoples National Liberation Front, with the communist Khmer Rouge.
56. See Rajendran, M., *ASEAN's Foreign Relations: The Shift to Collective Action*, arenabuku sdn. bhd., Kuala Lumpur, 1985, p. 87–130, for a summary of the refugee situation. Thailand received hundreds of thousands of mainly Cambodian refugees fleeing by land, while Malaysia bore the brunt of the Vietnamese 'boat people' – some 70,000 by the early 1980s. The other ASEAN nations received only a few thousand refugees each.
57. For a full discussion of the ASEAN position, see Tillman, R.O., *Southeast Asia and the Enemy Beyond*, Westview Press, Boulder, Colorado, 1987, p. 84–105.
58. For an Australian perspective on the origins of the peace process, see Evans, G., & Grant, B., *Australia's Foreign Relations in the World of the 1990s*, Melbourne University Press, Melbourne, 1991, p. 206–18.
59. Evans & Grant, op. cit., p. 209.
60. Chanda, N., 'Media manipulation', *Far Eastern Economic Review*, vol. 140, 30 June 1988, p. 28. See also the *Washington Post*, 18 June 1988.
61. Evans & Grant, op. cit., p. 209–10. The PICC brought together all four Cambodian factions, the six ASEAN nations, the five permanent members of the Security Council, Vietnam, Laos, Australia, Canada, India, Zimbabwe (as a representative of the non-aligned movement), and a representative of the United Nations Secretary-General.
62. Ibid., p. 210.

63. See also Pilger 1992a, op. cit., p. 200–2. According to Pilger, Solarz was a strong supporter of Sihanouk and had played a major part in shaping United States policy on Cambodia. This lends support to the thesis that the final settlement in Cambodia came about only because the United States decided it was time. See also Evans & Grant, op. cit., p. 210–1.

64. *Cambodia: an Australian Peace Proposal,* published by the Department of Foreign Affairs and Trade by the Australian Government Publishing Service, Canberra, 1990.

65. Chandler, D.P., *Brother Number One: A Political Biography of Pol Pot,* Allen & Unwin, St Leonards, NSW, 1992, p. 186.

66. *United Nations Peace-keeping Operations Information Notes 1993: Update No. 2,* p. 55.

67. McMullen and Norton, op. cit., p. 172.

68. See, for example, *New York Times,* 24 October 1991 and *The Times* (London), 24 October 1991.

69. Pilger 1992a, op. cit., p. 198.

70. Pilger, J., 'Peace in our time?', *New Statesman and Society,* 27 November 1992b, p. 10–1.

71. Scott, M., 'War and memory', *Far Eastern Economic Review,* vol. 155, 16 April 1992, p. 36–9.

72. Ponchaud, op. cit.

73. Pilger 1992a, op. cit., p. 203–29.

74. Ibid., p. 209–13. Pilger refers to Shawcross' book *The Quality of Mercy* (op. cit.) as an example of holding up American actions as reflecting the most humanitarian motives. Shawcross' theme is that it is the communists (in this case the Vietnamese) who thwarted the humanitarianism of the West.

75. Gomes, op. cit.

76. See Pilger 1992a, op. cit.

77. Silber, I., *Kampuchea: The Revolution Rescued,* Line of March Publications, Oaklands, Calif., 1986. According to Silber (p. 95) many Cambodians found the prospect of the return of the Khmer Rouge 'simply chilling.'

78. Scott 1992, op. cit.

79. Ibid. But Pilger claims to have made the comparison with both Maoism and Stalinism; see Pilger 1992a, p. 211.

80. Scott 1992, op. cit.

81. See *Cambodia: an Australian Peace Proposal,* op. cit., especially the foreword and p. 89. See also Pilger, 1992b, op. cit. Pilger took the Australian Commander of UNTAC, Lieutenant-General John Sanderson, to task for rejecting the use of the word 'genocide'

in relation to the Khmer Rouge. Pilger pointed out that the term had been applied by the United Nations in the recent past.

82. Quoted in Pilger 1992a, op. cit., p. 200.

83. Evans and Grant, op. cit., p. 212.

84. *United Nations Peace-keeping Operations Information Notes 1993: Update No. 2*, p. 55.

85. Despite the cease-fire, in early 1992 the Khmer Rouge continued to fight and to lay mines; see the *New York Times*, 5 March 1992; *The Times* (London), 8 April 1992.

86. *United Nations Peace-keeping Operations Information Notes 1993: Update No. 2*, p. 56.

87. Personal Interview, Lieutenant-General John Sanderson (UNTAC Force Commander), Canberra, April 1994. Evans also makes the point that deployment must take place quickly, and as soon as possible after the parties to a conflict have reached agreement, in order to build confidence and show that the United Nations is serious.; see Evans, G., *Cooperating for Peace*, op. cit., p. 108.

88. See, for example, *The Times* (London), 10 November 1992 and 14 November 1992. The Khmer Rouge was described as 'notoriously brutal' and Pol Pot had 'Stalin at his worst as his mentor.'

89. Pilger, J., 'Black farce in Cambodia', *New Statesman and Society*, 11 December 1992 (1992c), p. 10. Pilger criticised the United Nations for announcing trade sanctions but at the same time said it would 'leave the door open' for the Khmer Rouge to return to the peace process. He noted that the response of the Khmer Rouge was to take a team of United Nations' officials hostage.

90. *Asia Watch*, vol. 5, no. 14, 23 September 1993, p. 95.

91. *United Nations Peace-keeping Operations Information Notes 1993: Update No. 2*, p.56–8.

92. See *New York Times*, 18 August 1992. One of the main problems was the continuing refusal of the Khmer Rouge to disarm. By November 1992, Cambodians were allegedly disillusioned with UNTAC (see *The Times* (London), 26 November 1992). In an interview in early 1993, Sihanouk argued that UNTAC had alienated all the factions (see Chanda, N., 'Sharp words', *Far Eastern Economic Review*, vol. 156, 4 February 1993, p. 23).

93. Thayer, N., 'Moaners beware', *Far Eastern Economic Review*, vol. 155, 5 November 1992, p. 27.

94. *United Nations Peace-keeping Operations Information Notes 1993: Update No. 2*, p. 58–9.

95. *New York Times*, 10 May 93.

96. Heininger, Janet E., *Peacekeeping in Transition*, Twentieth Century Fund Press, New York, 1994, p.111.
97. *The Economist*, 'Stoning the press', vol. 327, 29 May 1993, p. 40. A photographer confronted by the sight of hundreds of voters rather than piles of corpses is reported to have announced 'This whole thing is a farce.'
98. *New York Times*, 1 June 1993; *The Australian*, 1 June 1993.
99. *United Nations Peace-keeping Operations Information Notes 1993: Update No. 2*, p. 60.
100. *The Australian*, 9 June 1993 and 11 June 1993.
101. *United Nations Peace-keeping Operations Information Notes 1993: Update No. 2*, p. 61.
102. Quoted in Pilger, J., 'Another UN triumph', *New Statesman and Society*, 21 July 1995, p. 14–5.
103. *The Australian*, 3 August 1993.
104. *The Australian*, 30 May 1994.
105. The United Nations had also accused the Cambodian police and military of using wanton brutality against the people. The *New York Times*, 11 July 1993, argued that the brutality could be explained by the fact that many army leaders were Khmer Rouge defectors.
106. Thayer, N., 'The honeymoon's over', *Far Eastern Economic Review*, vol. 157, 25 August 1994, p. 17–8; Hayes, M., 'Stop Press', *Far Eastern Economic Review*, vol. 157, 1 December 1994, p. 21. The colourful reporting includes calling co-prime ministers Prince Norodom Ranariddh and Hun Sen 'rats' and 'less than human excrement.'
107. *The Australian*, 30 May 1994. See also the *Weekend Australian*, 25–26 November 1995, for Shawcross' review of Cambodia's internal problem with official corruption. According to Shawcross, 'Cambodia is not threatened by the return of the Khmer Rouge; the threat comes from brutal corruption within the system. The Government appears to be acting with impunity and the outside world no longer shows any interest.'
108. Pilger 1995, op. cit.
109. *The Australian*, 16 January 1995, See also *The Australian*, 30 May 1994.
110. Pilger 1995, op. cit.
111. McMullen and Norton, op. cit., p. 172–3.
112. Tasker, R., 'Trading charges', *Far Eastern Economic Review*, vol. 157, 28 April 1994, p. 20; and *New York Times*, 19 December 1993. See also *New York Times*, 24 October 1991, which presented the peace accord as 'brokered' by the United States, the Soviet

Union and China. Thailand's close ties with the Khmer Rouge were always a cause for concern.

113. Pilger 1995, op. cit.
114. Pilger 1995, op. cit.
115. *The Economist*, reprinted in the *Weekend Australian*, 17-18 August 1996.

Chapter 13

1. Ollapally, D., 'The South Looks North: The Third World in the New World Order', *Current History*, vol. 92, no. 573, April 1993, p. 175-9.
2. *New York Times*, 14 January 1993.
3. Kumar, S., *US Intervention in Latin America*, Advent Books, New York, 1987, p. 111.
4. *Military Balance 1993/94*, IISS, London 1993, p. 187.
5. Knight, F., *The Caribbean: The Genesis of a Fragmented Nationalism*, Oxford University Press, New York 1978, p. 148.
6. Ibid., p. 156.
7. Morrisby, E., 'Papa Doc', *Quadrant*, vol. xxxvi, no. 4, April 1992, p. 58.
8. Calvert, P. (ed.), *The Central American Security System: North-South or East-West*, Cambridge University Press, Cambridge 1988, p. 40. See also Shiv Kumar, V., *US Intervention in Latin America*, Advent Books, New York 1987, p. 111.
9. Knight, op. cit., p. 181.
10. Larmer, B., et al. 'Should We Invade Haiti', *The Bulletin*, 19 July 1994, p. 63.
11. Knight, op. cit., p. 182.
12. Ibid., p. 183.
13. Morrisby, op. cit., p. 57. US State Department Travel Warning, 3 August 1994.
14. *Haiti: Selected Economic Data*, 1987.
15. *The Times* (London), 8 January 1991.
16. *The Times* (London), 1 October 1991.
17. Ollapally, op. cit., p. 178.
18. United Nations Security Council Resolution 841 (1993), 16 June 1993; See also *New York Times*, 17 June 1993. A proposed naval blockade in conjunction with the sanctions was dropped in the face of objections from Brazil.
19. *US State Department Report on Human Rights*, 1993.

20. *US State Department Report on Human Rights in Haiti*, 1993. See also *New York Times*, 4 July 1993.
21. *The Times* (London), 14 October 1993.
22. US State Department Briefing, 13 July 1994. The ICM did not return until January 1994.
23. *The Times* (London), 13 October 1993; *The Australian*, 14 October 1993.
24. *New York Times*, 14 and 16 October 1993.
25. *New York Times*, 4 April 1994.
26. White House Press Release, 16 May 1994; See also *Los Angeles Times*, 12 May 1994.
27. *New York Times*, 1 June 1994.
28. *New York Times*, 17 May 1994, 28 June 1994, and 6 July 1994; *The Times* (London), 11 July 1994; US State Department Briefing, 3 August 1994. The number of refugees eased somewhat from the peak in July, but in the six months prior to intervention, over 21,500 Haitians had fled by sea and 61,000 requests for asylum had been received by the US Embassy in Port-au-Prince.
29. US State Department Travel Warning, 3 August 1994.
30. *New York Times*, 22 July 1994.
31. *The Australian*, 19 October 1993.
32. AFP, 20 May 1994.
33. *New York Times*, 20 July 1994.
34. AAP/Reuters, 7 July 1994.
35. Reuters and *Sydney Morning Herald*, 15 June 1994.
36. AFP/AP, 16 July 1994.
37. *Report of the Secretary General on the United Nations Mission to Haiti*, 15 July 1994.
38. *New York Times*, 1 August 1994.
39. Reuters and *New York Times*, 1 August 1994; *Courier Mail* (Brisbane), 2 August 1994.
40. Roberts, A., 'Humanitarian War: Military Intervention and Human Rights', *International Affairs*, vol. 69, no. 3, 1993, p. 440.
41. UN Security Council Resolution 940 (1994). See also Evans, op. cit., p. 153
42. Roberts, op. cit., p. 444.
43. Ibid.
44. AFP and *New York Times*, 4 August 1994; *Weekend Australian*, 5 August 1994.
45. *Sydney Morning Herald*, 5 August 1994.
46. CNN, Reuters, and AFP reporting in the *Washington Post* and *The Australian*, 16–18 September 1994.

47. The seventeen nations pledging forces as of 15 September, were Antigua and Barbuda, Argentina, The Bahamas, Bangladesh, Barbados, Belgium, Belize, Bolivia, Dominica, Guyana, Israel, Jamaica, The Netherlands, Panama, St Vincents, Trinidad and the United Kingdom. US State Department and AP, 15 September 1994.
48. Reuters, 18 July 1994.
49. Reuters, reprinted *Sydney Morning Herald*, 16 September 1994.
50. Reuters, 16 September 1994.
51. *New York Times*, 2 August 1994; Reuters, AFP, *Weekend Australian*, 17–18 September 1994.
52. *New York Times*, 16 September 1994 and 17 September 1994. Carter enjoyed special status in Haiti, having been an observer at the 1990 elections which brought Aristide to power.
53. *Washington Post*, 19 September 1994.
54. *New York Times*, 19 and 20 September 1994; *The Australian*, 20 September 1994.
55. *The Australian*, 20 September 1994. Similar comments about the invasion being 'unpopular' with Americans were expressed in the *New York Times*, 19 September 1994.
56. *Los Angeles Times*, 19 September 1994; *New York Times*, 20 September 1994; *The Australian*, 21 September 1994.
57. *Sydney Morning Herald*, 21 September 1994.
58. *The Times* (London)/AFP, reprinted in *The Australian*, 19 October 1994.
59. *Sydney Morning Herald*, 27 September 1994.
60. *New York Times*, 15 July 1994.
61. Wilenz, A. 'Requiem', *The Nation* (New York), vol. 259, no. 8, 19 September 1994, p. 260–1. Wilenz describes the assassination of Haitian priest and reform worker, Father Jean-Marie Vincent, drew a typical picture of oppression and the bleak future facing Haiti. Father Vincent, the article said, '... was killed because of his past, but he was also killed because of his future. He was an organiser, a fundraiser, a field man ... Someone knew that Father Vincent was helping to lay the groundwork for a future Haiti, and that if democracy ever managed to inch its toe back through the door of the presidential palace, all his projects and people would be there waiting, ready for open conflict with Haiti's elite... Without Jean-Marie Vincent, Haiti's dark future grows more obscure.' Such writing leaves no room for debate about 'right' and 'wrong'.
62. *Washington Post*, 18 September 1994. The subsequent questions surrounding how Biamby came to know that the invasion force was on its way lends support to the argument that some form of news

blackout is necessary to ensure troop safety. See also *Washington Post*, 19 September 1994.

63. *Courier Mail* (Brisbane), 17 September 1994.
64. Co-authors survey of selected leading US, British and Australian newspapers, and AAP, 1 August–20 September 1994.
65. US State Department spokesman, Mike Curry, Washington 4 August 1994. 'Colour' was injected in a variety of ways. For example, the *New York Times*, 9 September 1994, carried a report that 'Haitian thugs loyal to the military regime have murdered hundreds of young orphaned children ... intent on wiping out even imaginary traces of Aristide.' The alleged motive for the killings was that Aristide had once started an orphanage.
66. Ibid.
67. *The Times* (London), 2 August 1994.
68. *The Australian*, 5 May 1994.
69. *Los Angeles Times*, 19 October 1994.
70. *New York Times*, 14 September 1994.
71. *Courier Mail* (Brisbane), 19 September 1994.
72. *Sydney Morning Herald*, 19 September 1994, quoting a *US Newsday* report attributed to a secret White House briefing.
73. Story datelined Washington. Reprinted *Courier Mail* (Brisbane), 21 September 1994.
74. *Los Angeles Times, Washington Post*, Reuters. Reprinted in the *Sydney Morning Herald*, 21 September 1994.
75. *Los Angeles Times, Washington Post*, Reuters. Reprinted in the *Sydney Morning Herald*, 21 September 1994.
76. AP, *Los Angeles Times*, 7 October 1994.
77. Reuters, *New York Times*, 12 October 1994.
78. Unsourced, *Courier Mail* (Brisbane), 12 October 1994.
79. Unsourced, *Courier Mail* (Brisbane), 5 October 1994.
80. AP, Reuters, *New York Times*, 1 October 1994.
81. AP/Reuters, AFP, 27 September 1994.
82. Reuters, 25 September 1994.

Chapter 14

1. Young, P., 'The Impact of the New High Technology Media on National Sovereignty', *Australian Journalism Review*, vol. 15, no. 2, 1993.
2. For an indication of present military policy that reflects this see Ad Hoc Media Group letter to Secretary of Defence Dick Cheney, 25

June 1991 (copy courtesy American Society of Newspaper Editors); *Defence Public Information Policy during Periods of Tension and Conflict*, Department of Defence, Australia; *Public Information in Limited Conflict, CLIC Papers*, US JCS Publications; the *Sidle Report*, US Defence Department, August 1984; *A Brief Guide to Public Relations (MODOS12)*, U.K. See also *Proposed Working Arrangements with the Media in Time of Tension and War*, Ministry of Defence, London, August 1987; and Young, P.R. (ed), *Defence and The Media In Time of Limited War*, Frank Cass, London, 1992.

3. *Discussion Paper: Relations Between the Media and the Australian Defence Force in Periods of Tension and Hostilities*, covering memo signed by Commodore M.S. Unwin, DPI, dated 29 August 1985. See also *ACCOR Joining Instructions for Participation in Exercise Kangaroo 86*, DPR15/86, October 1986; and the *Sidle Report* (see Office of the Assistant Secretary of Defence (Public Affairs), News Release No. 450/84, 23 August 1984).

4. See individual case studies.

5. Woodward, B., *The Commanders*, Simon & Schuster, New York, 1991, p. 315; Morris, M., *H. Norman Schwarzkopf: Road to Triumph*, Pan Books, London, 1991, p. 167.

6. LaMay, C., Fitzsimon, M., & Sahadi, J. (eds), *The Media At War: The Press and the Persian Gulf Conflict*, Freedom Forum Media Studies Center, New York, 1991, p. 86–97. See also individual case studies, especially Chapter 9, 'The Gulf Conflict: The Ascendancy of the Military'.

7. For an examination of this acceptance of war as a limiting factor in social contract obligations, see Chapter 1, 'The Changed Nature of War and Duties of the Citizen in Time of War'.

8. Rawls, J., *A Theory of Justice*, Clarendon Press, Oxford, 1972; Parekh, B., *Contemporary Political Thinkers*, Martin Robinson, Oxford, 1982. See also Chapter 1, 'The Changed Nature of War and Duties of the Citizen in Time of War'.

9. Orwell G., *Looking Back at the Spanish Civil War*, Mercury Books, London, 1961, p. 211. See also Waugh, E., *Evelyn Waugh in Abyssinia*, Longmans Green, London, 1937.

10. Knightley, P., *The First Casualty*, Quartet, London, 1975, p. 312. Also Personal interview, Dennis Warner, editor *Pacific Defence Reporter*, 17 October 1991.

11. Personal interview, M. Lucien Boz, Directorate of Information (1948–51), Paris, 11 March 1977; Giap, V., *People's War, People's Army*, Foreign Publishing House, Hanoi, 1975, p. 561.

12. See Fanon, F., *The Wretched of the Earth*, Penguin, Harmondsworth, Middlesex, 1965 and Special Operations Research Office, *Casebook on Insurgency and Revolutionary Warfare*, The American University, Washington, 1962. See also Chapter 3, 'Post War Self Determination: The Unheeded Warning'.

13. See Winchester, S., *In Holy Terror*, Faber & Faber, London, 1974; Dash, S., *A Challenge to Lord Widgery's Report on Bloody Sunday*, Defence and Education Fund of the International League of the Rights of Man, in association with the Council of Civil Liberties, August 1972; and *R v the Justices of the Peace for the County of the City of Londonderry (Ex Parte Hume and Others)*, unreported, judgement delivered 23 February, 1972 (see *Northern Ireland Legal Quarterly*, vol. 23, no. 2, Summer 1972, p. 206–7).

14. Knightley, op. cit., p. 4–7; Royle, T., *War Report*, Grafton Books, London, 1989, p. 19.

15. Merill, J., *Global Journalism*, Longman, New York, 1983, p. 302–53. See also Denton, R., & Woodward, G., *Political Communication in America*, Praeger, New York, 1985, p. 124–7.

16. See Chapter 5, 'Vietnam: Deception on a National Scale'.

17. Hallin, D., *The Uncensored War: The Media and Vietnam*, Oxford University Press, London, 1986, p. 99. See also Thayer, C., 'Vietnam: A critical analysis', paper delivered to the International Conference on Defence and the Media in Time of Limited Conflict, Brisbane, April 1991.

18. Evidence before the House of Commons Defence Committee, 27 October 1982. See also Moore, General Sir Jeremy, 'The Falklands war: A commander's view of the Defence/Media interface', paper delivered to the International Conference on Defence and the Media in Time of Limited Conflict, Brisbane, April 1991.

19. Mercer, D., Mungham, G., & Williams, K., *The Fog of War*, Heinemann, London, 1987, p. 48–52 and p. 210.

20. *Report on the Handling of the Press and Public Information during the Falklands Conflict*, (2 vols.), House of Commons Select Committee on Defence, HMSO, London 8 December 1982.

21. *Proposed Working Arrangements with the Media in Time of Tension and War*, MOD, London.

22. A working party on the issue of public information is reported to have been held in London in 1983 as part of the ABCA standardisation process. A second quadripartite special working group is known to have been held in the United States in November 1985, where work was done on the draft of a full ABCA public information policy.

23. *Washington Post*, 29 October 1983.
24. Personal interview, Admiral Metcalf, Brisbane, April 1991.
25. For background to the safety or otherwise of the American students, see *Grenada: Whose Freedoms?*, Latin American Bureau, London 1984.
26. OECS Statement, 25 October 1983. See also 'Documents on the Invasion', *Caribbean Monthly Bulletin*, Supplement No 1., October 1983, p. 17.
27. For the full text of the *Sidle Report*, see Office of the Assistant Secretary of Defence (Public Affairs), News Release No. 450/84, 23 August 1984. See also Chapter 7, 'Grenada: An Emerging Pattern of Control', for a list of the recommendations of the *Sidle Report*.
28. Woodward, op. cit., p. 178.
29. *The Australian*, 29 December 1989. See also Jaco, C., 'Missing the Action in Panama', *Quill*, November/December 1990; Cloud, S., 'How Reporters Missed the War', *Time Magazine*, January 1990.
30. See Chapter 8, 'Panama: A Deliberate Policy of Exclusion'.
31. *The Independent*, 2 January 1990; *The Australian*, 2 January 1990. See also Woodward, B., op. cit., p. 195.
32. Woodward, op. cit., p. 169–70. See also Darwish, A., & Alexander, G., *Unholy Babylon: The Secret History of Saddam's War*, Gollancz, London, 1991, p. 286.
33. Evidence of demonisation can be found in leading American, British and Australian newspapers. See, for example, *New York Times*, 26 August 1990, 30 September 1990, 6 January 1991 and 2 February 1991; *The Times* (London), 25 July 1990 and 3 March 1991; *The Age* (Melbourne), 13, 16, 22 and 24 January 1991; and *Courier Mail* (Brisbane), 26 January 1991.
34. LaMay et al., op. cit., p. 26–33.
35. Ibid.
36. Hallin, D., 'TV's Clean Little War', *Bulletin of the Atomic Scientist*, May 1991.
37. Personal interview, Colonel David Hackworth, defence correspondent, *News Week*, 2 April 1991.
38. O'Connor, T., 'Personal experiences of Australia's public information in wartime', paper delivered to the International Conference on Defence and the Media in Time of Limited Conflict, Brisbane, April 1991.
39. Draper, T., 'The True History of the Gulf War', *New York Review of Books*, 30 January 1992, p. 38–42.
40. *New York Times*, 6 May 1991. See also Neil, P., Annual Convention of the American Society of Newspaper Editors'.

41. Draper, op. cit., p. 43.

42. The United Nations Peace-keeping Force in Cyprus (UNFICYP), for example, has been in place for more than thirty years, supervising truce lines between Greek Cypriot and Turkish Cypriot forces. It is maintained at a strength of around 1,200 troops and support personnel and, as at 14 October 1993, had suffered 165 fatalities. See *United Nations Peace-keeping Operations Information Notes 1993: Update No. 2*, p. 7–9.

43. Ryan, H., 'A New Diplomacy', *Government Executive*, vol. 25, no. 2, February 1993, p. 36–8. See also Chapter 11, 'Somalia: The Uninvited Intervention'.

44. See, for example, *New York Times*, 15 July 1994. United Nations Security Council Resolution 940 (1994) was adopted on 1 August 1994, authorising a multi-national intervention in Haiti to end the crisis.

45. See Bonner, R., 'The dilemma of disarmament', *Time*, 28 December 1992, p. 24–5; *Washington Post*, 7 December 1992.

46. Stevenson, J., 'Hope restored in Somalia?' *Foreign Policy*, no. 91, Summer 1993, p. 138–54. Aidid was targeted in earnest from the latter part of 1992 when, after Secretary-General Boutros-Ghali made his unilateral decision to increase the peace-keeping force in Somalia, Aidid threatened to send the soldiers home in body bags. Interestingly, *The Times* (London) reduced Aidid to the rank of a 'crafty local chieftain' once he had thwarted the best efforts of the United States and the United Nations. See also *The Times* (London), 11 October 1993.

47. *The Australian*, 5 May 1994.

48. See Pilger, J., *Distant Voices*, Vintage, London, 1992, p. 171–249.

49. See Dobell, G., 'The media's perspective', in *Peacekeeping: Challenges for the Future*, H. Smith (ed.), Australian Defence Studies Centre, Australian Defence Force Academy, Canberra, 1993, p. 41–57.

50. *The Australian*, 1 June 1993.

51. LaMay et al., op. cit., p. 86–97.

52. See quote in Badsey, S., 'The media war', in Pimlott, J., & Badsey, S. (eds), *The Gulf War Assessed*, Arms & Armour, London, 1992, p. 219.

53. See individual case studies.

54. Cambodia is the exception, but it was a peace process rather than a conflict. Efforts were made to reverse the demonisation process to rehabilitate the Khmer Rouge and keep them within the peace process.

55. See individual case studies.

56. See case studies – Grenada, Panama and the Gulf War. In addition, it should be noted that the war establishments of the public information branches in the United States, the United Kingdom and Australia, now include military television crews whose operational role is to provide footage from areas denied to normal media or ACCOR on the grounds of the safety of the media.

57. Woodward, op. cit., p. 178. See also Davidson, S., *A Study of Politics and the Limitations of International Law*, Aldershot Publishing, Hants, U.K., 1987.

58. LaMay et al., op. cit., p. 26–33. See also Fialka, J., *Hotel Warriors: Covering The Gulf War*, Woodrow Wilson Centre Press, Washington, 1991.

59. In Australia, no television network presently maintains a dedicated defence specialist reporter and there remain only two dedicated specialist defence writers in the national print media. There are no full time defence reporters on national radio.

60. Network Ten, Canberra Bureau DMAG submission entitled *A Foreign Desk*, 9 July 1988.

61. LaMay et al., op. cit., p. xii and p. 86–97.

62. The Australian national broadcaster, the ABC, incurred the wrath of the government for attempting to present a balanced view of events during the Gulf war. See also *Sydney Morning Herald*, 24 January 1991 and the *Sunday Age* (Melbourne), 10 February 1991. The BBC in Britain came in for similar criticism during the Falklands campaign. See the *Sun*, 14 May 1982.

63. Co-authors content analysis of selected U.K., German and Australian national newspapers (courtesy Mr Andrew Scrimgeour).

64. *The Australian*, 4 September 1996.

65. *The Times* (London),

66. *The Australian*, 6 September 1996.

67. It may be ironic that the material cost of total war appears to have brought about its own demise. In the Iran-Iraq war, lives were wasted as a cheap substitute for technology.

68. The Milltown Cemetery killings in Northern Ireland gave the British government the opportunity to test its right to have third party national media hand over their film of events. The government secured film shot by the British media, but did not broach the third party question. See Chapter 4, 'Northern Ireland: A Classic Democratic Dilemma'.

SELECT BIBLIOGRAPHY

A Soldier's Eyewitness Account, Stackpoole Books, Harrisburg, 1990.

a'Court Repington, C., *The First World War*, Constable, London, 1921.

a'Court Repington, C., *Vestigia*, Constable, London, 1919.

Aaron R., *Peace and War: A Theory of International Relations*, (Trans) Doubleday, New York, 1966.

Aaron, R., *On War*, Anchor Books, New York, 1963.

Abbas Kelidar, *The Integration of Modern Iraq*, Croom Helm, London, 1979.

Adams, E., *Great Britain and the Civil War*, Longmans Green, London, 1925.

Adams, J., *The Financing of Terror*, New English Library, London, 1986.

Adams, V., *The Media and the Falklands Campaign*, Macmillan, London, 1986.

Adkin, M., *Urgent Fury: The Battle for Grenada*, Lexington Books, Massachusetts, 1989.

Akehurst, M., *A Modern Introduction to International Law*, Allen & Unwin, London, 1970.

Alexander, B., *Korea, the Lost War*, Arrow Books, London, 1986.

American Society of Newspaper Editors Annual Conference, Boston, May 1991.

Amter, J., *Vietnam Verdict*, Continuum, New York, 1982.

Andrews, J., *The North Reports the Civil War*, Pittsburgh University Press, 1955.

Arnett, P., *Live from the Battlefield*, Bloomsbury Publishing, London, 1994.

Aspinall, A., *Politics and the Press 1750–1810*, Home & Van, London, 1949.

Attorney-General v Heinemann, 62 ALJR 1988.

Australian Freedom of Information Act (1981)

Australian Law Review Journal, no. 55, 1981.

Bailey, G., & MacDonald, G., *Report or Distort: The Inside Story of the Media's Coverage of the Vietnam War*, Exposition Press, New York, 1973.

Ball, D., *The Intelligence War in the Gulf*, SDSC, Canberra, 1991.

Barbour, N., *A Survey of North West Africa (The Maghrib)*, Oxford University Press, London, 1959.

Barendt, E., *Freedom of Speech*, Clarendon Press, Oxford, 1987.

Barker, E., *Social Contract*, Dover Publications, New York, 1950.

Barker, E., *Social Contract*, World Classics, OUP, London, 1959.

Bean, C., *The Story of ANZAC*, vol. 11, Angus & Robertson, Sydney, 1935.

Becker, E., *When the War Was Over*, Simon & Schuster, New York, 1986.

Behar, D., & Godfrey, H., *Invasion, The American Destruction of the Noriega Regime in Panama*, Americas Group, Los Angeles, 1990.

Bennis, P., & Mousehabeck, M., *Beyond the Storm*, Olive Branch Press, New York, 1991.

Benthall, J., *Disasters, Relief and the Media*, I.B. Tauris & Co, London, 1993.

Bentham, J., *Constitutional Code*.

Bentley, N., Russell's *Despatches from the Crimea 1854–56*, André Deutsch, London, 1966.

Bing, P., *Contemporary Democracies*, Harvard University Press, Harvard, 1982.

Bishop, P., & Witherow, J., *The Winter War: The Falklands*, Quartet Books, London, 1982.

Bong-young Choy, *Korea: A History*, Charles Tuttle & Co, Rutland, 1971.

Bonnet, G., *Les Guerres Insurrectionelles et Revolutionnaires*, Payot, Paris, 1958.

Bonney, B., & Wilson, H., *Australia's Commercial Media*, Macmillan, Sydney, 1983.

Bowyer-Bell, J., *The Secret Army: The IRA 1916–1969*, Cambridge University Press, Cambridge, Massachusetts, 1980.

Boyd, A., *United Nations: Piety, Myth, and Truth*, Penguin, Harmondsworth, Middlesex, 1961.

Boyle, K., Hadden, T., & Hillyard, P., *Law and State*, Martin Robertson, London, 1975.

Boyle, K., *Ten Years on: Northern Ireland: The Legal Control of Political Violence*, Martin Robertson, London, 1980.

Brace, R., & Brace, J., *Ordeal in Algeria*, Princeton University Press, Princeton, NJ, 1960.

Braestrup, P., *The Big Story*, Westview Press, Colorado, 1977.

Brennan, E., & Harwood, S., *Desert Storm: The Weapons of War*, Fontana, London, 1991.

Brennan, G., & Buchanan, J., *The Reason of Rules: Constitutional Political Economy*, Cambridge University Press, Cambridge, 1985.

Brenner, E., & Harwood, W., *Desert Storm: Weapons of War*, Fontana, London, 1991.

Brizan, G., *Grenada: Island of Conflict, from Amerindians to People's Revolution 1498–1979*, Zed Books, London, 1984.

Browne, D., *International Radio Broadcasting*, Praeger, New York, 1982.

Brzezinksi, Z., & Huntington, S., *Political Power: USA/USSR*, Chatto & Windus, London, 1963.

Buchanan, J., *The Limits of Liberty: Between Anarchy and Leviathan*, University of Chicago Press, Chicago, 1975.

Bulloch, J., & Morris, H., *Saddam's War: The Origins of the Kuwait Conflict and the International Response*, Faber & Faber, London, 1991.

Burrows, R., *Revolution and Rescue in Grenada: An Account of the US Caribbean Invasion*, Greenwood Press, New York, 1980.

Buttinger, J., *A Dragon Embattled*, vol. 1, *From Colonialism to the Vietminh*, Praeger, New York, 1967.

Buttinger, J., *The Smaller Dragon, a Political History of Vietnam*, Praeger, New York, 1958.

Calvert, P. (ed.), *The Central American Security System: North-South or East-West*, Cambridge University Press, Cambridge, 1988.

Cambodia: an Australian Peace Proposal, published by the Department of Foreign Affairs and Trade by the Australian Government Publishing Service, Canberra, 1990.

Carpenter, T., *America Entangled: The Persian Gulf Crisis and its Consequences*, Cato Institute, Washington, 1991.

Carty, A., *The Decay of International Law?* Manchester University Press, Manchester, 1986.

Chanda, N., *Brother Enemy: The War after the War*, Collier Books, Macmillan Publishing, New York, 1986.

Chandler, D.P., *Brother Number One: A Political Biography of Pol Pot*, Allen & Unwin, St Leonards, NSW, 1992.

Chapman, C., *Russell of the Times*, Bell & Hyman, London, 1984.

Chomsky, N., *Necessary Illusions*, CBC Enterprises, Toronto, 1988.

Churchill, W., *London to Ladysmith Via Pretoria*, Longman, London, 1900.

Churchill, W., *The Second World War*, vols. v and vi, Penguin, London, 1985.

Clausewitz, *Vom Kriege*, Berlin, 1832.

CLIC Papers Series, JCS Publication 1–02, Army Air Force Centre for Low Intensity Conflict, Langley, Virginia, May 1988.

Cohen, S., *British Policy in Mesopotamia 1903–1914*, Ithaca Press, London, 1976.

Cole, A., (ed.), *Conflict in Indochina*, Cornell University Press, New York, 1956.

Collier, R., *The Sands of Dunkirk*, Collins, London, 1961.

Collier, R., *The WARCOS: War Correspondents of World War II*, Weidenfeld & Nicolson, London, 1989.

Constitutions of Australia, The United States, and West Germany.

Cooke, E., *Delane of the Times*, Constable, London 1915.

Cranston, M., *The Social Contract: By Jean Jacques Rousseau*, Penguin, London, 1968.

Crawley, A., *De Gaulle*, Collins, London, 1969.

Crispin Miller, M., *Spectacle: Operation Desert Storm and the Triumph of Illusion*, Poseidon Press, Washington, 1992.

Curran, J., Gurevitch, M., & Woollacott, J. (eds.), *Mass Communication and Society*, Edward Arnold, London, 1987.

Curtis, L., *The British Media and the Battle for Hearts and Minds*, Pluto Press, London, 1984.

Dalyell, T., *One Man's Falklands*, Cecil Woolf, London, 1982.

Darwin, J., *Britain and De-Colonisation: The Retreat of Empire in the Post War World*, Macmillan, London, 1965.

Darwish, A., & Alexander, G., *Unholy Babylon: The Secret History of Saddam's War*, Gollancz, London, 1991.

Davidson, B., & Davis, S., *Vision: Winning in the Information Economy*, Simon & Schuster, New York, 1991.

Davidson, S., *A Study of Politics and the Limitations of International Law*, Aldershot Publishing, Hants, U.K., 1987.

De La Billière, P., *Storm Command. A Personal Account of the Gulf War*, HarperCollins, London, 1992.

De Paor, L., *Unfinished Business: Ireland Today and Tomorrow*, Hutchinson Radius, London, 1990.

Denton, R., & Woodward, G., *Political Communication in America*, Praeger, New York, 1985.

Devilliers, P., *Histoire de Vietnam du 1940–52*, Seuil, Paris, 1952.

Devlin, J., *The Ba'athist Party: A History from its Origins in 1966*, Stanford University Press, Palo Alto, Calif., 1976.

Divine, D., *Dunkirk*, Faber and Faber, London, 1954.

Dizard, W., *The Coming Information Age*, Longman, New York, 1982.

Dobell, G., 'The media's perspective on peacekeeping'; in *Peacekeeping: Challenges for the Future*, ed. Hugh Smith, Australian Defence Studies Centre, Australian Defence Force Academy, Canberra, 1993.

Dulles, F., *American Policy Towards Communist China 1949–1969*, Thomas Crowell Co., New York, 1972.

Dunnigan, J., & Bay, A., *From Shield to Storm: High-Tech Weapons, Military Strategy and Coalition Warfare in the Persian Gulf*, Morrow, New York, 1991.

Earle, E. (ed.), *Makers of Modern Strategy: Military Thought from Machiavelli to Hitler*, Princeton University Press, Princeton, 1943.

Elegant, R., *How to Lose a War: Reflections of a Foreign Correspondent*, Encounter, London, 1981.

Evans, G., *Cooperating for Peace*, Allen & Unwin, St Leonards, NSW, 1993.

Evans, G., & Grant, B., *Australia's Foreign Relations in the World of the 1990s*, Melbourne University Press, Melbourne, 1991.

Eveleigh, R., *Peace Keeping in a Democratic Society*, C. Hurt & Company, London, 1978.

Fall, B., *Street without Joy*, Stackpole Publishing, Pasadena, 1958.

Fanon, F., *The Wretched of the Earth*, Penguin, London, 1967.

Faulkner, F., *'Bao Chi': The American News Media in Vietnam*, University of California Press, Los Angeles, 1981.

Ferro, M., *The Great War*, Macmillan, London, 1973.

Fialka, J., *Hotel Warriors: Covering The Gulf War*, Woodrow Wilson Centre Press, Washington, 1991.

Foot, P., *Why Britain Must Get Out*, Chatto and Windus, London, 1989.

Fowler, R., & Orenstein, J., *Contemporary Issues in Political Theory*, Praeger, New York, 1940.

Fox, R., *Eyewitness Falklands*, Methuen, London, 1982.

Frank, M., & Weisband, E., *Secrecy and Foreign Policy*, Oxford University Press, London, 1974.

Freedman, L., & Karsh, E., *The Gulf Conflict*, Faber & Faber, London, 1994.

Friedman, N., *Desert Victory: The War for Kuwait*, Naval Institute Press, Annapolis, 1991.

Frost, J., *2 Para Falklands*, Buchan & Enright, London, 1983.

Furneaux, R., *News of War*, London, 1964.

Furneaux, R., *The First War Correspondent*, Cassell, London, 1944

Gaddis, J.L., *Strategies of Containment*, Oxford University Press, Oxford, 1992.

Gavin, K., *War and Peace in the Space Age*, Harvard University Press, New York, 1958.

George, A., *The Chinese Communist Army in Action: The Korean War and its Aftermath*, Columbia University Press, New York, 1967.

Giap, Vo Nguyen, *People's War People's Army*, Foreign Publishing House, Hanoi, 1961.

Gibbs, P., *Adventures in Journalism*, Heinemann, London, 1923.

Gibbs, P., *Realities of War*, Heinemann, London, 1920.

Gillespie, J., *Algerian Rebellion and Revolution*, Praeger, New York, 1967.

Gilmore, W., *The Grenada Intervention: Analysis and Documentation*, Mansell Publishing, New York, 1984.

Glanz & Elan, *Der Propagandatruppen*, Die Welt, Berlin, 2 May 1970.

Godfrey, S., *Low Intensity Conflict Contingencies and Australian Defence Policy*, Canberra Papers on Strategy and Defence, No. 34, SDSC, ANU, Canberra, February 1985.

Gomes, C.M., *The Kampuchea Connection*, Grassroots Publisher, London, 1980.

Gough, J., *The Social Contract: A Critical Study of its Development*, Clarendon Press, Oxford, 1957.

Greaves, C., *The Irish Crisis*, Lawrence & Wishart, London, 1972.

Grenada, The Peaceful Revolution, Economical Program for Inter-America Community and Action (EPICA), Washington, 1982.

Grenada: Whose Freedoms?, Latin American Bureau, London, 1984.

Halberstam, D., *The Best and The Brightest*, Random House, New York, 1972

Hallin, D., *The Uncensored War: The Media and Vietnam*, Oxford University Press, London, 1986.

Halperin, M., *Limited War in the Nuclear Age*, Wiley, New York, 1966.

Halperin, M., *Strategy in the Nuclear Age*, Wiley, New York, 1983.

Hamill, D., *Pig in the Middle: The Army in Northern Ireland 1969–85*, Methuen, London, 1986.

Hammer, E., *The Emergence of Vietnam*, Institute of Pacific Relations, New York, 1947.

Hammer, E., *The Struggle for Indochina*, Stanford University, New York, 1947.

Hammond, G., 'Low Intensity Conflict: War by Another Name', *Small Wars and Insurgencies*, Frank Cass, London, vol. 1, no. 3, December 1990.

Hammond, M., *Public Affairs: The Military and the Media 1962–68*, Centre for Military History, Washington, 1988.

Hampton, J., *Hobbes and the Social Contract Tradition*, Cambridge University Press, 1985.

Hancock, A., & MacCullum, H., *Mass Communications: Australia and the World*, Longman, Sydney, 1971.

Harris, R., *Gotcha! The Media, the Government and the Falklands Crisis*, Faber and Faber, London, 1983.

Hart, L., *Liddell Hart's History of the Second World War*, Pan Books, London, 1970.

Hassan Quaid, *A History of Kuwait*, Dar Asharq Doha Quatar, 1990.

Hassan Shabr, *Political Parties in Iraq from 1908–1958*, Dar Al Turath Al Arabi, Beirut, 1989.

Hastings, M., & Jenkins, S., *Battle for the Falklands*, Michael Joseph, London, 1983.

Hatta, M., *Portrait of a Patriot*, Mouton Press, The Hague, 1972.

Hawkins, D. (ed.), *War Report: D Day to VE Day*, Aeriel Books, BBC, London, 1985.

Hayes, C., *Nationalism, A Religion*, Macmillan, New York, 1960.

Herman, S., & Chomsky, N., *Manufacturing Consent: The Political Economy of the Mass Media*, Pantheon, New York, 1988.

Herr, M., *Dispatches*, Picador, London, 1977.

Higgins, M., *The Report of a Woman Combat Correspondent*, Doubleday, New York, 1951.

Hill, Lord, *Behind the Screen*, Sidgwick and Jackson, London, 1974.

Hilsman, R., *George Bush vs. Saddam Hussein*, Lyford Books, Novato, California, 1992.

Hilvert, J., *Blue Pencil Warriors*, University of Queensland Press, Brisbane, 1984.

Hiro, D., *The Longest War*, Grafton Press, London, 1989.

Hiro, D., *Desert Shield to Desert Storm: The Second Gulf War*, Paladin, London, 1992.

History of the Righteous War of Korean People for the Liberation of the Fatherland, History Research Centre, Pyongyang, North Korea, 1971.

Hobbes, T., *Leviathan, or the Matter, Forme and Power of a Commonwealth, Ecclesiastical and Civil*, C. McPherson (ed.), Penguin, London, 1975.

Hobson, J., *Imperialism: A Study*, London, 1902.

Hoepli, N., *Aftermath of Colonialism*, H. Wilson Publishing, New York, 1973.

Honey, P. (ed.), *North Vietnam Today, A Profile of a Communist State*, Praeger, New York, 1962.

Hood, M., & Ablin, D.A., 'The path to Cambodia's present', in *The Cambodian Agony*, Ablin, D.A., & Hood, M. (eds), M.E. Sharpe, Inc., Armonk, New York, 1987.

Horne, A., *A Savage War of Peace: Algeria 1945–62*, Macmillan, London, 1969.

Hung, N.T, & Schecter, J.L., *The Palace File*, Perennial Library (Harper & Row), New York, 1989.

Iskander Amir, *Saddam Hussein: The Fighter, The Thinker and the Man*, Hachette, Paris, 1980.

Joint Low Intensity Conflict Project: Final Report, US Army Training and Doctrine Command, Fort Monroe, Virginia, August 1986.

Jones, C., (ed.), *The Reagan Legacy*, Chattam Publishing, New Jersey, 1988.

Julien, C., *L'Afrique Du Nord en Marcle*, Juillard, Paris, 1952.

Jullian, M., *The Battle of Britain*, Jonathan Cape, London, 1967.

Kamin, G., *Nationalism and Revolution in Indonesia*, Ithaca, New York, 1952.

Karnow, S., *Vietnam. A History*, Penguin, London, 1984.

Kelly, K., *The Longest War: Northern Ireland and the IRA*, Zed Books, London, 1982.

Kempe, F., *Divorcing the Dictator*, G.P. Putnam's Sons, New York, 1990.

Khan, H., *Escalation, Metaphors and Scenarios*, Pall Mall Press, London, 1965.

Khan, H., *On Thermonuclear War*, Princeton University Press, Princeton, NJ, 1963.

Khan, H., *On Escalation, Metaphors and Scenarios*, Praeger, New York, 1959.

Kiljunen, K. (ed.), *Kampuchea: Decade of the Genocide*, Report of a Finnish Inquiry Commission, Zed Books, London, 1984.

Kim Chun Kon, *The Korean War*, Kwangmyong Publishing, Seoul, South Korea, 1973.

Kipling, R., *From Sea to Sea*, London, 1900.

Kissinger, H., *Diplomacy*, Simon & Schuster, New York, 1994.

Kissinger, H., *Nuclear Weapons and Foreign Policy*, Harper, New York, 1957.

Knight, F., *The Caribbean: The Genesis of a Fragmented Nationalism*, Oxford University Press, New York, 1978.

Knightley, P., *The First Casualty*, Quartet, London, 1975.

Knorr, R., & Read, T., *Limited Strategic War*, Pall Mall Press, London, 1962.

Koch, T., *Journalism in the 21st Century: Online Information, Electronic Databases and the News*, Adamantine Press, Twickenham, UK, 1991.

Kolko, G., *Vietnam, The Anatomy of a War 1940–75*, Allen & Unwin, London, 1986

Kraft, J., *The Struggle for Algeria*, Doubleday, New York, 1961.

Kris, E., & Spier, H., *German Radio Propaganda and the Media*, Oxford University Press, London, 1944.

Kumar, S., *US Intervention in Latin America*, Advent Books, New York, 1987.

LaMay, C., Fitzsimon, M., & Sahadi, J. (eds), *The Media At War: The Press and the Persian Gulf Conflict*, Freedom Forum Media Studies Centre, New York, 1991.

Laslett, P., *Locke's Two Treatises of Government*, Clarendon Press, London, 1960.

Laslett, P., & Fishkin, J. (eds), *Philosophy, Politics and Society*, Blackwell, Oxford, 1979.

Lauterpacht, E., *The Kuwait Crisis: Basic Documents*, Cambridge International Documents Service, Cambridge, 1991.

Lawrenson, J., & Barber, L., *The Price of Truth. The Story of Reuters Millions*, Sphere Books, London, 1985.

Lebedoff, B., *The New Elite*, Franklin Watts, New York, 1981.

Leebert, D. (ed.) *The Future of Computing and Communications*, MIT Press, New York, 1991.

Legrand, J., *L'Indochine à l'heure Japonaise*, Legrand, Paris, 1963.

Lerner, A., *The Passing of Traditional Society*, Free Press, Glencoe, 1958.

Lessnoff, M., *Social Contract*, Macmillan, London, 1986.

Levering, R., *The Public and American Foreign Policy 1918–1979*, William Morrow & Co, New York, 1978.

Lively, J., & Reev, A., *Modern Political Theory from Hobbes to Marx*, Routledge, New York, 1989.

Luddendorf, F., *My War Memoirs 1914–18*, (trans.), London, 1919.

Lunn, H., *Vietnam: A Reporter's War*, University of Queensland Press, Brisbane, 1985.

Lyons, F., *Culture and Anarchy in Ireland 1819–1939*, New York, 1979.

MacArthur, D., *Reminiscences*, McGraw Hill, New York, 1964.

MacArthur, J., *Second Front: Censorship and Propaganda in the Gulf War*, Hill & Wang, New York, 1992.

MacDonald, J., *Television and the Red Menace*, Praeger, New York, 1985.

Maclear, M., *Vietnam: The Ten Thousand Day War*, Methuen, London, 1981.

Magdoff, H., *Imperialism: From the Colonial Age to the Present*, Monthly Review Press, New York, 1978.

Mansfield, P., *Kuwait: Vanguard of the Gulf*, Hutchinson, London, 1990.

Marwick, A., *Britain in the Century of Total War*, Macmillan, London, 1968.

Marwick, A., *War and Social Change in the Twentieth Century*, Bodley Head, London, 1974.

Mathams, R., *Sub Rosa*, Allen & Unwin, Sydney, 1982.

Mathews, L., (ed.), *Newsmen and National Defense*, Brassey's, McLean, Virginia, 1991.

Maurice Bishop Speaks, *The Grenada Revolution 1979–83*, Pathfinder Press, New York, 1983.

McKenzie, J., *Propaganda Boom*, John Giffard, London, 1938.

McMurrin, S., *John Rawls: Liberty, Equality and Law*, Tanner Lectures on Moral Philosophy, Cambridge University Press, Cambridge, 1987.

Mechjer, H., *Imperial Quest for Oil: Iraq 1910–1928*, Ithaca Press, London, 1976.

Mercer, D., Mungham, G., & Williams, K., *The Fog of War*, Heinemann, London, 1987.

Merill, J., *Global Journalism*, Longman, New York, 1983.

Meyer, A., *Marxism, the Unity of Theory and Practice*, Michigan University Press, Michigan, 1963.

Mezerick, A., (ed.), *Algeria Development 1959: De Gaulle, FLN, UN*, International Review, New York, 1960.

Michael, H., *Restraints on War*, Oxford University Press, Oxford, 1978.

Middlebrook, M., *Operation Corporate*, Viking, London, 1985.

Millar, T., *Australia in Peace and War*, ANU Press, Canberra, 1978.

Miller, D., *Queen's Rebels, A Historical Study of Ulster Loyalism*, Praeger, New York, 1978.

Miller, J., & Carroll, J., *Korea 1951–53*, Office of the Chief of Military History, Washington, 1956.

Morris, M., *H. Norman Schwarzkopf: Road to Triumph*, Pan Books, London, 1991.

Morrison, D., and Tumber, H., *Journalists at War*, Sage Publications, London, 1988.

Morrison, D., *Television and the Gulf War*, John Libbey, London, 1992.

Mueller, J., *Retreat from Doomsday*, Basic Books, New York, 1989.

Murrow, E., *This is London*, Cassell, London, 1941.

Musicant, I., *The Banana Wars*, Macmillan, New York, 1990.

Nguyen, Tien Hung, & Schecter, J., *The Palace File*, Harper & Row, New York, 1986.

Northern Ireland Emergency Provisions Act.

O'Ballance, E., *Malaya: The Communist Insurgent War*, Faber & Faber, London, 1966

O'Ballance, E., *The Algerian Insurrection, 1954–62*, Faber & Faber, London, 1967.

O'Brien, W., *The Conduct of Just and Limited War*, Praeger, New York, 1981.

O'Shaugnessy, H., *Grenada: An Eyewitness Account of the US Invasion and the Caribbean History that Provoked It*, Dodd Mead, New York, 1984.

Oakeshott, M., *Hobbes on Civil Association*, University of California Press, Los Angeles, 1975.

Olsen W., 'The Concept of Small Wars', in *Small Wars and Insurgencies*, Frank Cass, London, vol. 1, no. 1, April 1990.

Orwell, G., *Looking Back on the Spanish Civil War*, Collected Essays, Mercury Books, London, 1961.

Osanka, F., *Modern Guerrilla Warfare: Fighting Communist Guerrilla Movements*, Free Press, Glencoe, 1962.

Osborne, M., *Before Kampuchea: Preludes to Tragedy*, George Allen & Unwin, Sydney, 1979.

Osborne, M., *Region of Revolt: Focus on Southeast Asia*, Penguin, Harmondsworth, Middlesex, 1970.

Osgood, R., *Limited War*, University of Chicago Press, Chicago, 1957.

Osgood, R., *Strategic Thought in the Nuclear Age*, Heinemann, London, 1979.

Parekh, B., *Contemporary Political Thinkers*, Martin Robertson, Oxford, 1982.

Parrish, R., & Andreacchio, N., *Schwarzkopf: An Insider's View of the Commander and his Victory*, Bantam, New York, 1992.

Pilger, J., *Distant Voices*, Vintage, London, 1992.

Pimlott, J., & Badsey, S. (eds), *The Gulf War Assessed*, Arms & Armour, London, 1992.

Plamenatz, J., *Man and Society*, vol. 2, McGraw Hill, New York, 1963.

Ponchaud, F., *Cambodia: Year Zero*, Holt, Rinehart & Winston, New York, 1977.

Porter, A., & Holland, R., *Money, Finance and Empire 1790–1960*, Frank Cass, London, 1985.

Powell, C., *A Soldier's Way*, Hutchinson, London, 1995.

Privileges, J., *The Making of Modern Ireland*, Faber & Faber, London, 1968.

Proposed Working Arrangements with the Media in Time of Tension and War, MOD, London.

RAAF Air Power Manual 1990.

Rajendran, M., *ASEAN's Foreign Relations: The Shift to Collective Action*, arenabuku sdn. bhd., Kuala Lumpur, 1985.

Rapaport, A., *Three Principles of War*, Introduction to *Clausewitz On War*, Pelican, London, 1968.

Rawls, J., *A Theory of Justice*, Clarendon Press, Oxford, 1972.

Reynolds, C., *Modes of Imperialism*, Oxford University Press, London, 1981.

Rice, D., & Gavshon, R., *The Sinking of the Belgrano*, Secker & Warburg, London, 1984.

Ridgeway, M., *The Korean War*, Doubleday, New York, 1965.

Rolston, B., (ed.), *The Media and Northern Ireland: Covering the Troubles*, Macmillan, London, 1991.

Rose, R., *Governing Without Consensus: An Irish Perspective*, Faber & Faber, London, 1971.

Rosen, B., *Holding Government Bureaucracies Accountable*, Praeger, New York, 1982.

Rousseau, J., *The Social Contract or Principles of Political Right*, chaps. v, vii.

Roy, J., *The War in Algeria*, Knopf, New York, 1957.

Royle, T., *War Report*, Grafton Books, London, 1989.

Russell, W., *My Diary during the Last Great War*, Routledge, London, 1874.

Russell, W., *My Diary. North and South*, Bradbury & Evan, London, 1863.

Ryan, H., 'A New Diplomacy', *Government Executive*, vol. 25, no. 2, February 1993.

Salinger, P., *Secret Dossier: The Hidden Agenda Behind the War*, Penguin, New York, 1991.

Schnabel, J., & Watson, R., *The History of the Joint Chiefs of Staff and National Policy*, vol. 3, *The Korean War*, Joint Secretariat, Joint Chiefs of Staff, Washington, 1978–79.

Schnabel, J., *Policy and Direction: The First Year*, Office of the Chief of Military History, Washington, 1962.

Schumpeter, J., *Capitalism, Socialism and Democracy*, Harper & Row, New York, 1982.

Schwarzkopf, N., *It Doesn't Take a Hero*, Bantam, New York, 1993.

Sciolino, E., *The Outlaw State: Saddam Hussein's Quest for Power*, Wiley, New York, 1992.

Seabury, P., & McDougall, W., *The Grenada Papers*, Institute for Contemporary Studies, Washington, 1991.

Semmler, C. (ed.), *The War Diaries of Kenneth Slessor*, University of Queensland Press, Brisbane, 1971.

Serle, G., *John Monash, A Biography*, Melbourne University Press, Melbourne, 1982.

Shapiro, M. (ed.), *The Pentagon Papers and the Courts. A Study in Foreign Policy Making and the Freedom of the Press*, Chandler Publishing, 1982.

Shawcross, W., *The Quality of Mercy: Cambodia, Holocaust and Modern Conscience*, Simon & Schuster, New York, 1984.

Shiv Kumar, V., *US Intervention in Latin America*, Advent Books, New York, 1987.

Sihanouk, Prince Norodom, *War and Hope: The Case for Cambodia*, Pantheon Books, New York, 1980.

Silber, I., *Kampuchea: The Revolution Rescued*, Line of March Publications, Oaklands, Calif., 1986.

Singer, J., *Deterrence, Arms Control and Disarmament*, Ohio State University Press, Ohio, 1962.

Sixsmith, E., *Eisenhower as Military Commander*, Batsford, London, 1973.

Smith, H., (ed.), *Peacekeeping: Challenges for the Future,* Australian Defence Studies Centre, Australian Defence Force Academy, Canberra, 1993.

Smith, P., *How CNN Fought the War*, Carroll Publishing, New York, 1991.

Snepp, F., *Decent Interval*, Vintage Books, New York, 1978.

Special Operations Research Office, *Casebook on Insurgency and Revolutionary Warfare*, The American University, Washington, 1962.

Spigelman, J., *Secrecy and Political Censorship in Australia*, Angus & Robertson, Sydney, 1972.

Steevens, G., *With Kitchener to Khartoum*, Blackwood, London, 1898.

Steiner, Z., *Britain and the Origins of the First World War*, Macmillan, London, 1977.

Stoessinger, J., *Why Nations Go To War*, Macmillan, London, 1985.

Stone, G., *War Without Honour*, Jacaranda Press, Sydney, 1972.

Struve, W., *Elites Against Democracy*, Princeton University Press, Princeton, 1973.

Sunday Times Insight Team, *The Falklands War*, Sphere Books, London, 1982.

Swinton, E., '*Eyewitness*', Hodder & Stoughton, London, 1923.

Taylor, P., *War and the Media: Propaganda and Persuasion in the Gulf*, Manchester University Press, Manchester/New York, 1992.

Thayer, C., 'Vietnam: A critical analysis', International Conference on Defence and the Media in Time of Limited Conflict, Brisbane, April 1991.

The British Press and Northern Ireland, Socialist Research Centre, London, 1971.

The Times: Past, Present and Future, (The History of *The Times*), *The Times* (London), 1952.

Thomas, H., *An Unfinished History of the World*, Hamish Hamilton, London, 1981.

Thompson, G., *Blue Pencil Admiral*, Sampson Low, London, 1947.

Thompson, L., *Low Intensity Conflict, An Overview*, Lexington Books, Lexington, Massachusetts, 1989.

Thompson, R., *Cry Korea*, Macdonald, London, 1951.

Thompson, R. (ed.), *War in Peace*, Orbis, London, 1981.

Thorndike, T., *Grenada: Revolution and Invasion*, Francis Pinter, London, 1985.

Tillman, R.O., *Southeast Asia and the Enemy Beyond*, Westview Press, Boulder, Colorado, 1987.

Towle, P., 'The Debate on Wartime Censorship in Britain 1902–1914', *War and Society*, 1975.

Trager, F., *Why Vietnam*, Praeger, New York, 1966; Giap, Vo Nguyen, *Unforgettable Days*, Foreign Languages Publishing House, Hanoi, 1978.

Trevelyn, H., *The Middle East in Revolution*, Macmillan, London, 1970.

Turner, K., *Lyndon Johnson's Dual War: Vietnam and the Press*, University of Chicago Press, Chicago, 1985.

United Nations Convention on Human Rights, 1954.

United Nations Yearbook 1955, May Edition.

United Nations Yearbook 1950, New York, 1950.

US Army *FM–100 Operations series*, especially *FM100–5 and FM100–10 Low Intensity Conflict*, HQ Department of the Army, Washington, 1976.

US News & World Report Staff, *Triumph Without Victory: The Unreported History of the Persian Gulf War*, Times Books/Random House, New York, 1992.

Vagts, A., *A History of Militarism*, Meridian Books, New York, 1959.

Vaizey, J., *The Squandered Peace*, Hodder & Stoughton, London, 1983.

Valienta, J., & Ellison, H., *Grenada and Soviet Cuban Policy: Internal Crisis and US/OEC Intervention*, Westview Press, Boulder, 1986.

Vatcher, W., *Panmunjon*, Praeger, New York, 1958.

Vaughan, C., *Jean Jacques Rousseau, Political Writings*. Blackwell, Oxford, 1962.

Vaught, E., *The Political Writings of Jean Jacques Rousseau*, Cambridge University Press, Cambridge, 1915.

Vickery, M., *Cambodia 1975–1982*, George Allen and Unwin, North Sydney, NSW, 1984.

Wallace, E., *Unofficial Dispatches*, Hutchinson, London, 1901.

Waller, W., *War in the 20th Century*, Dryden Press, New York, 1940.

Ward, J., *Military Men*, Michael Joseph, London, 1972.

Ward, J. *The American Way of War*, Macmillan, New York, 1973.

Warner, D., *Not With Guns Alone*, Hutchinson, Sydney, 1977.

Watson, B., & Tsouras, P., *Operation Just Cause: The US Intervention in Panama*, Westview Press, Boulder, 1991.

Watson, B., *Military Lessons of the Gulf War*, Greenhill Books, California, 1991.

Weigley, R., *History of the United States Army*, Macmillan, New York, 1967.

Westmoreland, W., *A Soldier Reports*, Dell Publishing Company, New York, 1976.

Wichert, S., *Northern Ireland since 1945*, Longman, London, 1991.

Williams, E., *From Columbus to Castro: The History of the Caribbean 1492–1969*, Deutsch, London, 1970.

Wilson, T., *Ulster: Conflict and Consent*, Blackwell, London, 1989.

Winchester, S., *In Holy Terror*, Faber & Faber, London, 1974.

Winkler, A., *The Politics of Propaganda*, Yale University Press, New Haven, Conn., 1978.

Wolfson, S., *The Untapped Power of the Press*, Praeger, New York, 1985.

Woodman, S., 'Defining Limited Conflict: A case of mistaken identity', paper delivered to the International Conference on Defence and the Media in Time of Limited Conflict, Brisbane, April 1991.

Woodward, B., *The Commanders*, Simon & Schuster, New York, 1991.

Woodward, S., with Robinson, P. *One Hundred Days*, HarperCollins, London, 1992.

Wright, J., *Terrorist Propaganda: The Red Army Faction and the Provisional IRA*, St Martin, 1991.

Yass, M., *This is Your War, Home Front Propaganda in the Second World War*, HMSO, London, 1973.

Yates, L., *Power Pack: US Intervention in the Dominican Republic 1955–66*, Combat Studies Institute, Kansas, July 1988.

Young, P., & Lawford, J., *History of the British Army*, Barker Ltd, London, 1970.

Young, P R (ed.), *Defence and The Media In Time of Limited War*, Frank Cass, London, 1992.

INDEX

A

B